"How I wish I had [this] guidebook with me when I sang my debut in Wien [Vienna]! It provides fascinating insight to the tourist who is also a music lover. And for the tourist-musician, your guide is a 'must.'"

ELLEN SHADE, American soprano, Metropolitan Opera, Chicago Lyric Opera, Vienna Staatsoper, Frankfurt Opera, Paris Opéra

The Opera Lover's Guide to Europe "is a treasure-trove for opera lovers, entertainingly written, beautifully illustrated, and full of practical advice on what to see and where to stay in operatic Europe.... It is a must for any devotee of the lyric art."

MYRON S. FINK, Composer in Residence, San Diego Opera, 1995–97

"Carol Plantamura's *Opera Lover's Guide to Europe* tells us everything we want to know—it also tells us everything we need to know... it is informative as well as entertaining. What more could we ask for?"

LUKAS FOSS, composer and conductor

"Carol Plantamura has expertly met the needs of the opera-minded traveler... with Plantamura's guide in hand, you can confidently put together your own Grand Tour of European opera houses. For experienced operagoers and neophytes alike, Plantamura illuminates the performance history of opera in a lively... informative manner."

ROGER PINES, Lyric Opera of Chicago

"*The Opera Lover's Guide to Europe*...should be in the suitcase, briefcase, or backpack of every opera lover visiting Europe, as well as on the bookshelf of anyone who wants to know more about operatic history...it provides such a lucid introduction to the major operatic cities and the history of the important performances they hosted, that I regretted I did not have it available when I was last traveling in Europe myself....For the first-time traveler the information about local hotels and eating places will be a more valuable asset, and will serve to make that first visit to these operatic capitals even more enjoyable and less daunting. For the experienced traveler, insights on each city provide much new stimulation which will make a return visit even more rewarding....Altogether it is a much-needed contribution to the field of opera..."

    IAN D. CAMPBELL, General Director, San Diego Opera

"I have sung in so many of the opera houses mentioned in [*The Opera Lover's Guide to Europe*]...I learned so much about them that I hadn't known before...a fascinating and timely book..."

    CATHERINE MALFITANO, American soprano, Metropolitan Opera, Vienna
    Staatsoper, Paris Opéra, Munich Opera, La Monnaie, Deutscher Oper
    (Berlin)... films of *Tosca* and *Salome*

The Opera Lover's Guide to Europe

To Jane on our wedding anniversary – Gordon

The Opera Lover's Guide to Europe

Carol Plantamura

Annette Poitau, Maps
Michael Waterman, Drawings

A CITADEL PRESS BOOK
Published by Carol Publishing Group

A Citadel Press Book
Published by Carol Publishing Group
Citadel Press is a registered trademark of Carol Communications, Inc.

Editorial, sales and distribution, rights and permissions inquiries should be
addressed to Carol Publishing Group, 120 Enterprise Avenue, Secaucus, N.J.
07094

In Canada: Canadian Manda Group, One Atlantic Avenue, Suite 105,
Toronto, Ontario M6K 3E7

Carol Publishing Group books may be purchased in bulk at special discounts
for sales promotion, fund-raising, or educational purposes. Special editions
can be created to specifications. For details, contact Special Sales
Department, 120 Enterprise Avenue, Secaucus, N.J. 07094.

Manufactured in the United States of America
10   9   8   7   6   5   4   3   2   1

Library of Congress Cataloging-in-Publication Data

Plantamura, Carol.
    The opera lover's guide to Europe / Carol Plantamura.
      p.   cm.
    "A Citadel Press book."
    ISBN 0-8065-1842-1 (pbk.)
    1. Opera—Europe. 2. Theaters—Europe—Guidebooks.
3. Europe—Description and travel. I. Title.
ML1720.P53   1996
782.1'094—dc20   96—31531
                                                   CIP
                                                   MN

Contents

Acknowledgments

This book could not have been written without the passion of Betsy Jolas, the involvement of Alberto Rossatti and Karen Ringnalda Altman Flusty, the patience and fortitude of Cheryl Brown, and the generous help of Karen Christenfeld, Sylvia Dimiziani, Margaret Eastman, Genette Foster, Tatjana and Vinko Globokar, Romana Jaroff, Kathy Offerding, Susan Rands, Dr. John Stewart, and the UCSD Academic Senate.

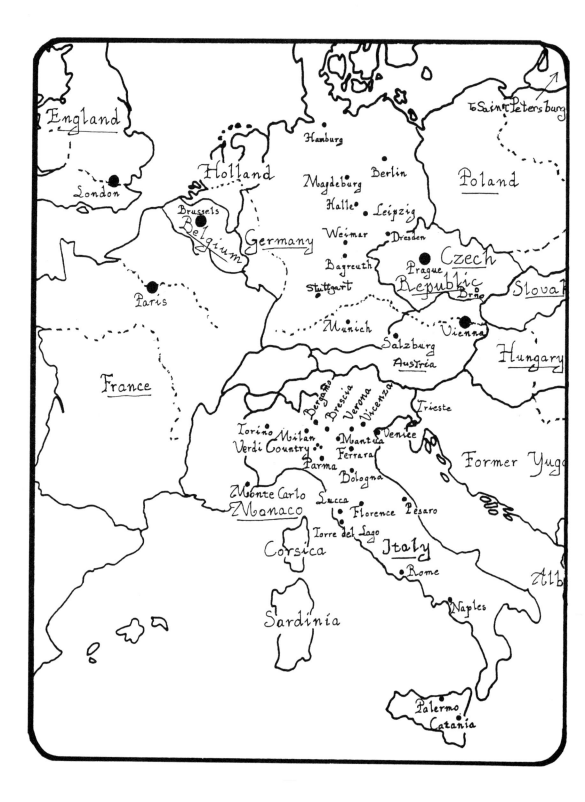

Preface

The locals don't always know. In Mantua once, at the palace where *L'Orfeo* was first performed, I drew a blank with the guide. He had no idea it was an opera and asked, "Monteverdi who?"

So this book is dedicated to those who want to know the "who," "where," and "when" of opera. It is a grand tour of Europe's opera houses where the great operas had their premieres.

The focus is the composers we all love, the towns where they lived, and the theatres where they had their hits or disasters. The text explains what happened where, when, and to whom, embracing museums dedicated to the great conductors as well as composers of these stupendous productions, the European opera houses of today and their schedules, plus interesting festivals. Detailed maps direct the reader to these operatic hot spots, while a list of nearby places for eating and sleeping takes care of creature comforts.

Opera anywhere outside Italy is an imported form. Granted, Paris, very early on, developed its own kind of opera—but the *idea* came from Italy. In fact the relationship of opera theatres to the cities in which they stand varies enormously from country to country and city to city. Outside Italy, until well into the nineteenth century, opera (and we are speaking of Italian-style opera) made its greatest impact in the larger cities: Vienna, Munich, and London.

Opera was in general more popular in the Catholic areas of Germany, Austria, and Prague. In the eighteenth century, before the birth of nationalism, the Lutheran Prussian courts did not go for its extravagances in the same way as did the great Saxon courts of Catholic Germany and Austria.

Twelve years of singing (and living, eating, and sleeping) in Europe have informed the author, who takes delight in sending you on an exciting musical adventure. Opera awaits you in the countries of its birth and development.

So immerse yourself in this unique guide and enjoy the rich and fascinating world of opera. Follow its maps to historic sites (and stop along the way to enjoy typical mouth-watering regional foods). Your guide tells all—the dirt on the best-known operas; the who-did-what-to-whom; the cultural background; the trivia.

Buon Viaggio! Gute Reise! Bon Voyage!

The Opera Lover's Guide to Europe

ITALY
The Birthplace of Opera

※ ⫷

Italy and opera are inextricably bound: expressive, expansive, exciting, exaggerated, and, above all, beautiful. The Italian language evokes the sound of singing; the small towns look like opera sets; the irrepressible Italian spirit is operatic. Italy is opera and opera is Italy.

Ever since opera was "invented" in Italy in the late sixteenth century, it has been the quintessential Italian art form, even though it is also composed and enjoyed in other countries.

By the end of the seventeenth century opera was so popular that over forty towns and cities throughout Italy had *at least* one opera house. Most of these theatres were constructed in the tiered horseshoe shape today called *teatro all'italiana*.

By the eighteenth century the theatre, and opera in particular, succeeded in uniting Italian intellectuals into a relatively cohesive force which proceeded to inform the rest of the population of the latest developments in humanistic thought and politics. By the 1790s opera became the voice for the emerging force of public opinion against foreign domination.

It is interesting that although opera was certainly *the* musical art form of eighteenth-century Italy, and although there were literally hundreds of Italians writing thousands of operas for the opera houses of Italian cities, most of this operatic music—except that by Vivaldi and Pergolesi in the beginning of the century—is no longer performed. Opera throughout the rest of Europe in the eighteenth century was written in the Italian style. Some composers were Italians writing outside of Italy, such as Antonio Salieri, who had been recruited by the Austrian occupation government of Venice for the court and opera houses of Vienna. But the musicians we now consider the great eighteenth-century composers of Italian-style opera are the Germans, Handel and Gluck, and the Austrian, Mozart. It took the genius of Rossini, Donizetti, Bellini, the mastery of

Teatro all'italiana

Verdi, and the synthesis of Puccini's creativity to put great Italian opera back into the hands of the Italians.

This paucity of memorable Italian opera from eighteenth-century Italy is due partially to the political and ecclesiastical forces influencing the peninsula during the century; to the somewhat ingenuous Italian librettos that generated rather forgettable operas; and to the current passion for nineteenth-century Italian opera that precludes rediscovery of eighteenth-century Italian operatic conventions.

By the end of the eighteenth century more than one hundred opera theatres dotted the peninsula, and by the end of the first quarter of the nineteenth century the number had risen to well over two hundred. Strangely, more than one hundred new opera theatres were built during the political unrest of the Risorgimento in the second quarter of the nineteenth century, and by the 1890s 1,055 theatres flourished in 755 cities and towns! To some degree this incredible number can be accounted for by the fact that the repertories of spoken drama and opera were not counted separately during the nineteenth century. Only a few of these 1,055 theatres were considered first-class opera houses and presented solely opera. Interestingly, with only a few exceptions, these continue to be the great opera theatres of Italy today. They are: Teatro Comunale, Bologna, Teatro Carlo Felice, Genoa, La Scala, Milan, Teatro San Carlo, Naples, Teatro Regio, Parma,

Teatro Costanzi (known today as Teatro dell'Opera), Rome, Teatro Regio, Turin, Teatro La Fenice, Venice.

These theatres, and many others, continue to put on fabulous opera seasons. They do this against heavy odds: opera is a hybrid art made up of theatre, orchestral music, solo singing, choral singing, staging, lighting, costuming, and sometimes ballet; these activities plus the concomitant requirements for management, publicity, etc., make opera the most expensive to produce of all the performing arts. When it is well done, it is well worth the expense.

But today, even the great houses listed above have cut back on the number of operas they present in a season. Even Rome's enormously popular Terme di Caracalla (Baths of Caracalla) have been closed for the foreseeable future, and Palermo's glorious Teatro Massimo has been "under repair" for the past twenty years! In Italy, as in the rest of the world, there's the danger that live opera performances may go the way of the dinosaur. The potential loss of such a heritage is both real and disturbing. The less opera is performed, the fewer singers will train to sing opera, conductors to conduct, orchestras to play, theatres to present. Then, for lack of artists and locations, opera as a living art form will exist no more.

Although this guide is by no means a scholarly book, even the most learned of opera lovers should find it extremely valuable for discovering the opera theatres of both yesterday and today as well as for discovering how to gain access to these sites.

For people of our auto-dependent society, accustomed to large, amorphous, suburbial cities, it is particularly remarkable to see that opera houses of yesteryear were so central to everyday life. As well as being a comprehensive guide to many of today's opera theatres in Europe, this book also points out the location of theatres that no longer exist, thus providing a sense of the vital role opera once played in the normal life of Italians by demonstrating the abundance of theatres and their physical proximity to one another.

From the seventeenth to the early twentieth century opera was *the* musical art form of the Italian peninsula—symphonic and chamber composition ran a very distant second. Each neighborhood's opera house was centrally located, usually in or near the same large square that housed the principal church. Often the church and the theatre had the same names: for example, Rome's Sant'Andrea della Valle and Teatro Valle; Venice's San Cassiano and Teatro San Cassiano; and Milan's La Scala, which was built where the church of La Scala once stood. The character of the neighborhood was defined by its church *and* its theatre.

In Italy, until not very long ago, opera and theatregoing was an essential part of the everyday life of all classes of people. Laborers rubbed elbows with aristocrats. It was as usual to attend the opera as it was to attend Mass, and for the similar reasons of enlightenment, social contact, and people watching. Throughout Italy and, for that matter, Europe, the opera house was the secular center of civility and public sociability. The neighborhood opera house was once as ubiquitous as the neighborhood movie theatre was to those of us growing up in the 1940s and 1950s in U.S. urban areas. Further exemplifying this social aspect, the seats of these opera houses were often removed on New Year's Eve and during *Carnevale* to enable the theatre to hold the town's public grand ball celebration called the *Veglione,* or the grand vigil. The custom is still observed on New Year's Eve in some of Italy's smaller towns.

Every town and city on the Italian peninsula has its via, viale, or piazza G. Verdi, G. Donizetti, V. Bellini, G. Rossini, or G. Puccini. Imagine every U.S. town with a G. Gershwin, C. Porter, I. Berlin, or O. Hammerstein Street!

A critical "hit" premiere was not mandatory for an opera's, or even a composer's, survival (just as with movies today). With so many different theatres clamoring for new works, a composer always had another opportunity for a new production and thus a chance for it to become a hit. And a hit, of course, almost guaranteed many more productions.

Unfortunately, because of the various and burgeoning entertainment media today, even the Italians have lost their habit of regularly attending the opera. As a consequence, just as in the United States, opera theatres are often forced to present only the "old chestnuts" in order to fill the house. It is as if today's public does not want to judge what is new and exciting but rather whether something is as exciting as it was last time. Italian opera houses, obviously at the demand of their publics, presented seasons full of *new* works well into the late 1940s.

All opera lovers know of the summer performances at the Arena di Verona and Rome's Terme di Caracalla (unfortunately closed in 1994 for the foreseeable future. See Rome, page 12 for further information). This guide offers other less well-known summer operatic possibilities and year-round performances and also provides the telephone numbers and addresses needed to get tickets.

General Pointers on Getting About in Italy With Ease

- When you arrive in Italy, the first thing to do is find a newspaper stand (there's one in every airport) and ask for an *Orario Ferroviario* (a train schedule). The easiest to read is called *Orario Generale* by Veltro. It costs about $3.00 and is an invaluable tool for traveling in Italy. Only one area described here cannot be *easily* reached by train. (To get to the towns of Le Roncole, Busseto, and Sant'Agata, you can rent a car in any nearby city— for example, Parma or Mantua.) Since parking in Italian cities can be hell, I cannot recommend too strongly that you take the train. This also means do not bring too much to carry. Remember, the clothes you need for a week are plenty for two months (plus a coat and a change of shoes).
- When you arrive in a city, pick up a map of the city at the train station. You will be pleased to see, in terms of opera, how many places are a four-to-five-minute walk from each other.

- City bus tickets, and airport bus tickets, are purchased at newspaper stands. Be sure to slip the ticket in the slot of the yellow box on the bus to validate it. All tickets are valid for 90 minutes.
- A bus stop is called a *fermata* and is clearly marked by a *fermata* sign: ⌒
- A word about looking for a restaurant:

   An *osteria* is usually the least expensive place to have a good meal. They probably will not have white tablecloths and candles on the tables.

   A *trattoria* is similar to an *osteria* in that it often serves excellent simple food for a relatively low price without a lot of fuss paid to ambience.

   A *ristorante* will have white tablecloths and most likely will be more expensive than a *trattoria*. However, many *ristoranti* are worth the price.
- In a "caffe" or a "bar" Italians always stand at the counter when having a coffee or a drink. If you want to blend in, stand.
- In the cities of Italy, as in all the cities of Europe, dress is slightly more formal than in the United States (particularly West Coast United States). To feel comfortable in Italy's cities, and to be treated with respect, women should wear relatively conservative skirts and men casual trousers. Relatively conservative means do not show a lot of skin unless you are interested in being ogled. Leave your shorts, skintight Lycra dress, and bright polyester pantsuits at home.
- The telephone code for Italy is 39 + the city code; minus its 0 outside of the country; minus 39 but with its 0 within Italy.
- All the large train stations, Turin, Genoa, Milan, Venice, Bologna, Rome, Naples, have a *diurno* or a day hotel, where you can take a shower after a long trip. They also have very clean toilets which can be used for a small fee.

ROME (Roma)

Rome was named the capital of Italy only after the unification of the country in 1860. Although the city has had a lively operatic tradition since the seventeenth century, its operatic history is less important than that of Milan or Venice in the north or Naples in the south. Perhaps this is because Rome was ruled by the Pope, and although he may have been artistically enlightened, he still was the standard-bearer for the Church and its morals. It is an interesting dichotomy, for many of the Popes came from Rome's richest and most noble families— Barberini, Pamphili, Chigi, Rospiglioso—and were themselves great patrons of the arts and specifically of opera. Because of the influence of the Church, however, Roman drama and opera forbade women to appear on the stage throughout the seventeenth and early eighteenth centuries. Women's roles were played by young castrati, and many of the famous operatic castrati of the eighteenth century got their start in the papal states.

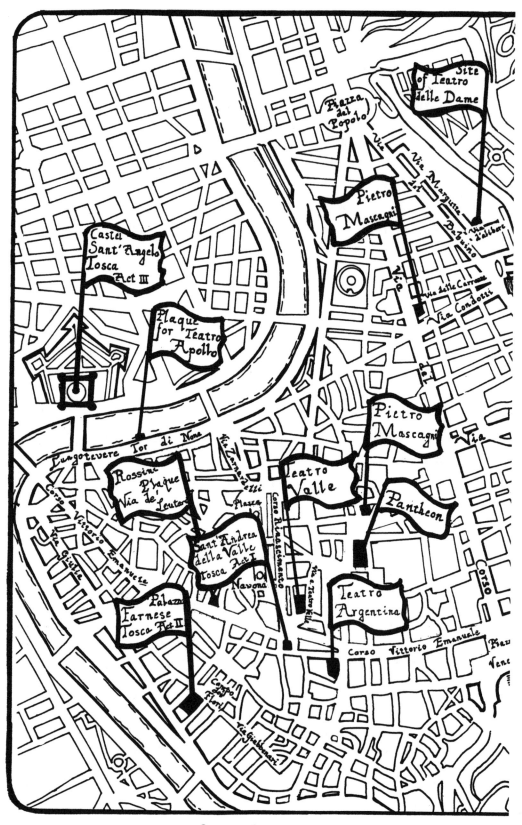

Operatic Rome

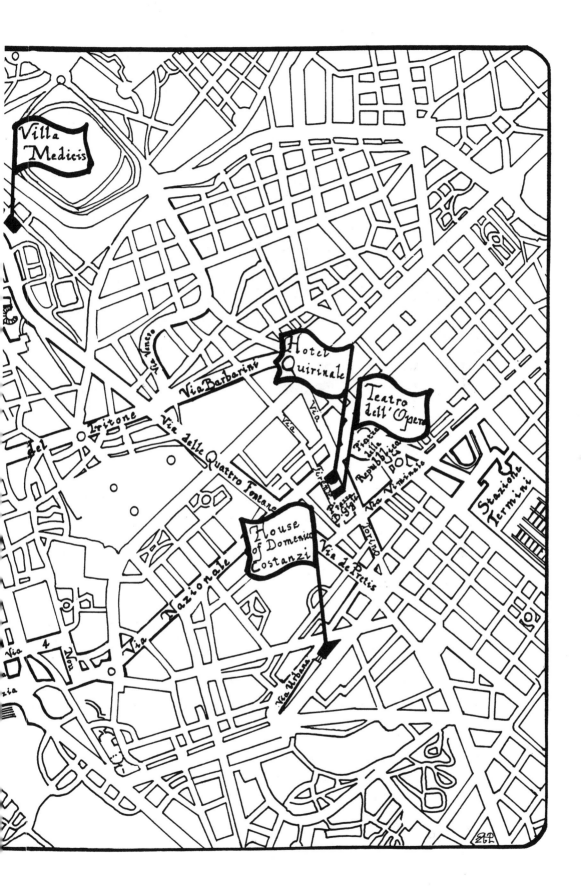

Villa Medicis

Hotel Quirinale

Teatro dell'Opera

House of Domenico Costanzi

Via Veneto

Via Barbarini

del Tritone

Via delle Quattro Fontane

Via

Via

Via della Repubblica

Piazza Figli

Via Viminale

Via Nazionale

Via de Pretis

Torino

Via Urbana

Stazioni Termini

Via 4 Nov

Via

zia

7

Sant'Andrea della Valle Seen From the Back of Teatro Argentina

Because of a decree by Pope Innocenzo V, all Roman public theatres were closed in 1679. Thus, during the 1680s any operatic performances in Rome were given in private palace theatres. In the 1690s, when opera was again allowed to flourish in Rome's public theatres, the city's favorite composer was Alessandro Scarlatti.

In the nineteenth century, political and religious censorship of opera continued to be stronger in Rome than in other Italian cities. Consequently, many opera librettos had to be changed to appease the Roman censors.

Rome is the setting for Puccini's glorious and bloody *Tosca*: the opera's three acts take place right in the center of the *centro storico* (historic center) and each act is a five-minute walk from its predecessor:

Act I: the Attavanti Chapel in the church of Sant'Andrea della Valle (above) in corso Vittorio Emanuele behind Teatro Argentina.
Act II: Palazzo Farnese in piazza Farnese, open daily from 10:00 A.M.–1:00 P.M. (today it is the French embassy and a museum).
Act III: Castel Sant'Angelo in largo del Castello, open daily from 9:30 A.M.–4:00 P.M.; holidays, 9:30 A.M.–1:00 P.M.

The Antico Albergo del Sole al Pantheon, 63, piazza della Rotonda (which is piazza del Pantheon), has a plaque stating:

Palazzo Farnese

In questo albergo	In this hotel
Dal nome augurale	With its auspicious name
Pietro Mascagni	Pietro Mascagni
Volle soggiornare nel MDCCCXC	In 1890
Nell'ansiosa vigilia	Anxiously awaited
Dell'ambito riconoscimento	The longed-for recognition
Che segnò il trionfo	Which accompanied the triumph
Della Cavalleria rusticana.	Of *Cavalleria rusticana.*

(The hotel, which has stood in the same place since the late fifteenth century, also hosted Lodovico Ariosto in 1513. He was the Ferrarese poet who wrote *Orlando furioso,* on which many eighteenth-century opera librettos are based.)

After the big successes of his operas *Cavalleria rusticana* and *L'amico Fritz,* Mascagni lived in via del Corso. Today, at the broadening of the Corso, called largo San Carlo al Corso, at the corner of via delle Carozze, right above the music store called Messaggerie Musicali, there is a bust of Mascagni and a plaque:

Pietro Mascagni	Pietro Mascagni
Da questa casa	From this house,
Dove a lungo	Where for many years
Visse e operò	He lived and wrote,
Il 2–VII–1945	On July 2, 1945
Passò alla	Passed into
Immortalità.	Immortality.

Georges Bizet (1838–75) won the Prix de Rome and spent about three years in Rome at the French Academy, situated in the Villa Medicis, next to the

Borghese Gardens in viale Trinità dei Monti, 1. There he wrote his third opera, *Don Procopio*.

Richard Wagner and his wife Cosima stayed down the street from piazza di Spagna at the Albergo d'America in via del Babuino, 79 (now apartments and offices) for a month. The old carriage entrance to the hotel can still be seen in via Margutta, 67.

Domenico Costanzi, the land developer who built Rome's Teatro dell'Opera, built his own home, which still stands near the opera in via Urbana, 167.

Like all Italian cities, Rome contained many private opera theatres, the majority of which remained the exclusive sphere of the nobility. There were also a good number of public opera houses, however, four of which presented more than a few premieres.

Teatro Argentina, built in 1731 and inaugurated January 13, 1732, originally belonged to the Sforza-Cesarini family. Duke Francesco Sforza-Cesarini was a theatre fanatic and, even though he was losing money, ran Teatro Argentina from 1807 until his death in 1816, just before the premiere of Rossini's *Il barbiere di Siviglia*. Teatro Argentina has always been known for its excellent acoustics, and the architect Gianantonio Selva used the theatre as his model when he built Venice's Teatro La Fenice.

(I once lived in a penthouse in the building next door to Teatro Argentina. Some of the windows looked out on the roof of the theatre, while others overlooked Sant'Andrea della Valle, the church in which the first act of *Tosca* takes place. Surrounded by opera as I was, I could hardly help but be compelled to write this book.)

Today Teatro Argentina is the home of Rome's Teatro Stabile, the municipal theatre repertory company, and rarely produces musical presentations.

Teatro Argentina premiered (details of the premieres appear at the end of the section) *Il barbiere di Siviglia* (1816), Gioacchino Rossini; *La battaglia di Legnano* (1849), Giuseppe Verdi; *I due Foscari* (1844), Giuseppe Verdi.

Teatro Argentina, largo di Torre Argentina, on the west side
tel: (06) 687–5445

In 1816, while preparing the premiere of *Il barbiere di Siviglia* at Teatro Argentina, Gioacchino Rossini stayed in nearby via de'Leutari, 35. There is a plaque, put up in 1872, on the front of the building:

Abitando in questa casa	While living in this house
Gioacchino Rossini	Gioacchino Rossini
Trovò le armonie	Created the ever fresh
Sempre nuove	Harmonies of
Del Barbiere di Siviglia.	*The Barber of Seville.*

The small and elegant Teatro Valle, built in 1726, originally belonged to the Capranica family. In the nineteenth century it was regularly open for Carnevale, as well as for spring and autumn opera seasons. The theatre was rebuilt in 1821 and the façade, designed by Gaspare Servi, was added in 1845. The theatre presented the premieres of two works by Rossini, four by Donizetti, and many others by lesser-known or local composers. Since about 1850 Teatro Valle has presented spoken drama and has only occasionally been used for operas. It was restored in 1936–37 to its original style and is still a beautiful small theatre used today mostly for drama. (Note the placement of the theatre: The church of Sant'Andrea della Valle stands just across Corso Vittorio Emanuele; Teatro Argentina is three minutes on foot; Teatro Apollo was a five-minute walk across piazza Navona.)

Teatro Valle premiered (details of the premieres appear at the end of the section) *La Cenerentola* (1817), Gioacchino Rossini; *Demetrio e Polibio* (1812), Gioacchino Rossini.

Teatro Valle, viale Teatro Valle, 23a
tel: (39–6) 6880–3794

Teatro Costanzi (1880), renovated in 1926–27, reopened in 1928 as Teatro Reale dell'Opera and is now called Teatro dell'Opera. Teatro dell'Opera, as well as the nearby Hotel Quirinale, was built by the real estate speculator and developer Domenico Costanzi as a commercial venture in the late 1870s when the central city of Rome began to expand east toward the newly built train station. The theatre was inaugurated November 27, 1880, with a performance of Rossini's *Semiramide.* Perhaps because of the very nature of its purely commercial beginning, or simply because it was built so late, the theatre has never been considered as artistically important as Milan's La Scala, Venice's La Fenice, or Naples's San Carlo. The theatre is an *ente autonomo,* (a public body) publicly financed and state-supported. Because of its historical importance, since 1975 the theatre has been called an *istituzione nazionale* (a national institution).

The Milanese music publisher Edoardo Sonzogno was impresario of Teatro Costanzi when he organized his second famous verismo competition, which Mascagni's *Cavalleria rusticana* won in 1890. The theatre became the unofficial headquarters of verismo opera with its premieres of *Cavalleria rusticana* (1890) and *Tosca* (1900). And the Italian premiere of Richard Wagner's *Parsifal* took place in the theatre in 1914.

The *scandale* of Maria Callas's famous nonperformance of *Norma* (January 2, 1958) also took place in the theatre. The President of the Republic of Italy specially attended this performance at which Callas was scheduled to sing. Ill with an inflamed throat, she asked the management to replace her, which they declined to do. So she heroically, perhaps foolishly, sang the first act, during which she lost her voice. She refused to continue the performance. Because she had been seen dancing in the New Year, only two nights before, this provoked an enormous uproar, after which Callas was banned from the Teatro dell'Opera. With an incensed mob booing her, she managed to escape through a tunnel from the theatre's backstage to the Hotel Quirinale where she was staying. Subsequently she sued the theatre and won 2.7 million lire in restitution.

A plaque on the front of Hotel Quirinale attests to the fact that Giuseppe Verdi appeared on the balcony of his room, on April 13, 1893, to greet a crowd that gathered after the first Rome performance of *Falstaff.*

Hotel Quirinale
via Nazionale, 7 (down via Torino from the Teatro dell'Opera)

Teatro Costanzi (today's Teatro dell'Opera) presented premieres of (details of the premieres appear at the end of the section) *L'amico Fritz* (1891), Pietro Mascagni; *Cavalleria rusticana* (1890), Pietro Mascagni; *Tosca* (1900), Giacomo Puccini.

The entrance to Teatro dell'Opera is in piazza Beniamino Gigli.

Teatro dell'Opera, piazza Beniamino Gigli, 1, 00184 Roma
mailing address:
via Firenze, 63, Roma 00184
tel, box office: (39–6) 481–7003 (also for update of summer season)
tel, information: (39–6) 474–2595
Opera season from December through June.

Le Terme di Caracalla (The Baths of Caracalla): At one time the summer opera productions here were the place to go for three weeks of opera (eight performances) in the evenings of late July through mid-August. Unfortunately, opera can no longer be performed at the Baths because the city decided that the vibrations of the music and the masses of people who attended these performances were damaging the masonry of the Roman ruin. Since abandoning the Baths, the summer opera performances have been presented in the gardens of Villa Borghese, in piazza di Siena, in front of the Borghese Gallery and just to the north of the large *galoppatoio* (horseback riding ground).

For information call: Teatro dell'Opera: (39–6) 481–7003

Two theatres no longer standing but very important in the history of opera in Rome were Teatro Apollo and Teatro Alibert.

Teatro Apollo, originally called Teatro di Tor di Nona, was built in 1671 and was one of the first public theatres in Rome. Before 1680 almost all opera was presented as court entertainments. The theatre was Rome's first attempt to mount more cosmopolitan productions by using nonlocal singers. It was rebuilt in 1732 on the banks of the Tiber opposite Castel Sant'Angelo.

On January 29, 1781, Teatro di Tor di Nona was destroyed by fire, again rebuilt, and opened in 1795 and named Teatro Apollo. At first the theatre was used for light opera; however, in the course of the nineteenth century more serious works by Rossini, Saverio Mercadante, Donizetti, Giovanni Pacini,

Verdi, Meyerbeer, Gounod, Ambroise Thomas, and Massenet were performed there. The first Italian performances of Beethoven's *Fidelio* and the world premieres of Verdi's *Il travatore* and *Un ballo in maschera* took place at the Apollo. Wagner's *Lohengrin* was first heard in Rome at the Apollo in 1878, and his entire *Ring* cycle was performed in German (!) in 1883. Unfortunately, the theatre was demolished in 1889 because of seasonal flooding that was yearly becoming worse and in order to make way for the widening of Lungotevere Tor di Nona between Ponte Sant'Angelo and Ponte Umberto. The widening of the embankments of the Tiber was done in imitation of what Paris had done with the banks of the Seine several years earlier. Even though it is no longer standing, it is interesting to note the theatre's proximity to the other theatres in the city.

A large, freestanding marble plaque on the *river side of Lungotevere* between Ponte Sant'Angelo and Ponte Umberto states:

> *Teatro Apollo*
> *Sulle Pietre della antica Torre Orsina*
> *A fasti e glorie d'arte musicale*
> *Aprì le dorate scene*
> *E dove foscheggio Torre di Nona*
> *Libera si difuse la pura Melodia Italica*
> *Del Trovatore—il XIX Gennaio del MDCCCLIII*
> *Di Un Ballo in Maschera—il XVII Febbraio in DCCCLN*
> *Qui dove sul teatro demolito*
> *Passa la nuova strada Romana*
> *Il Genio di Giuseppe Verdi*
> *Affida l'eterna melodia canora*
> *All'aria al sole, al cuore umano*
> *A ricordanza della Torre*
> *Del Teatro del genio creatore*
> *Il comune di Roma pose*
> *Anno Domini MCMXXV.*

Here on the ruins of the ancient Orsina Tower
Teatro Apollo
Dedicated its golden stage
To the triumphs and glories of the art of music.
And just where the dark Tower of Nona once stood,
The pure Italian melodies
Of *Il trovatore*—January 19, 1853,
Of *Un ballo in maschera*—February, 17, 1859
Freely echoed.
Here where this new Roman road
Now passes over what was once the theatre,

The genius of Giuseppe Verdi
Offered the eternal art of bel canto
To the air, the sun, and the human heart.
Placed in memoriam of the tower,
The theatre, and that of creative genius
By the city of Rome
1925.

Among the operas Teatro Apollo premiered were (details of the premieres appear at the end of the section) *Un ballo in maschera* (1859), Giuseppe Verdi; *Il trovatore* (1853), Giuseppe Verdi.

The history of Teatro Alibert is an interesting footnote. The theatre was renamed Teatro delle Dame, in 1726, because it was the first theatre in Rome where female operatic parts were sung by women, not by castrati or *sopranisti*. Unfortunately, the theatre was destroyed by fire in 1863. Teatro delle Dame stood on the corner of via d'Alibert and via Margutta, where the present-day via d'Alibert, 2, has its *portone* (doorway).

Details of the premieres presented at Teatro Argentina

Il barbiere di Siviglia, commedia in two acts, February 20, 1816.
Gioacchino Rossini (1792–1868)
Libretto Claudio Sterbini, after Pierre-Augustin Beaumarchais's *Le barbier de Séville.*

The Beaumarchais play had been the subject of operas by a number of composers before Rossini, the most successful being Paisiello's. So, for the first performances Rossini called the opera *Almaviva, ossia L'inutile precauzione* (Almaviva, or the Useless Precaution). The title fit the plot, which recounts the passionate wooing of Rosina, ward of the possessive Doctor Bartolo, by Count Almaviva, aided by Figaro, Seville's barber and general factotum. (For the story's continuation in *Le nozze di Figaro,* see Vienna, page 174.) The premiere was conducted by Rossini at the harpsichord and proved a disaster because friends and followers of Paisiello constantly interrupted with catcalls and the like. (It was even reported that a cat was thrown on the stage during the performance.) Not until the first performance in Bologna, in August 1816, two months after Paisiello's death, was the present title used. *Il barbiere di Siviglia* was commissioned by the impresario of Teatro Argentina, Duke Sforza-Cesarini, who died just two weeks before the first performance. Rossini received the text from his librettist on January 25, 1816, and delivered the completed music to the first rehearsal February 6, 1816, writing the entire opera in twelve or thirteen days! It is said that the orchestra of the theatre was made up of thirty-five poorly paid amateurs. The Almaviva was the famous Spanish tenor Manuel García, father of the famous soprano Maria

Malibran. Notwithstanding its disastrous premiere, the opera became a great success throughout Europe, including Russia, and was the first opera to be sung in Italian in New York, at the Park Theatre in November 1825. It was Adelina Patti, whose unusually florid rendering of "Una voce poco fa" was met by Rossini's polite inquiry, "Very nice, my dear, and who wrote the piece you have just performed?"

La battaglia di Legnano, *tragedia lirica* in four acts, January 27, 1849.
Giuseppe Verdi (1813–1901)
Libretto Salvadore Cammarano, after Joseph Méry's play *La Bataille de Toulouse.*

Verdi wrote *La battaglia di Legnano* as an overtly political statement. Throughout Europe, 1848 had been a year fraught with revolutionary fervor. As a result, the opera's premiere was an enormous success and the whole of Act IV was demanded as an encore. Because of counterrevolutionary repression in other cities, however, it proved nigh to impossible to perform the opera outside of Rome. Even later in the century the opera did not become as popular as other Verdi creations, perhaps because it was too closely associated with an anguished period in Italian history.

I due Foscari, *tragedia lirica* in three acts, November 3, 1844.
Giuseppe Verdi (1813–1901)
Libretto Francesco Maria Piave, after Lord Byron's play *The Two Foscari.*

Verdi began writing *I due Foscari* soon after the premiere of *Ernani.* Verdi wanted his librettist, Piave, to concentrate on complex personal confrontations rather than grand scenic effects. Because Verdi did not yet trust Piave's abilities completely, and because of his demanding theatrical instincts, Verdi perhaps intervened too much in the making of the libretto. The premiere was not a great success, most likely because the audience's expectations were too high after the stunning triumph of the opera's immediate predecessor, *Ernani.*

Details from some premieres presented at Teatro Valle

La Cenerentola, *ossia La bontà in trionfo* (Cinderella, or Goodness Triumphant), *dramma giocoso* in two acts, January 25, 1817.
Gioacchino Rossini (1792–1868)
Libretto Jacopo Feretti, after Charles Perrault's *Cendrillon* and librettos by Charles-Guillaume Etienne for Nicolas Isouard's *Cendrillon* (Paris, 1810) and Francesco Fiorini for Stefano Pavesi's *Agatina, o La virtù premiata* (Agatina, or The Prize of Virtue) (Milan, 1814).

It took Rossini three weeks to write *La Cenerentola.* Instead of composing a new overture for the opera, he reused the one to *La gazzetta* (The

Newspaper), an opera buffa he had written in 1816 in Neapolitan dialect that had been premiered in Naples in September 1816. *La Cenerentola*, which loosely follows the fairy tale of the sweet young girl forced to be a servant to her two stepsisters and their vapid father, quickly became popular in Italy and the rest of Europe and in the Americas. In 1844 it became the first Italian opera to be presented in Australia (February 12, 1844). Teresa Berganza and Frederica von Stade are both well known for their interpretations of the title role.

Demetrio e Polibio, *dramma serio* in two acts, May 18, 1812 (written before 1808).
Gioacchino Rossini (1792–1868)
Libretto Vincenzina Vaganò-Mombelli (this is one of two women librettists in this book!).

This is Rossini's first full-scale opera, though it was not the first to be performed. He wrote *Demetrio e Polibio* as a student at the conservatory in Bologna. Even though it is such an early work, one can already see in it signs of his future compositional facility and musical greatness.

Details of the operas premiered at Teatro del Opera

L'amico Fritz, *commedia lirica* in three acts, October 31, 1891.
Pietro Mascagni (December 7, 1863, Livorno–August 2, 1945, Rome)
Libretto P. Suardon (pseudonym for Nicola Daspuro), from Erickmann-Chatrian's story *L'ami Fritz.*

The triumphant premiere of *L'amico Fritz* was hailed as the most important operatic event since the premiere of Verdi's *Otello* in 1887. Strange, because the opera's action is innocuous, with no intense drama or passion, unlike *Otello.* Mascagni's music is very detailed and subtle, with a great deal of attention paid to atmospheric effects rather than the broad dramatic strokes he used in *Cavalleria rusticana.* It is almost as if he deliberately wrote a contrast to *Cavalleria. L'amico Fritz* is not a repertory opera today but has been presented in the past ten years at the Metropolitan Opera.

Cavalleria rusticana (Rustic Chivalry), *melodramma* in one act, May 17, 1890.
Pietro Mascagni (1863–1945)
Libretto Giovanni Targioni-Tozzetti and Guido Menasci, after a novel of the same name by Giovanni Verga.

Mascagni wrote *Cavalleria rusticana* for the music publisher Sonzogno's second competition for a one-act opera. Puccini was sent the libretto before Mascagni but did not find it interesting! (Remember, Puccini did not even get honorable mention for *Le villi* in the first competition. See page 93.) Mascagni won the competition hands down and the opera was a resounding success; within months it had been performed to wild acclaim in the principal opera houses of Europe and America. (Gustav Mahler conducted it in Budapest.) *Cavalleria rusticana* is a pseudonationalistic opera that displays a primitive, stylized, rustic, blood-and-guts type of violence. The opera begins on Easter morning with Turiddu singing of his love for Lola, who is married to Alfio. Santuzza, another young villager, appears. She has been seduced and abandoned by Turiddu and begs him to return to her but to no avail. She tells Alfio of the affair between Lola and Turiddu, and Alfio kills Turiddu. Although he tried very hard to do so, Mascagni was never able to write another blockbuster success. (He went so far as to set the story of Lady Godiva as an opera called *Isabeau,* in 1911.) Since a performance at Teatro Costanzi (Teatro dell'Opera) in 1893, *Cavalleria rusticana* has usually been paired with Leoncavallo's *I pagliacci,* a duo often referred to as *Cav-Pag.*

Tosca, melodramma in three acts, January 14, 1900.
Giacomo Puccini (1858–1924)
Libretto Luigi Illica (libretto) and Giuseppe Giacosa (versification) after Victorien Sardou's play *La Tosca.*

In 1889, after reading Sardou's play *La Tosca,* Puccini begged the publisher Giulio Ricordi to obtain permission for him to set it as an opera, saying, "In this *Tosca* I see the opera that will fulfill all my expectations: one without excessive proportions or decorative spectacle..." With this comment Puccini was rejecting the grand opera spectacle popular in Italy at the time. In 1895, after he saw the great Sarah Bernhardt perform the title role (it was written for her) in Florence he became even more insistent. When the libretto was finally prepared by Illica, Puccini considered it an improvement on the original play. Puccini's theatrical instincts were correct. The opera is dramatically gripping throughout. The singer (Floria Tosca) and the painter (Mario Cavadarossi) are vividly characterized, while the chief of police (Baron Scarpia) is a true villain. When Tosca kills him in Act II one wants to cheer. In Act III Mario's death by firing squad and Tosca's suicide are some of the most riveting moments in all of opera. The title role contains Puccini's most varied and interesting dramatic music, music that in the hands of a great operatic actress (such as Maria Callas) makes the character Floria Tosca credible, dignified, passionate, and intelligent. In a Covent Garden production in 1925, the famous soprano Maria Jeritza began the tradition of singing "Vissi d'arte" lying on her stomach, full-length on the floor, because Scarpia had accidentally knocked her down.

Ricordi arranged the premiere in Rome, probably because of the opera's Roman setting. Some critics objected to the brutality of the plot, but the opera was an unprecedented public success, playing twenty nights to a packed house. The premiere was somewhat marred by a bomb scare and threats to the singers by Roman musicians who were jealous of Puccini. Two months later, *Tosca* was given in Milan at La Scala, conducted by Arturo Toscanini, and its success was indeed confirmed. In *Tosca* Puccini combined his lyricism with the Wagnerian leitmotiv technique. This speeds up the action of Sardou's rather silly melodrama and makes the title role a very compelling dramatic vehicle.

Details of the operas premiered at Teatro Apollo

Un ballo in maschera, melodramma in three acts, February 17, 1859.
Giuseppe Verdi (1813–1901)
Libretto Antonio Somma, after Eugène Scribe's libretto *Gustave III, ou Le bal masqué,* which Scribe wrote for Auber's opera of the same name in 1833.

    Verdi originally set out to write *Un ballo in maschera* for a commission from Teatro San Carlo in Naples. Under Spanish control, the Neapolitan censors were even stricter than those in Rome, so Verdi decided to have the opera performed in Rome. To meet the demands of the Roman censors, who objected to the assassination of a king during a masked ball, Verdi and Somma changed the locale of the action from Sweden to North America, giving the heroic tenor role to Riccardo, Count of Warwick, rather than to Gustavus III, King of Sweden. Somma was upset by this and other things and refused to let his name appear on the printed libretto. The premiere, however, was a great success, and the opera became one of Verdi's most popular works. It remains in the international repertory today.

Il trovatore, dramma in four parts, January 19, 1853.
Giuseppe Verdi (1813–1901)
Libretto Salvatore Cammerano (with additions by Leone Emanuele Bardare after Cammerano's death in July 1852), after Antonio Garcia Gutierrez's play *El trobador.*

    Il trovatore is the second of the three operas that from 1851 to 1853 propelled Giuseppe Verdi to stardom. The violent story about the witch Azucena and her "son" Manrico hinges on Manrico's love for Leonora, who is also loved by the Count di Luna. Eventually the Count di Luna is in charge and while Azucena waits to be burnt at the stake, Leonora poisons herself, and Manrico is beheaded. At the very end Azucena cries out exultantly that the Count di Luna has just killed his own brother. Verdi saw Azucena as akin to Rigoletto, a bizarre and vengeful character, fired by filial love. The opera was a huge success and soon became the most popular of Verdi's works, both in Italy and around the world. For a production in Paris in 1857 Verdi prepared a French version of the opera (*Le Trouvère*) that included a ballet after the opening chorus of Act III. *Il trovatore* remains in the international repertory, although it is not as popular as the other two operas of the 1851–53 trilogy, *Rigoletto* and *La Traviata*.

The premiere of *Il trovatore* took place even though the public had to wade to the theatre's entrance through the floodwaters of the Tiber River!

LODGING

Since the mid 1980s traffic has been limited in Rome's *centro storico*. This is by no means to say that there is no traffic, but vehicles at least move and the air seems better, making Rome still a nice city to walk in. It is most definitely best to stay in the center of Rome, even though the present-day opera house is to the east of the city center. To understand what I mean by center, look at the map of Rome and use the Pantheon as the center; go north to piazza del Popolo, south to the Tiber, east to via del Babuino, and west to the west side of piazza Navona. This is the area of Renaissance Rome. Rome is a *very* popular tourist city, so reserve a hotel well in advance to get what you want.

Hotel Margutta, via Laurina, 34, Roma 00187
tel: (39–6) 322–3674 or 679–8440
The only thing wrong with this lovely hotel is that it is a twenty-minute walk from the center of most of Rome's past operatic action. It is just off via del Babuino (Street of the Baboon) between piazza di Spagna and piazza del Popolo. It is a real bargain and *quiet* to boot!

Hotel Arenula, via Santa Maria de' Calderari, 47, Roma 00186
tel: (39–6) 687–9454   fax: (39–6) 689–6188
Just down the street from Teatro Argentina, this is a lovely hotel with *very good* prices for a long stay in Rome. Remember to ask for a quiet room. Its only problem is that it has no elevator.

Hotel Santa Chiara, via Santa Chiara, 21, Roma 00186
tel: (39–6) 654–0142   fax: (39–6) 687–3144
The Santa Chiara is right in back of the Pantheon on a relatively quiet street.

Hotel Teatro di Pompeo, largo del Pallaro, 8, Roma 00186
tel: (39–6) 687–2812   fax: (39–6) 654–5531
This hotel is built into the curve of the Roman Theatre of Pompeo where Julius Caesar met his end. It is a stone's throw from Campo dei Fiori, an open market that has been in use since early Roman times.

Albergo del Sole al Pantheon, piazza della Rotonda, 63, Roma 00186
tel: (39–6) 678–0441   fax: (39–6) 684–0689

Quite expensive, but since it has been a hotel since the fifteenth century it positively reeks with history!

Hotel Senato, piazza della Rotonda, 73, Roma 00186
tel: (39–6) 679–3231   fax: (39–6) 684–0297
Much less expensive than the Sole and not as nice, still, this hotel is very comfortable and overlooks piazza del Pantheon.

SNACKS

Rome has wonderful *rosticcerie* (fast food and food to take out). Although none of this food will do your arteries any good, it tastes wonderful, it is relatively cheap and fast, and you can take it to your hotel room or a sunny piazza. Some of their specialties are not to be missed:

> *supplì al telefono* (balls of savory rice with a center of creamy, melted mozzarella, breaded and deep-fried—that, when bitten into make "telephone wires" of melted cheese)
> *arancini fritti* (slightly larger breaded and deep-fried balls of rice)
> *crochette di patate* (balls of savory mashed potatoes, breaded and deep-fried)
> *zucchini fritti* (battered and deep-fried strips of zucchini)
> *carciofi fritti* (thin slices of Italian artichokes, battered and deep-fried)
> *mozzarella in carozza* (a mozzarella "sandwich," dipped in egg and deep-fried)

One of the better *rosticcerie* is:

Il Delfino, corner of via di Torre Argentina and corso Vittorio Emanuele.
Closed Mondays.

FOOD

Once upon a time it was cheaper to eat in Rome's restaurants than to cook for oneself. Alas, those days have long passed, but there are still excellent restaurants that have good prices. Some *specialità romane* are:

> *stracciatella* (hot chicken broth with egg and Parmesan beaten in)
> *spaghetti all'amatriciana* (spaghetti in a tomato sauce with bacon, onions, and herbs that has its origins in the town of Amatrice in Lazio)
> *maccheroni alla carbonara* (macaroni with a "sauce" of eggs, bacon, and cheese)
> *spaghetti alle vongole* (spaghetti with a garlicky tomato-based clam sauce, or simply with olive oil, garlic, clams, and parsley)

paglia e fieno con piselli, funghi e prosciutto (literally "straw and hay," plain and spinach egg noodles, served with cream, peas, mushrooms, and ham; add a good quantity of Parmesan)

abbacchio alla romana (baked lamb with rosemary and garlic)

patate al forno (small potatoes baked with olive oil, garlic, and rosemary, or in the same pan as the abbacchio; they go perfectly with the abbacchio)

stufato alla romana (a tasty Roman version of beef stew)

involtini di vitello (stewed veal rolls containing vegetables)

spezzatino di vitello (tasty veal "stew")

carciofi alla romana (small roman artichokes stewed in herbs, olive oil, and garlic; served hot or cold)

piselli al prosciutto (fresh green peas cooked with butter and ham; the peas that grow near Rome are known for their tender sweetness)

Trattoria dal Cav. Gino, vicolo Rosini, 4 (at the corner of the piazza del Parlamento)
tel: (39–6) 687–3434
Closed Sundays.

The cooking in this popular restaurant is *casareccia* (home cooking). They have excellent wines. The street in front of this small *trattoria* is always full of Romans waiting for a table. *Most definitely* reserve.

Al Moro, vicolo delle Bollette, 13
tel: (39–6) 678–3495

This is an excellent small restaurant that specializes in Roman cooking. As soon as you are seated, they will bring a plate of appetizers consisting of:

fiori di zucchini fritti (fried zucchini flowers)

supplì (balls of savory rice, breaded and deep-fried)

Definitely reserve.

La Buca di Ripetta, via di Ripetta, 36
tel: (39–6) 321–9391
Closed Sunday nights and Mondays, and the month of August.

I used to walk halfway across Rome to come to this simple and excellent restaurant situated not far from the Spanish Steps. Reserve.

Il Buco, via Sant'Ignazio, 8
tel: (39–6) 679–3298
Closed Mondays, and from August 15 through September 1.

This lovely restaurant specializes in Tuscan food: excellent steaks, meat, sausages, and bean dishes. It is situated right around the corner from via del Piede del Marmo with its *large* marble foot. Reserve.

Da Giggetto, via del Portico d'Ottavia, 21/a–22
tel: (39–6) 686–1105

Da Giggetto al Portico d'Ottavia is the full name of this restaurant that stands in the middle of Rome's ancient and present ghetto. The specialties are Jewish-Roman:

> *carciofi alla giudia* (crunchy, fried, Italian-Jewish-style artichokes)
> *baccalà fritto* (fried codfish; salted, dried cod, soaked and desalted before being battered and fried)
> *fiori di zucca fritti* (fried zucchini flowers)
> *rigatoni con la pajata* (rigatoni with a sauce made of the intestine of milk-fed calf)

BERGAMO

Bergamo is situated in Italy's north, in Lombardia, fifty kilometers northeast of Milan. Approaching Bergamo by train you become aware of the Alps rising up from the plain; the old part of the city, Bergamo Alta, is perched on the top of a hill overlooking Bergamo Bassa. The evocative city center of Bergamo Alta, with its Byzantine palaces, owes much to the fact that Venice ruled Bergamo for over 350 years.

To get to Bergamo Alta: After first getting a bus ticket from the newspaper stand in the station, take the number 1 bus from in front of the train station to the funicular railway (*funicolare*). Your bus ticket is also good for the *funicolare,* and the view of the valley below is fantastic.

In Bergamo Alta

Gaetano Donizetti (November 29, 1797–April 8, 1848) was born and died in Bergamo, although he spent most of his adult life in other parts of Italy and in Paris. The son of an indigent family, because of his potential talent he was taken under the wing of the expatriate German composer and teacher Simone Mayr (1763–1845) from whom he took charity lessons in music from 1806 to 1815 at the Lezioni Caritatevoli (the Charitable School) in Via Arena, 20, behind the church of Santa Maria Maggiore. A plaque in front of the building states:

In questa casa	In this house
Gaetano Donizetti	Gaetano Donizetti
fequentò	attended
dal 1806 al 1815	from 1806 to 1815
le Lezioni Caritatevoli	the Charitable School
di Simone Mayr	of Simone Mayr
che indovinò il genio	who recognized his genius
e ne predisse la gloria.	and predicted his glory.

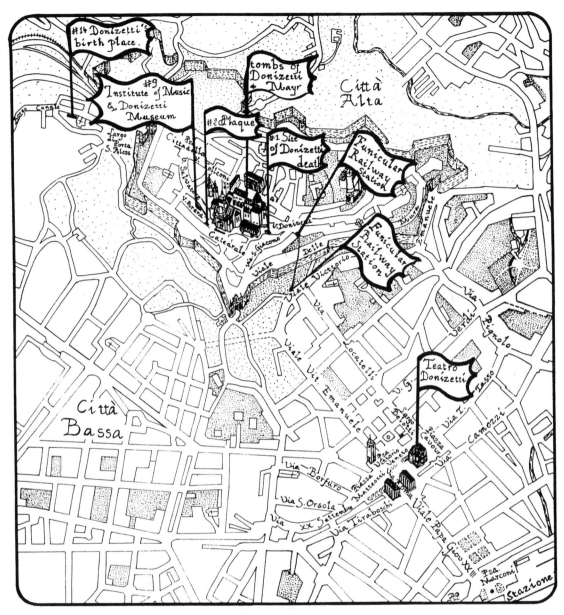

Operatic Bergamo

All music conservatories were closed in the French-ruled parts of Italy during the Napoleonic period in the first decade of the nineteenth century. The Lezioni Caritatevoli was begun to surreptitiously fill the void left by the closings as well as to offer education to poor and orphaned children. Mayr was so convinced of Donizetti's prospects as a composer that he underwrote the young man's further studies in Bologna.

In his relatively short career, Donizetti wrote sixty-six operas and between 1820 and 1830 was the most performed operatic composer in Italy. Only about seven of his operas are generally known in this century: *Don Pasquale, Linda de Chamounix, La favorite, La fille du régiment, Lucia di Lammermoor, Maria Stuarda,* and *L'elisir d'amore*; today only two, *L'elisir d'amore* and *Lucia di Lammermoor*, are performed with any frequency outside of Italy.

Donizetti went insane at the end of his life (due to cerebrospinal syphilis) and returned to Bergamo, paralyzed and unable to speak. An unfortunate and not often mentioned manifestation of his condition was that he was in an unrelieved state of sexual arousal for the last several months of his life. He spent his last days cared for in the palace of the Baronessa Scotti in the present Via Gaetano Donizetti, 1 (to the left immediately upon exiting the *funicolare*).

Further up the hill both Donizetti and his teacher, the composer Simone Mayr, are buried in the Church of Santa Maria Maggiore. Their beautifully decorated tombs are well worth a visit. A plaque in the church also commemorates the tenure of Amilcare Ponchielli (1834–86, of *La gioconda* fame) as organist there from 1882 until his death in 1886.

The Donizetti Museum, with a collection of manuscripts and mementos, is situated in the Istituto Musicale (Institute of Music). Although rather dowdy, it is a strangely evocative place. The paintings of Donizetti at various stages of his life are interesting, as are the paintings and sculptures of many of the singers that made Donizetti's music live. The museum also exhibits posters from the premieres of many of his operas, his letters, some original manuscripts of his work, and quite a few opera reductions for voice and piano. (For a full experience go to the museum on a weekday of the school year and you are likely to hear some wonderful singing in the background!)

Museo Donizetti (in the **Istituto Musicale di Bergamo**), via Arena, 9 Open Monday–Friday, 9:00 A.M.–12:30 P.M. and 3:30–6:00 P.M.

The museum is not clearly marked, so just enter the doors of the Istituto Musicale, go up the stairs, turn immediately to the right, then turn left and go to the end of the hallway; the museum is there.

Donizetti's birthplace, just outside the gates of the old city, in via Borgo Canale, 14, is now a national monument open to the public from May to September. The house stands next to the Ristorante Colombina, so called because Bergamo is reputed to be the home of Brighella, who, along with Pierrot, Colombina (Columbine) and Arlecchino (Harlequin), is a character of the Italian commedia dell'arte.

To get to the house, walk out the western gates of Bergamo Alta and go up a little hill to Borgo Canale. Call the porter at 237–374 to gain entrance (be sure to tip!).

Both Donizetti and Vincenzo Bellini conducted operas in Bergamo's Teatro Ricordi, in Bergamo Bassa. Built in 1791, the theatre is now naturally called Teatro Donizetti and seats 1,164. Since 1982 an annual city homage to Donizetti, called Donizetti e il suo tempo (Donizetti and his age), takes place for four weeks from mid-September to early October, during which at least one of his operas is

Donizetti's tomb

always performed as well as three or four others by his contemporaries. The concert season extends from October through May. For information write:

Teatro Donizetti, Donizetti e il suo tempo, piazza Cavour, 15, 24100 Bergamo, Italy
tel, information: (39–35) 399–320 or 399–20
tel, tickets: (39–35) 249–631   fax: (39–35) 217–560

LODGING

Hotel Excelsior San Marco, piazza della Repubblica, 6, Bergamo 24122
tel: (39–35) 366–111   fax: (39–35) 223–201
This is a particularly pleasant hotel near the theatre and the *funicolare* in Bergamo Bassa.

FOOD

Taverna Valtellinese, via Tiraboschi, 57
tel: (39–35) 243–331
　　Closed Sunday nights and Mondays and the first two weeks in August.
This moderately priced restaurant is a five-minute walk from the theatre.

Ristorante Da Vittorio, viale Papa Giovanni XXIII, 21
tel: (39–35) 218–060
Closed Wednesdays and the month of August.
　　Da Vittorio is a world-class restaurant only a five-minute walk from
the theatre. Although it is quite expensive, it is worth the price.

Ristorante La Mariana, largo Colle Aperto, 214
tel: (39–35) 237–027
Closed Mondays and the first two weeks in January.
　　This restaurant is in Bergamo Alta near the western gate that leads to
Donizetti's birthplace. The view from largo Colle Aperto is breathtaking. (Just pretend that the ugly housing development in the distance is
nonexistent.)

BOLOGNA

Bologna is the capital and largest city of Emilia-Romagna, the region just north
of the Apennines, at the southeastern end of the val Padana, the valley of the Po
River. The principal railway linking all of Italy to the south to most of the rest of
Europe goes through Bologna's Stazione Centrale (Central Station). For many
years as I passed through the train station of Bologna I thought, "Ugh! what an
ugly city." Only in 1970 did I alight from the train to sing in Teatro Comunale.
To my delight and surprise, I found that Bologna is an extraordinarily beautiful
city of vaulted sidewalks lined with fourteenth- through seventeenth-century
palaces. The University of Bologna, founded in 425, is one of the oldest, if not
the oldest, in Europe. Bologna's north-central geographic location has always
allowed for easy contact with other musical centers in Italy and the rest of
Europe.
　　In the library of the Conservatorio di Musica G.B. Martini (formerly the
Liceo Filarmonico) in piazza Rossini, down via Zamboni from the Teatro
Comunale, one finds the original exercise prepared by Wolfgang Amadeus
Mozart for entry into Bologna's distinguished Accademia Filarmonica on
October 9, 1770. He received a *low* but passing mark! A plaque attesting to his
presence can be seen in the conservatory's library. Open Monday–Saturday, 9:00
A.M.–1:00 P.M.

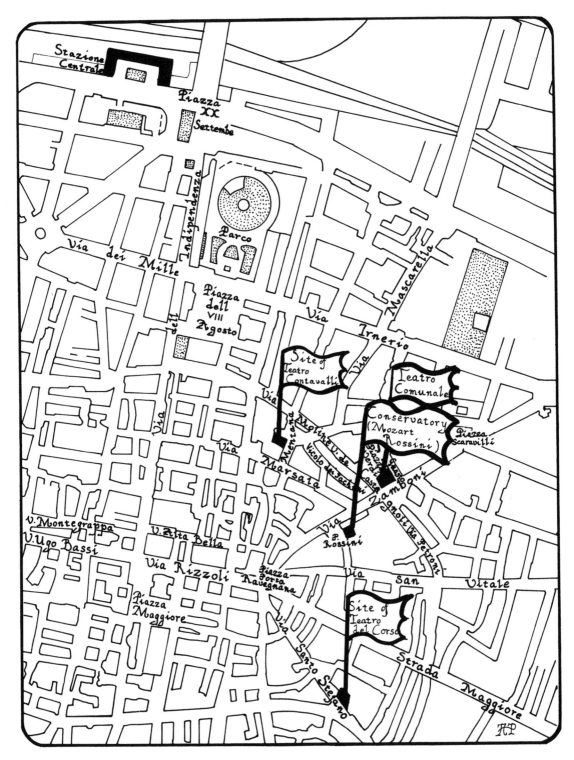

Operatic Bologna

Gioacchino Rossini served as an administrator at the conservatory from 1839 to 1843. A plaque near the entrance recounts his connection with the institution both as a student and then as *consulente perpetuo* (permanent consultant). The importance of opera to the city is also reflected by the fact that the most important treatise on singing in eighteenth-century Europe was written by the famous Bolognese castrato, teacher, and writer, Pier Francesco Tosi. This 1723 treatise was entitled *Opinioni de' cantori antichi e moderni* (Opinions of Singers of Yesterday and Today).

The only opera house still standing and used for the presentation of opera in Bologna is Teatro Comunale (seating capacity 1,500). Originally called Teatro Malvezzi, the theatre opened in 1653 and was renovated and enlarged in 1697 by the Galli-Bibiena family, famous architects and stage designers. This theatre burned down in 1745, and Teatro Comunale, constructed in its place, was inaugurated May 14, 1763, with a performance of Christoph Willibald Gluck's *Il trionfo di Clelia*. The theatre quickly became the most important operatic institution in the city, presenting three seasons a year, each composed of up to four new productions that were repeated thirty to forty times.

Unlike the many Italian theatres built in the rather broad horseshoe shape of the *teatro all'italiano*, Teatro Comunale is built with more curves, more in the shape of a cello. It is somewhat reminiscent of Mantua's Teatro Scientifico (see page 68), which was also built by the Galli-Bibiena family about the same time.

Wagner's music was first presented in Italy in an 1871 performance of *Lohengrin* at the Teatro Comunale. Tannhäuser received its Italian premiere in 1872 (Verdi, who traveled all the way from Parma to hear the opera, wrote that Wagner was "mad !!!"), and *Tristan und Isolde* in 1888. The theatre also mounted the Italian premiere of Verdi's *Don Carlo* in 1867, six months after its world premiere in Paris.

The theatre was severely damaged by Allied bombing in 1944 but was rebuilt and again renovated recently, in 1980–81; it has one of the most splendid interiors in all of Italy. Be sure to enter the foyer of the first floor (American second) where a mock-up of how the theatre's floor was constructed shows why the acoustics are so superb.

Today Teatro Comunale presents one of Italy's most interesting opera seasons.

Teatro Comunale, largo Respighi, 1 (entrance in via Zamboni 28–30), 40126 Bologna
Box office open Monday–Friday, 3:30–7:00 P.M.; Saturday, 9:30 A.M.–12:30 P.M. and 3:30–7:00 P.M.
tel: (39–51) 529–999

Most of the many Bolognese opera houses dating from the seventeenth and eighteenth centuries were destroyed by fire or in World War II Allied bombing. Two of these theatres are of note because of their relationship to Gioacchino Rossini:

Teatro Contavalli opened in 1814 on the grounds of the Convent of the Carmelite Fathers near the church of San Martino. From 1815 to 1826 and 1840 to 1843, Rossini directed many performances of his works there. In 1938 the theatre was transformed into a cinema. The building was destroyed January 29, 1944, by Allied bombs. One can see where it once stood. Where Viccolo de' Facchini makes a T with via Mentana, across the street from Bar Contavalli and Farmacia Contavalli, there is a large empty space flanked by a very modern building and the church of San Martino.

Teatro del Corso opened May 19, 1805, with Napoleon Bonaparte in attendance and Gioacchino Rossini singing a minor role in an opera by Ferdinando Paer, one of the composers responsible for the development of *opera semiseria* at the beginning of the nineteenth century. The theatre also presented the Italian premiere of Offenbach's *Les Contes d'Hoffmann*, September 28, 1903. Unfortunately the building was severely damaged by Allied bombing in 1944, and the city, impoverished by the war, repaired only Teatro Comunale. One can see where Teatro del Corso once stood on via Santo Stefano across from the flank of the church of Santo Stefano near the Farmacia del Corso.

Teatro del Corso presented the premiere of:

L'equivoco stravagante, (The Curious Misunderstanding), *dramma giocoso* in two acts, October 26, 1811.
Gioacchino Rossini (1792–1868)
Libretto Gaetano Gasbarri.

Rossini was nineteen when he wrote *L'equivoco stravagante*, his first full-scale opera in two acts. The police in Bologna banned the opera after its third performance; its libretto was considered too risqué because it dealt with a transsexual disguise and an army deserter, as well as clandestine love. Ricordi published this very long opera (over 300 pages) in 1847. Unfortunately, as is the case with Mozart's early operas, one seldom has the opportunity to hear the work of the young and prolific Rossini. (Today *L'equivoco stravagante* can be heard on a CD, Claves 50–9200.)

Ruggiero Raimondi was born in Bologna, and Mirella Freni, born in nearby Modena, studied at the Conservatorio G. B. Martini.

LODGING

The Palace Hotel, via Montegrappa 9/2, Bologna 40121
tel: (39–51) 237–442   fax: (39–51) 220–689
This hotel is charming, clean, reasonably priced, and very centrally located. It is a ten-minute walk from Teatro Comunale and only a minute away from da Nello!

Hotel Cavour, via Goito, 4, Bologna 40126
tel: (39–51) 228–111   fax: (39–51) 222–978

This comfortable, centrally located hotel is a three-minute walk from Teatro Comunale.

SNACKS

For afternoon coffee go to any *pasticceria* (pastry–coffee shop) in the center of town near the two towers.

FOOD

Bologna is home of some of the world's greatest food. Some typical specialties are:

> *mortadella* (Bologna's unique pink salami laced with pistachios)
> *passatelli* (hot chicken broth into which egg, bread crumbs, and Parmesan cheese have been added through a special sieve)
> *gramigna con salsiccia* (curly pasta with sausage in a cream sauce)
> *budino di pollo in brodo* (chicken mousse in broth)
> *tagliatelle con ragù* (broad egg noodles with bolognese meat sauce)
> *tortellini con ragù* (little pasta cakes filled with meat and served with a bolognese meat sauce)
> *lasagne verdi* (spinach lasagne with *ragù*)
> *cotolette al marsala* (veal cutlets in a marsala sauce)
> *petti di pollo alla bolognese, cotolette alla bolognese, petto di tacchino alla bolognese* (chicken breasts, veal cutlet or turkey breast, gently flattened and floured and sautéed in butter, then topped with prosciutto and Parmesan cheese; often served with a few sautéed mushrooms)

For consistently fine meals try:

Da Nello, via Montegrappa, 2
tel: (39–51) 236–331
Closed Mondays.

Their tortellini in a cream sauce with a shaving of *tartufi bianchi* (white truffles) is to die for. The house pasta specialty, *gramigna*, is wonderful. The restaurant is a ten-minute walk from Teatro Comunale.

Dal Duttòur Balanzon, via Fossalta, 3
tel: (39–51) 232–098
Closed Saturdays and the month of July.

This centrally located restaurant has wonderful and rich bolognese specialties. It is a five-minute walk from Teatro Comunale.

BRESCIA

Brescia lies on the plain between Milan and Verona, in Lombardy, on the principal train line from Milan to Venice. The center of the city has a friendly, open atmosphere. It is an easy walk from the train station to Teatro Grande, in the city's center.

Teatro Grande faces corso Zanardelli near the corner of via delle X Giornate (the official address is via Panagora, 19a). The theatre, seating 1,070, was built of wood in 1710 but was covered with stucco and gilded in the 1860s. After its disastrous premiere at La Scala, Giacomo Puccini's *Madama Butterfly* was successfully produced here.

Madama Butterfly, *tragedia giapponese* (Japanese tragedy), May 28, 1904 (a mere three months after its Milan premiere).
Giacomo Puccini (1858–1924)
Libretto Luigi Illica and Giuseppe Giacosa, based on a play by David Belasco, *Madame Butterfly*, which was itself based on a short story by John Luther Long, which in turn was based partly on Pierre Loti's story "*Madame Chrysanthème.*"

After the La Scala disaster, Puccini revised the score of *Madama Butterfly*. Among other things he added Pinkerton's arietta, "Addio fiorito asil," in a vain attempt to make him less of a cad. The second performance, at Teatro Grande, was a triumph. Then, before the Paris premiere on December 28, 1906, Puccini further removed some of Pinkerton's more xenophobic phrases (but he remains a racist and misogynist). He also made Kate more sympathetic by excising her confrontation with Butterfly. This last version appears in the printed score. Today *Madama Butterfly* is one of Puccini's most performed operas. (While composing *Madama Butterfly*, Puccini was almost killed in an automobile accident, for like many men of his time, he was fascinated by the powerful motors of cars and boats!)

Teatro Grande's entrance belies the beauties within. Its three narrow doors lead to one of Italy's finest baroque theatres. The foyer is of beautiful pink marble, and the *ridotto* (lounge) is a delight of pink and green marble with pastoral paintings and mirrors set into the walls. The ceiling holds a gallery (no longer used) from which one once could hear concerts of "soft" instruments like the harpsichord.

The *portiere*, whose office is at the theatre's entrance in via Paganora, 19a, is very helpful and will show you the theatre. Be sure to give him a good tip.

Opera season from October through December. For information:

Teatro Grande, box office: corso Zanardelli
information: via Panagora, 19a, 25100 Brescia
tel: (39–30) 42–400

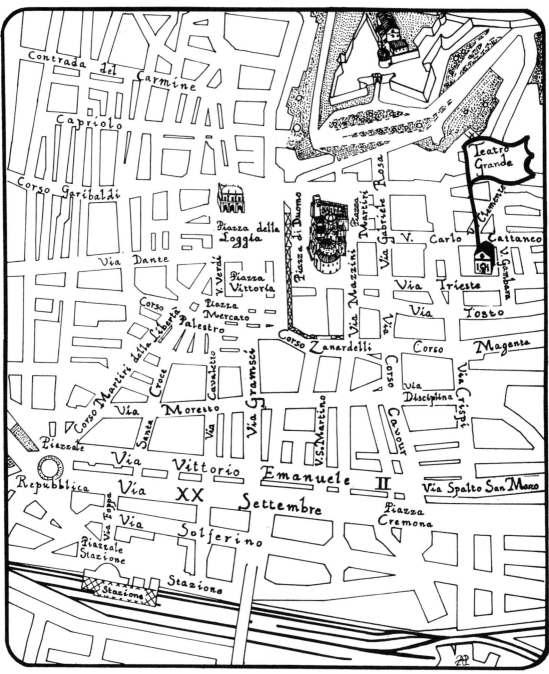

Operatic Brescia

LODGING

Hotel Vittoria, via delle X Giornate, 20, Brescia
tel: (39–30) 280–061   fax: (39–30) 280–065

This hotel is smack-dab in the center of old Brescia and a one-minute walk from the theatre, features that make it worth the slightly higher price than that of other nice hotels in town.

SNACKS

For a quick bite, go into one of the lovely *rosticcerie* (fast food and takeout) in via Gramsci. Try deep-fried stuffed olives!

FOOD

The food of Brescia is similar to that of Milan.

Trattoria al Frate, via Musei, 25
tel: (39–30) 375–1469
This charming *trattoria* is a five-minute walk from Teatro Grande and is open after the opera. Be sure to reserve!

Don Rodriguez, via Cavallotti, 6 (right in front of the theatre)
tel: (39–30) 377–4452
This lovely *ristorante* is also open after the opera. Be sure to reserve!

Ristorante Raffa, corso Magenta, 15
tel: (39–30) 200–2367
Yet another lovely restaurant, this one is a two-minute walk from the Teatro Grande. Reserve!

BUSSETO, LE RONCOLE, and SANT'AGATA DI VILLANOVA SULL'ARDA

Busseto, Le Roncole, and Sant'Agata are at the western edge of Emilia-Romagna, about thirty-five kilometers northwest of Parma, or about twenty-five kilometers south of Cremona. The land here is flat and filled with open fields of vineyards, wheat, sugar beets, and occasional clumps of tall trees. The climate is humid, so the summers are very hot and the winters achingly cold. It is, however, a timelessly evocative area. The rich color of the green fields in the early spring light is like none other. And the silence in the fall, when *foschia* (ground fog) blankets the land, is almost palpable. It was here that Bernardo Bertolucci filmed his *1900*.

Although Busseto can be reached by train, the only way to see all of Verdi country is to rent a car in nearby Parma, Fidenza, or Cremona for the day.

Busseto

When Verdi was ten, he moved to the slightly larger town of Busseto to attend the *ginnasio*, where he studied Italian, Latin, humanities, and rhetoric. Two years later he began musical studies with the director of the municipal music school. During this period in Busseto he attracted a patron, Antonio Barezzi, a wealthy

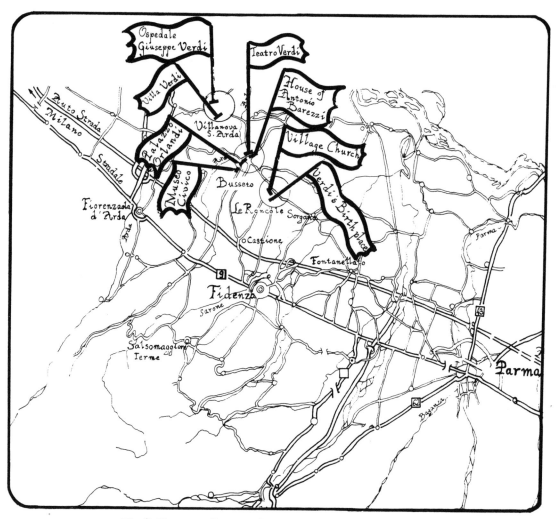

Verdi Country: Busseto, Le Roncole, and Sant'Agata

merchant and the founder of Busseto's Philharmonic Society. He housed Verdi in Busseto, aided him when he went to Milan, and, in 1836, gave him the hand of his daughter Margherita in marriage. The wedding took place next door to the Barezzi home in the Oratorio della SS Trinità, right off Busseto's piazza Verdi. Antonio Barezzi's house still stands at:

119 via Roma.

Verdi and Margherita had two children, neither of whom lived to see their second birthday. Margherita died in 1840 after giving birth to their second child. The Barezzi house, open from April through October, contains Verdi memorabilia including a drawing of Verdi as a young man by Stefano Barezzi, Margherita's uncle. In the hall in front of the door to the Barezzi apartment hang numerous opera posters with names of performers such as Tebaldi, Del Monaco, and Bruson.

A plaque mounted in 1913 on Barezzi's house, on the first centenary of Verdi's birth, states:

Antonio Barezzi di Busseto	Antonio Barezzi of Busseto
comprese il genio	understood the genius
incoraggiò i cimenti	encouraged the efforts
presagi la gloria di	and foresaw the glory of
Giuseppe Verdi.	Giuseppe Verdi.
Benedisse il connubbio	He blessed the marriage
della propria figliola	of his daughter
Margherita	Margherita
coll'artista povero e ignoto.	with the poor and unknown artist.
Il fiero Maestro	The proud Maestro
lo venerò come padre	venerated him as a father
lo riconnobbe sempre	and always recognized
con divota umiltà	with devoted humility
suo benefattore.	his benefactor.

In May 1832, at the age of eighteen, Verdi went to Milan and applied for permission to study at the conservatory. He was refused entry, owing to his unorthodox piano technique and because he was four years older than the usual entrance age. So he became the private student of Vincenzo Lavigna, who had been a conductor at La Scala. Slowly but surely he emerged as the most influential composer of Italian opera and the dominant figure in nineteenth-century Italian cultural life.

In 1849 Verdi moved back to Busseto with his mistress, Giuseppina Strepponi (1815–97), and occupied Palazzo Orlandi in the town's center, almost next door to Barezzi's house. The two years he and Strepponi lived in Busseto provoked a *scandale* in the small country town. Strangely enough, it was Antonio Barezzi, his former father-in-law, who quenched the flames of outraged provincial public opinion. Finally, in the spring of 1851 Verdi and Strepponi moved to the villa he had commissioned in Sant'Agata di Villanova sull'Arda, about two miles northwest of Busseto.

Directly off piazza Verdi stands Teatro Verdi (1868), a small theatre seating 600, built into the right wing of the palace Rocca dei Marchesi Pallavicino (now the city hall). Arturo Toscanini conducted a performance of *Falstaff* in 1913 in Teatro Verdi to celebrate the centennial of Verdi's birth and to raise funds for a Verdi monument. The large monument of a seated Verdi now stands directly in front of the palace and the theatre. Teatro Verdi was recently renovated and reopened in November 1994.

Teatro Verdi, piazza Giuseppe Verdi 10, 43011 Bussetto, Province of Parma

Teatro Verdi

A veritable cult of Verdi exists in Busseto, a group of men who meet in the central bar in via Roma and know all of the Maestro's music by heart. They say that the young people today don't like Verdi's music, but when they grow up "it will change... it is inevitable."

Busseto's Museo Civico Verdiano in Villa Pallavicino holds a few items from Verdi's life. Signs abound to lead you to the villa.

> **Museo Civico Verdiano,** Open daily, April through September, 9:30 A.M.–12:30 P.M. and 3:00–7:00 P.M.; October and November, 9:30 A.M.–noon and 2:30–5:00 P.M.

The tenor Carlo Bergonzi was born in nearby Polisene (on July 13, 1924) and now runs one of Busseto's hotels, called *I due Foscari* after the title of Verdi's sixth opera. It is situated right next to the Teatro Verdi. There is also a restaurant.

> **Albergo I due Foscari,** 43011 Busseto, Province of Parma
> tel: (39–524) 92337 or 92205   fax: (39–524) 91625

Le Roncole

A few kilometers outside of Busseto, one finds Le Roncole, the birthplace of Giuseppe Verdi (1813–1901). The humble house in which Verdi was born is now a national monument and contains some memorabilia from his life (all the rest are in the museum of La Scala in Milan). The house stands in the middle of the little hamlet of Le Roncole, near the church and the bar. It is on the main road and cannot be missed. The house is open daily from April through October.

The church's baptismal register for October 11, 1813, records Verdi as "born yesterday." His father was an innkeeper and his mother a spinner of yarn. A year after Verdi's birth, the defeat of Napoleon brought victorious allied armies through northern Italy. The story has it that the pursuing Austrian and Russian forces indiscriminately killed many of the local folk of Busseto, including those who had taken refuge in the church of San Michele. Verdi's mother, however, had had the foresight to climb into the bell tower, and thus she and her son, Giuseppe, were spared. The church still stands, with a plaque that says:

In questa torre vetusta e gloriosa
L'anno 1814
Luigia Uttini Verdi
Scampava il suo piccolo BEPPINO
Dalle orde sanguinarie
Di Russia e di Austria
Devastante questa fertile plaga
E conservava
All'arte un arcangelo sublime
All'auspicata redenzione d'Italia
Un bardo potente
Alla terra di Roncole
Una fulgida gloria imperitura
Un secolo dopo
Il prevosto Don Remiglio Zardi
L'opera parrocchiale
E il Circolo Popolare Cattolico
Commemorando la fausta data
Come ricordo
Questo marmo posero.

In this ancient and glorious tower,
In 1814,
Luisa Uttini Verdi
Saved the little Beppino
From the bloody hordes
Of Russia and Austria
That were laying waste to this fertile region,
And saved for art and the land of Roncole
A lofty archangel,
And for the fortunate redemption of Italy,
A powerful bard
Who was a shining, everlasting glory.
A century later
The parish priest, Don Remigio Zardi,

As part of his parish work
And by other Catholic organizations
Commemorated the propitious date
By hanging this plaque.

Of his youth Verdi said simply: "It was hard."

Before he was four, Verdi began musical and scholastic instruction with the local priests of Le Roncole. When he was nine, he took on the position of organist of the village church of San Michele, situated directly across the road from his house.

Plaques inside say that Verdi played the organ in the church and was baptized there.

Sant'Agata di Villanova sull'Arda

In 1851 Verdi and Strepponi moved to a villa in Sant'Agata di Villanova sull'Arda, a village two miles outside of Busseto (Provincia di Piacenza). In 1859 Verdi and Strepponi finally married, and this was their home until her death in 1897. Verdi was obviously happy in Sant'Agata, for he quickly finished the "trilogy" of *Rigoletto* (1851), *Il trovatore* (1853), and *La traviata* (1853) that released him from the artistic prison he felt held him captive during the years in which he wrote his first sixteen operas. (He considered it a prison in that he could not advance beyond the musical heritage of Bellini and Donizetti.)

The Church of San Michele, Le Roncole

The farmland around the villa had been owned by Verdi's ancestors for many years. Even today one can see the love and care that Verdi poured into his home. The trees around the villa were all planted by him, and he spent a great deal of time laying out the garden, which has been maintained as he left it. Verdi obviously loved the land and loved working it; in 1900 when he made his last will and testament, he left two four-year scholarships for two promising students of agriculture.

Verdi's villa in Sant'Agata di Villanova sull'Arda is open for guided tours:

Open daily, May through October, 9:30 A.M.–noon and 3:00–7:00 P.M. Entrance is restricted to a *guided* tour; the last tour of the morning sets out at 11:40, the last of the evening at 6:40.

Verdi also founded a hospital near villa Sant'Agata, Ospedale Giuseppe Verdi, for the populace of the surrounding country.

Verdi is undoubtedly the most internationally known figure of nineteenth-century Italy. The old thousand-lira bill had Verdi's picture on it, and his picture, complete with a musical quote from Aïda's "Triumphal March," appears on a wrapped specialty cake of the region called *spongata*.

For more information about any of these towns connected with Verdi, contact:

Ufficio Turistico, piazza G. Verdi 24, Busseto, Province of Parma
tel: (39–524) 92487

LODGING

The nicest and most comfortable way to visit these three small places is to stay in Parma, rent a car, and take a day trip to Verdi country.

SNACKS

Be sure to buy a *spongata;* the carton has Verdi's picture on it. It is said that Verdi adored *spongata,* a sweet tart filled with raisins, seeds, and nuts.

FOOD

Two rustic but world-class restaurants near Busseto serve the delicious, hearty, *and* subtle traditional cooking of the area. Be sure to try the *culatello* (rump of pork cured in a distinctive manner), by far the tastiest Italian ham, ever.

Trattoria Vernizzi, (in Frescarolo di Busseto, three miles from Busseto)
tel: (39–524) 92–423
Closed Tuesdays.

Exit the autostrada at Fidenza in the direction of Busseto.

Among the specialties of this restaurant are *cappellotti, spalla cotta* (cooked, cured pork shoulder), and prosciutto. Be sure to reserve!

La Buca, (four miles northeast of Busseto in Zibello)
tel: (39–524) 99–214
Closed Monday nights and Tuesdays.
Exit from the autostrada at Fidenza, then take the direction for Soragna, and then toward Cremona and then straight into Zibello.

Some of La Buca's specialties are:

cappelletti (little filled pasta "hats")
tortelli di zucca (pasta stuffed with pumpkin)
pasticcio di maccheroni (savory pasta encased in a slightly sweet crust)
lingua con funghi (tongue with mushrooms)
rane (frog's legs)
anguilla (eel)

CATANIA

Catania, very far away from the rest of Italy, is situated in the middle of the east coast of Sicily with Mount Etna looming on its northern horizon. Sicily's second largest city, it is built of the blackish-gray volcanic rock of Mount Etna. Catania was settled by early Greek colonists in 729 B.C. and became so influential that its laws were adopted by all the western colonies of Magna Grecia. An eruption of Mount Etna in 1669 totally engulfed the city and the harbor. Then, in 1693, an earthquake devastated all of southeastern Sicily. Much of the city as we see it today dates from when it was rebuilt in the eighteenth century and from after World War II. It is by no means a pretty town.

If you find yourself in Sicily, you will discover that the city of Catania has done much to honor its great native composer of nineteenth-century opera, Vincenzo Bellini (November 3, 1801, Catania—September 23, 1835, the Paris suburb of Puteaux), even though he returned to the city only once after leaving at the age of eighteen. The public gardens, the opera house, and its central piazza bear his name. His statue dominates the central piazza Stesicoro, surrounded by figures from his most famous operas, *Norma, I puritani, Il pirata,* and *La sonnambula.* In his short life Bellini wrote ten operas and several revisions of three of them, including his popular *I puritani.*

All accounts of Bellini begin with the fact that he was very handsome and, indeed, the present-day five-thousand-lira bill has the striking young Bellini's picture on it.

It is said that he possessed an amiable and passionate character and seemed to know exactly what he wanted from his music and from his life. Some

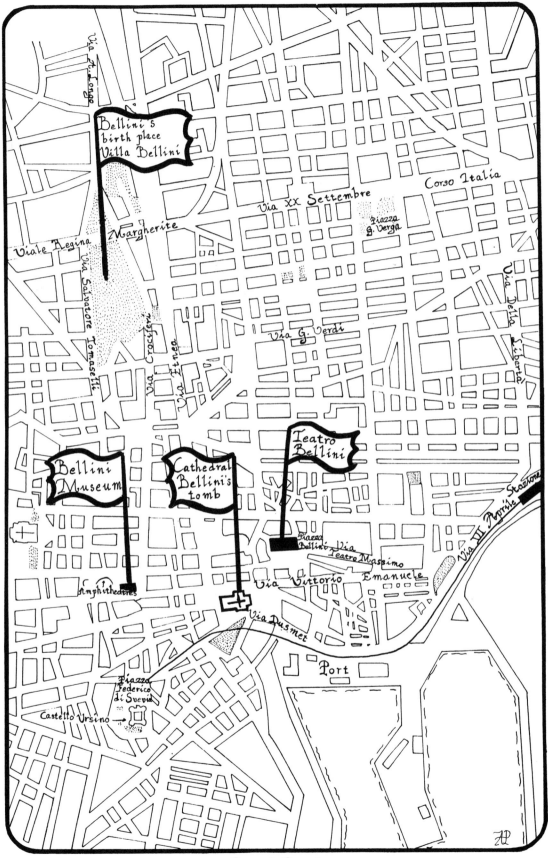

Operatic Catania

contemporaries criticized him as being calculating, particularly in matters of love, and it seems he suffered genuine feelings of envy toward his slightly older contemporary Donizetti.

He left Catania to study in Naples in 1819 and then went on to Milan in 1827 at the invitation of La Scala's impresario Domenico Barbaja. He began a seven-opera collaboration with the librettist Felice Romani, and his first opera for La Scala, *Il pirata,* was a wild public success. Although it might be difficult to perceive its novelty today, his style as a composer was considered very new and exciting. He was totally dedicated to composing and, unlike Rossini, he never held a position in a conservatory but lived solely by composing operas.

During the last eight years of his life, 1827 to 1835, Bellini was considered the most genuinely original composer of opera in Italy and he celebrated constant successes. Productions of his works were also enormously successful outside of Italy—in London from 1833 to 1834 and in Paris from 1834 to 1835. During the last year of his life in Paris he became friends with Gioacchino Rossini, Frédéric Chopin, and the poet Heinrich Heine. Early in 1835 *I puritani* was a total triumph at Paris's Théâtre des Italiens. In August of that year he fell ill and died alone—he was thought to have cholera—in a country house in the Parisian suburb of Puteaux. An autopsy, however, revealed intestinal inflammation and an abscess of the liver.

Between 1825 and 1835 Bellini had written ten operas. Forty-one years after his death, his body was moved from Paris's Père Lachaise Cemetery and buried in the Duomo (cathedral) of Catania.

A small Bellini Museum in the house where Bellini was born and spent his youth stands in piazza Francesco d'Assisi, 3, in Palazzo dei Gravina Cruvlas. The museum contains fascinating Bellini memorabilia.

Teatro Bellini was inaugurated in 1890 with Bellini's *Norma.* The theatre, closed at the beginning of World War II, escaped damage during the fighting. When the British began their occupation of Catania, on August 5, 1943, the commanding officer insisted that the theatre be reopened and the performance of operas resumed. Scenery was flown in from Palermo courtesy of the United States Air Force.

Teatro Bellini, via Perrotta, 12
tel: (39–95) 715–0200   fax: (39–95) 321–830

LODGING

If you want to visit the Bellini memorabilia of Catania, I suggest you stay in Taormina, a beautiful resort town an hour north of Catania, from which you can make a short day trip.

Villa Paradiso, via Roma, 2, Taormina
tel: (39–942) 23–922   fax: (39–942) 625–800

FERRARA

Ferrara, in the eastern Po River valley, lies forty kilometers north of Bologna, a half hour's train ride, and is one of the most elegant towns in northeastern Italy. The town was the seat of the dukes of Estense, who were patrons of many of the principal artists and musicians of the fifteenth and sixteenth centuries in northern Italy. Ferrarese support of the arts and humanities ended in the seventeenth century when the ruling Este family failed to produce an heir and the town effectively died. Throughout the eighteenth century it was said to be a sort of ghost town that had no soul. By the beginning of the nineteenth century, however, its fortunes revived, and one of the city's two opera houses presented the premiere of *Ciro in Babilonia*, an early opera by Gioacchino Rossini.

Teatro Comunale, built between 1786 and 1792 by the architect Antonio Foschini, diagonally across from the moated castle (*Palazzo Comunale*), is a gem of a theatre (capacity 990), and an ideal space for eighteenth-century opera. There is a short opera season from January through February, when three operas are produced.

Teatro Comunale premiered:

Ciro in Babilonia, ossia La caduta di Baldassare (Cyrus in Babylon, or the Fall of Belshazzar), March 14, 1812.
Gioacchino Rossini (1792–1868)
Libretto Francesco Avento, partly based on the biblical Belshazzar's feast.

This libretto, in which a Babylonian king is attracted to the wife of his enemy, the Persian king, and in which the prophet Daniel appears, is not representative of the excellent librettos Rossini usually chose. There is some nice music, including an aria written on a single repeated B-flat that foreshadows Rossini's more mature genius. Rossini was twenty when he wrote this, his fifth opera.

Teatro Comunale, offices: piazzetta Sant'Anna
tel: (39–532) 202–312
Ticket office: Rotonda Foschini 4 (next to the theatre)
tel: (39–532) 247–353
Opera season from November through January. In July, ATER Forum (Association of Theatres of Emilia-Romagna) presents a music series that sometimes includes operas.

Besides being the town in which Donizetti's historical opera *Lucrezia Borgia* is set, Ferrara's other operatic claim to fame is that Giulio Gatti-Casazza (Udine 1869—Ferrara 1940) lived at Corso della Giovecca, 157 (there is a plaque near the door).

Gatti-Casazza began his career by succeeding his father as impresario in Ferrara at Teatro Comunale. He then went to La Scala where, along with the

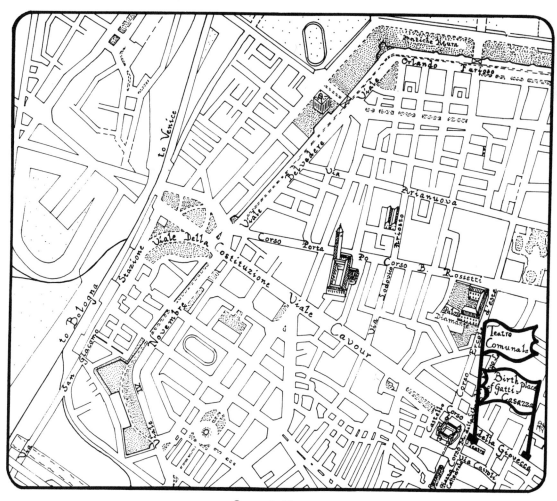

Operatic Ferrara

young Arturo Toscanini, he revitalized the theatre. Finally, from 1910 to 1935, he was general manager of the Metropolitan Opera. The years 1910 to 1915, when Toscanini was also at the Met, are considered the finest in the history of the house.

Gatti-Casazza was a clever manager able to raise the kind of funds necessary to put La Scala back on the map and to make New York's Metropolitan Opera the focal point of the new Italian opera at the beginning of the twentieth century. He was one of the music world's rare visionaries, a businessman with the knowledge of artists, music, and the public that made what he did possible.

Giulio Gatti-Casazza is buried in the *certosa* (cemetery) of Ferrara.

Lodging

Because Ferrara is a center for the surrounding agribusiness, its hotels are often full.

Hotel Annunziata, piazza della Repubblica, 5, Ferrara 4410
tel: (39–532) 201–111   fax: (39–532) 203–233

This moderately priced hotel is located right in the historic center of Ferrara, two-minutes' walk from Teatro Comunale, one minute from the cathedral, and half a minute from the *castello*.

SNACKS

For a different kind of breakfast, be sure to go to Bar Boni in viale Cavour near the corner of via Ariosto and try some of their delicious small sandwiches with a cappuccino. Also ask if they have small *pasticcio*. These delights contain savory pasta in a sweet crust.

FOOD

Ferrara is considered one of the food capitals of the world. Ferrarese specialties include:

> *coppa* (a specially cured ham)
> *pasticcio di maccheroni* or *di tortellini* (savory pasta encased in a sweet crust and baked)
> *lasagne verdi al forno* (spinach lasagna with *ragù*, meat sauce, cooked in the oven)
> *cappellacci in brodo* (filled pasta "hats" in broth)
> *anguille alla griglia* or *in umido* (grilled eel or stewed eel)
> *salama da sugo* (Ferrara's juicy, cooked salami spiced with nutmeg, cloves, salt, and pepper, served hot and usually with mashed potatoes)
> *coppia* (Ferrara's *absolutely* unique bread)

Ristorante La Centrale, via Boccaleone, 8
tel: (39–532) 206–735
Closed Sundays, Wednesday nights, and the first two weeks of July.

This restaurant, three minutes from Teatro Comunale, specializes in ferrarese cooking. If you ask in advance they can prepare you a *pasticcio*. In the fall and winter, try the *tortelli di zucca* (large pumpkin ravioli). Eel, a specialty of the area, is best *alla griglia* (grilled). Reserve.

Ristorante Max, piazza della Repubblica, 16
tel: (39–532) 209–309

Max serves good, basic cooking and is three minutes from Teatro Comunale.

FLORENCE (Firenze)

The city of Florence began its life under Julius Caesar in 59 B.C. as the Roman colony Florentia. The Roman street plan still governs the area lying between the Duomo and piazza della Signoria. During the Middle Ages the landed nobility around Florence was constantly battling for land rights. Florence gave birth to the famous conflict between the propapal Guelphs and the pro-imperial Ghibellines that tore thirteenth-century Italy apart. In 1348 the Black Plague destroyed half the city's population. Only with the rise of the Medici family under Cosimo de' Medici did Florence gain a certain balance between landed nobility and a new, burgeoning middle class. Under the Medici family the arts reigned supreme in Florence. The same Florence often thought of as the capital of the Italian Renaissance, famous for its art, music, and philosophy, is also *the* birthplace of opera.

Camerata de' Bardi, Camerata Fiorentina, Florentine Camerata: all of these names refer to a single group of musicians, poets, philosophers, and literary thinkers responsible for the creation of *opera*. From 1579 to 1592 they met as a group in the house of Count Giovanni Maria Bardi (1534–1612). The thinkers of the Camerata changed the relationship between poetry and music in a way that emulated the manner of the great writers of tragedy in the Golden Age of Greece, the fifth century B.C.. They sought to recapture the power of the ancient Greek dramas as described by Aristotle and his contemporaries, trying to create drama that represented the passions of man in moments of greatness through the heightened language of sublime poetry delivered with "rhythm, tone, and meter." They felt that the music of the sixteenth century—in particular the polyphonic Italian madrigal, based upon highly complex musical theories— could never manage to express this power because the text, as well as the force of its words and its story, was obscured by the complex polyphony in which it was set.

So the men of the Camerata "invented" a musical setting for great texts called *monody,* in which texts are sung in declamatory rhythm over slow harmonic progression called *recitar cantando* (singing speech). In early seventeenth-century monody the words are the master of the music and reign supreme. The first operas, made up of many monodies strung together, were based on this kind of vocal writing. The word *opera* is the plural of *opus.* One piece of music, a song, or monody, is an opus. Thus, many pieces of music, songs, or monodies, strung together delineating a drama, make up an opera.

Count Bardi himself was a man of many diverse interests. In 1580 he published a treatise on the particular kind of *calcio* (football) played in Florence. He was also renowned as a military man. His house still stands in via de' Benci, 5.

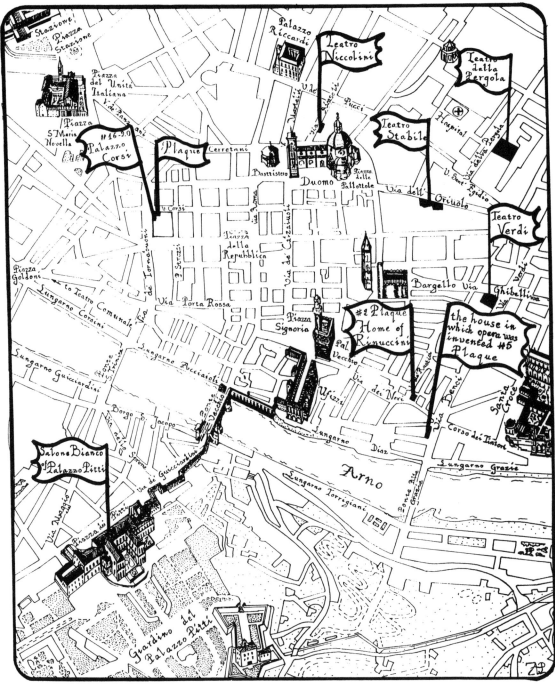

Operatic Florence

Although the outside of the house has recently been redone in neobrutalistic cement blocks, one can still see a glorious courtyard through the street doors. On the house's exterior wall a plaque states:

In questa casa dei Bardi
Visse Giovanni, Conte di Vernio,
Che al valor militare
Mostrato negli assedi di Siena e di Malta,
Congiunse lo studio delle scienze e l'amore delle lettere
Coltivò la poesia e la musica
E accolse e fu l'anima di quella celebre Camerata
La quale intese a ripartire l'arte musicale
Imbarrata dalle stranezze fiamminghe
Alla sublimità della Greca melopea
Di cui scrissero gli storici della antica civiltà
Aprì la via già chiusa da secoli
E con la reforma del melodramma
Fu la culla dell'arte moderna
MDXXXII–MDCXII.

In this house of the Bardi family
Lived Giovanni, Count of Vernio,
Who showed great military valor
In the battles of Siena and of Malta.
He followed the study of the sciences and his love of the humanities
He cultivated poetry and music
He gathered together and was the soul of the celebrated Camerata
Which was intent on releasing the art of music
From its Flemish bonds
To arrive at the sublime Greek melopoeia
That the ancient historians wrote of.
They opened the way that had been closed for centuries
And with the invention of melodrama
They were the cradle of the new art.
1534–1612.

When Count Giovanni Bardi left Florence for Rome in 1592, the wealthy and noble Jacopo Corsi became the city's leading patron of music. Corsi, a successful businessman in the silk and wool trade, helped write and sponsored the first performance of *La Dafne*, which is considered *the* first opera. After its first private showing in 1598, it was presented at the Medici court for *Carnevale* in 1599 and 1600. Almost all of its music has been lost.

A room in the enormous Renaissance Palazzo Corsi was the site of the 1598 performance of *La Dafne*. (For many years it was said to have taken place in 1596.) The first fruit resulting from the ideas of the Camerata, *La Dafne* was a dramatic poem to be sung on the stage in *stile rappresentativo* (representational or dramatic style). It was a collaborative work with music by Jacopo Peri (August 20, 1561, Rome or Florence—on or before August 12, 1633, Florence) and Jacopo

Corsi (1561, Florence—December 29, 1602, Florence), and lyrics based on a dramatic poem by Ottavio Rinuccini based on the Greek myth of *Dafne.*

Today Palazzo Corsi, which covers an entire city block, houses the Banca Commerciale Italiana. On the second floor, most of which has been completely renovated as modern offices, stands the Stanza del Teatro. Although it is not entirely certain, it is most likely that this double room, with its arched middle, is where the first opera, *La Dafne,* was performed.

Upon entering the bank take the staircase to the right to the first (American second) floor and ask the man seated at a desk at the top of the stairs if you may see the Stanza del Teatro. (Don't forget to tip him!)

On many maps of Florence the neighboring Palazzo Strozzi is marked. The two palaces are separated by via Strozzi.

Palazzo Corsi, (Banca Commerciale Italiana), via Tornabuoni, 16–20
Open 8:30 A.M.–1:15 P.M. and 2:30–4:00 P.M.

Palazzo Corsi in 1650

Palazzo Corsi Today

On the side of Palazzo Corsi that faces via Corsi a plaque says:

Jacopo Corsi	Jacopo Corsi
Patrizio Fiorentino	Patrician Florentine
Nelle sue vicine case	In his neighboring houses
Già da tempo demolite	Long since demolished
Accolse nella seconda	Gathered during the second
Metà del secolo XVI	Half of the sixteenth century
Il fiore dei letterati,	The flower of the humanists
Musici, e poeti	Musicians and poets.
Fu delle loro discipline	He was a learned scholar
Dotto cultore	Of these arts
E favoreggiatore generoso	And a generous patron.
E ivi fece rappresentare	There he put on
Nel MDLXXXXIV	In 1594 [sic]
Con musica sua	With his own music
E di Jacopo Peri	And music by Jacopo Peri

LA DAFNE	LA DAFNE
dramma di Ottavio Rinuccini	Drama by Ottavio Rinuccini,
Primo frutto de' sapienti	The first fruit of the careful studies
Studi della CAMERATA	Of the CAMERATA
del Conte Bardi	Of Count Bardi
E prima opera	And the first work
Del rinnovato melodramma.	Of the new melodrama.

(The term "demolition," in line 4, refers to the fact that via Tornabuoni was *sistemata* [renovated] in the early nineteenth century.)

Ottavio Rinuccini, the poet and librettist for *La Dafne,* lived behind the Palazzo Vecchio in via de' Rustici, 2.

There is a plaque on the wall of the house in which he lived:

Ottavio Rinuccini	Ottavio Rinuccini
Patrizio Fiorentino	Patrician Florentine
Letterato illustre	Illustrious humanist
e gentile poeta	And noble poet
Scrisse in questa casa	In this house wrote
La Dafne, *Favola Pastorale*	*La Dafne,* a pastoral fable,
Primo de' suoi	The first of his
drammatici componimenti	Dramatic works
Che messo in musica da	Set to music by
Jacopo Corsi e Jacopo Peri	Jacopo Corsi and Jacopo Peri
E rappresentato in casa Corsi	And performed in Palazzo Corsi
Con plaudente	With great success
Universal Maraviglia	And universal acclaim
Nel MDLXXXXIV	In 1594 [*sic*]
Spirò nell' arte	Gave to art
Un alito di nuova vita	A breath of new life
è fu l'opera memorabile	It was this memorable work
Onde s'iniziò	That gave birth
La reforma melodrammatica.	To melodrama.

The old no. 2 and the plaque are right on the corner of via de' Rustici and via dei Neri.

The second opera coming from the Camerata was entitled *Euridice.* Its first performance took place in Palazzo Pitti in the rooms of Antonio de' Medici, today called Il Salone Bianco:

Euridice, opera in a prologue and five scenes (the first opera for which the music is preserved), October 6, 1600.
Jacopo Peri (1561–1633) and Giulio Caccini (October 8, 1551, Rome or Tivoli—buried December 10, 1618, Florence). Caccini wrote Euridice's arias, some arias for the nymphs and shepherds, and three choruses. The

rest is by Peri. Libretto Ottavio Rinuccini, based on the Greek myth of Orpheus and Euridice.

Euridice is the earliest opera for which the music survives. The libretto adds many pastoral scenes to the myth of the death of Euridice and Orpheus's descent into the underworld to rescue her from its king, Pluto. Orpheus fails at the last moment, but Rinuccini's version ends happily with his success and general rejoicing. Jacopo Corsi, Florence's chief patron of music, sponsored the opera's performance at the wedding festivities of Maria de' Medici and Henry IV of France. He also helped negotiate the marriage. The performance of *Euridice* took place in the rooms of Antonio de' Medici in Palazzo Pitti. The composer Jacopo Peri sang the role of Euridice, Corsi himself played the harpsichord, and several of Caccini's family, all noted singers and later composers in their own right, played roles.

In 1549 the Medici family moved to Palazzo Pitti. The palace still bears the name of Luca Pitti for whom it was built, circa 1457, most likely using a design intended for Palazzo Medici by the architect Brunelleschi which had been rejected by the Medici as too grand! Today the rooms of Antonio de' Medici are called Il Salone Bianco (the large white room). The east walls of this very large room face the inner courtyard of the palace.

Go up four flights of stairs to the first floor. The room is directly to the right of where the books and postcards are sold.

One can visit the room by reserving in advance:

Palazzo Pitti / Salone Bianco
tel: (39–55) 284–272 or 238–8611

Although the 1600 performance of *Euridice* was by no means a great hit, the concept of "drama in music" caught on with composers, poets, and the courts that supported them. Opera was well on the road to becoming the most important musical art form of the seventeenth and early eighteenth centuries.

Construction on Teatro della Pergola (seating capacity 1,000) was begun in 1651. The theatre opened in December 1656 with one of the first examples of opera buffa, *Il podestà di Colognole,* by Jacopo Melani. Until 1718, when it became a professional public theatre, it was used for theatricals exclusively by several groups of noblemen—the Accademia degli Immobili, the Accademia dei Nobili, and the Medici court.

Originally constructed of wood, the theatre was rebuilt of brick in 1755. Teatro della Pergola became *the* theatre for serious opera in Florence in the eighteenth century. Between 1782 and 1784 it staged three premieres by the Florentine opera composer Luigi Cherubini before he left Italy and became the dominant figure in early nineteenth-century French musical life. When Florence was under Napoleonic rule, from 1810 to 1814, the Pergola was designated an Imperial Theatre. In 1925 it was declared a national monument. The Accademia degli Immobili still exists and remains in charge of the theatre's archives.

Teatro della Pergola is horseshoe-shaped, but the curve of the "shoe" is tighter than that of other theatres, which makes it much more oval-shaped and narrow.

Teatro della Pergola premiered three operas by Luigi Cherubini (September 8, 1760, Florence—March 15, 1842, Paris) between 1782 and 1784.

Macbeth, opera in four acts, March 14, 1847.
Giuseppe Verdi (1813–1901)
Libretto Francesco Maria Piave, with additional material by Andrea Maffei, after Shakespeare's play.

Verdi wrote the opera *Macbeth* without a heroic tenor role. Instead, the title role demands a fine baritone actor-singer. The composer took great interest in the libretto of *Macbeth*, so much so that he asked his friend Andrea Maffei to reset certain passages of Piave's text that he felt were not exactly right. Verdi also took inordinate time and care in making sure that the premiere was well rehearsed, with every nuance that he wanted. A resounding success, the opera soon appeared throughout Italy. In 1864 Verdi was aked to prepare a version of *Macbeth* in French for the opera at the Théâtre Lyric in Paris. It is the Paris version, albeit in Italian, that is generally heard today.

Other special events occurring at Teatro della Pergola were the first Italian performances of Mozart's *Le nozze di Figaro,* in 1788, two years after its premiere in Vienna; *Don Giovanni,* in 1792, five years after its premiere in Prague; and *Die Entführung aus dem Serail,* in 1935, 153 (!) years after its premiere.

Today Teatro della Pergola mainly presents spoken drama. The stage's main curtain has an over-curtain, painted by Gaspare Martellini in 1828, which is used only on special occasions.

The bell in via della Pergola, 20, marked *Portineria,* will sometimes fetch the custodian; if not, ask in the offices, in via della Pergola, 12, for someone to show you the theatre. (Don't forget to tip whoever guides you!)

Teatro della Pergola, main entrance: via della Pergola, 30, offices: via della Pergola, 12, Florence 50121
Office open Tuesday–Saturday, 9:30 A.M.–1:00 P.M. and 3:45–6:45 P.M.; Sunday 10:00 A.M.–1:00 P.M. Closed Monday.
tel: (39–55) 247–9651 or 247–9652   fax: (39–55) 247–7969
The ticket office is also open two hours before the beginning of an event for tickets to that day's event.

Performances for Maggio Musicale Fiorentino (established in 1933) regularly take place in Teatro della Pergola, Teatro Comunale (1852), and the Palazzo dei Congressi each year from late April through July. Festival headquarters are in:

Teatro Comunale, corso Italia, 16, 50137 Florence
Open Tuesday–Saturday, 9:00 A.M.–1:00 P.M. and 2:30–6:30 P.M.
tel: (39–55) 277–9236 or 211–158

Teatro Comunale opened in 1852 as an outdoor theatre. It was covered in 1882–83, modernized in 1930, and now seats 2,500. It has none of the physical charm of Teatro della Pergola, but its acoustics are very good.

Florence was home to many other theatres that performed operas. Two are still in existence and present plays or cabaret.

Teatro del Cocomero (built between 1650 and 1654) was home to the premiere of George Frideric Handel's opera *Rodrigo* in November 1707. In 1858 it was renamed Teatro G. B. Niccolini, and is today the home of the Teatro Regionale Toscano (the Tuscan Regional Theatre).

Teatro Niccolini, via Ricasoli, 5
tel: (39–55) 213–282 or 239–6653

Teatro Verdi, originally the seventeenth-century Teatro Pagliano, which today presents Italian-style cabaret:

Teatro Verdi, via Ghibellina, 101
tel: (39–55) 212–320 or 239–6242

LODGING

Florence is one of those cities where, because there are so many tourists, it is *very* important to reserve a nice room well in advance. All of the following hotels are very comfortable, relatively reasonably priced, and within walking distance of all of historic and operatic Florence:

City Hotel, via Sant'Antonino, 18, Florence 50123
tel: (39–55) 211–543   fax: (39–55) 295–451
The City Hotel is close to the station, the central market, and one of the better *trattoria* in Florence, Trattoria Antellesi (more about this below).

Hotel Fiorino, via Osteria del Guanto, 6, Florence 50122
tel: (39–55) 210–579   fax: (39–55) 210–579
Hotel Fiorino is close to where the poet Rinuccini and Count Bardi lived.

Hotel Della Signoria, via delle Terme, 1, Florence 50123
tel: (39–55) 214–530   fax: (39–55) 216–101
Hotel della Signoria is close to the piazza della Signoria.

Hotel Cavour, via del Proconsolo, 3, Florence 50122
tel: (39–55) 282–461   fax: (39–55) 218–955

SNACKS

If you crave a snack, try a small *vinaio* (wine shop) or a *fiaschetteria* (flask shop) where you can have a glass of local wine (usually from the owner's own vineyard) and a small sandwich or tasty *crostini* (crusts). Some places offer a few more items to eat. Custom has it that you consume everything standing at the bar.

FOOD

Florentine and Tuscan specialità:

> *finocchiona* (Florentine salami seasoned with fennel)
> *bistecca alla Fiorentina* (grilled steak)
> *arista di maiale* (roast pork with rosemary)
> *braciole di vitello* (grilled veal chops)
> *fritto misto fiorentino: cervello, animelle, petti di pollo, carciofi, e mozzarella* (brains, sweetbreads, chicken breasts, tiny Italian artichokes and mozzarella, tastily battered and deep-fried)
> *salsiccie e fagioli* (sausages and beans)
> *finocchio e salsicce* (cooked fennel and sausages)

And of course try the local Chianti.

Most of the following restaurants are very popular, so it pays to phone for a reservation or to show up early.

Trattoria Antellesi, via Faenza, 9
tel: (39–55) 216–990
Closed Sundays.

Trattoria del Fagioli, corso Tintori, 47
tel: (39–55) 244–285
Closed Sundays, the month of August, and both Saturday and Sunday in the summer.

Buca dei Lapi, via del Trebbio, 1
tel: (39–55) 213–768
Closed Sunday, and Monday for lunch.

GENOA (Genova)

Genoa is the capital city of Liguria, known as the Italian Riviera, on the northwestern coast of Italy. With a natural harbor strategically located near France and Spain, the city was a medieval shipping center and the archrival of the republics of Venice and Pisa. And, of course, Genoa was the birthplace of

Cristoforo Colombo (Christopher Columbus). The city was occupied by France and then Austria in the seventeenth and eighteenth centuries. During the French-governed Jacobin regime (1797–99), most all Genoese theatres were closed.

Although the theatres of Genoa did not stage premieres of any of the very famous eighteenth- or nineteenth-century Italian operas, the city is still of operatic interest. Rossini and Verdi were the favorite composers of the nineteenth-century Genoese. Two operas about Columbus premiered in Teatro Carlo Felice: Francesco Morlacchi's *Colombo* (1828) and Baron Alberto Franchetti's *Cristoforo Colombo* (October 6, 1892), commissioned by the city of Genoa to celebrate the four-hundredth anniversary of Columbus's voyage. The commission was originally given to Verdi, who, because he was busy writing his last two operas, deferred to Franchetti. In 1894 the Carlo Felice hosted a marathon, conducted by Arturo Toscanini, of sixty-four opera performances in fifty-eight days! It was Toscanini who introduced the operas of Wagner and Strauss to the Genoese opera public. Until the 1940s no Mozart, Beethoven, or Weber had ever been performed in the city!

Teatro Carlo Felice, with a seating capacity of 2,000, was named after King Carlo Felice. The theatre opened April 7, 1828, with a performance of Bellini's *Bianca e Fernando*. During World War II, it was partially destroyed in the 1943–44 incendiary air raids and was finally reopened October 18, 1991, in time for the gala year 1992 celebrating the five-hundredth anniversary of Columbus's voyage to the New World. Of the original nineteenth-century structure, only a part of the external walls and the wide Doric-columned downstairs vestibule remain.

The newly rebuilt Teatro Carlo Felice is most certainly worth a visit. The exterior of the theatre was built to resemble the façades of ancient Genoese palaces and the interior to resemble a Genoese piazza. Inside the walls are of gray marble streaked with blue and white, not unlike Genoa's via Garibaldi; the ceiling resembles the night sky, and extending up through each floor's foyer there is a *campanile genovese* (a Genoese bell tower). Although the architects abandoned the cozy *teatro italiana* shape, the Carlo Felice most definitely has architectural allure. The theatre features state-of-the-art equipment, raked stage, and a raked orchestra.

The Genoese are very proud of their newly rebuilt theatre, and rightly so. There are, however, some problems:

If you are seated in the first three rows of the balcony, the rail is directly in your sight line. To overcome this the theatre provides very firm, large cushions so you can see above the rail. This works, but your legs are apt to fall asleep because your feet do not touch the floor. But the theatre's acoustics are fabulous, particularly in orchestra seats.

Even if there is no production to see, go to the artists' entrance in *paseo del Teatro,* to the right of the columned front of the theatre, and politely ask if someone can schedule a guided tour of the theatre.

Teatro Carlo Felice

Carlo Felice has an excellent and long—November to June—opera season enthusiastically attended by the Genoese public.

Teatro Carlo Felice, piazza Raffaele de Ferrari
tickets: via XXV Aprile, 1, 16121 Genoa
tel: (39–10) 538–1225   fax: (39–10) 538–1233
    Tickets are generally available even at the last moment.

Some tips on getting around in Genoa:
Take the train to Genova Brignole station, which is the closest station to the center where the Carlo Felice stands.
    When going down into the lower, medieval city, "hold on to your purse" (as a nice shopkeeper said to me). The area is full of jewelry shops and evocative street names such as via Orefici (Street of the Goldsmiths) and vico degli Indoratori (Alley of the Gold-painters).

LODGING

City Hotel Genova, via San Sabastiano, 6, 16123 Genoa
tel: (39–10) 592–595   fax: (39–10) 586–301
    The City Hotel is directly across the street from Teatro Carlo Felice. It is a medium-priced hotel with a very friendly staff; its rooms are quiet and very nicely appointed.

SNACKS

For a snack when browsing in the port area, under the long arches of via Gramsci in the old city, have a piece of *baccalà fritto* (fried codfish).

Don't miss the *farinata,* a pizza unique to Genoa made with the flour of *ceci* (garbanzo beans). Drink a glass of cold white wine with this treat. The best *farinata* and *baccalà fritto* can be had in the Frigitoria Corega under the arches of via Gramsci. The mole-tunnel streets are safe during the day.

FOOD

Genoese food was profoundly influenced by the cuisine of southern France. Both are characterized by the use of the basil, oregano, lavender, olives, olive oil, etc., that grow indigenously. You must try *linguine con pesto* made with the basil and oil of northwestern Italy. Almost any restaurant can whip up a delicious bowl in no time.

And try *cima,* a cold slice of veal breast stuffed with pistachios, peas, and other delicious things. *Cima* is a real home-cooking delight. If it is not on the menu of a restaurant you like, ask them to prepare it for you for the next night.

LUCCA

Lucca is a beautiful walled city set down among the western Tuscan mountains. Situated in a small fertile plain between Florence and the Ligurian Sea, the area has always been the heart of one of Italy's richest agricultural regions and is especially known for the quality of its olive oil. During the Middle Ages it was the center of the Italian silk trade. Besides all this, Lucca has always had a fertile artistic climate.

Giacomo Puccini (December 22, 1858, Lucca—December 29, 1924, Brussels) represents the fifth generation of composers named Puccini. He is considered the most successful composer of Italian opera after Verdi. Opera was unquestionably *the* musical art form of the nineteenth century, but although Puccini had been trained from infancy as a musician and composer, it was only when he saw Verdi's *Aïda,* in Pisa in 1876, that he decided to be a composer of opera.

Puccini's birthplace, Casa Puccini, is situated just down via del Poggio from the church of San Michele where he, his father, and his grandfather were organists. Casa Puccini contains a museum on the second floor above an unlikely ground-floor butcher shop. A plaque (above the butcher shop) says:

> Da lunga progenie di musici degni
> Della viva tradizione patria
> Qui nacque il 22 Dicembre 1858
> Giacomo Puccini
> Che alle nuove voci di vita
> Accordo note argute di verità e leggiadria

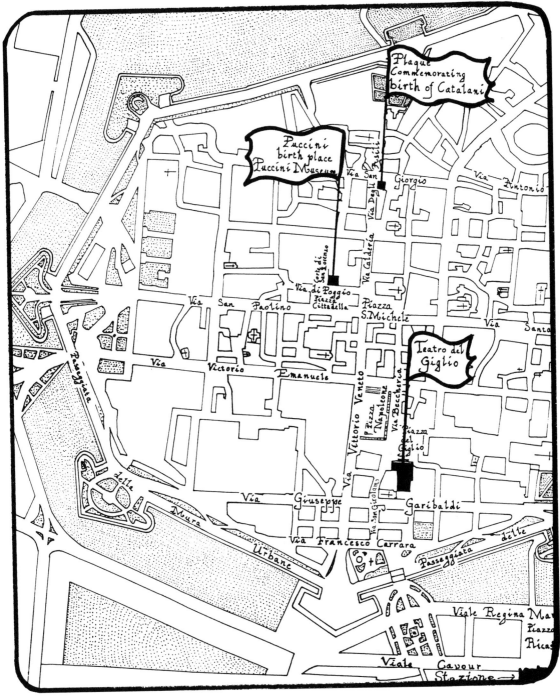

Operatic Lucca

Riaffermando con le schiette
Agili forme la nazione dell'arte
Nel suo primato di gloria nel mondo.
La città orgoliosa di lui nel trigesimo della morte, 29 Dic. 1924.

From a long line of musicians,
Worthy of the great Italian tradition,
Giacomo Puccini
Was born here on December 22, 1858.
He responded to the new currents of his time
With subtle sounds full of grace and truth
Reconfirming with his unadorned lovely lines
Italy's first rank in the world's glory.
On the 29th of December, 1924, one month after his death,
His city remembers him with pride.

The museum holds the Steinway on which Puccini composed *Turandot*, many original scores, including early symphonic works, a Mass, songs, and chamber music. There are photographs, posters from premieres, and correspondence from Puccini to his librettists and vice versa. There are also sketches for the original costumes for all his well-known operas as well as original set designs. It is very evocative and a lovely place to visit. You know you are near the museum when you hear Puccini's music in the street. The museum is run by students of the conservatory, and they play the music of the master all day, which lends a wonderfully exuberant feeling to the place. The premieres of Puccini's twelve operas took place in Turin, Milan, Rome, Monte-Carlo, and New York City. The first successful performance of *Madama Butterfly* was in Brescia.

Casa Puccini, via di Poggio, 30
Open Tuesday through Sunday—April through September, 10:00 A.M.–1:00 P.M. and 3:00–6:00 P.M.; October through March, 11:00 A.M.–1:00 P.M. and 3:00–5:00 P.M.
Entrance is free.

Also born in Lucca was Alfredo Catalani (June 19, 1854—August 7, 1893, Milan), composer of *La Wally,* and Giacomo Puccini's almost exact contemporary. His birthplace, marked only with his name, is four hundred feet from Puccini's. His career was unfortunately overshadowed by the debilitating disease hemoptysis combined with tuberculosis. Arturo Toscanini championed Catalani's compositions and so admired *La Wally* that he gave his daughter the very un-Italian name of Wally. Although the opera is rarely performed today, surely we all remember the performance of the heroine's principal aria "Ebbene? Neandrò lontana," so beautifully sung by the soprano Wilhelmena Wiggens Fernandez in the 1980s film *Diva.* A plaque attests to the fact that Catalani lived in via degli Asili, 16.

Teatro Comunale del Giglio was originally built in 1692 as Teatro San Gerolamo. The theatre collapsed in 1817 and was rebuilt in its present form in 1819. The Giglio (Lily) in the name of the theatre comes from the Bourbon family coat of arms, as they were occupying Lucca in the nineteenth century when the theatre was rededicated. A number of Puccini artifacts can be found in the theatre's left foyer, including a wonderful family tree of the long dynasty of Puccinis.

Teatro Comunale del Giglio, piazza del Giglio
tel: (39–583) 442–103
Opera and theatre season from November through April.

LODGING

Lucca is a quiet example of such a beautiful walled Tuscan town that I suggest you stay here, rather than in crowded Florence, and make day trips to Florence, Viareggio, Torre del Lago, and come back to eat well and sleep peacefully in this lovely city. Everything in the town is within walking distance of everything else. Directly across via del Poggio from the Puccini museum, right in the town's center, is:

Piccolo Hotel Puccini, via del Poggio, 9, 55100 Lucca
tel. and fax: (39–583) 55–421 or 53–487
This centrally located hotel is reasonably priced and even has a place to park.

Hotel Universo, piazza del Giglio, 1, 55100 Lucca
tel: (39–583) 493–678
This lovely hotel is reasonably priced and right next to the theatre.

FOOD

Try some of the wonderful Lucchese specialties, similar to those of Florence, with an emphasis on excellent beans, meats, and sausages; stuffed chicken; *cappelletti in brodo* (little stuffed pasta "hats" in broth), etc.), after which a stroll through the lovely, quiet town is a must.

Buca di Sant'Antonio, via della Cervia, 1/5
tel: (39–583) 55–881
Closed Sunday night and Monday, and the last two weeks of July.
The Buca di Sant'Antonio is a two-minute walk from the Hotel Puccini and is a world-class restaurant.

Giglio, piazza del Giglio
tel: (39–583) 494–058
Closed Tuesday night, Wednesday, and the first two weeks of February.
The Giglio is situated right next to the theatre.

PUCCINI COUNTRY

Torre del Lago Puccini

After his first big success with *Manon Lescaut,* Puccini built a villa in Torre del Lago, on the shores of Lago di Massaciuccoli. Torre del Lago is five kilometers southeast of the elegant Tuscan resort town of Viareggio. The composer lived here while writing *La bohème, Tosca,* and *Madama Butterfly.* His presence was so important that the town's name has been changed to include Puccini.

To reach Torre del Lago Puccini, take the train from Lucca to Viareggio (twenty minutes). In Viareggio, exit from the train station, go to the bar directly across the large avenue, and get a round-trip (*andata e ritorno*) ticket to Torre del Lago Puccini. The bus ride takes about twenty-five minutes.

Villa Puccini is the site of the Puccini Museum, which holds memorabilia including a special piano that has a desk built right into it for writing music. Puccini's tomb is in the chapel of the villa, as are the tombs of his wife, son, and daughter-in-law.

Puccini was a *very* dashing, handsome man. In her attempts to keep him from straying, it is said that his wife sewed cloves of garlic into his clothing so its stink would make him less attractive to women. He was also an adventurous sort and loved to speed along in the new horseless carriages; he was almost killed in an automobile accident while composing *Madama Butterfly.* During his life Puccini smoked fifty (!) cigarettes a day and died after an operation for throat cancer. The museum contains a note handwritten to his wife (after the operation he had no voice) just before he died: *"Elvira povera donna finì"* (Elvira, poor woman, it is finished). We assume he was apologizing for the suffering he must have caused her during his life.

Puccini Museum, viale Puccini, 266, Torre del Lago (Provincia di Lucca)

Open 9:00 A.M.–noon and 3:00–7:00 P.M. in the summer; winter closure at 5:30 P.M.

In the winter the present owners seem willing to show the museum only to groups of more than five or six people. Most of the time that number has gathered before the gates open. If you find yourself alone outside the gates, however, a little begging will get you in.

Torre del Lago Puccini also hosts a summer festival which presents Puccini's works in an open-air theatre.

Festival Pucciniano, belvedere Puccini, 4, 55048 Torre del Lago Puccini tel: (39–584) 359–322

Fourteen opera performances in three weeks, late July to mid-August.

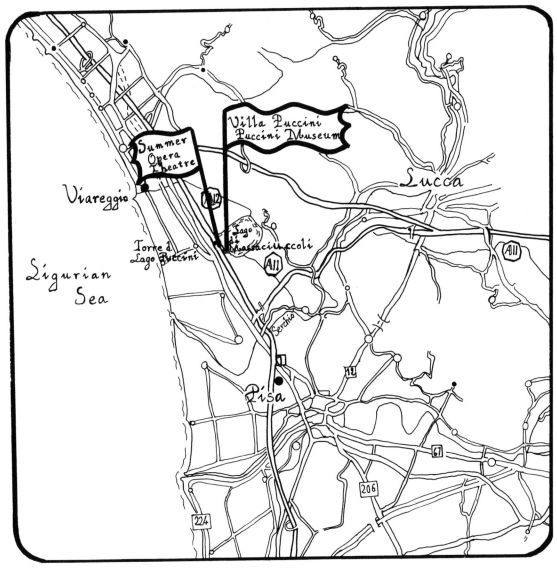

Villa Puccini
Puccini Museum

Summer
Opera
Theatre

Lucca

Viareggio

Lago
di
Massaciuccoli

Torre d.
Lago Puccini

Ligurian
Sea

Serchio

Pisa

Puccini Country

Lodging and Food

Torre del Lago Puccini is a summer vacation spot with many small, rather basic, hotels and restaurants. Once again: were I attending the operas at the festival, I would rent a car and stay in the beautiful and uncrowded town of Lucca.

A nice spot for a coffee or a glass of wine is in the same piazza as Villa Puccini and near the festival entrance:

Bar Butterfly, hotel/restaurant/bar, belvedere Puccini, 24
tel. and fax: (39–584) 341–024

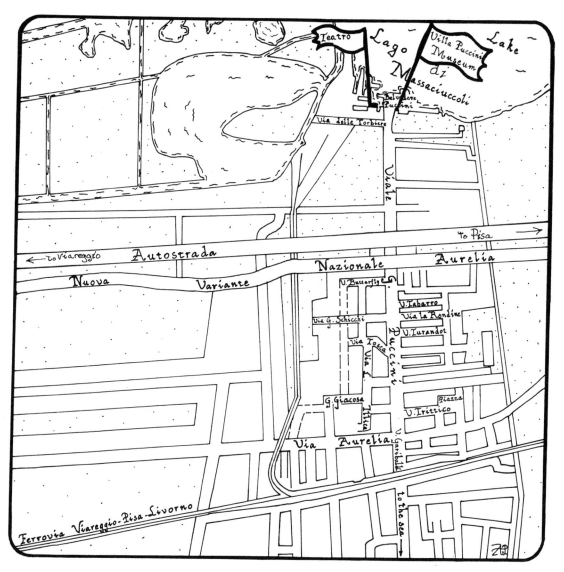

Torre del Lago Puccini

MANTUA (Mantova)

Mantua has a rich history dating back to Etruscan times (ca. sixth century B.C.). The poet Virgil (70–15 B.C.), author of the *Aeneid*, was born in the Mantua area. In his *Eclogues* and *Georgics*, he describes the beautiful fertile plain on which Mantua is situated, and the misty light, so common in the val Padana (the Po River valley), caused by ground fog (*foschia*). Aldous Huxley called Mantua the most romantic city in the world. Its setting amid three lakes, created in 1198 when an architect changed the course of the slow-moving Mincio River, is undeniably evocative even today.

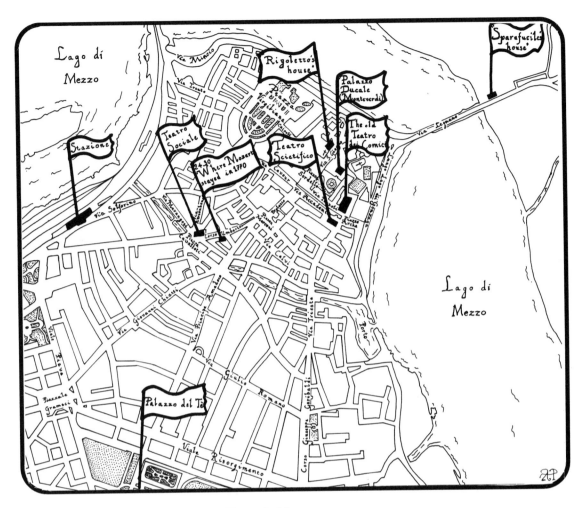

Operatic Mantua

From the fifteenth through the seventeenth centuries, Mantua was a center of the arts in Italy, owing to the patronage of the ruling Gonzaga family, dukes of Mantua from 1328 to 1708. Isabella d'Este (1474–1539), wife of Francesco Gonzaga, marquis of Mantua, was a great patroness of the arts and gathered around her the likes of Raphael, Andrea Mantegna, and the architect Giulio Romano. Through her family connection to the courts of Ferrara and Milan, she played an important role in the development of the Italian madrigal, considered by many to be *the* musical art form of the sixteenth century.

In 1590 Duke Vincenzo I hired Claudio Monteverdi as a court musician, first to be *suonatore di viuola* (a player of viola da gamba), and then in 1601, appointed *maestro di cappella,* with full control over the music of the court and cathedral of Mantua.

Today, Monteverdi is known as the father of modern music for musical developments he initiated while in Mantua. He was the first composer to give instruments rhetorical power of their own apart from the text; the first to write

Palazzo Ducale

dynamics and bowings for string instruments into the score; the first to notate for specific instruments.

Outside the Sala degli Specchi (Hall of the Mirrors) in the Palazzo Ducale (Duke's Palace), a small sign states: *Ogni Venere di Sera Si Fa Musica Nella Sala degli Specchi* (Every Friday evening there will be music in the Hall of Mirrors), signed: *Cl. Monteverdi to Cardinal Ferdinand Gonzaga of Mantua, 22 June, 1611.*

Mantua premiered two operas by Claudio Monteverdi. Both took place in the Palazzo Ducale.

L'Orfeo, favola in musica (a fable in music), February 24, 1607.
Claudio Monteverdi
Libretto Alessandro Striggio, based on the tale of Orpheus as told in Ovid's *Metamorphoses.*

L'Orfeo set Monteverdi completely apart from other composers of opera. It was written as an entertainment for the *Carnevale* season of 1607 at the Mantuan court. The performance was prepared under the auspices of Francesco Gonzaga, elder son of the duke of Mantua, for a select group called the Accademia degli Invaghiti (Group of the Charmed Ones). *L'Orfeo* was performed in a room in the apartments occupied by the duke's sister, Margherita Gonzaga. Tradition says the room was the Salone dei Fiumi (Room of the Rivers), a long and rather narrow, loggia-like room connected by floor-to-ceiling French windows to a large *giardino sospeso* (hanging garden), planted some forty feet above the ground.

L'Orfeo is considered the first "popular" opera, in that it played in various venues outside of Mantua very soon after its premiere and continued to be performed regularly up through a 1646 production in Genoa. Then it fell into obscurity until the beginning of the twentieth century, when composers such as Vincent d'Indy, Carl Orff, Ottorino Respighi, Gian Francesco Malipiero, Paul Hindemith, Bruno Maderna, Luciano Berio, and several others rediscovered it and made modern editions.

Because of the extraordinary success of *L'Orfeo*, Duke Vincenzo ordered a second performance for March 1, 1607, then asked Monteverdi to prepare a similar work the following year. In 1608 Monteverdi wrote two more theatrical works: *Arianna* (Ariadne), May 28, 1608, from which comes the famous "Lamento d'Arianna: Lasciatemi morire," the only extant part of the opera; and *Ballo delle ingrate, Mascheratea delle ingrate* (Dance or Masque of the Ungrateful Ones), June 4, 1608, a dramatic and sung ballet. Both of these works were based on librettos by Florence's Ottavio Rinuccini.

The performances of these two works were given as part of the festivities celebrating the important political alliance forged by the marriage of the duke of Mantua's elder son, Francesco Gonzaga, to Margherita, daughter of Duke Carlo Emanuele of Savoy.

Perhaps because the performances were fraught with political importance, particular care was taken concerning the choice of the singer-actress for the title role of Arianna. Monteverdi chose Caterina Martinelli, a famous young singer from Rome (she was fourteen!). The duke sent an envoy to Rome to escort her back to Mantua. The entourage was hosted by several towns during the long return, and after each stop, and when she reached Mantua, the girl was examined by a doctor to ascertain that she was still a virgin! She passed the tests and began rehearsals with Monteverdi. Then, only days before the performance, she contracted smallpox and died. (Earlier that year Monteverdi had lost his own wife in the same epidemic.) Monteverdi quickly prepared another singer-actress, the older, more experienced Virginia Archilei, to play Arianna. She was obviously successful, for her singing of the famous "Lament of Arianna" was said to have brought "even the strongest man to tears."

A large temporary structure holding 6,000 (!) was erected on the palace grounds, most likely in the hanging garden, for the event.

Palazzo Ducale, (Duke's Palace)
Open October through April, 9:00–3:00 P.M.; Sundays and holidays, 9:00 A.M.–noon.
guided tours: 9:00–11:30 A.M. and 2:30–6:00 P.M.
Closed Mondays, May 1, June 2, August 15, Easter, and Christmas.
   You must specifically ask to see Salone dei Fiumi.

In 1613, Monteverdi left Mantua for a better position in Venice as *maestro di cappella* of Saint Mark's Cathedral. After his departure, the artistic climate of the city began to decline; in 1630 the Duke's Palace was sacked and the city was occupied by the Hapsburgs.

Mantua is also the setting for Giuseppe Verdi's *Rigoletto* (1851). It seems that the ruling Gonzaga family passed on a predisposition for the weakening in the spine that causes a hunchback. Thus, when Verdi's librettist Francesco Maria Piave was forced by the censors in Venice to change the original setting for *Rigoletto*, which involved a French king, he must have remembered his history. It was Duke Vincenzo I himself whose debauchery and corruption provided the inspiration for the lecherous duke of the opera. Although *all reference to Mantua is purely fiction*, the present town of Mantua has made the most of the story, claiming that the house with a veranda and walled garden at piazza Sordello, 23, standing on the same piazza as the Palazzo Ducale, is supposed to be the garden from which Gilda was abducted. Right over the eastern bridge across the Lago di Mezzo on "the road to Verona" stands a building (an "inn") with a square tower and a dock on the lake. This is supposed to be the home of the hired assassin, Sparafucile, and his sister Maddalena. It is certainly evocative even if it is spurious. Today the tourist bureau of Mantua is located in "Rigoletto's house."

Mantua's Conservatorio di Musica, in piazza Dante Alighieri, is connected to the small, elegant Teatro Scientifico (seating ca. 200). Built in 1769 to house a private club (accademia), the Accademia Virgiliana, by the famous Galli-Bibiena family of architects, it is also called Teatro Bibiena. Like several of their theatres (see Bologna, page 28) Mantua's theatre is cello-shaped, in contrast to the typical teatro all'italiana. Wolfgang Amadeus Mozart inaugurated the hall in 1770, when he was fourteen, during his first journey to Italy. The theatre today

"Rigoletto's House"

"Sparafucile's Inn"

presents a year-round concert series and the entrance is around the corner from the conservatory.

Teatro Bibiena (Teatro Scientifico), via dell' Accademia, 47
Open 9:00 A.M.–12:30 P.M. and 3:00–5:30 P.M.
tel, office: (39–376) 327–653 or 323–849, for concert schedule

While in Mantua, Mozart and his father stayed in the Hotel Croce Verde, now a private house in corso Umberto I, 24–30. Corso Umberto I radiates off of piazza Cavallo, where Mantua's present-day opera theatre, Teatro Sociale, stands.

Teatro Sociale, piazza Cavallo, 15
tel: (39–376) 323–860
ticket office (for information and tickets): corso Umberto 12/b, 46100 Mantua
tel: (39–376) 362–739
Theatre and opera season from November to April.

LODGING

Mantua is a very pleasant city in which to stay.

Hotel Broletto, via Accademia, 1
tel: (39–376) 326–784   fax: (39–376) 221–297

This hotel is centrally located near piazza Sordello and a stone's throw from Teatro Bibiena.

Hotel Mantegna, via Fabio Filzi, 10/b
tel: (39–376) 350–315 or 16 or 17   fax: (39–376) 367–259
This very comfortable, pleasant hotel is a five-minute walk from piazza Sordello.

SNACKS

The best snack food of Mantua is the *sbrisolona,* a delicious, hard, sweet, almond biscuit. Perfect with an afternoon coffee. The best are found in any bar near piazza Sordello.

FOOD

The food of Mantua is uniquely delicious. Be sure to try *tortelli di zucca al burro fuso e salvia,* largish tortellini filled with pumpkin, Parmesan cheese, and crumbled *amaretto* cookies. In Mantua, there is the addition of *mostarda,* a sweet-savory condiment made with candied fruit in a slightly piquant mustard syrup. *Rane* (grilled frog's legs) and eels are also specialties. Also try *anguilla in umido* (stewed eel) and *luccio alla griglia* (grilled lake pike).
Everything goes very well with the local tart *Lambrusco.*

Antica Osteria ai Ranari, via Trieste, 11
tel: (39–376) 328–431
Closed Monday.

Aquila Nigra, vicolo Bonacolsi, 4
tel: (39–376) 350–651
Closed Sundays and Mondays and the first two weeks in January.

Two Places of Operatic Interest Near Mantua

Sabbioneta

Accessible by car: Take the 420 southwest in the direction of Casalmaggiore.
For the real culture buff, the late sixteenth-century town of Sabbioneta, thirty-three kilometers (21 miles) southwest of Mantua, is a must. The town is almost exactly as it was in the late sixteenth century, when it was called the "little Athens" because of the refinement of the court of Duke Vespasiano Gonzaga (1531–91), a minor member of Mantua's Gonzaga family. At the town's center stands Teatro all'Antica, completed in 1590, and surely one of the most perfect small theatres in the world; this gem is well worth a short side trip. The

architect, Vicentino Scamozzi, assisted Palladio in building Vicenza's Teatro Olimpico. The theatre is also similar to Parma's Teatro Farnese.

Teatro all'Antica
Open daily, 10:00–11:30 A.M. and 3:00–5:30 P.M.; in October, November, March, and April, till 4:30 P.M.

Legnano

Due east of Mantua, on the train line between Mantua and Padua (Padova), stands the town of Legnano, the birthplace of Antonio Salieri (1750–1825). In Salieri's time the town was under Venetian rule and Venice itself was under Austrian rule. Salieri, orphaned when very young, was sent to Venice, the capital of the province, to study in one of that city's large orphanages. Discovered to have true creative genius, he was taken to Vienna where he became the composer who shaped Viennese operatic life from 1870 to well into the nineteenth century. He also became the successor to Christoph Willibald Gluck for the Paris stage. The German opera public considered him the composer able to "bind all the power of German music to the sweet Italian style." He is, of course, infamous to those who saw the film *Amadeus*.

MILAN (Milano)

In the fourth century the Emperor Constantine signed the Edict of Milan granting Christians throughout the Roman Empire, for the first time, the freedom to worship as they wished. Through the interest of its ruling dukes, the city of Milan has long been important in the arts. The Duchess of Milan, Beatrice d'Este (1475–97), sister of Isabella d'Este of Mantova, wife of Ludovico Sforza, Duke of Milan, managed in her short life to be a patroness of such artists as Leonardo da Vinci, Niccolo da Correggio, Donato Bramante, and many others. The Renaissance splendor of the Castello of Milan and several other famous buildings in Lombardy owe their beauty to her good taste and patronage.

Milan fell to the French in 1499, marking the beginning of almost four centuries of foreign rule. Interestingly, in the eighteenth century, while under Hapsburg (Austrian) rule, Milan became a principal center of Italian opera.

Wolfgang Amadeus Mozart visited Milan early in 1770 as a child prodigy, when commissioned to write and conduct his opera *Mitridate, re di Ponto*, which was first performed December 26, 1770, for the Regio Ducal Teatro. He returned again in 1771, August 21 to December 5, to write and conduct *Ascanio in Alba,* first performed October 17, 1771. *Ascanio in Alba* was commissioned as a *festa teatrale* to celebrate the marriage of Archduke Ferdinand of Austria and Maria Ricciarda Beatrice d'Este of Modena. Mozart returned for the last time in

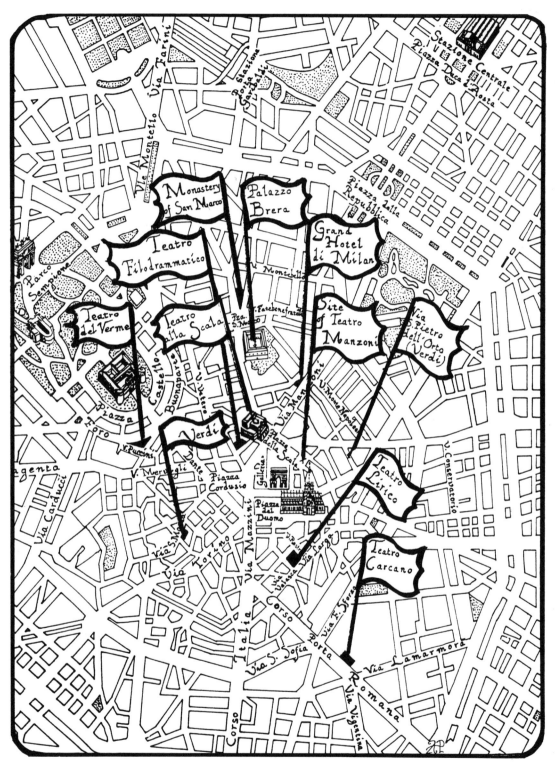

Operatic Milan

1772–73 for the premiere of *Lucio Silla,* December 26, 1772, at the Regio Ducal Teatro. The original theatre, built in 1717, was destroyed by fire in 1776 and rebuilt.

During their first three-month visit Mozart and his father stayed at the thirteenth-century Augustinian Monastery of San Marco. The monastery is found next to the Church of San Marco in piazza San Marco (enter from via Pontaccio) behind palazzo Brera. A plaque commemorates their stay:

Wolfgang Amadeus Mozart	Wolfgang Amadeus Mozart
qui fu ospite	was guest here
dei padri Augustini	of the Augustinian fathers
durante il primo	during his first
soggiorno Milanese,	stay in Milan,
23 Gennaio–15 Marzo 1770.	January 23–March 15, 1770.

Giuseppe Verdi's *Requiem,* written to honor the great nineteenth-century Risorgimento patriot and writer Alessandro Manzoni, was premiered in the same church in 1874 on the first anniversary of his death. The church was completely rebuilt in 1690 and again in 1873 in a conventional Lombard-Gothic style.

Milan really is the city of Giuseppe Verdi. During his early years in Milan (1832–45), he lived in several apartments around La Scala, and all the buildings still standing have plaques honoring him. Some of the addresses with plaques are via S. Marta, 19, 1832–34; via S. Pietro all'Orto, 17, 1834–35; via Corrente, 15, 1839–40 (where he lived with his first wife, Margherita, and their two children, who died in infancy; Margherita died in 1840 from complications following childbirth, after which Verdi moved frequently); via Montenapoleone, 1, 1844–45 (Verdi was famous by this time, and this neighborhood is more upscale).

Milan also houses the home for retired musicians founded by Verdi in 1889, called the Casa di Riposo dei Musicisti, or Casa Verdi.

Casa di Riposo dei Musicisti (Casa Verdi), piazza Michelangelo Buonarroti, 20.

Because he lived as long as he did (1813–1901), Verdi saw many of his contemporaries fall ill and become destitute. In 1869 when his former librettist Francesco Maria Piave was paralyzed by a stroke, Verdi contributed to his support and to that of his family, even after the poet died. In a time before any kind of Social Security, Verdi made it possible for old musicians to retire with dignity. When it was built, the Casa Verdi must have stood at the edge of Milan with open country nearby. The splendid documentary film *Tosca's Kiss,* shot at Casa Verdi, features many of its residents, attesting to the continuing success of the place. Any Italian musician, or foreign musician who has become Italian, may live in Casa Verdi.

A monument to Giuseppe Verdi stands in the center of piazza Michelangelo Buonarroti. The architect of Casa Verdi was Camillo Boito, son of Arrigo Boito (opera composer and Verdi's librettist for *Otello* and *Falstaff*). The courtyard contains a monument depicting Arrigo Boito, and both Giuseppe Verdi and his second wife, the soprano Giuseppina Strepponi, are buried in the crypt. Just inside the doorway to the home is a large plaque saying:

> *Giuseppe Verdi*
> *Sommo nell'arte grande nella vita civile*
> *Fondava*
> *Questa casa di riposo per musicisti*
> *Il 16 Dicembre MDCCCIC*
> *Defunto a dì XXVII Gennaio MCMI*
> *Qui fu deposto nel trigesimo della morte*
> *Con solenne onoranza.*
> *Il Re Vittorio Emanuele III e la Regina Elena*
> *Riverente*
> *Visitarono la tomba nell' 8 Ottobre dello stesso anno.*
> *Il X Ottobre MCMII.*
> *LXXXIX Natalizio del fondatore*
> *Si apriva la casa ai Beneficati.*

> Giuseppe Verdi,
> As great in civil life as in art,
> Founded
> This retirement home for musicians
> December 16, 1899.
> He died on the day of January 27, 1901
> And was buried here on the thirtieth day after his death
> With solemn honors.
> King Victor Emanuel III and Queen Elena
> Reverently
> Visited the tomb
> On October 8th the same year.
> October 10, 1902,
> On the 89th birthday of the founder,

Verdi died on January 27, 1901, at 2:30 A.M. in a suite in Milan's Grand Hotel et de Milan, in via Manzoni, 29, at the corner of via Croce Rossa (metro stop Montenapoleone). The hotel has named the suite, number 105, Sala Verdi. A plaque on the front of the hotel at the corner of via Manzoni and via Croce Rossa reads:

> *Questa casa fece nè secoli memoranda*
> *Giuseppe Verdi*
> *Che vi fu ospite ambito*

E vi spirò il dì 27 di Gennaio del 1901.
Nel primo anniversario di tanta morte
Pose il comune per consenso unanime di popolo
A perpetuo onore del sommo
Che avvivò nei petti Italici con celestiali armonie
Il desiderio e la speranza di una patria.

This house should be held in memory in the coming centuries.
Giuseppe Verdi
Lived here as a guest.
He died here January 27, 1901.
On the first anniversary of his death
The city put up this plaque with unanimous support of the people
To forever honor the greatness
That excited the hearts of Italians with celestial harmony
The desire and hope for one nation.

Three days after he died, on January 30, 1901, in accordance with his wishes to avoid a lot of fuss, Verdi's body was taken secretly at dawn and buried in a temporary grave. Then on February 27, both the bodies of Verdi and his wife Giuseppina Strepponi were escorted to their final resting place in the crypt in the Casa di Riposo. Twenty-eight thousand mourners followed the funeral cortege. "Va pensiero sull'ali dorate" (Go, my thoughts, on golden wings) from *Nabucco* was softly sung by the assembled masses.

Grand Hotel

Casa Verdi in piazza Michelangelo

To commemorate Verdi's death, the great turn-of-the-century poet Gabriele D'Annunzio wrote:

Let mourning and hope echo forth:
He died and wept for all men.

The Milan Conservatory of Music, founded in 1808 on the site of the convent of the Laterans, also carries Verdi's name. Conservatorio di Musica Giuseppe Verdi is found in via del Conservatorio, 12, next to the church of Santa Maria della Passione. During his lifetime Verdi refused to have the conservatory named after him. After all, he was denied entry when he was an eighteen-year-old student! The library contains over one hundred thousand volumes, including operatic manuscripts of Mozart, Paisiello, Rossini, Meyerbeer, Donizetti, Bellini, Verdi, Ponchielli, Catalani, Boito, and others. The conservatory also hosts a small museum displaying precious instruments and more manuscripts.

Teatro alla Scala in piazza della Scala was built on the site of the church of Santa Maria della Scala, which was torn down in 1775 when work on the new opera house began. This placed the theatre right in the center of the Milan of its day: ten-minutes' walk from the Palazzo Sforzesco; five minutes' walk from Palazzo Brera and Palazzo Cusani, both in via Brera; and five minutes from Palazzo Crivelli, in via Pontaccio. The new theatre was inaugurated on August 3, 1778, with a specially commissioned work, *Europa riconosciuta*, by Antonio Salieri. In its early days the theatre overlooked a narrow street. Finally, in 1857 the houses on the other side of the street were torn down and the piazza was opened out to its present size.

Originally Teatro Ducale alla Scala, it soon was called simply Teatro alla Scala and became the most famous opera house in Italy, if not in the world, and the principal center for the development of Italian opera in the nineteenth century. The horseshoe-shaped theatre has 194 boxes in five tiers, a large six-tier gallery, and a sizable royal box. Visibility is excellent and acoustics are very good throughout the theatre. The seating is rather tight (see end of section on La Scala).

Around 1820, cycles of Mozart's operas began to be mounted at La Scala. The performance of such "old" works by a dead, non-Italian composer was a historical first. The young Rossini wrote four operas for the house, Bellini three, and seven out of sixty-six of Donizetti's operas were premiered there. Likewise, Giuseppe Verdi's first four operas premiered there, as well as three important revisions, and finally his triumphant final two operas, *Otello* (1887) and *Falstaff* (1893). Although Verdi's name is very closely associated with La Scala, his career there was checkered. A disagreement Verdi had with the management of La Scala at the time of the premiere of *Giovanna d'Arco* (1845), as well as some financial misdealings on the part of his publisher Ricordi, seemed to alienate Verdi from Milan. Hissing and chattering marred the Milan premieres of *La forza del destino*, *Un ballo in maschera*, and *Aïda*, and Milanese critics accused Verdi of not knowing how to write for singers and of imitating Wagner. After the 1845 premiere of *Giovanna d'Arco* his works, with the exception of revisions, had their premieres elsewhere, until *Otello* in 1887 and *Falstaff* in 1893. Teatro alla Scala suffered during this period, and the years of Verdi's "strike" (1845–87) are among the theatre's least brilliant.

Throughout the nineteenth century alterations and improvements were made to the theatre: the stage was enlarged in 1807; overall restoration took place in 1838; gas lighting was installed in 1860 and electric lighting in 1883.

The great Italian conductor Arturo Toscanini (March 25, 1867, Parma—January 16, 1957, New York City) was artistic director of La Scala from 1898 to 1903 and from 1920 to 1929. During his first period as artistic director, Toscanini took it upon himself to educate the Milanese public, the musicians, and the administration of La Scala to treat opera seriously as a great art form. He fought against singers' bad habits and the administrative cutting of corners to save money, and above all, he insisted upon following the directions of the composer as given in the score. He started the tradition of lowering the lights in the theatre so that the audience would focus on the stage. He also abolished the obligatory ballet that traditionally concluded an evening of opera and tried to eliminate encores. In fact, he walked out on La Scala the last night of the 1903–04 season when the audience insisted on an encore during a performance of Verdi's *Un ballo in maschera*, which he rightly felt would break up the dramatic flow of the opera.

La Scala Today

In 1920, the same year that the theater became a self-governing body called Ente Autonomo del Teatro alla Scala, Toscanini was again made artistic director of La Scala, but this time before accepting the position, he insisted that he be given complete and unprecedented power over what the theatre presented. "The Great Toscanini Period" established the theatre's reputation for consistent excellence in performances. He formed an orchestra of 100 players and a chorus of 120.

In 1922, he refused to allow Mussolini's portrait to be hung at La Scala and regularly defied the new Fascist government by refusing to conduct the official Fascist hymn "Giovinezza." Finally he resigned from La Scala at the end of the 1929 season because his passionately anti-Fascist position was increasingly putting him and the theatre in danger. Mussolini interpreted his refusal to conduct "Giovinezza" as a threat to his power and had Toscanini beaten up by a mob in Bologna, then confiscated his passport and held him under de facto house arrest for several weeks. During this time some fifteen thousand messages of support were delivered to him. Toscanini's fame saved him from a worse fate. When he was released, he left Italy and refused to conduct in Italy or anywhere the Fascist or Nazi regimes were in power, saying he "would rather die" than do so. (See Parma, page 112 for more on Toscanini.)

La Scala was seriously damaged by Allied bombing in 1943. As soon as the war ended in Italy, the theatre was among the first buildings to be rebuilt. It was reconstructed to its original design and now has a seating capacity of 3,000. It reopened on May 11, 1948, with a gala concert conducted by Toscanini (who had personally contributed a large sum of money toward its reconstruction) and debuting the young Renata Tebaldi, who remained a member of the theatre's repertory company until 1955.

Teatro della Scala, via Filodrammatici, 2, 20121 Milan
Ticket office open daily, noon–7:00 P.M.
tel: (39–2) 7200–3744
Opera season from November through May.

If you are in Milan and want to go to a production at La Scala, *go directly to the ticket office, where it is almost always possible to get some kind of ticket for any given event.* If you call on the telephone, you are most likely to be put on hold indefinitely. In the wall in front of the ticket office is an interactive computer that works in Italian, English, French, German, and Japanese, so you can see what seats are available for any performance.

The interior of La Scala is gorgeous, and from most seats the acoustics are wonderful. However, the seats in the *platea* (orchestra) are *very* close together, both in terms of leg room and seat width. As a consequence, it is virtually impossible to get to seats in the middle of a row if the side seats are already occupied, which makes for a lot of ups and downs and milling around. Even though the *palchi* (boxes) have their own problems, anyone who is slightly claustrophobic or over 5 feet 10 inches would be *much* more comfortable in a box. Row K in the *platea* is a broad aisle row and thus has leg room.

The Piccola Scala, a small theatre in back of La Scala, had 600 seats and was built in 1955 for performances of early opera and small-scale contemporary works. Unfortunately, it was closed in 1983.

The Museo Teatrale alla Scala, which opened in 1913, has inner rooms containing many treasures. Among them are the Verdi items I had thought to find in Busseto: the spinet (a small, short-octave piano) given to him by his patron and first father-in-law, Antonio Barezzi, on which he wrote his first operas, and a later piano of Verdi's that the impresario Giulio Gatti-Casazza donated to the museum; the passport, signed by Maria Luigia of Parma, allowing Verdi to go to Milan to apply for entry into the conservatory; many first editions of his scores; everything that was in his hotel suite when he died; the original manuscript of his *Requiem*; wonderful photos of the first cast of *Falstaff*.

Besides the Verdi memorabilia, there are many costumes and copious amounts of stage jewelry; material on Rossini; an enormous library of books on opera and theatre; photos of La Scala after it was bombed; a poster announcing a performance of *Nerone*, by Boito, with a sign slashed across it saying the performance was canceled because of the death of Puccini; and wonderful photos and paintings of singers including a charcoal drawing of a very dramatic Maria Callas.

A video in one room shows a La Scala production while in another a recording continually plays some famous interpretation of an opera. The museum often has exhibits illustrating particular periods and aspects of the theatre's history and since 1988 has published a quarterly *Rivista illustrata del Museo alla Scala*.

Museo della Scala
Open weekdays, 9:00 A.M.–noon and 2:00–6:00 P.M.; holidays,
9:30 A.M.–12:30 P.M. and 2:30–6:00 P.M.

Teatro alla Scala premiered, among many others (details of these premieres can be found at the end of this section) *Dialogues des Carmélites* (1957), Francis Poulenc; *Don Carlo* (Italian premiere, 1884), Giuseppe Verdi; *Falstaff* (1893), Giuseppe Verdi; *La figlia del reggimento,* Italian premiere (1840), Gaetano Donizetti; *La forza del destino,* Italian premiere (1863), Giuseppe Verdi; *La gazza ladra* (1817), Gioacchino Rossini; *La gioconda* (1876), Amilcare Ponchielli; *Un giorno di regno* (1840), Giuseppe Verdi; *Giovanna d'Arco* (1845), Giuseppe Verdi; *I lombardi alla prima crociata* (1843), Giuseppe Verdi; *Lucrezia Borgia* (1833), Gaetano Donizetti; *Madama Butterfly* (1904), Giacomo Puccini; *Mefistofele* (1868), Arrigo Boito; *Nabucco* (1842), Giuseppe Verdi; *Nerone* (1924), Arrigo Boito; *Norma* (1831), Vincenzo Bellini; *Oberto* (1839), Giuseppe Verdi; *Otello* (1887), Giuseppe Verdi; *La pietra di paragone* (1812), Gioacchino Rossini; *Il pirata* (1827), Vincenzo Bellini; *Simon Boccanegra,* reorchestrated and revised (1881), Guiseppe Verdi; *La straniera* (1829), Vincenzo Bellini; *Turandot* (1926), Giacomo Puccini; *Il turco in Italia* (1814), Gioacchino Rossini; *La Wally* (1892), Alfredo Catalani.

Since 1960 Teatro della Scala has presented several adventurous premieres including *Donnerstag aus Licht* (1981), Karlheinz Stockhausen (born August 22, 1928, Burg Mödrath, near Cologne); *Montag aus Licht* (1988), Karlheinz Stockhausen (Both of these full-length operas are part of a large cycle entitled *Licht* that Stockhausen began in 1974 and plans to finish by 1999.); *Passaggio* (1963, Teatro Piccolo Scala), Luciano Berio (born October 24, 1925, Oneglia, Imperia); *La vera storia* (1982), Luciano Berio.

From 1812 on, Milan's musical history became virtually one with that of Italian opera. La Scala was undeniably the most notable center and has had since then a world-class reputation. Milan, however, hosted several other opera houses that premiered many of the operas that are popular today. Some of these theatres still stand though they rarely, if ever, present opera.

Teatro Filodrammatico sits just across a narrow street from La Scala. In this theatre, literally twenty feet from the front doors of La Scala, the young Giuseppe Verdi conducted the performance of Haydn's *Creation* that first put him in the eye of Milan's concertgoing public.

Teatro della Cannobiana (1779), now called Teatro Lirico, was inaugurated August 21, 1779, on a site adjoining a school of painting founded by Paolo Cannobio in 1554. The theatre, a mere five-minute walk across the piazza del Duomo from La Scala, had an audience capacity of 2,000, with four tiers and a gallery. In 1894 it was renovated and renamed Teatro Lirico Internazionale. The theatre burned in 1939 but was rebuilt in 1945. Today known simply as Teatro Lirico, it is a squat, dirty yellow building that presents only prose theatre.

Teatro Filodrammatico

Teatro Lirico, via Rastrelli, 5 (corner of via Rastrelli and via Largo)
tel: (39–2) 8646–4823

Teatro Lirico premiered (details of these premieres are at the end of the chapter) Adriana Lecouvreur (1902), Francesco Cilea; *L'elisir d'amore* (1832), Gaetano Donizetti; *Zazà* (1900), Ruggero Leoncavallo.

Teatro Carcano is a ten-minute walk from Teatro Lirico. Teatro Carcano, built in 1803, was modeled after La Scala and until the end of the nineteenth century was a quite successful opera theatre. Among the premieres presented here was the first Milan concert of Richard Wagner's music in 1882. The theatre, now devoted to prose drama, has not been used for music since the first decade of the twentieth century.

Teatro Carcano presented the premieres of (details of the premieres are at the end of the chapter) *Anna Bolena* (1830), Gaetano Donizetti; *La sonnambula* (1831), Vincenzo Bellini.

> **Teatro Carcano,** corso di Porta Romana, 63
> tel: (39–2) 5518–1377
> metro stop: Crocetta

Teatro dal Verme was originally a private theatre dating from the eighteenth century. It was acquired by Count Francesco dal Verme, who demolished and then rebuilt it in 1872. At its reopening it was considered the most modern theatre of its time as well as being a beautiful building. The theatre is a five-minute walk from La Scala in the direction of the Castello Sforzesco. In 1989 Teatro dal Verme was purchased by the RAI (Italian Radio and TV) of Milan and since 1990 has been under reconstruction. Unfortunately, the Italian radio has had financial problems and recently the work on this beautiful theatre halted. Via Puccini borders it on the left, reminding us that Puccini's first opera, *Le villi*, was performed there. The garden of Palazzo dal Verme where the count lived still stands next to via Puccini, 5. Teatro dal Verme is on the corner of via San Giovanni sul Muro and via Puccini.

Teatro dal Verme presented the premieres of (details of the premieres are at the end of the chapter) *I pagliacci* (1892), Ruggero Leoncavallo; *Le villi* (1884), Giacomo Puccini.

A footnote that simply reiterates the importance of opera in Milan is Teatro Manzoni, a theatre that presented opera buffa and stood just across piazza della Scala from Teatro La Scala in piazza San Fedele. Teatro Manzoni opened in 1873. It ceased to function as an opera house soon after 1900 and became a prose theatre. From 1900 to 1930 it presented the broadest scope of Italian and foreign theatre in Milan. In 1930 it was given to the music-publishing company Suvini-Zerboni. All that stands in piazza San Fedele today is a plaque to Manzoni.

Details of Teatro alla Scala premieres

> *Dialogues des Carmélites, opera* in three acts, January 26, 1957.
> Francis Poulenc (January 7, 1899, Paris—January 30, 1963, Paris)
> Libretto by the composer after the play of the same title by Georges Bernanos.
>
> The premiere of the *Dialogues des Carmélites* was performed in an Italian translation of Poulenc's original. The opera reflects the nuns' experiences under the Terror, for which they were later beatified. Today, it is an internationally standard repertory work in French.

Don Carlo, opera in four acts, Italian premiere, January 10, 1884 (*Don Carlos* premiere at Paris L'Opéra, in five acts, March 11, 1867).
Giuseppe Verdi (1813–1901)
Libretto Joseph Méry and Camille Du Locle (Italian translation by Achille de Lauzières and Angelo Zanardini), after a dramatic poem by Friedrich Schiller, *Don Carlos, Infant von Spanien*.

The shorter four-act Italian translation of *Don Carlos* is the one usually heard outside France today. However, a wonderful recording in the original French conducted by Claudio Abbado is truly a revelation, in particular, the two arias of Princess Eboli. The music is from Verdi's middle period, his most sophisticated, and contains some of his most exciting before *Otello*. *Don Carlo* has recently become more popular and is now presented with some regularity throughout the world.

Falstaff, *commedia lirica* in three acts, February 9, 1893.
Giuseppe Verdi (1813–1901)
Libretto Arrigo Boito, after William Shakespeare's plays *The Merry Wives of Windsor* and *Henry IV*.

Falstaff is Verdi's twenty-eighth and last opera. In his later years Verdi often spoke of writing a comic opera, even though his one *melodramma giocoso* (comic opera), *Un giorno di regno*, had been a disaster at La Scala in 1840. Two years after the success of *Otello*, Arrigo Boito suggested a work based on Shakespeare's *Merry Wives of Windsor*. From 1887 to 1891, Verdi composed the music and wrote the libretto (with Boito); between 1891 and 1892 he orchestrated the score. The premiere was a triumph that capped a career spanning three-quarters of the nineteenth century. Verdi's genius for translating drama into music reached unprecedented heights in *Falstaff*. Although it is riotously funny, the great Italian actress Eleonora Duse was said to have wept throughout the premiere because of the touching themes Verdi brought so wisely to life. It remains part of the international repertory but is less performed than his dramatic operas.

La figlia del reggimento, *opera buffa* in two acts, Italian premiere of revised opera, October 3, 1840.
Gaetano Donizetti (1797–1848)
Libretto Jules-Henri Vernoy de Saint-Georges and Jean-François-Alfred Bayard, revised and translated into Italian by Calisto Bassi.

The fact that the revised and translated *La figlia del reggimento* received its Italian premiere only eight months after its Paris premiere attests to Donizetti's popularity. For the La Scala premiere Donizetti substituted recitative for the spoken dialogue required by L'Opéra Comique, cut some pieces, and added others. Except in France, the Italian version is usually performed today. (See Paris, page 247.)

La forza del destino, *opera* in four acts, Italian premiere, February 27, 1869.

Giuseppe Verdi (1813–1901)

Libretto Francesco Maria Piave after the play by Angel de Saavedra, Duke of Rivas, *Don Alvardo, o la fuerza del sino* (influenced by Victor Hugo) and a scene from Friedrich von Schiller's play *Wallensteins Lager,* translated by Andrea Maffei and additional text added to the revised edition premiered in Italy by Antonio Ghislanzoni.

La forza del destino was commissioned by the Imperial Theatre (Mariinskij Teatr) in Saint Petersburg, Russia, where its world premiere on October 29, 1862, was modestly successful. Verdi began revisions to the score and Piave's libretto in 1863, and the Italian premiere at La Scala in 1869 fared much better. Verdi called *La forza* an "opera of ideas," alluding to the looseness of the narrative, and perhaps to the libretto's many sources. In the story, Don Carlo di Vargas hunts down his sister Leonora and her lover Don Alvaro because he believes they were responsible for his father's death. At the end of the first version everyone lay dead on the stage. Verdi felt this was too much for Italian audiences and asked Piave to allow Alvaro to survive. No matter how you look at it, the story is very confusing, so Verdi made use of a "fate motif," which recurs throughout the opera, giving the orchestra a larger role than in any of his preceding works. Since the 1930s the opera has become one of Verdi's most popular after his middle-period masterpieces *Rigoletto, La traviata,* and *Il trovatore.*

Un giorno di regno (King for a Day, known also as *Il Finto Stanislao,* The False Stanislaus), *melodramma giocoso* in two acts, September 5, 1840.

Giuseppe Verdi (1813–1901)

Libretto Felice Romani (probably revised by Temistocle Solera) after Alexandre Vincent Pineu-Duval's play *Le Faux Stanislas* (The False Stanislaus).

Verdi's second opera, *Un giorno di regno,* was a complete fiasco. It was withdrawn from the stage after only one performance. The opera was Verdi's only comic work until he wrote *Falstaff* some fifty-three years later.

La gazza ladra (The Thieving Magpie), *melodramma* in two acts, May 31, 1817.

Gioacchino Rossini (February 29, 1792, Pesaro—November 13, 1868, Paris)

Libretto Giovanni Gherardini after *La Pie voleuse* by J. M. T. Badouin d'Aubigny and Louis-Charles Caigniez.

La gazza ladra is a kind of Italian "rescue opera"—the heroine is saved from execution at the eleventh hour and everyone lives happily ever after. In the French original she dies on the gallows. The orchestration for the march to the scaffold anticipates Berlioz's use of the orchestra for a similar setting. Rossini revised this, his twenty-first opera, several times, even though it had a successful premiere. The opera in its entirety is performed only rarely. The overture, however, is a standard opening piece for symphony concerts.

La gioconda (The Happy One), *dramma lirico* in four acts, April 8, 1876.
Amilcare Ponchielli (August 31, 1934, Paderno, now called Paderno Ponchielli—January 16, 1886, Milan)
Libretto Tobia Gorrio (a pseudonym of Arrigo Boito using his name in an anagram) after Victor Hugo's play *Angelo, tyran de Padoue* (Angelo, the Tyrant of Padua).

The publisher Ricordi commissioned *La gioconda* and hired Arrigo Boito (the famous librettist of Verdi's *Otello* and *Falstaff*) to prepare the libretto. The opera is modeled after the French style of grand opera, with large choral scenes, spectacular historical framework, many contrasts, and a central ballet. Boito made the title role far less important than in the original Hugo play and elevated the role of the Venetian spy to a more "operatic" character, a rather lurid, satanic figure. It is a truly Gothic story of lust, revenge, murder, and suicide. The premiere received a "cordial reception" and critics wrote that, apart from Verdi, only Ponchielli was capable of writing a work of such importance. For the subsequent performances in Venice, Rome, and Genoa, Ponchielli made many modifications, and it is the Genoa version, first performed on November 29, 1879, that is considered definitive. Today, performances of this one Ponchielli opera that remains in the repertoire are restricted to opera houses that can' afford the many resources it requires. Its most universally known music is its "Danza delle ore" (Dance of the Hours).

Giovanna d'Arco, *dramma lirico* in a prologue and three acts, February 15, 1845.
Giuseppe Verdi (1813–1901)
Libretto Temistocle Solera after Friedrich von Schiller's *Die Jungfrau von Orleans* (The Maid of Orleans).

Giovanna d'Arco is Verdi's seventh opera. The premiere was a great public success, but the direction of La Scala did not adhere to the high standards Verdi set for the production; as a result, he refused to have his operas premiered at the theatre for many years. His next fifteen operas were premiered elsewhere. *Giovanna d'Arco* is not in today's repertory.

I Lombardi alla prima crociata (The Lombards on the First Crusade), *dramma lirico* in four acts, February 11, 1843.
Giuseppe Verdi (1813–1901)
Libretto Temistocle Solera after Tommaso Grossi's poem of the same title.

Even though the Archbishop of Milan felt the opera was a sacrilege, the premiere of *I Lombardi,* depicting the battle between "true believers and the infidels," was a smashing public success, most likely because of the political climate in a Milan occupied by Austria. As with *Nabucco,* performed eleven months earlier, the public intensely felt the parallel between their situation and the story of the opera. The opera was frowned upon by the religious censors of Milan because of factual changes Solera made for dramatic impact and plot development, but it ultimately escaped with relatively few minor alterations. Verdi made a revised French version of the opera given in Paris in 1847 as *Jérusalem. I Lombardi* is Verdi's fourth opera. It does not appear today as a repertory opera, although the Met produced it for the first time in that theatre's history in January 1994.

Lucrezia Borgia, *melodramma* in a prologue and two acts, originally entitled *Alfonso, Duca di Ferrara* (Alfonso, the Duke of Ferrara), December 26, 1833.
Gaetano Donizetti (1797–1848)
Libretto Felice Romani, after Victor Hugo's play *Lucrèce Borgia.*

Lucrezia Borgia, Donizetti's thirty-ninth opera in nine years, was one of the major successes in his career. The scene that particularly captures the greatness of Donizetti's imagination is where the six coffins of Lucrezia's victims appear. The Milanese censors refused to permit this scene at the premiere. In fact, the whole subject matter of the opera was regarded as suspect. As a consequence, between the first production at La Scala and the second, three years passed. For a time the work was given under a number of aliases, and in one version the action was even transferred to a non-Christian country. Donizetti's use of a dialogue duet, over an orchestral melody, anticipates Verdi's later use of the technique in the famous scene in *Rigoletto* between Rigoletto and Sparafucile. Unfortunately, *Lucrezia Borgia* is seldom made available to today's operagoing public.

Madama Butterfly, *tragedia giapponese* (Japanese tragedy), February 17, 1904.
Giacomo Puccini (1858–1924)
Libretto Luigi Illica and Giuseppe Giacosa, based on a play by David Belasco, *Madame Butterfly,* which was itself based on a short story by John Luther Long, which in turn was based partly on Pierre Loti's story "*Madame Chrysanthème.*"

Madama Butterfly tells of the Japanese "wife" of a sailor, Pinkerton, who leaves her after Act I to return to the United States. Butterfly, who has given birth to Pinkerton's son, awaits his return, spurning other offers of marriage and support. She is first overjoyed when she hears Pinkerton has returned and then devastated when she learns he has brought an American wife. As the Pinkertons enter her house she kills herself. La Scala's premiere of

Madama Butterfly was a total disaster. Not only did a claque disrupt the performance with catcalls and laughter, but Puccini was accused of plagiarizing himself and other composers. He withdrew the opera after the first performance, and a revised version was successful in Brescia. (See Brescia, page 31.)

Mefistofele, *dramma lirico,* March 5, 1868.
Arrigo Boito (February 24, 1842, Padua—June 10, 1918, Milan)
Libretto by the composer after Goethe's *Faust.*

The first performance of *Mefistofele* was a disaster chiefly because Boito was relatively inexperienced as an opera composer. The performance was far too long and the cast undistinguished. Consequently Boito revised and shortened the work. The first revised version was performed in 1875 in Bologna. Boito continued to revise, and the opera as it is known today was first performed in London at Her Majesty's Theatre July 6, 1880. *Mefistofele* returned to La Scala May 25, 1881, this time with great success. The opera requires a charismatic bass, and since 1969 Samuel Ramey has sung the title role internationally with some regularity.

Nabucco, *dramma lirico* in four parts, March 9, 1842.
Giuseppe Verdi (1813–1901)
Libretto Temistocle Solera, after the ballet *Nabuccodonoor* by Antonio Cortese and the play *Nabuchodonoor* by Auguste Anicet-Bourgeois and Francis Cornu.

Nabucco is Verdi's third opera and his first unqualified success. It was immediately revived for the fall of 1842. Verdi made only very slight changes after the first performances, changes made more to suit a specific singer than to alter the opera. At the premiere the rousing chorus "Va pensiero sull'ali dorate" was perceived by the Milanese public as a proclamation of their liberty. The Milanese, under the control of Austria, identified with the story of the captive Jews in Babylonia longing for their freedom and homeland. The Austrian censors knew there would be trouble if they tried to prohibit performances of the opera, so, its subject matter notwithstanding, the opera ran for a record fifty-seven performances after its fall 1842 revival. "Va pensiero" gradually assumed something like iconic status as the hymn behind the movement for the unification of Italy. Verdi's name itself became an acronym of the vocabulary for the unification of Italy against foreign domination and for an Italian king:

Viva VERDI = Viva Vittorio Emanuele Re *d'Italia* (Long Live Victor Emanuel King of Italy).

This acrostic message was written on walls throughout Italy. Anyone caught writing it could always claim to be merely an opera lover! *Nabucco* contains some splendid music but unfortunately is not often performed today.

Nerone (Nero), *tragedia* in four acts, May 1, 1924.
Music and libretto Arrigo Boito (1842–1918).

Left unfinished by Boito, *Nerone* was put into working shape after his death under the direction of Arturo Toscanini. The opera was not particularly successful and never became part of general repertory.

Norma, *tragedia lirico* in two acts, December 26, 1831.
Vincenzo Bellini (1801–35)
Libretto Felice Romani after Alexandre Soumet's verse tragedy of the same name.

Bellini was paid an enormous sum of money to write his eighth opera, *Norma.* He obviously felt it was an important commission and interrupted the preparation of the premiere, revising and trimming the libretto and changing the music. "Casta diva" alone is reputed to have had eight versions. The story concerns a beautiful Druid high priestess, Norma, who, though required to be chaste, in actuality has had two children with a Roman officer, Pollione. Tired of Norma, Pollione attempts to go off with her best friend Adalgisa but is caught and brought to Norma to be killed. Unable to kill him herself, she offers him his life if he will renounce Adalgisa. He refuses, so Norma confesses their relationship to the Gauls, and the two are led off to be burnt at the stake. The premiere was a flop, due in part to the fact that Bellini offended the operagoing public by defying tradition and ending the first act with a trio instead of a more complex ensemble. The opera quickly became popular, however, and remains in today's repertory. The title role is an excellent vehicle for an agile and dramatic soprano such as Maria Callas, who made her debut as the Druidess of the title role in London, Chicago, and New York's Metropolitan Opera.

Oberto, *dramma* in two acts, November 17, 1839.
Giuseppe Verdi (1813–1901)
Libretto Antonio Piazza and Temistocle Solera.

Verdi originally tried, without success, to get *Oberto,* his first opera, performed in both Parma and Milan. Only after revisions was it premiered successfully at La Scala. Immediately after the premiere the music publisher Giulio Ricordi bought the publishing rights and La Scala's director, Bartolomeo Merelli, commissioned three more operas from the young Verdi. The first, *Un giorno di regno,* was a failure and was withdrawn after its first performance in 1840, but *Nabucco* (1842) and *I Lombardi alla prima crociata* (1843) were great successes. In fact, the music of both *I Lombardi* and *Nabucco* came to represent the drive toward the unification of Italy, and the great patriotic choruses of the operas, such as "Va pensiero sull'ali dorati," from *Nabucco,* often incited demonstrations in the theatre.

Otello, *dramma lirico* in four acts, February 5, 1887.
Giuseppe Verdi (1813–1901)
Libretto Arrigo Boito after Shakespeare's play *Othello, or the Moor of Venice.*

In 1879 the music publisher Giulio Ricordi, together with Arrigo Boito, suggested that Verdi base an opera on Shakespeare's *Othello.* Verdi had not written an opera since *Aïda,* in 1871, and seemed unwilling to consider a new work after composing his *Requiem* in 1874. Verdi had a lifelong passion for Shakespeare, whose name he wrote as "Shachespeare," and a year later, when Boito had drafted a libretto, he set to work. Given the complexity of the score, he composed the opera in a relatively short period of time. The premiere was an extraordinary success with the public, though some critics lamented that the new sophistication in Verdi's music lacked the immediacy found in that of his middle period. *Otello* is an extraordinary work in which Verdi used musical motivic material, not unlike Wagner's use of a leitmotiv, to highlight Otello's passion for Desdemona. Iago's "Credo," interpreted by a great baritone-actor, is truly one of the most frightening arias ever written. The opera was soon given in all the major opera houses in Europe and today remains a staple in the international repertory. (The young Arturo Toscanini was the second cellist, and the young Tullio Serafin was in the violin section in the orchestra of La Scala at the premiere of *Otello.*)

La pietra di paragone (The Touchstone), *melodramma giocoso* in two acts, September 26, 1812.
Gioacchino Rossini (1792–1868)
Libretto Luigi Romanelli.

Rossini was only twenty when he wrote *La pietra di paragone,* his sixth opera performed in a public opera house. Rossini was already entering his prime. The author Stendhal considered the opera's Act I finale the funniest of all Rossini's comic finales, for it is full of nonsensical patter and in the aria "Ombretta sdegnosa," the refrain of "Misippi ipipi, pipi, pipi" appears over and over again. The opera is full of quotable jokes that made him the toast of Milan. After the big success of *La pietra di paragone,* Rossini was exempted from Italian military service and established the kind of reputation where simply his name guaranteed a public!

Il pirata, *melodramma* in two acts, October 27, 1827.
Vincenzo Bellini (1801–35)
Libretto Felice Romani after J. S. Taylor's play *Bertram, ou Le pirate* (Bertram, or the Pirate).

Il pirata was Bellini's second professional production and his first collaboration with Felice Romani. He took a great deal of time and care in preparing the score, much more than was usual for him and for other composers of the time, because he felt it was essential to have a major triumph at La Scala at this point in his career. The production was a hit, Bellini was hailed as an exciting new voice in Italian opera, and by 1830 the opera had been performed in Vienna, London, and Paris. *Il pirata* is a splendid operatic vehicle for an agile and dramatic soprano with a great voice. Notable performances in this century have been given by Maria Callas and Montserrat Caballé, but the opera is by no means part of standard repertory in the twentieth century.

Simon Boccanegra, opera in a prologue and three acts, March 24, 1881.
Giuseppe Verdi (1813–1901)
Reorchestrated, text revised by Arrigo Boito, and scenes added to Piave's original libretto.

This second "premiere" was a great success. The premiere of the first version took place March 12, 1857, at Venice's Teatro La Fenice.

La straniera, melodramma in two acts, February 14, 1829.
Vincenzo Bellini (1801–35)
Libretto Felice Romani, after Victor-Charles Prévôt's novel *L'Etrangère* (The Stranger).

This opera was Bellini's second great success at La Scala after *Il pirata*. *La straniera* quickly became popular in Italy with performances in Palermo, Naples, Venice, Rome, Trieste, and other cities. It reached London in 1832. Bellini described the tenor lead as *un disperato* (a desperate character). Rather than the usual stylized music of his more popular operas, Bellini wrote an extremely colorful and dramatic score for *La straniera* that enhances the very dramatic plot. *La straniera* is rarely performed today.

Turandot, dramma lirico in three acts, April 25, 1926 (completed by Franco Alfano at the suggestion of Arturo Toscanini).
Giacomo Puccini (1858–1924)
Libretto Giuseppe Adami and Renato Simoni after Carlo Gozzi's dramatic fairy tale of the same title.

Turandot is Puccini's twelfth and final opera. Puccini and his librettists decided to base an opera on Gozzi's most celebrated fairy tale, devising a libretto that would "modernize and bring human warmth to the old cardboard figures." The story concerns the beautiful "Ice Princess," Turandot, who refuses every one of her many suitors; she asks them three riddles and eliminates them, literally, when they cannot answer. Enter the exiled Prince Calaf, who bumps into his disguised, old, blind father, and their serving girl, Liù, all in flight from their enemies. Calaf wants Turandot (and presumably her kingdom) and answers the three riddles. When Turandot still refuses to marry him, he offers her an escape: if by the next morning she can discover his name, he will consent to be beheaded. Calaf's father and Liù are captured and tortured for Calaf's name. Liù, who loves Calaf, says she alone knows his name but refuses to tell it. Driven beyond endurance, she grabs a knife and kills herself. In the end Calaf and Turandot seem headed for living happily ever after. The character of Liù was added by the librettists to insert some "human warmth." The problem was and is Calaf, who persists in wooing a woman of whom he knows nothing and whom he has every reason to dislike, given the treatment of his father and the slave girl. Puccini died before his librettists had come up with a successful ending and the problem remains, some glorious music notwithstanding. At the premiere of the opera, a year and a half after Puccini's death, Toscanini—even though he had been responsible for the completion of the opera by Franco Alfano—laid down his baton after the death of Liù, the last music written by Puccini. The score was finally published with a shortened version of Alfano's ending. Although Puccini died before completing the opera, *Turandot* is considered the summit of his musical-dramatic achievement. The style is secure in its nineteenth-century roots, but it is broadened by "modern elements" such as bitonality (the opera's beginning is starkly bitonal) and the use of whole-tone, modal, and pentatonic ("oriental") harmonies. The principal roles in the opera, Turandot, Liù, and Calaf, are favorites of many sopranos and tenors, and *Turandot* is a firmly established part of the repertory today.

Il turco in Italia, *dramma buffo* in two acts, August 14, 1814.
Gioacchino Rossini (1792–1868)
Libretto Felice Romani after Caterino Mazzola's novel of the same title.

After the extraordinary success of *L'italiana in Algeri,* the smaller scale *Il turco in Italia* should have been a runaway success, but it received only moderate critical acclaim, probably because the piece is dominated by ensembles and conversations in a type of "drawing-room chatter" rather than portraying a character with whom the public can identify. The text and music combine in double meanings that express hypocrisy, smothered anger, forced smiles, and asides through clenched teeth. Some of the solo numbers are absolutely fabulous. *Il turco in Italia* is rarely heard today.

La Wally, *dramma musicale* in four acts, January 20, 1892.
Alfredo Catalani (1854–93)
Libretto Luigi Illica after Wilhelmine von Hillern's story *Die Geyer-Wally.*

La Wally is Catalani's masterpiece. Its sound lies halfway between earthy, early verismo opera and Puccini's elegant operas of the late 1890s. It is a wonderfully decadent story, some of the music is quite splendid, but the plot lacks dramatic interest and is a bit too long. Some people, however, liked the opera. As noted earlier, Arturo Toscanini so admired it that he named his daughter Wally, a very un-Italian name.

Luigi Illica, the librettist of *La Wally*, led quite a dramatic life. He was a patriot and a notorious womanizer who lost part of an ear in a duel, which is the reason the few photographs we have of him are in profile.

Details of Teatro Carcano's premieres

Anna Bolena, *tragedia lirica* in two acts, December 26, 1830.
Gaetano Donizetti (1797–1848)
Libretto Felice Romani after Pindemonte's *Enrico VIII, ossia Anna Bolena* and Pepoli's *Anna Bolena*.

Anna Bolena put Donizetti on the international operatic map with performances in Paris and London. At this point in his career, he became the most important opera composer between Bellini and Verdi's middle period. For the first time Donizetti was able to write incredibly gripping music. He even makes use of "Home, Sweet Home" in a little aria that then explodes into an amazing cabaletta at the end of the opera.

La sonnambula, *melodramma* in two acts, March 6, 1831.
Vincenzo Bellini (1801–35)
Libretto Felice Romani after Eugène Scribe and Jean-Pierre Aumer's ballet-pantomine *La somnambule, ou L'arrivée d'un nouveau seigneur* (The Sleepwalker, or the Arrival of the New Lord).

Bellini started *La sonnambula* January 2, 1831, and wrote the whole second act between February 9 and February 23. Odd physio-psychological phenomena such as somnambulism, the stuff of which Gothic stories are made, were popular subjects in the nineteenth century. The opera was instantly successful, and the role of Amina has since been a favorite of sopranos such as Renata Scotto, Maria Callas, Amelita Galli-Curci, and Luisa Tetrazzini.

Details of Teatro Lirico premieres

Adriana Lecouvreur, *opera* in four acts, November 6, 1902.
Francesco Cilea (July 23, 1899, Palmi, Reggio Calabria—November 20, 1950, Varazze, Savona)
Libretto Arturo Colautti, after the play *Adrienne Lecouvreur* by Eugène Scribe and Ernest Legouvé.

The premiere was an outstanding success. The opera was a commission by the publisher Edoardo Sonzogno following the success of Cilea's *L'arlesiana*. *Adriana Lecouvreur* is the only one of Cilea's three surviving operas to remain in general repertory.

L'elisir d'amore, *melodramma giocoso* in two acts, May 12, 1832 (when the theatre was called Teatro Cannobiana).
Gaetano Donizetti (1797–1848)
Libretto Felice Romani after Eugene Scribe's text for the opera by Daniel-François-Esprit Auber's *Le Philtre* (1831, Paris).

Donizetti composed *L'elisir d'amore* in six weeks. The story depicts Nemorino, who purchases an elixir guaranteed to make him irresistible to women, and his love, Adina, who makes him wait to get her. The same plot had been used the previous year for an opera by the French composer Auber. It is, however, Donizetti's opera that has been a huge success from its first performance and continues to be a favorite today. Donizetti's music proved so popular in Italy that between 1838 and 1848, one out of every four productions in Italy was a work by Donizetti!

Zazà, *commedia lirica* in four acts, November 10, 1900.
Ruggero Leoncavallo (1857–1919)
Libretto by the composer after the play of the same name by Pierre Berton and Charles Simon.

Arturo Toscanini conducted the premiere of *Zazà*, and for many years the opera was a favorite for star sopranos. It has recently enjoyed something of a revival in Italy.

Details of Teatro dal Verme premieres

I pagliacci, *dramma* in a prologue and two acts, May 22, 1892.
Ruggero Leoncavallo (1857–1919)
Libretto by the composer based on a newspaper crime report.

Motivated by the success of Mascagni's *Cavalleria rusticana*, the music publisher Sonzogno commissioned Leoncavallo to write an opera on another verismo subject and was very pleased with the libretto of *Pagliacci's* story of love and jealousy. Leoncavallo tried to follow Mascagni's example by making it a one-act opera but found it necessary to close the curtain to make clear the distinction between the real life of the opera's first half and the second half in which the play is performed. Arturo Toscanini conducted the triumphant premiere, and within two years it had been translated into all the European languages (and even into Hebrew for a 1924 performance in Tel Aviv). *I pagliacci* and *Cavalleria rusticana* are often paired on the stage and are the two prime examples of verismo opera.

Le villi (The Will-o'-the-Wisp), *opera-ballo* (*leggenda drammatica*) in two acts, May 31, 1884.
Giacomo Puccini (1858–1924)
Libretto Ferdinando Fontana after Alfonse Karr's short story *"Les Willis."*

Le villi is Puccini's first opera and is markedly eclectic, as many composers' early works are. The subject matter is anything but Italian and if anything is reminiscent of the *Giselle* story. Written as a one-act opera for a competition sponsored by the music publisher Edoardo Sonzogno, *Le villi* did not even receive honorable mention. The music publisher Giulio Ricordi, however, was in no doubt that Puccini was the successor of Giuseppe Verdi and persuaded Puccini and his librettist to expand the opera to two acts. Because of the success of *Le villi,* modest though it was, Ricordi provided Puccini with a monthly stipend so that he could compose at his leisure and remained Puccini's guide and friend to the end of his life in 1912. Sonzogno was enraged that Ricordi saw what he, Sonzogno, missed.

Music publishers were making so much money because of opera's popularity in the late nineteenth century that they not only commissioned new operas but also held competitions to find exciting, new, young talent. The object was to sign up these potential star composers, thus assuring their publishing company of all the profits from their future operas. As opera was still *the* popular art form in Italy, these contests were good investments.

LODGING

Milan is a northern industrial city in which it is very important to stay in the right places and to eat in the right restaurants. All the "right" places are within walking distance of La Scala.

Hotel London, via Rovello, 3, Milano 20121
tel: (39–2) 7202–0166   fax: (39–2) 805–7037
Closed from December 23—January 3, and for the month of August.
   This hotel is definitely one of the better deals in Milan. The hotel is family run and is very nice, very clean, nicely maintained, near good restaurants, quite inexpensive (considering how expensive Milan is), and a five-minute walk from La Scala.

Hotel Giulio Cesare, via Rovello, 10, Milano 20121
tel: (39–2) 7200–3915   fax: (39–2) 7200–2179
   This hotel is located right across the street from Hotel London and its price range is the same, quite inexpensive considering where it is located.

Hotel Manzoni, via Santo Spirito, 20, Milano 20121
tel: (39–2) 7600–5700   fax: (39–2) 784–212
   This is a lovely hotel, relatively inexpensive and near everything, including Milan's most elegant shopping street, via Montenapoleone. It is a seven-minute walk to La Scala.

Hotel Star, via dei Bossi, 5, Milano 20121
tel: (39–2) 801–501   fax: (39–2) 861–787
Closed the month of August.

This ever-so-slightly more expensive hotel is a two-minute walk from La Scala and near many good restaurants.

Grand Hotel et de Milan, via Manzoni, 29, Milano 20121
tel: (39–2) 72314.1   fax: (39–2) 8646–0861

If expense is no problem, stay in this elegant and newly restored hotel a ten-minute walk from La Scala and very near the elegant shopping street, via Montenapoleone. Walking down via Manzoni toward the theatre, you will follow in the footsteps of Giuseppe Verdi. And for about $600 you can even stay in the suite where he died.

SNACKS

For a quick bite before a performance at La Scala try:

Il Panino del Conte, *bar-paninoteca* corner of via Broletto and via Bossi (almost next door to the Hotel Star)
tel: (39–2) 8646–3869
Closed Sundays.

This unique *panino* (sandwich) shop offers over seventy-five original and excellent sandwiches. Fully thirty of them are vegetarian! Do try the delicious offerings made with the cheese *scamorza* (a smoked, low-fat kind of mozzarella) and those made with *bresaola* (a delectable cured beef). They also serve good wines and beer on tap.

FOOD

Good Milanese cuisine is hard to beat. It combines the best of Austria, France, and indigenous cooking. Some specialties not to miss are:

bresaola (thin slices of cold, cured beef on which you squeeze lemon and pour a bit of fresh olive oil)

Salame milanese (salami of pork and beef, seasoned with pepper, garlic, and white wine)

risotto alla milanese (creamy Arborio rice cooked in white wine and veal broth with saffron, which gives it a lovely yellow hue, added at the end)

ossobuco alla milanese (veal shanks with their marrow browned in butter and braised with white wine; usually served with peas and *risotto milanese*)

cotolletta alla milanese (veal cutlets, pounded very thin, coated with
bread crumbs and sautéed in butter; should be served with slices of
lemon to squeeze over them and alongside a risotto)

casoeula milanese (pork stewed with pork sausage, cabbage, carrots and
white wine)

Several excellent Milanese restaurants are:

Ristorante Casolare, via dell'Orso, 12
tel: (39–2) 805–3581
Closed all day Monday and Tuesdays at noon.
  Tucked away about a ten-minute walk from La Scala, this restaurant is
a real find. The owner really cares about the food he serves, as evidenced
by the restaurant's large and local clientele. Do reserve.

Ristorante Il Garfagnino, via Cherubini, 8
tel: (39–2) 4800–4483 or 481–4191
Closed Mondays.
  This excellent restaurant is only a ten-minute walk from the Casa di
Riposo Verdi. It's a five-minute taxi ride from La Scala and well worth
whatever you spend getting here. It has excellent regional dishes. Do
reserve.

Trattoria dell'Angolo, corner of via Fiori Chiari and via Formentini
tel: (39–2) 8646–0152
Closed Saturday evenings and Sundays, the first week in January, and the
three middle weeks of August.
  This charming restaurant is a ten-minute walk from La Scala.

Ristorante Don Lisander, via Manzoni, 12a
tel: (02) 7602–0130
Closed Saturdays and Sundays, December 24 to January 15, and the last
two weeks in August.
  This upscale, elegant restaurant is situated just down the street from
the place of Giuseppe Verdi's death in the Grand Hotel et de Milan. It is
also a five-minute walk from La Scala. Be sure to reserve.

Biffi Scala, piazza della Scala
tel: (39–2) 866–651
Closed Sundays and December 25 through January 6.
  The Biffi Scala is located right inside the building of Teatro della
Scala. It is a lovely, somewhat expensive restaurant in which to have a
light supper after the opera with other operagoers. Be sure to reserve.

NAPLES (Napoli)

Naples was *the* city of eighteenth-century Italian opera. In the early eighteenth century any reference to Italian opera meant Neapolitan opera. The most lasting examples of this genre were written by the distinctly non-Neapolitans George Friderich Handel, and Christoph Willibald Gluck, to name only two.

By the beginning of the 1700s opera no longer carried the idealistic view of its originators in Florence. The meaning of the text and literary concerns were no longer primary considerations; rather, Neapolitan opera had become a series of beautifully tuneful arias strung together by dialogue in the form of recitative. The human voice—its prowess, its sensuous capacities, and its agility—was of overriding importance. Bel canto opera (opera of beautiful singing), "singer's opera" or "number opera" (so called because the opera was simply a parade of great vocal tunes, or "numbers"), became the rage throughout Europe. All this notwithstanding, foreign visitors to Naples in the early nineteenth century complained that the Neopolitans went "to see, not to hear an opera" because the audience talked all through the performances!

Neapolitan audiences were insatiable in their appetite for the two kinds of opera their local composers wrote: Metastasian *opere serie* (after the local librettist Pietro Metastasio, who eventually settled in Vienna) and *opere buffe* in Neapolitan dialect. In the eighteenth century alone, more than forty local composers wrote over two thousand operas that were performed in the city. With the exception of *La serva padrona*, by the short-lived Giovanni Battista Pergolesi (see Teatro San Bartolomeo), most of these locally composed operas were written by composers unknown today and rely upon operatic conventions we, today, find mostly tedious.

Interestingly, although presentations of Venetian opera in Naples in the mid-seventeenth century occurred under the auspices of the viceroy, the viceroy did not pay the complete expenses of the singers and musicians, so the performers had to charge admission to make a living wage. Thus, from its beginning, the presentation of opera in Naples had a mixture of courtly and public support.

At the beginning of the eighteenth century, Naples had four conservatories of music, all originally founded as institutions for orphaned children. Much like the orphanages of Venice in vogue at the same time, these were places where children could learn to carry out a musical role in society. Most Neapolitan opera composers had some connection with these institutions, either as students or as teachers. Many of the great castrati of the early eighteenth century had first been heard as boy sopranos in these orphanages. The boys with the most beautiful voices were encouraged to undergo surgery to maintain the beauty of their high voices to adulthood, and thus almost certainly find gainful employment as adults. The castrato is known to have had extraordinary agility, power, and beauty of sound and was the favorite medium for "singer's," or Neapolitan opera. Today it is

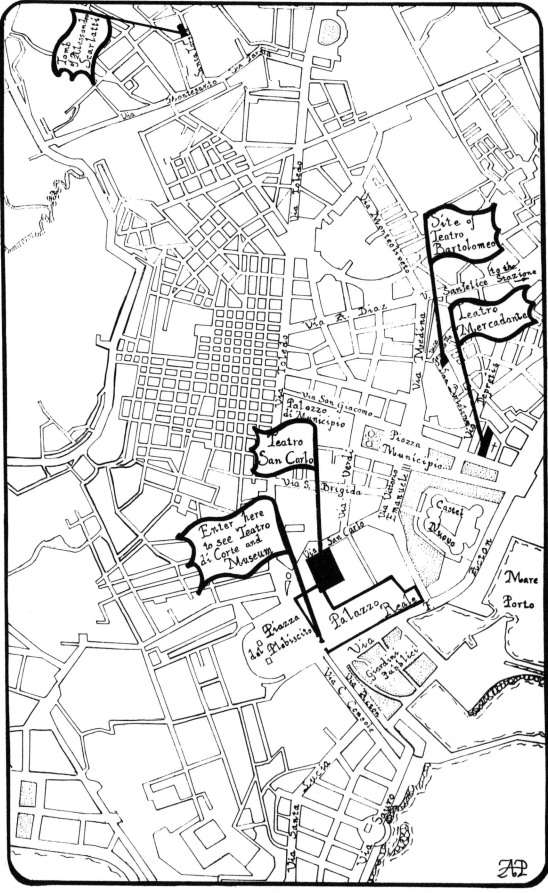

Operatic Naples

hard to understand the attraction to this "unnatural" sound. One can only imagine the power of a male voice mixed with the purity and smoothness of a superb boy soprano and the agility of a coloratura soprano or mezzo. The castrati were highly prized and tended with great care. (They were also highly regarded as lovers in a period before birth control!) In opera the castrato went out of vogue by 1830. Church music in Italy, however, made use of the voice into the twentieth century, and there are recordings of the last castrato in the papal choir of San Pietro in Rome.

Musical life in Naples is still very focused on singing. The sound of bel canto is intrinsic in the sound of Neapolitan dialect. When I first went there I was astonished by the full-throated "singing" I heard *everywhere!*

The most prolific, if not the most famous, Neapolitan opera composer is undoubtedly Alessandro Scarlatti (1660–1725). Although born in Palermo and spending a good while in Rome, Scarlatti was really *the* composer who codified Neapolitan-style opera with his own sixty-six works plus about fifteen contributions to other composers' operas. The codified conventions of Neapolitan-style opera included upbeat tempos for overtures, fast-moving dialogue set in *recitativo secco*, and arias made up of very tuneful harmonic and melodic formulae. Scarlatti's tomb is in a small chapel on the left side of the church of Santa Maria Montesanto in piazza Montesanto.

From 1815 to 1822, Gioacchino Rossini was principal composer at Naples's Teatro San Carlo, during which time eight of his operas were premiered there. It was in Naples that he became involved with his future wife, the Spanish soprano Isabella Colbran, who was at that time the mistress of the famous impresario of Teatro San Carlo, Domenico Barbaja. (The two men maintained their cordial working relationship.) Colbran was an extraordinary singer admired for both her dramatic stage presence as well as the brilliance and power of her voice. Rossini had originally met Colbran in Bologna in 1807 during his school days, and later wrote some of his most powerful and dramatic roles for her. From 1815 to 1822 they carried on a volatile courtship. They were finally married (March 16, 1822) but formally separated in 1837. Later, Rossini married the beautiful Parisian Olympe Pélissier, who had been an artist's model and mistress to the French painter Antoine Charles Vernet.

Note: Domenico Barbaja was such a character and so important in the development of opera in the nineteenth century that he inspired an opera by the French composer Auber, *La sirène* (1844), and a novel (written in Vienna in 1937) by Emil Lukas. During his illustrious career he was impresario of Naples's San Carlo and of Milan's Teatro della Scala.

Ruggero (sometimes spelled Ruggiero) Leoncavallo (April 23, 1857, Naples—August 9, 1919, Montecatini) was a native of Naples, though his fame was gained principally in Rome and Milan. Inspired by Richard Wagner's aesthetic concerning the relationship between *Wort-Ton-Drama* (words, music, drama), Leoncavallo went so far as to begin to write an Italian *Ring* cycle called *Crepusculum* (Twilight). The first of the cycle was called *I Medici*, but he did not complete his plan for an Italian tetralogy. Instead, he turned his attention to Mascagni's success with *Cavalleria rusticana* in 1890 and wrote his first big hit, *I pagliacci*, in 1892, saying he felt that verismo was the way of the future.

Between 1893 and 1897, after a bitter controversy with Puccini over who had the idea to set the text first, he wrote his version of *La bohème* and then *Zazà*, which achieved international success.

By the early 1900s Leoncavallo's operas were more popular in Germany than in Italy, and he even wrote an opera in German based on the Hohenzollern dynasty called *Der Roland von Berlin*. In all he wrote ten operas and several operettas (including one in French). When he died, the poet Gabriele D'Annunzio, who so eloquently praised Verdi after his death (see Milan, page 74), wrote that Leoncavallo had died "suffocated by melodic adiposity"!

Enrico Caruso (February 25, 1873—August 2, 1921) was born in Naples, the nineteenth child of an impoverished laborer. He achieved fame principally in Milan, London, and, particularly, at the Metropolitan Opera in New York City where, in 1910, he created the role of Dick Johnson in Puccini's *La fanciulla del West* (The Girl of the Golden West). In 1901, on the one occasion when he did return to Teatro San Carlo, to sing Nemorino in Donizetti's *L'elisir d'amore* and Des Grieux in Massenet's *Manon*, he was not greeted with the kind of enthusiasm he had enjoyed elsewhere. As a consequence, he never sang again in Naples. He returned only when he was dying, in 1921.

The original Teatro San Carlo, built in 1737 under the direction of King Charles III, burned down in 1816 and was immediately rebuilt in 1817. Teatro San Carlo is second only to La Scala in its importance in the history of opera, and in the early nineteenth century, both the San Carlo and La Scala were run by the same manager, the wheeler-dealer Domenico Barbaja.

In 1906 a Teatro San Carlo performance of *Tess*, by Frédéric d'Erlanger, an opera unknown today, was cut short by the eruption of Mount Vesuvius! And, in 1943, as war raged immediately north of Naples, the theatre was reopened and operas were presented as matinees to avoid the nightly curfew and blackout.

Teatro San Carlo presented the premieres of (details of these premieres appear at the end of this section) *Alzira* (1845), Giuseppe Verdi; *Bianca e Fernando* (1826), Vincenzo Bellini; *La donna del lago* (1819), Gioacchino Rossini; *Lucia di Lammermoor* (1835), Gaetano Donizetti; *Luisa Miller* (1849), Giuseppe Verdi; *Poliuto* (1848), Gaetano Donizetti.

Today Teatro San Carlo presents an excellent season (December through June).

Teatro San Carlo, via San Carlo, 80121 Naples
tel: (39–81) 797–2331
    The auditorium and foyer are open to visitors daily from 9:00 A.M.–noon.

Teatro San Carlo

The present-day Teatro Mercadante was originally called Teatro del Fondo. The theatre was constructed in 1779 and presented the premiere of:

Otello, *ossia Il moro di Venezia, dramma* in three acts, December 4, 1816.
Gioacchino Rossini (1792–1868)
Libretto Francesco Berio di Salsa after Shakespeare's play of the same name.

Unlike Verdi's *Otello,* Rossini's libretto follows Shakespeare's play only in very broad outline. At the time he wrote the opera, Rossini's decision to set Shakespeare's *Othello* was considered bold and original, and most of the opera's ending was censored because operatic tradition of the time forbade violence on the stage. Nonetheless, the opera achieved huge popularity in the nineteenth century due mostly to its final violent act. The French opera composer Meyerbeer wrote: "The third act of *Otello* established its reputation so firmly that a thousand errors could not shake it. This third act is really godlike, and what is so extraordinary is that its beauties are quite un-Rossini-like. First-rate declamation, continuously impassioned recitative, mysterious accompaniments full of local color..." Such a description makes one long to see a fine production of the opera!

Teatro del Fondo (Teatro Mercadante), piazza Municipio
tel, ticket office: (39–81) 551–3396   fax, administrative offices: (39–81) 552–4214
     The theatre is still used for concerts.

Teatro San Bartolomeo was constructed in 1620 in strada San Bartolomeo, near the church of San Bartolomeo. Before it became the first public opera theatre of Naples, in 1654, it was the city's major public theatre. The San Bartolomeo seems to have been the first public theatre regularly attended by royalty, who realized that the operatic fare at a public theatre was far better than that offered in private court theatres.
     In 1683 Alessandro Scarlatti, then twenty-three, was appointed by the court to be *maestro di cappella* of the court *and* director of music at the San Bartolomeo, thus solidifying the relationship between courtly and popular culture. It was Scarlatti who, by presenting his "southern"-style operas, broke the dominance of Venetian-style opera.
     Because of an agreement between the theatre's managers and Charles III, King of Naples and Sicily, who was responsible for the construction of Teatro San Carlo in 1737, the San Bartolomeo was destroyed in 1738 to allow the total predominance of the San Carlo. The small church of Santa Maria delle Grazie o della Mercede was built in its place, so one can still see its position of physical importance in the city. Because of its small size and charming proportions, the church is known as la Graziella and is situated directly off the central city's main street, strada Medina. La Graziella can be reached by descending the stairs of via Graziella directly off strada Medina. The church stands about twenty-five feet in where via Graziella and via San Bartolomeo make a Y.

Teatro San Bartolomeo presented the premiere of:

La serva padrona (The Maid as Mistress), *intermezzo* in two parts, August 28, 1733.
Giovanni Battista Pergolesi (January 4, 1710, Iesi, in le Marche—March 16, 1736, Pozzuoli, near Naples)
Libretto Gennaro Antonio Federico after Jacopo Angello Nelli's play of the same title.
     La serva padrona was originally performed as a comic intermezzo between the acts of Pergolesi's opera seria *Il prigioniero superbo* (The Proud Prisoner),

commissioned for the birthday celebration of Empress Elisabeth Christina, consort of Spain's Charles VI. *La serva padrona* has long outlived its opera seria companion piece in the repertory, and with minimal changes. Its popularity was most unusual for a throw-away intermezzo. Between 1752 and 1754 the work was often performed in Paris and had a profound impact upon the development of opéra comique which, like *La serva padrona,* is opera with spoken dialogue. *La serva padrona* continued to be performed throughout the second half of the eighteenth century in Paris and London. The melodies and the patter manifest a perfect inflection of the text. The musical buffo (comic) writing for the character Uberto, with its exaggerated vocal line, is very much a musical role model for all further *basso buffo* roles and really gave credence to the form of opera buffa as opposed to simply comic intermezzos. Interestingly, Charles III not only tore down Teatro Bartolomeo in 1738, but in 1741, five years after the premiere of *La serva padrona,* he also banned the performance of comic intermezzos. Because it is a short work with only two singing characters, *La serva padrona* is often performed today by small opera companies and student workshops. The music is wonderful, and one is lucky to see a professional production of the opera.

Although it presented no opera premieres of note, Teatro di Corte (Court Theatre of the Royal Palace) in the Palazzo Reale is worth a visit. The theatre stands just around the corner from the San Carlo. (Enter the Palazzo Reale in piazza del Plebiscito.) The room was designed and built in 1768 and is decorated with statues of the Muses. The ceiling was destroyed by Allied bombing in World War II but has been restored to its original beauty. In fact, the whole palace has just undergone extensive restoration and is well worth seeing. The theatre regularly puts on chamber operas, chamber music, and ballet.

Teatro di Corte, Palazzo Reale
Open Monday–Saturday, 10:00 A.M.–4:00 P.M.
tel: (39–81) 418–744

Details of Teatro San Carlo premieres

Alzira, *tragedia lirica* in a prologue and two acts, August 12, 1845.
Giuseppe Verdi (1813–1901)
Libretto Salvatore Cammarano, after Voltaire's play *Alzire, ou Les Américains.*

In the spring of 1845 Salvatore Cammarano was the most famous librettist living in Italy. Giuseppe Verdi, most eager to work with the eminent librettist, accepted a commission from Teatro San Carlo for his eighth opera, *Alzira.* Verdi completely trusted Cammarano's highly professional theatrical instincts (after all, he was principally known for a string of operatic successes with Gaetano Donizetti) and involved himself only in writing the music. The cast for the premiere included some of the finest singers in Italy, but the performance was a flop and the opera soon disappeared from the repertory. In later life Verdi referred to *Alzira* as *"proprio brutta"* (downright ugly).

Bianca e Fernando, *melodramma* in two acts, May 30, 1826.
Vincenzo Bellini (1801–1835)
Libretto Domenico Gilardoni, after Carlo Roti's play *Bianca e Fernando alla tomba di Carlo IV duca di Agrigento.*

Bianca e Fernando is Bellini's first professionally performed opera, this event occurring when he was the relatively old age of twenty-five. In 1828 Felice Romani helped Bellini revise the opera for new performances in Genoa at Teatro Carlo Felice. It is a rescue opera without a love story.

La donna del lago (Lady of the Lake), *melodramma* in two acts, October 24, 1819.
Gioacchino Rossini (1792–1868)
Libretto Andrea Leone Tottola, after Sir Walter Scott's poem *The Lady of the Lake.*

Rossini's twenty-ninth opera, *La donna del lago*, contains some of Rossini's most lyrically imaginative music. During the six operas he wrote for Teatro San Carlo, Rossini's style changed and he is considered to have become a radical and pioneering artist, one capable of developing the techniques necessary to confront the new array of theatrical subjects posed by the postrevolutionary and Napoleonic Europe of the early nineteenth century. At the time Teatro San Carlo had some of the most dramatically intelligent singers in Italy, and they inspired Rossini. *La donna del lago*, needless to say, was a success.

Lucia di Lammermoor, *dramma tragico* in three acts, September 26, 1835.
Gaetano Donizetti (1797–1848)
Libretto Salvatore Cammarano, after Sir Walter Scott's novel *The Bride of Lammermoor.*

The Bride of Lammermoor truly inspired Italian opera librettists—it had already been set three times before Cammarano adapted it. In the story, because of old family feuds, Lucia is forbidden to marry Edgardo, whom she loves, and forced to marry Arturo, whom she kills on their wedding night before enacting her celebrated Mad Scene. The opera ends with Edgardo's killing himself at Lucia's tomb. The highly successful premiere of Donizetti's forty-fourth opera was given with the San Carlos's best singers. *Lucia*, considered the apogee of Romantic sensibility, was quick to win success in the rest of Europe. In 1839 Donizetti reworked the score to fit a French translation, the version first given in the United States—in New Orleans in

1841. The Italian original was given its U.S. premiere a year later, also in New Orleans, by a touring company from Havana, Cuba. The opera's famous Mad Scene not only calls for enormous technical prowess from the title character but contains an extraordinarily psychological treatment of musical themes: Lucia, in her disorientation, distorts melodies heard earlier in the opera. *Lucia* remains very much in today's repertory wherever there is an agile and dramatically artistic soprano to take on the role.

Luisa Miller, *melodramma tragico* in three acts, December 8, 1849.
Giuseppe Verdi (1813–1901)
Libretto Salvatore Cammarano, after Friedrich von Schiller's play *Kabale und Liebe.*

After the disaster of *Alzira,* Verdi tried to extricate himself from a commitment to write another opera for the San Carlo. The authorities held him to his contract, however, and at Cammarano's suggestion, Verdi agreed upon Schiller's play *Kabale und Liebe.* He knew the play and already considered its subject matter operatic. Verdi came to Naples to oversee the rehearsals, and the performance was most likely a success, although no press reports are extant. The opera did not become popular in the nineteenth century. In the twentieth century, however, *Luisa Miller,* along with *Ernani* and *Macbeth,* are some of the few pre–1851 scores of Verdi to enjoy a place in today's international repertory.

Poliuto, *tragedia lirica* in three acts, Italian premiere, November 30, 1848.
Gaetano Donizetti (1797–1848)
Libretto Salvatore Cammarano, after Pierre Corneille's play *Polyeucte.*

Originally planned for a world premiere at the San Carlo in 1838, *Poliuto* was banned by the religious censors because it depicted the martyrdom of a Christian saint. Donizetti soon after went to Paris, where Eugène Scribe reworked the libretto. Donizetti added extensive ballet music and a new overture, and the premiere took place in Paris. Finally, the original Italian three-act form was premiered at Teatro San Carlo in 1848, soon after Donizetti's death and ten years after its Paris premiere. This original three-act opera is preferred today.

Tourist note

Naples is reputed to be a place where everyone is out to rob you. If you use common sense, however, you can enjoy the beauty of the city without suffering.

- Be aware but do not appear frightened, as if you expect trouble.
- Take only cabs that are *actually in line* at the station; or that are procured for you by your hotel or by the restaurant where you have eaten.

- Avoid walking through groups of young children. Cross the street if necessary.
- Do not carry large amounts of money, or your tickets, credit cards, or passport in your pocket or purse. Leave them in the hotel safe.
- Do not walk in deserted areas.

LODGING

The part of the city pertinent to the opera lover is quite small, all (except for the tomb of Alessandro Scarlatti) in the area from via Medina down to piazza del Plebiscito. The following hotels and restaurants are right in this area:

Hotel Jolly, via Medina, 70, Napoli 80133
tel: (39–81) 416–000   fax: (39–81) 551–8010
   This hotel stands in the seventeenth-to-eighteenth-century center of Naples and actually overlooks the San Carlo, the Royal Palace, piazza del Municipio, and even the street where Teatro Bartolomeo once stood. It is a ten-minute walk to the doors of the San Carlo.

Hotel Miramare, via N. Sauro, 24, Napoli 80132
tel: (39–81) 764–7589   fax: (39–81) 764–0775
   This hotel is on the water of the bay and is a ten-minute walk back up the hill to the San Carlo.

SNACKS

Naples is, of course, home of the *pizza napoletana* so dear to the hearts of many Americans. Real *pizza napoletana* has garlicky tomato sauce with oregano, anchovies, and mozzarella on it. Try any of the numerous Neapolitan *pizzerie* for a slice.
   Calzone, the deep-fried folded pizza of Naples, can also be had at most *pizzerie.*
   Across the busy street fron Teatro San Carlo, piazza Trieste e Trento has several elegant bars frequented by operagoers before a performance. Try a *babà al rum con panna* (rum baba with whipped cream). Or have *una sfogliatella* (flaky pastry shaped like a scallop and filled with sweetened ricotta with tiny pieces of candied fruit). Both are Neapolitan sweet specialties. Try both with an espresso. Neapolitan coffee is known to be unusually excellent.
   Gelati napoletani raise the concept of ice cream to new heights.

FOOD

Some classical examples of the cuisine of Naples are:

   mozzarella di bufala con pomodori e basilico (buffalo milk mozzarella, with slices of tomato, basil, olive oil, and salt and pepper) *zuppa di pesce* (fish soup)

spaghetti all'aglio e olio (spaghetti with garlic [and sometimes hot red peppers] lightly tossed in olive oil, served with a handful of fresh, chopped parsley)

spaghetti alle vongole (spaghetti with clams, garlic, olive oil, and parsley)

spaghetti alla marinara (spaghetti with a simple tomato sauce with garlic and parsley)

sartù di riso (a monumental rice dish made with tomato sauce, chicken giblets, mushrooms, peas, tiny meatballs, and mozzarella)

bistecca alla pizzaiola (thin beefsteak with a tomato and garlic sauce)

Several excellent restaurants are near the San Carlo:

San Carlo, via Cesario Console, 18/19
tel: (39–81) 764–9757
Closed Sundays and the month of August.

San Carlo is situated just down the hill from the entrance of the Royal Palace and is a five- to seven-minute walk from the Teatro San Carlo. *Definitely* reserve; it is the perfect place to eat after a performance.

Rosolino, via N. Sauro, 5/7
tel: (39–81) 415–873   fax: (39–81) 405–457
Closed Sundays and the last three weeks of August.

This restaurant overlooks the bay and is a ten-minute walk from Teatro San Carlo, just down the hill of via Cesario Console and to the right on via Sauro. Reserve.

PALERMO

Palermo is the capital of Sicily (Sicilia), the largest island in the Mediterranean. Colonized in the eighth century B.C. by the Greeks, Palermo has a richly diverse heritage, drawing from the Greeks, the Romans, the Normans, the Arabs, the French, and the Spanish. Like the rest of Sicily, Palermo is very far away from the other operatic hot spots on the Italian peninsula.

Nevertheless, Palermo hosted Richard Wagner (1813–1883), who passed the winter of 1881–1882 at the Hotel des Palmes, now called the Grand Hotel et des Palmes, where he used a harmonium now on display in the *salone* of Teatro Massimo, while completing Parsifal.

Grand Hotel et des Palmes, via Roma, 398
tel: (39–91) 583–933

Palermo is also the setting for *Les Vêpres siciliennes* (*I vespri siciliani,* The Sicilian Vespers), an opera Giuseppe Verdi wrote for L'Opéra of Paris in 1855. The opera's revolutionary subject is set in the Palermo of A.D. 1282 and juxtaposes victorious French soldiers against a resentful Sicilian people and Spanish forces who are ready to aid the Sicilians. The revolutionary Sicilians kill off the French ruler of the city. Needless to say, when the opera was presented in an Italian translation in 1855 in Parma's Teatro Regio, the subject matter caused the censors to cut it radically.

In 1897, after the unification of Italy, Teatro Massimo became Palermo's leading opera house. This world-class theatre is the third largest in Europe, after Vienna's Staatsoper and Paris's Palais Garnier. Sadly, the theatre has "been under restoration" since 1974 and in the spring of 1994 showed absolutely no sign of being completed.

Teatro Massimo, via Riccardo Wagner, 2, Palermo, Sicily
tel: (39–91) 605–3111

PARMA

Parma is considered to have the highest standard of living in Italy. It is the home of the famous *parmigiano, the* cheese of Italy. Parma has a highly developed artistic past because of the lengthy reigns of two particularly devoted patrons. The Farnese family ruled from 1545 to 1727, promoting and protecting the arts and the humanities. And from 1816 to 1846 Marie Louise (called Maria Luigia by the Italians) of Austria, the wife of Napoleon and Duchess of Parma, oversaw an enlightened administration of the city. "Verdi country" is in the province of Parma, so it was Maria Luigia who signed the passport (hanging in the Museum of La Scala in Milano) allowing the young Giuseppe Verdi to leave the province to study in Milan.

Maria Luigia also founded the court orchestra and was the motivator behind the construction in 1829 of Teatro Regio (the Royal Theatre), now found in via Garibaldi, 16 (seating 1,300). By all means get a ticket for *any* opera performance in the theatre. Parma's operatic public has a reputation as particularly demanding, famous for being very unforgiving of any singer not in good voice, and it is a real experience for well-behaved Americans to attend an opera here! The theatre also has a beautiful interior and a Greenroom worth a visit in itself.

For its inaugural performance in 1829 Teatro Regio presented the premiere of:

Zaira, tragedia lirica in two acts, May 16, 1829.
Vincenzo Bellini (1801–1835)
Libretto Felice Romani, after Voltaire's tragedy *Zaire.*

Zaira, Bellini's fifth opera, was commissioned for the opening of Teatro Regio. Second choice for the commission after Rossini, he seemed to have little enthusiasm for writing the opera and declined to come from Paris for rehearsals and the premiere, which was a disaster even though the Grand Duchess of Parma, Maria Luigia, attended the first performance. The piece

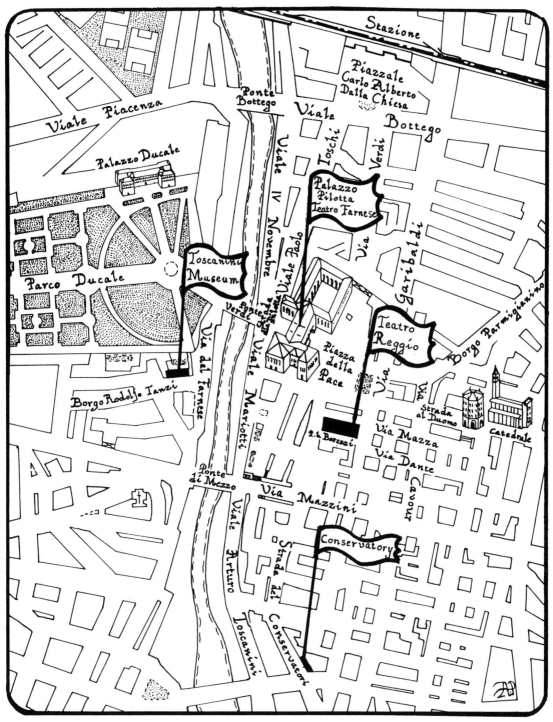

Operatic Parma

was revived only once after Bellini's death, and is his only lasting operatic failure. Bellini, however, cannibalized the score of *Zaira*, using sections of it for *I Capuleti e i Montecchi*, *Norma*, and *Beatrice di Tenda*.

The theatre also presented the first Italian performance of Verdi's *I vespri siciliani*. The city was never able to mount a world premiere of a Verdi opera, even though he became a dominant figure in the city late in his life.

Teatro Regio, via Garibaldi, 16, 43100 Parma
tel: (39–521) 218–678
Ticket office open (*biglietteria*): Tuesday–Saturday, 9:30 A.M.–12:30 P.M. and 4:00–7:00 P.M., and two hours before the beginning of a performance.
Opera season from December through May; five productions.
   If you go to the ticket office for any given production, you will get a ticket. You need not bother to call.

Since 1963 Parma has been home to the Istituto di Studi Verdiani, and since 1989 a Verdi Festival has been held annually in September and October.

Verdi Festival, Fondazione Verdi Festival, Teatro Regio (*biglietteria*), via Garibaldi, 16, Parma 43100
tel: (39–521) 218–678
Late September through October.

In 1618 the Gran Teatro dei Farnese was built in Palazzo della Pilotta to honor a proposed visit to Parma by Cosimo II de' Medici (the visit did not take place). It was inaugurated in 1628 at the marriage of Odoardo Farnese and Margherita de' Medici, for which the entertainment was a royal tournament (*torneo regale*) with music by Claudio Monteverdi—the lost *Mercurio e Marte*—for which the arena area below the seats was flooded to a depth of two feet in order to represent sea battles!
   In my view this theatre is the Holy Grail of opera houses. Its beautiful structure shows clearly the architectural origins of the horseshoe-shaped Italian opera theatres. Toward the end of the seventeenth century, as public opera houses became more important, performances were phased out of Teatro Farnese and the theatre was dark from 1732 onward. On May 13, 1944, the theatre was severely damaged by American bombs but has since been rebuilt on its original model.
   Today all of Palazzo Pilotta is a museum. You enter through doors under the portico of the city gates in via della Pilotta 4. You can buy a ticket to see only Teatro Farnese or two tickets to see the whole palace.

Palazzo Pilotta
Open Tuesday–Friday, 9:00 A.M.–2:00 P.M.; Sundays and holidays 9:00 A.M.–1:00 P.M.

Arturo Toscanini (March 25, 1867—January 16, 1957, New York City) was born in Parma. The house of his birth in borgo Rodolfo Tanzi, 13, just across the river from Palazzo Pilotta, is a beautiful museum.

Teatro Regio

Teatro Farnese (Interior)

On June 30, 1886, in Rio de Janiero, the nineteen-year-old Toscanini replaced an ailing conductor in a production of *Aïda*, for which he had been playing the cello. His outstanding performance established his fame as a conductor. From 1886 to 1898 he conducted in various Italian theatres, directing the premieres of *I pagliacci* (1892, Milan, Teatro dal Verme) and *La bohème* (1896, Turin, Teatro Reggio). He was a staunch champion of Wagner, calling him "the greatest composer of the nineteenth century." From 1898 to 1903 and from 1920 to 1929, Toscanini was artistic director of Milan's La Scala (see Milan, page 78).

In 1908 Toscanini became the artistic director of New York's Metropolitan Opera, where he stayed for seven years. In 1910 he conducted its first world premiere, Puccini's *La fanciulla del West*. In 1930 he became conductor of the New York Philharmonic. For the rest of his career he conducted only symphonic music, with the exception of some concert versions of opera, in particular the live recording of *Falstaff* made in Carnegie Hall in 1950. As budgets grew smaller for the production of operas, he felt he could no longer do justice to the art form.

Some of the tributes in the Toscanini Museum are very moving and attest to the extraordinary character of the man. Among them is a letter from Albert Einstein, who wrote of Toscanini's stand against Fascism that he was "happy to be the contemporary of such greatness," even though it made him feel so small. And a letter from the Philharmonic Society of New York lauds Toscanini with the following:

> the supreme artist depends for his spiritual
> sustenance upon elements no less rare than
> simplicity, selflessness and faith.

The city has taken great care with the heritage of Toscanini. The museum is beautifully maintained and the guides are very knowledgeable, sympathetic, and willing to speak in English. The museum and guided tour are free.

Toscanini Museum, borgo Rodolfo Tanzi, 13
to reserve for a group, tel: (0521) 285–499 or 218–593
Open Tuesday–Sunday 10:00 A.M.–1:00 P.M. and 3:00–6:00 P.M.

LODGING

Hotel Torino, via Mazza, 7
tel: (39–521) 281–046 or 28–1074   fax: (39–521) 230–725
The Hotel Torino is located in a small quiet street directly across via Garibaldi from Teatro Regio and Palazzo della Pilotta. It is relatively inexpensive, clean, and friendly—a perfect place for an opera lover to stay.

Park Hotel Stendhal, piazzetta Bodoni, 3
tel: (39–521) 531–216   fax: (39–521) 285–655

This slightly more expensive hotel is a five-minute walk from Teatro Regio and two minutes from Palazzo della Pilotta.

The restaurant La Pilotta is on the premises and is closed Sunday. The hotel reminds us that Stendhal's *La Chartreuse de Parme* was written about Parma.

SNACKS

Parma has its own kind of *spongata,* a filled pie-like sweet that is a perfect pick-me-up with afternoon coffee or tea.

FOOD

Parma's standard of living can be fully appreciated in its cuisine. A few specialties are:

Parmigiano, eaten with a fresh pear (a simple but unforgettable treat)
prosciutto di Parma, with Parma-style bread
culatello and *salame felino* (two delicious antipasti, cold meat dishes)
fesa col prosciutto (veal stewed with prosciutto, carrots, wine, and sage)
una bomba di riso (a large mound of savory rice with all kinds of goodies mixed in, Parmesan, braised chicken or pigeon, onion, and covered with bread crumbs gratinée)
stracotto di manzo (beef gently cooked with wine and vegetables for a *long* time, so tender you can cut it with a fork)
lambrusco (the slightly tart red sparkling wine of the region that really enhances Parmigiano food)

Two excellent places to eat, filled with natives, are:

Trattoria Corrieri, via Conservatorio, 1
tel: (39–521) 234–426
Be sure to reserve or go very early. Closed Sundays.

Ristorante Croce di Malta, borgo Palmia, 8
tel: (39–521) 235–643
Closed Sundays. Be sure to reserve.

PESARO

Pesaro is situated midway down the east coast of the Italian peninsula, just north of the large port city of Ancona. It is one of the principal cities of Le Marche (The Marshes), the area between the eastern foothills of the Apennines and the

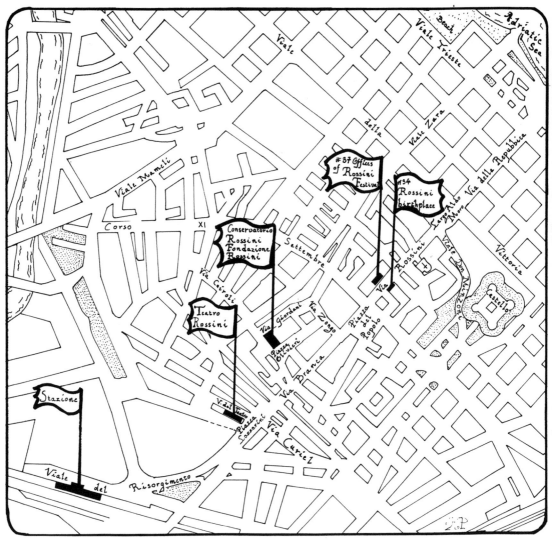

Operatic Pesaro

Adriatic Sea. Pesaro is an elegant town containing many art deco villas as well as Gothic and Renaissance palaces in the *centro storico* (historic center). The hills around the city make it much more attractive than any of the nearby beach towns.

Pesaro is the birthplace of Gioacchino Rossini (February 29, 1792—November 13, 1868, Passy, Paris). Rossini always said that his eternally youthful spirit was due to the fact he celebrated his birthday only every four years. Both his parents were professional musicians: His father was the public trumpet player of Pesaro and eventually taught French horn at the Accademia Filarmonica (conservatory) in Bologna; his mother was a soprano with a career in regional opera houses.

By the time he was twelve, Rossini had already begun to write with a distinctive personal style. He is a singer's composer, even when he writes for instruments (as in his Duet for Cello and Bass Viol, in which the instruments take on the character of operatic voices). His music demands great technique, flair, and imagination from those who perform it. Samuel Ramey and Marilyn Horne are two fine examples of the kind of singer it takes to perform his works successfully.

In the first decades of the nineteenth century, Rossini was the most popular composer of the Western world's most popular art form—opera. No poet, novelist, or composer had wider circulation.

For many years Rossini lived with the Spanish soprano Isabella Colbran, for whom he wrote some of his most elaborate and powerful roles. They married in 1822 but were formally separated in 1837. (See Naples, page 99.)

Rossini truly understood the sheer beauty of vocal sound, and because of this unusually heightened aesthetic he was adviser to many of the leading singers in Europe from 1813 to the time of his death. He wrote thirty-nine operas in nineteen years; his first, *La cambiale di matrimonio*, was written in 1810, and his last, *Guillaume Tell*, in 1829. From 1825 to 1855 he divided his time between Paris and Bologna, and then from 1855 he spent the rest of his life in Paris.

Rossini's birthplace hosts a small museum of Rossini memorabilia.

Rossini Museum, via Rossini, 34, 61100 Pesaro
Open weekdays, 10:00 A.M.–noon, and 4:00–6:00 P.M.; and Saturdays, 10:00 A.M.–noon.

Right across the street from the museum stand the offices of the Rossini Opera Festival with a large statue of the seated Rossini in the courtyard. The festival takes place the last three weeks of August each year and presents the operas of Rossini, many of which had lain dormant during this century until they were performed here.

The Accademia Rossiniana, which starts during the last week in July and extends through the festival, conducts free seminars open to singers, professional theatre people, and scholars. Subjects that might be covered include the interpretation of the music of Rossini, bel canto: history, development, ideology, stage problems of Rossini's music, concepts of modern interpretation.

Entry to rehearsals of the operas is provided as well. For an opera lover, this is most definitely the place to be in August!

Rossini Opera Festival, offices: via Rossini, 37, 61100 Pesaro
Open Monday–Friday, 9:00 A.M.–1:00 P.M. and 3:00–5:00 P.M.; Saturday, 9:30 A.M.–1:00 P.M.
booking information, tel: (39–721) 30–161   fax: (39–721) 30–979

The festival performances are projected simultaneously on a giant video screen installed in the courtyard of the Palazzo Ducale.

The Fondazione Rossini is headquartered in the conservatorio. A beautiful hall in the building, Salone Pedrotti, is often used for concerts during the summer Rossini Festival. The foundation is a scholarly research organization, not really set up for tourists, but, if you are interested, they will guide you through a very small "museum" of Rossini's manuscripts.

Fondazione Rossini and Rossini Museum, Conservatorio Rossini, piazza Oliveri 5 (first floor), Pesaro 61100
tel: (39–721) 30–053 or 33–818   fax: (39–721) 31–220
Open Monday–Friday, 9:00 A.M.–noon and 4:00–7:00 P.M.; Saturday, 9:00 A.M.–noon.

Pesaro's theatre, Teatro Comunale G. Rossini, is a gem. It was built in 1637 and reinaugurated as Teatro Rossini in 1855. Since the 1980 opening of the Rossini Festival, the theatre has hummed with new life.

The entry foyer, white with crimson carpeting, is an airy marvel of light and glass. The first-floor (American second) foyer displays all the posters for all the operas presented by the festival. Some are quite special. The piano Rossini used as a boy when living in Pesaro is also in the foyer. (The first-floor foyer is the only place smoking is allowed in the theatre, so be forewarned!)

The exterior of the theatre looks like a church. It isn't!

Teatro Comunale G. Rossini, piazza Lazzarini, Pesaro 61100
tel, box office: (39–721) 33–184   fax: (39–721) 30–979

For further information contact:

Azzienda di Turismo, Open daily, 9:00 A.M.–1:00 P.M. and 3:00–6:00 P.M.
tel: (39–721) 64–302

Not only was Pesaro the birthplace of Rossini but also of Renata Tebaldi, born on February 1, 1922.

ROSSINI AND FOOD

Rossini, known as a *bon vivant,* loved excellent food. It is said that one of the reasons he continued to consult in Bologna, long after he took up residence in Paris, was the extraordinary Bolognese cooking. In letters to colleagues and friends in Italy, he lamented that the French had absolutely no idea of how to make pasta. He said: "To eat, to love, to sing and to digest; in truth, these are the four acts in this *opéra bouffe* that we call life, and which vanish like the bubbles in a bottle of champagne."

In the nineteenth and twentieth centuries, the great culinary artists of Paris frequently celebrated their favorite musicians by creating special dishes. Dishes named after him generally include foie gras and truffles.

Tournedos alla Rossini—the exquisite small end of the beef fillet, grilled and then placed on top of a slice of bread fried in butter or an artichoke heart, topped

Teatro Rossini

with warm foie gras, covered with truffles and a delectable Madeira sauce—was created for Rossini.

(Two other "operatic" recipes that immediately come to mind are *Chicken alla Tetrazzini*, created for the late-nineteenth- and early-twentieth-century diva Luisa Tetrazzini, and *Pêche Melba*, created for Dame Nellie Melba, the great Australian soprano of the late nineteenth and early twentieth centuries who sang at the Met from 1893 to 1910.)

Food

Pesaro is famous for its fish dishes in general and for its *brodetto* (fish soup) in particular. Many excellent pasta dishes also originate in this region of Italy. And in the fall and winter, if you are lucky, you will find *tartufi bianchi* (white truffles) from the nearby eastern slopes of the Apennines, served on pasta with butter and

Parmesan. The waiters in all of the restaurants included below are very willing to discuss local specialties.

Ristorante da Teresa, viale Trieste, 180
tel: (39–721) 30–222   fax: (39–721) 31–636
Closed Mondays and from November to March.

Ristorante Lo Scudiero, via Baldassini, 2
tel: (39–721) 64–107
Closed Thursdays and the month of July.

This extraordinary retaurant is a five-minute walk between the *centro storico* and the beach. You *must* reserve.

Ristorante Uldergo, via Venturini, 24
tel: (39–721) 33–180
Closed Mondays and from July 20 to August 30.

This restaurant, in the *centro storico,* is almost right next to the theatre. Unfortunately it is closed the month of August.

LODGING

Because Pesaro is a beach resort in addition to a town with an opera festival, it is imperative that you book your hotel far in advance. Early booking is also important because some of the nicest hotels are right down on the beach on viale Trieste.

Hotel Principe, viale Trieste, 180
tel: (39–721) 30–096   fax: (39–721) 31–636

Hotel Principe is a simple, neat, and clean beach hotel containing a world-class restaurant, Ristorante Teresa (see above), that specializes in fish (but has much more to offer).

Hotel Vittoria, piazzale della Libertà, 2
tel: (39–721) 34–343   fax: (39–721) 68–874

This is a slightly more luxurious hotel situated directly in front of Hotel Principe on the beach. It also has a restaurant (closed Sundays and from October to May).

Hotel Mamiani, via Mamiani, 24
tel: (39–721) 35–541

Hotel Mamiani is located right where viale Rossini enters the *centro storico*, which is principally an *isola pedonale* (pedestrian island). It is less than one hundred feet from the Rossini Festival offices, and, because it is not on the beach, is quieter in the summer than hotels on viale Trieste.

TRIESTE

In terms of the rest of the Italian peninsula, Trieste is the back of beyond. With its gray northern architecture, the city physically looks more like Ljublana, the capital of Slovenia, than an Italian city. In a *pasticceria* you are more likely to find strudel or its cousin, *Presnitz*, than any of the customary Italian sweets made of ground almonds. Culturally and physically Trieste is closer to Vienna than to Rome. In fact, Trieste was an unaligned city from 1060 A.D. until the beginning of the fourteenth century, when it came under Venetian rule. Then from 1382 until 1918 it was under Hapsburg rule, and only after World War I did it become a part of Italy. A World War I song summed up the view of many Italians about Trieste:

> *Il General Cadorna ha scritto alla Regina:*
> *"Se vuol' veder Trieste la ved'in cartolina."*
> General Cadorna wrote the Queen:
> "If you want to see Trieste, look at a postcard."

Trieste holds a Festival of Operetta, but operetta is definitely something that most Italians do not relate to at all! This festival serves to highlight the fact that Trieste was a part of the Austro-Hungarian Empire until 1918 and only became fully a part of Italy after a United Nations settlement in 1954.

If you should find yourself in Trieste, by all means go to the city's Teatro Comunale Giuseppe Verdi. The theatre was built in 1801 by the architect of Venice's La Fenice and named Teatro Nuovo. In 1821 it was renamed Teatro Grande. On January 29, 1901, two days after the death of Giuseppe Verdi, the city council spontaneously decided to rename the house after the master of nineteenth-century Italian opera: Teatro Comunale Giuseppe Verdi. The theatre was extensively renovated from 1990 to 1995. Performances were scheduled to begin again in October 1995.

Two of Verdi's operas received their premieres in Teatro Grande:

Il corsaro, *opera* in three acts, October 25, 1848.
Giuseppe Verdi (1813–1901)
Libretto Francesco Maria Piave, based on Lord Byron's poem *The Corsair.*

The premiere of *Il corsaro,* a commission from the music publisher Ricordi's archrival, Francesco Lucca, was a total flop. In order to rid himself of a contractual obligation, Verdi wrote the opera in haste and gave the score to Lucca with no idea where the first performance would take place or who the singers might be. This from a composer who was usually almost fanatic about the details of the premieres of his operas!

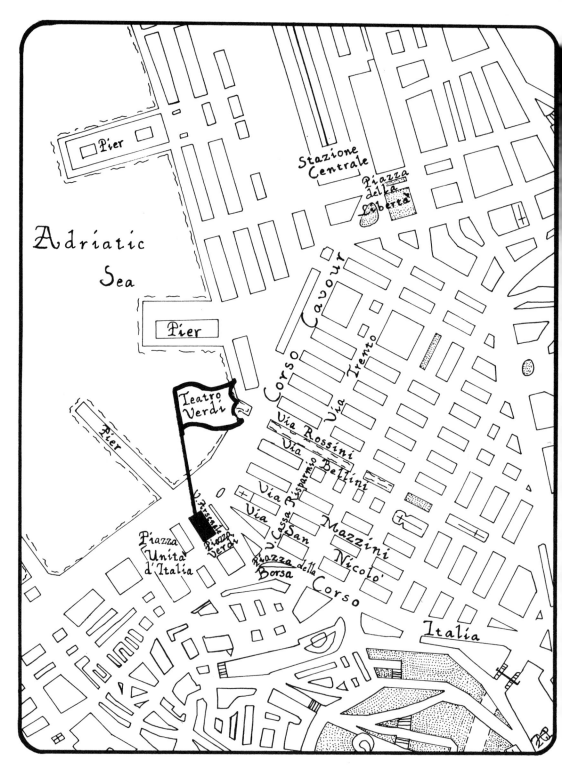

Operatic Trieste

Stiffelio, opera in three acts, November 16, 1850 (revised as *Araldo*, with a new last act, and performed in Rimini, Teatro Nuovo, August 16, 1857).
Giuseppe Verdi (1813–1901)
Libretto Francesco Maria Piave, based on Emile Souvestre and Eugène Bourgeois's play *Le Pasteur, ou L'Évangile et le foyer.*

As of this writing, *Stiffelio* is enjoying a comeback with performances at the Metropolitan Opera, the Los Angeles Opera, and many other theatres. The opera was a commission from the music publisher Ricordi. The plot is realistic and set in Verdi's own day, foreshadowing *La traviata*. Stiffelio himself is a Protestant minister whose wife is unfaithful to him. The action takes place in Salzburg, and the ruling Austrian censors had a field day cutting up the thrust of the drama. The censors particularly objected to the moment that Stiffelio randomly opens the Bible to take inspiration from whatever passage he finds. He reads the story of an adulterous wife whom Jesus forgives. The chorus then joins in, repeating that she is forgiven. Needless to say, this was a part of the Bible the censors did not want the local populace to dwell on. The drama of *Stiffelio* was so mutilated by the censors that the opera was not received well at all, so Verdi withdrew it from circulation. In 1857 he changed the plot, making it far less "sensitive," and called it *Araldo*. Act II of both *Stiffelio* and *Araldo* contains a quartet, "Ah no, è impossibile," that immediately prefigures the famous quartet from *Rigoletto*.

Teatro Comunale Giuseppe Verdi, piazza Verdi, 1, 34121 Trieste
tel: (39–40) 672–2111   fax: (39–40) 366–300
During the December through May season there are ten performances each of seven operas.

Festival dell'Operetta, Teatro Comunale Giuseppe Verdi, ticket office: riva III Novembre, 1, 34121 Trieste
tel: (39–40) 62–931
Season is six weeks, from late June to early August.

The Civic Theatrical Museum is housed in:

Teatro Comunale Giuseppe Verdi, piazza Verdi, 1
Open Tuesday–Saturday, 9:00 A.M–1:00 P.M. Tuesday–Saturday
tel: (39–40) 62–931

LODGING

Hotel Duchi d'Aosta, via dell'Orologio, 2, Trieste 34121
tel: (39–40) 7351   fax: (39–40) 366–092
Hotel Duchi d'Aosta is a three-minute walk from Teatro Verdi in the

center of town. Since the area of Trieste near the train station is rather grungy, this hotel is well worth its slightly higher price.

Harry's Grill is on the premises of the hotel.

SNACKS

Do sit down in one of Trieste's many outdoor cafés, which feel positively Viennese, to have an afternoon coffee and a slice of *Presnitz*, a sweet similar to strudel.

FOOD

Ristorante Città di Cherso, via Cadorna, 6
tel: (39–40) 366–044
Closed Tuesdays and the month of August.

This excellent restaurant is a five-minute walk from Teatro Verdi and two minutes from Hotel Duchi d'Aosta. *Definitely* reserve!

TURIN (Torino)

The region of Piemonte (the foothills) stands in the northwest of Italy on the southern slopes of the Swiss Alps and the eastern slopes of the French Alps. The source of the famous Po River that meanders through Turin and gave birth to the fertile plain known as the *val Padana* (the valley of the Po) originates in the Alps above the city. Turin is strategically situated on the main train line from France to Milan and is the area's largest and most important city. French was the lingua franca of the region until the beginning of the twentieth century. Besides housing Fiat (Fabbrica Italiana di Automobili Torino, the Italian Automobile Factory of Turin), Turin has been home to the Dukes of Savoy since 1574, and to Victorio Emanuele, a direct descendent of the original dukes who became Italy's first king in 1870, after the Risorgimento, during which period Turin was the capital of the "kingdom of Italy." The city suffered great destruction by Allied bombing in World War II. Today, Turin's beautifully rebuilt center lies around the Palazzo Reale and piazza Castello.

The original Teatro Regio, inaugurated in 1738, had a seating capacity of 2,500 and was designed to be the cultural and artistic center for the city of Turin. The current Teatro Regio was built in 1973 to replace the original eighteenth-century theatre destroyed by fire in 1936. All the other Torinese theatres were destroyed or badly damaged in the war. Today's Teatro Regio looks a bit like New York's Lincoln Center, 1970s new and spiffy, glass and chrome, not as inviting as the horseshoe-shaped theatres. But the acoustics are great, it has a long and exciting season, and it still acts as the city center's focal point.

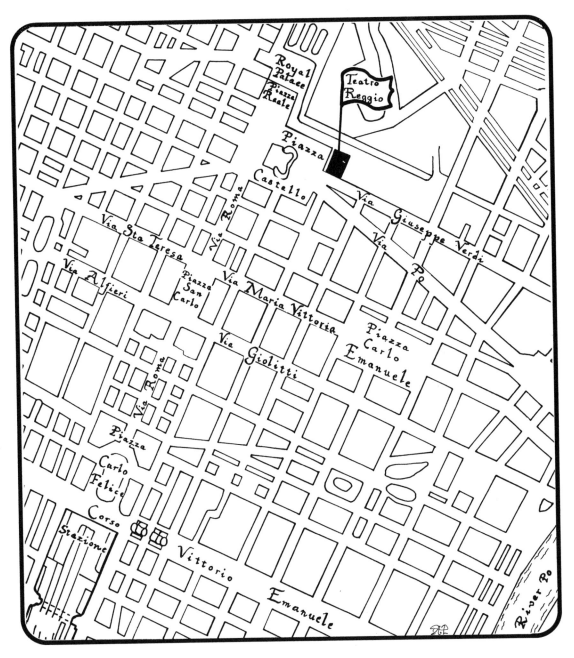

Operatic Turin

The original Teatro Regio presented the premieres of:

Ifegenia in Aulide, January 12, 1788, Luigi Cherubini.

La bohème, *opera* in four acts, February 1, 1896.
Giacomo Puccini (1858–1924)
Libretto Luigi Illica and Giuseppe Giacosa, after Henri Murger's novel
Scènes de la vie de bohème.

In the winter of 1892–93 Puccini decided to write an opera based on
Murger's novel, a decision that at once involved him in a controversy with
the composer Ruggero Leoncavallo (of *Pagliacci* fame), who claimed he had
had the idea first. It took the librettists until the winter of 1893–94 to put
together something that Puccini felt could be the basis for a convincing
opera. The libretto beautifully contrasts the tender love between the young
poor poet Rodolfo and the mortally ill Mimi, with the volatile love between
the young, poor painter Marcello and shrewd Musetta. Although often
unrestrainedly emotional, *La bohème* achieves an almost perfect balance of
pathos and comedy, realism and romanticism, and is a wonderfully satisfying
opera. (The guillotine C-sharp minor chords that close the opera are
unutterably moving.) Puccini began to write the music to *La bohème* in the
summer of 1894 and finished on December 10, 1895. At this time La Scala
was under the management of the music publisher Edoardo Sonzogno, who
excluded all Ricordi scores from the repertory. So the premiere was in Turin
in the same theatre where *Manon Lescaut* premiered. Arturo Toscanini
conducted. The reaction to the opera was mixed. Most critics felt that
Puccini nearly approached triviality in his music for *La bohème*. The public,
however, seems to have liked the opera; it was presented immediately with
great success throughout Italy and then Europe. The French composer
Claude Debussy thought that *La bohème* perfectly captured the Paris of the
time. The American premiere of the opera took place in Los Angeles, in
1897, performed by a touring Italian opera company and then by New York's
Metropolitan Opera in 1898. In 1951 the work achieved its thousandth
performance at the Opéra-Comique in Paris, where it was first presented in
1898 as *La vie de bohème*. Today, internationally, *La bohème* is the central
opera of the late nineteenth-century Italian repertory.

Manon Lescaut, *Dramma lirico* in four acts, February 1, 1893.
Giacomo Puccini (1858–1924)
Libretto Domenico Oliva and Luigi Illica, after Antoine-François
Prévost's novel *L'histoire du chevalier des Grieux et de Manon Lescaut* (The
Story of the Chevalier des Grieux and Manon Lescaut).

Although *Manon Lescaut*, Puccini's third opera, was his first immediate
success, it had a difficult birth. Four librettists (including Ruggero Leoncavallo) were involved in rendering the text. Although the final product was
effectively the work of Oliva and Illica, it was finally decided to publish the
libretto without attribution. At the premiere the critics were unanimous in
their praise (even though the text speaks of the "desert" of Louisiana!).
When it reached London in 1894, music critic George Bernard Shaw wrote
that in the opera "the domain of Italian opera is enlarged by an annexation of
German territory" and that "Puccini looks to me more like the heir of Verdi
than any of his rivals," implying that *Manon Lescaut* used techniques from
Wagner and set forth where Verdi left off. After the premiere of *Manon*

Lescaut, Puccini's financial problems were at an end and he purchased the villa at Torre del Lago that remained his home and workplace for the rest of his life.

Teatro Regio Torino, piazza del Castello, 215, 10124 Torino
tel: (39–11) 881–5241   fax: (39–11) 881–5214
   Opera season from September through June (both matinees and evenings).

LODGING

Hotel Venezia, via XX Settembre, 70, 10122 Torino
tel: (39–11) 562–3384   fax: (39–11) 562–3726
   This moderately priced hotel is a stone's throw from Teatro Regio.

Hotel des Artistes, via Principe Amedeo, 21, 10123 Torino
tel: (39–11) 812–4416   fax: (39–11) 812–4466
   This pleasant and economically priced hotel is a ten-minute walk from Teatro Regio. Many of the theatre's guests stay here.

SNACKS

   Before the opera have a *panino* (sandwich) at Cafe Regio in via Verdi right next to the theatre.
   From a *paneficio* (bread bakery) buy some *grissini torinese* (Turin-style breadsticks) to snack on. They are very different from breadsticks elsewhere in Italy!

FOOD

   The food of Turin is rightly famous as the perfect blend of French and Italian cuisines. The city abounds with excellent restaurants!
Some of the culinary delights to try are:
   The winter fondue-like dish *bagna cauda* (an unlikely but delicious sauce made of oil, butter, garlic, anchovies, and capers), served hot and into which raw vegetables and cooked meat are dipped.
   Also in fall or winter, *anything* that has a scraping of *tartufi bianchi* (white truffles) over it. The *real* treat is something bland, like *riso in bianco con tartufi* (white rice cooked in a light broth and served with butter, Parmesan, and truffles), or, simpler yet, an omelette with Parmesan and truffles.
   Fonduta con tartufi (a fondue made of *fontina,* a *piemonte* cheese) served with wedges of toast and a scraping of white truffles.
   Be sure to try the local Nebiolo, Barbera, Freisa, and Barolo wines.

Ristorante Del Cambio, piazza Carignano, 2
tel: (39–11) 546–690
Closed Sundays and the month of August.

   Piemonte, where Turin is located, has some of the most extraordinary
food in Italy, and this is one of Italy's *great* restaurants. In autumn and
winter do try something with truffles. It is a five-minute walk from
Teatro Regio. Definitely reserve!

Ristorante Spada Reale, via Principe Amedeo, 53
tel: (39–11) 832–835
Closed Sundays and the first three weeks of August.

   This is an excellent, popular restaurant with reasonable prices.

VENICE (Venezia)

Venice, situated on Italy's northeast coast, is the jewel of the Adriatic Sea. It's
lagoon is a natural port, and the city's location gave it ready-made protection,
making it the most important shipping center for the eastern Mediterranean on
the peninsula. Not by chance did Marco Polo come from Venice. The land first
settled in Venice was the island of San Marco. Because it contains most of
Venice's opera houses, from our perspective it is the most interesting.

   Venice was an independent republic until 1797, when it came under
Austrian rule. The city thus avoided the extreme Catholic conservatism of the
counter-Reformation that characterized the papal states on the peninsula. Venice
was, in fact, antipapist and stood up to the Pope in several disputes, including
exiling all Jesuits from the city for the year 1605–06. With its large, literate
merchant class, Venice was able to maintain its humanistic predilection
throughout the seventeenth and early eighteenth centuries.

   Opera had been a courtly affair since its beginnings in Florence in 1600. In
1637 Venice gave birth to the world's first public opera house, a theatre anyone
could attend by paying a fee. Up until that time, though often presented to
socially mixed audiences, operatic performances were invitational.

   For the first years of their existence, these early public opera houses paid for
production costs by dunning the members of the companies. This proved difficult
and unreliable, and it took only a few years before the cost of presenting opera
was left in the hands of a theatre's owner, to whom an impresario reported. The
impresario was responsible for the artistic health of the theatre's productions.

   From the seventeenth through the eighteenth centuries, Venice maintained a
good number of theatres for such a small city. At the beginning of the nineteenth
century, however, when the republic fell first to Austria, then to France
(Napoleon)—under whom Italy was called the Kingdom of Italy—and then back
again to Austria, the number of opera theatres in the city was drastically

reduced, because opera offers the potential for expressing political sentiment, forthrightly or in "code" (think of V-E-R-D-I, as described in the chapter on Milan). The French proposed to reduce the number of theatres to four, then the Austrians prohibited the construction of new theatres, thus tightening the belt on the Venetians' natural insatiable operatic appetite while not resorting to an outright ban.

The first public opera house, with a box office and a paying public, also presented commedia dell'arte. The theatre, which opened in 1581, was originally called Teatro Tron. Because it was situated near the church of San Cassiano, it became known as Teatro San Cassiano (most theatres in Italy were given the name of the nearby neighborhood church).

The theatre was built in the round, with seats set up on ascending steps around a semicircular space, in a style similar to the architecture of Parma's Teatro Farnese. After a fire in 1619, it was rebuilt in stone (1636), most likely in the horseshoe-shaped style of the typical *teatro all'italiana* but still without a proscenium arch. (The proscenium arch was "invented" in England in the 1670s.) The first performance in Teatro San Cassiano as a public opera house took place for Carnevale 1637 with a production of the opera *Andromeda*, music by Francesco Manelli, libretto by Benedetto Ferrari, with Manelli and his wife playing four roles between them.

A far more important performance took place in 1641, a year after its premiere in another opera theatre (probably Teatro SS Giovanni e Paolo): Claudio Monteverdi's penultimate opera, *Il ritorno di Ulisse in patria* (The Return of Ulysses to His Homeland), *dramma per musica* in a prologue and three acts, 1640, with a libretto by Giacomo Badoaro after books 3 to 23 of Homer's *Odyssey*.

Monteverdi had left Mantua for Venice in 1613 to become *maestro di cappella* of San Marco, the cathedral of Venice. We know he wrote several large-scale dramatic works during his Venetian years, but all that remain today are his *Il ritorno di Ulisse in patria*, *L'incoronazione di Poppea*, and the curious dramatic study *Il combattimento di Tancredi e Clorinda*. *Il ritorno di Ulisse* contains some of Monteverdi's finest dramatic music; certainly the scene where the three suitors press Penelope to forget Ulysses, and her response of "Non voglio amar" ("I don't want to love"), is one of his most memorable operatic moments. Monteverdi and Badoaro molded each character with great care, and one is moved by the individuals' plights in a way never achieved before 1640 in opera.

By the end of the seventeenth century Venice had no fewer than sixteen public theatres that produced opera!

Unfortunately Teatro San Cassiano was destroyed in 1812. The land on which the theatre stood lies between the rio delle Due Torri and rio di San Cassiano, where corte del Teatro and calle della Commedia join. Today a garden and the street numbers 2301 to 2302 mark the site of the theatre.

Since the late eighteenth century serious opera performances in Venice have

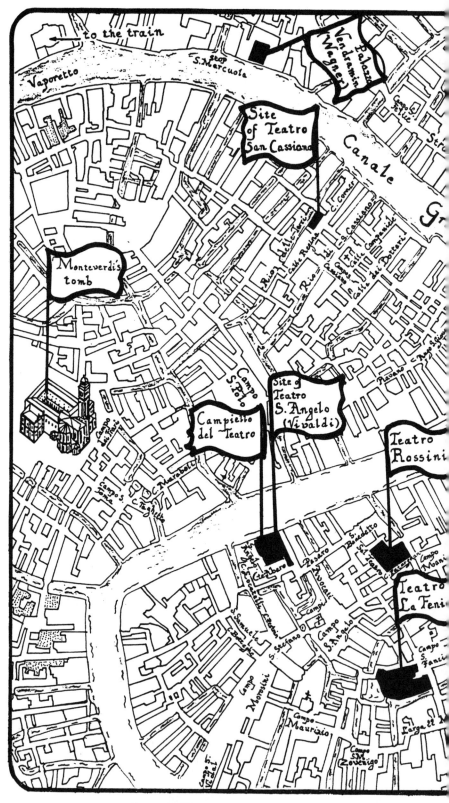

Operatic Venice

Site
of Teatro
San Giovanni
e Paolo

Teatro
Malibran

Teatro
Goldoni

Nuova

Campo S.
Apostoli

Caciano

S. Maria
Nova
Corovado

Rio de Mendicanti

Fondamenta dei Mendicanti

Fondamenta nuove

Calle Rotta

Rio della Panada

Calle Stella

Calle della Testa

Rio di

S. Marina

S.s. Giov. Crisostomo

Bartolomio S.

S. Salvador

Campo S. S. Giov.
e Paolo

Rio-li

Ponte
Rialto

San Marco

Palazzo Dandolo
(Monteverdi)
today's Hotel
Daniele

Hotel
Metropole
(Vivaldi)

S. Maria
della Pietà
Vivaldi's
Church

Doge's Palace

Calle Fabbri

Site
of Teatro
S. Moise &
Rossini

Sal. Moise

S. Moise

Piazza

S. Marco

Rio della Zecca

Royal
gardens

Molo, Riva degli Schiavon

stop
Zaccaria

Canale Grande

been presented at Teatro La Fenice (the Phoenix), and today the theatre is the only opera house left in the city. La Fenice, with a seating capacity of 1,500, was built in 1792 as the result of a competition held to replace the recently burned-down Teatro San Benedetto. (Teatro San Benedetto was also rebuilt, but its importance was diminished by the new La Fenice.) The first really significant premiere given at La Fenice did not take place until Rossini's opera seria, *Tancredi*, in 1813. La Fenice, along with Milan's La Scala and Naples's San Carlo, became one of the most notable opera theatres on the Italian peninsula. The original theatre burned down in 1837 but was quickly rebuilt that same year without much alteration of the original design. The interior of La Fenice is sumptuous and positively jewel-like. The ceiling and the royal box are held up by bare-breasted caryatids that look a bit like hefty-chested singers!

Alas, on the night of February 29, 1996, at the moment of this book's writing, Teatro La Fenice was razed by fire. The canals that normally act as the city's fire hydrants had been drained around the theatre in order to remove a heavy fifty-year buildup of silt. Fireboats had to pump water from the Grand Canal, which is at least five hundred feet away! The city was saved, but all that remains of the theatre is a blackened shell. The irony is that Venice is usually threatened by too much water. To date the Italian government has pledged $12.5 million toward the theatre's reconstruction, a job they promise will be completed in two years.

Teatro La Fenice premiered (details of the premieres are at the end of the chapter) *Attila* (1846), Giuseppe Verdi; *Beatrice di Tenda* (1833), Vincenzo Bellini; *La bohème* (1897), Ruggero Leoncavallo; *I Capuleti e i Montecchi* (1830), Vincenzo Bellini; *Ernani* (1844), Giuseppe Verdi; *Intolleranza 1960* (1961), Luigi Nono; *The Rake's Progress* (1951), Igor Stravinsky; *Rigoletto* (1851), Giuseppe Verdi; *Semiramide* (1823), Gioacchino Rossini; *Simon Boccanegra* (1857), Giuseppe Verdi; *Tancredi* (1813), Gioacchino Rossini; *La traviata* (1853), Giuseppe Verdi; *The Turn of the Screw* (1954), Benjamin Britten.

Teatro La Fenice, Campo S. Fantin, 2519, 30124 Venezia
Box office open 9:30 A.M.–noon and 4:00–6:00 P.M.
tel: (39–41) 521–0161 or 521–0336   free from other cities in Italy: (167) 853-043   fax: (39–41) 522–1768
Opera season October through June.

Besides La Fenice, many other important opera theatres sprang up in Venice. Among them are:

Teatro San Benedetto, built in 1755, was the immediate forerunner of La Fenice. It was damaged in a fire in 1774, after which a competition was organized for the design of a new theatre. La Fenice (the phoenix, reborn from the ashes) won the competition, but Teatro San Benedetto was also rebuilt. In the early nineteenth century, although La Fenice was the foremost theatre in Venice, Teatro San Benedetto presented two premieres by Rossini and, on May 6, 1854, the second production—but first successful one—of Verdi's revised *La traviata*. In 1868 the theatre was renamed Teatro Rossini. Today it is a cinema, but even as a cinema it has a claim to fame: In 1929 the theatre presented the first sound movies in Venice. In 1951 the building was completely torn down and has since been rebuilt.

> **Cinema Rossini,** San Marco 3988, (surrounded by calle San Patergnan, calle Sant'Andrea, calle delle Monache, salizada Teatro, and rio di San Luca).
> tel: 523–0322

Teatro San Benedetto (Cinema Rossini) premiered (details of the premieres are at the end of the chapter) *L'italiana in Algeri* (1813), Gioacchino Rossini; *Eduardo e Cristina* (1819), Gioacchino Rossini.

The double name of Teatro San Luca–San Salvador derives from its location next to the church of San Salvador in the parish of San Luca. The theatre was originally constructed by the noble Vendramin family (in whose palace Richard Wagner died). In terms of seventeenth-century Venetian opera, the theatre was second in importance only to SS Giovanni e Paolo and presented operas by the second generation of Venetian composers such as Francesco Cavalli, Antonio Cesti, and Giovanni Legrenzi. From 1752 to 1762 the theatre was the seat of the theatrical company of the great Venetian playwright Carlo Goldoni. It was closed under Napoleon in 1807, then reopened under the Austrians in 1815. For most of the rest of the nineteenth century, it played a role equal to that of La Fenice, alternating opera and prose theatre. In 1833 the name was changed to Teatro Apollo, and in 1834 it was the first Italian theatre to have gas lighting. When La Fenice burned in 1836, its whole season was transferred to Teatro Apollo. In 1875 the name was again changed, this time to Teatro Goldoni. After World War II the theatre was declared unsafe. Restored in 1974, Teatro Goldoni today is the home of Teatro Stabile. Although it is built on the foundation of the original theatre, the present building has been completely renovated in late-twentieth-century chrome and glass.

> **Teatro Stabile,** San Marco 4650 (facing calle del Teatro just around the corner from campo San Luca)
> tel: (39–41) 520–5422

Teatro SS Giovanni e Paolo was where many of the premieres of the first seventeenth-century Venetian operas took place. The theatre was constructed between 1635 and 1637 in contrada di San Marina between calle della Testa and rio della Panada, near the Fondamenta Nuove, putting it between the two very populated neighborhoods of Castello and Cannaregio. Eighty-eight operas premiered here between 1637 and 1715, when it was closed. The theatre was eventually abandoned and torn down in the middle of the nineteenth century.

Teatro SS Giovanni e Paolo most likely presented the premiere of:

L'incoronazione di Poppea, dramma musicale in a prologue and three acts, 1643.
Claudio Monteverdi (1567–1643)
Libretto Giovanni Francesco Busenello, primarily based upon Tacitus's *Annals* (books 13–16), but also upon Suetonius, *The Twelve Ceasars* (book 6); Dio Cassius, *Roman History* (books 61–62); and pseudo-Seneca, *Ottavia.*

L'incoronazione di Poppea is the first opera *not* to be modeled after a myth or classical poem. This is an opera about the bloody and terrible reign of Nero, Roman emperor from A.D. 54–68. We all know what *he* did while Rome burned. This opera fills us in on more of his dastardly deeds, in particular his lust for Poppea, the wife of one of his noblemen. (Incidentally, Poppea, a nickname, must have referred to either a highly voluptuous derriere, *la poppa* being Italian for a ship's poop deck or stern, or else shapely breasts, *poppe* being Italian for teat. Unless it alluded to the fact that the ship is directed from the stern...) Certainly Monteverdi's Nero is goaded in every step by Poppea. The opera depicts Nero's lust for her and his machinations to rid himself of his wife Ottavia; a death sentence to his adviser Seneca (who slits his wrists in a bath); and the exile of Poppea's husband Ottone. Today it is common knowledge that other composers, younger contemporaries of Monteverdi, probably wrote portions of what we today know as the score of the opera. This does not detract from Monteverdi's achievement. The opera contains the materials that operas should be built upon—lust, ambition, jealousy, and human beings with strong emotions, desires, and fears. The setting of the text displays remarkable sensuality and is often downright sexy. The story has a broad moral compass and great psychological conviction.

The score of *L'incoronazione di Poppea* has been edited many times in this century by such noted musicians as Vincent d'Indy, Ernst Krenek, Raymond Leppard, Nikolaus Harnoncourt, and Alan Curtis, to name only a few. It was Harnoncourt's version, conducted by him and directed by Jean-Pierre Ponnelle, given in collaboration with the Zurich Opera, that was filmed and widely shown on public television in the United States. It takes true masters to direct and conduct the opera successfully, and slowly but surely such collaborations are helping early masterpieces enter the operatic mainstream.

Teatro San Giovanni Girostomo, built in 1678, was considered the most magnificent Venetian theatre of the late seventeenth to the mid-eighteenth century. During its early period it was home to the premiere of Handel's *Agrippina,* December 26, 1709. The theatre was reconstructed in 1834 and renamed Teatro Emeronittio (Theatre of Day and Night). In 1835, after the great Spanish diva Maria Malibran sang Bellini's *La sonnambula* in the theatre just before her untimely death at age twenty-eight, it was renamed Teatro Malibran. In 1984, only ten years before the writing of this book, Teatro Malibran was the site of a performance of Antonio Cesti's *Il tito* (Venice, 1666, Teatro SS Giovanni e Paolo) conducted by Alan Curtis. Today, alas, it is sadly derelict and smells of mold and cat urine.

Teatro Malibran, Calle del Teatro o dell'Opera off of salizada S. Giovanni Gristostomo directly across from Hotel Malibran.

Teatro San Moisè (Teatro Giustinian a San Moisè) opened in 1620. *Arianna*, one of the lost operas of Claudio Monteverdi, was performed here in 1639. After various ownerships and renovations, in 1772 the theatre was completely restored and began to present *opere buffe*. By the end of the eighteenth century the theatre was known as *the* Venetian theatre for comic opera. Teatro San Moisè was one of four theatres allowed to continue productions under Napoleon's government in the early 1800s. In the early twentieth century it became a cinema but was demolished just before World War II.

Today we think of Teatro San Moisè as being the place that Gioacchino Rossini (1797–1868) tried out his creative wings, learning how to set humor in music. All of his works presented at the theatre were one-act farces. (All five of these farces can be heard on one CD, Claves 50–9200.)

The location of Teatro San Moisè was off rio S. Moisè near the church of San Moisè off today's via XXII Marzo near where the hotel Bauer Grünwald now stands. (calle del Traghetto della Trinità detta del Forno near the Canal Grande.)

Teatro San Moisè premiered (details of the premieres are at the end of the chapter) *La cambiale di matrimonio* (1807), Gioacchino Rossini; *L'inganno felice* (1812), Gioacchino Rossini; *L'occasione fa il ladro* (1812), Gioacchino Rossini; *La scala di seta* (1812), Gioacchino Rossini; *Il signor Bruschino* (1813), Gioacchino Rossini.

Palazzo Dandolo is situated on the riva degli Schiavoni. The building is in a Gothic palace that was remodeled in the seventeenth century and became a hotel in 1822. It is here, in the apartments of G. Mocenigo, where Claudio Monteverdi's dramatic madrigal *Il combattimento di Tancredi et Clorinda* (1624) was first performed. Monteverdi invented new instrumental techniques which enabled instruments to go beyond simple accompaniment and to take on character and drama in their own right. This dramatic style of instrumental writing is called *stile concitato*.

Il combattimento di Tancredi e Clorinda, *epic,* three days of Carnevale, February 18–20, 1624.
Claudio Monteverdi (1567–1643)
Libretto Monteverdi, setting sixteen stanzas of the twelfth canto (52–68; omitting stanza 63) from Torquato Tasso's epic poem *Gerusalemme liberata* (The Liberation of Jerusalem).

Il combattimento di Tancredi e Clorinda is not really an opera, in that it is a through-composed narrative, without various arias and recitatives, almost entirely written in *recitar cantando* (singing speech). The principal role is that of the narrator, Testo (meaning the text), who describes the action; Tancredi and Clorinda sing only a very few short phrases. The piece contains very specific theatrical instructions for the singing actors *and* the small instrumental ensemble (basically a string quartet with a harpsichord). In *Il combattimento*, Monteverdi was stretching the limits of his experience and experimenting. He created a new style, a new category, by giving dramatic sense to the accompaniment, which heretofore had only supported the vocal parts. Some of the performers actively disliked the work, in particular the vigorous reiteration of one note that pointedly represented Monteverdi's idea of how anger and aggression should sound in music. The work is a scenic madrigal or a scenic cantata and in every sense it is a dramatic piece of musical theatre. It was most likely performed in Palazzo Dandolo, where Monteverdi himself was living. Today Palazzo Dandolo is the Hotel Danieli and stands on riva degli Schiavoni just east of the Doge's Palace.

Palazzo Dandolo (Hotel Danieli), riva degli Schiavoni, 4196, 30122 Venice
tel: (39–41) 522–6480   fax: (39–41) 520–0208

The Church of S. Maria Gloriosa dei Frari in the Cappella of Saint Ambrogio, in campo dei Frari: The tombstone the third to the left of the choir is the tomb of Claudio Monteverdi, who died November 29, 1643. (Tiziano [Titian] and Canova are also buried in the church.)

The great Venetian composer Antonio Vivaldi (1678–1741) was the impresario of Teatro Sant'Angelo from 1714 to 1739 and wrote eighteen operas that were premiered there. Then, between 1749 and 1753, the theatre played a central role in the career of the famous Venetian playwright Carlo Goldoni, producing many of his plays. The infamous Giacomo Casanova (see Portoguaro and Lorenzo Da Ponte) was impresario in 1780. The theatre closed in 1803. Where it stood can be found where contrada Sant'Angelo and corte dell'Albero meet campiello del Teatro on the Grand Canal at the St. Angelo vaporetto stop.

Vivaldi's presence can also be felt on the riva degli Schiavoni (almost next door to Hotel Paganelli). The famous conservatory for orphan girls was housed in what is today's Hotel Metropole. A plaque on the front of the building states:

La Capella Musicale del	The Musical Chapel of
conservatorio della Pietà	the Conservatory of the Pietà
dove il genio di	where the genius of
Antonio Vivaldi	Antonio Vivaldi,
allora non pienamente	not yet fully appreciated,
compreso operó quale	acted as

Hotel Danieli (Palazzo Dandolo)

"Maestro di' Concerti"	Maestro of Concerts
dal 1703–1740	from 1703–1740
donando a Venezia	giving to Venice
ed al mondo	and to the world
l'incomparabile richezza	the uncomparable richness
della sua musica di cui	of his music of which
"Le 4 Stagione"	"The Four Seasons"
sono il fiore e il suggello.	are the flower and the seal.
Il suo tempo é venuto.	His time has come.

Next to the hotel is Santa Maria della Pietà, now called Vivaldi's Church.

Richard Wagner (1813–83), like so many nineteenth-century northern Europeans, loved Italy and spent a good portion of his productive life there. While writing *Tristan und Isolde,* he stayed in Palazzo Giustinian, situated just to the west of piazza San Marco. On February 13, 1883, while staying in the sixteenth-century Palazzo Vendramin-Calergi, he died of a heart attack following a bitter row with his wife Cosima. The row was provoked by the announced visit of Pauline Horson, one of the Flower Maidens in *Parsifal,* with whom Wagner was probably having an affair.

Wagner was renting a suite of fifteen rooms, which made up only a part of the mezzanine level of the palace. The palace, situated on the left bank of the Grand Canal near the train station, is now the Casino of Venice. A plaque on the front of the building and on the Grand Canal is accompanied by a bust of the composer.

Some of the other places Wagner stayed in Italy

South of Macerata in the Marche, he stayed in an eighteenth-century villa next to a Cistercian abbey, Abbazia di Fiastra.

In Rome, he lived in Albergo d'America in via del Babuino, 79. Today the hotel is an office building. The entrance for carriages in Wagner's day can be seen in via Margutta, 67.

In Palermo, in 1881–82 while composing *Parsifal*, the composer stayed in what today is called Grande Hotel e des Palmes in via Roma 398. The harmonium he used to facilitate his writing is now on display in Teatro Massimo in via Riccardo Wagner 2. (We will be able to see it again if they ever finish the theatre's renovation.)

Details of the premieres at Teatro La Fenice

Attila, *dramma lirico* in a prologue and three acts, March 17, 1846.
Giuseppe Verdi (1813–1901)
Libretto begun by Temestocle Solera and finished by Francesco Maria Piave, after Zacharias Werner's play *Attila, König der Hunnen.*

Strangely enough, from our vantage point today, *Attila*, although a bit of a flop at its premiere, went on to become one of Verdi's most popular operas of the 1850s. Then it went out of mode and has been revived only recently in Italy. The writing was fraught with difficulties. Verdi fell seriously ill; after writing only an outline of the last act, Solera went off to live in Madrid; Piave had to be called in to rescue the situation. As a result, several of the principal characters in the opera are never clearly delineated. It is very much one of Verdi's few "formula" operas.

Beatrice di Tenda, *tragedia lirica* in two acts, March 16, 1833.
Vincenzo Bellini (1801–1835)
Libretto Felice Romani, after Carlo Tedaldi-Fores's play of the same name.

Beatrice di Tenda was a commission from La Fenice. Bellini wrote the title role expressly for the great nineteenth-century soprano Giuditta Pasta and had high hopes for the opera's success. When he arrived in Venice to work with the librettist, however, he found Romani had not even begun *Beatrice di Tenda*, being busy on five other librettos. The premiere appears to have been attended by an orchestrated claque that hissed and carried on. Pasta, it seems, stopped singing and stepped forward to address the audience, asking them to at least respect her even if they disliked the opera. The first performances of the opera were mostly unsuccessful. Bellini blamed Romani, Romani blamed Bellini, and the opera was their last collaboration. The opera is not in today's repertory.

La bohème, *commedia lirica* in four acts, May 6, 1897.
Ruggero Leoncavallo (Naples, 1857—Monte catini, 1919)
Libretto by the composer, after Henry Murger's novel *Scenes de la vie de bohème,* revised in 1913 as *Mimi Pinson.*

Leoncavallo wrote his *La bohème* in direct competition with Puccini, whose opera premiered fifteen months earlier. Both operas are based on the Murger novel, but Leoncavallo's *Bohème* is more superficial, with all the lovers constantly fighting and making up. After all, he called it a "lyric comedy," and even though Mimi dies at the end, it completely lacks the pathos that Puccini demanded from his librettists and that he managed to instill musically in the opera. This pathos is what audiences to this day respond to with tears. The premiere of Leoncavallo's *Bohème* was a success and the opera coexisted with Puccini's *Bohème* for about ten years, after which it dropped out of the performance arena. In the last few years several productions have been staged in Italy, but the opera shows no signs of a major revival.

I Capuleti e i Montecchi, *tragedia lirica* in two acts, March 11, 1830.
Vincenzo Bellini (1801–1835)
Libretto Felice Romani, roughly based on the play *Giulietta e Romeo* by Luigi Scevola.

Although the title implies that the libretto is after Shakespeare's *Romeo and Juliet,* Felice Romani's star-crossed lovers have Italian Renaissance sources. The theme was very popular in Italian opera at the beginning of the nineteenth century (four different librettos had already dealt with the same subject by the time Romani first set it for the composer Vaccai). Bellini wrote his score in about six weeks, reworking tunes from his unsuccessful opera *Zaira.* Later he said, "*Zaira* hissed at Parma [1829] was avenged by *I Capuleti,*" for the premiere at La Fenice was a wild success.

Ernani, *dramma lirico* in four parts, March 9, 1844.
Giuseppe Verdi (1813–1901)
Libretto Francesco Maria Piave, after Victor Hugo's play *Hernani.*

In 1843, after receiving a commission from La Fenice, Verdi became interested in setting Victor Hugo's play *Hernani,* despite the likelihood that the Venetian-Austrian Church censors would most likely object strongly to a story of adultery and conspiracy. In this, Verdi's fifth opera, he shows his incredible musical and dramatic command over the entire flow of each act and ultimately of the whole opera. Such command was a new achievement and not again equaled until his great operas of the early 1850s. Verdi wrote the role of Don Carlo (the king) for a dramatic baritone, one of the first roles written for a lower voice constantly singing *tutta forza* (as strongly as possible) in its highest range and creating an emphatic dramatic sound, with a heavier dramatic accompaniment; this innovation put the baritone voice on the map, distinguishing it entirely from the bass voice. *Ernani* is also the origin of the typical nineteenth-century operatic setup, a triangle formed by a soprano, tenor, and baritone. Because he was unsure of Piave's dramatic abilities, Verdi actively participated in the writing of the libretto. Piave was then quite inexperienced; this was his first professional engagement. The opera was an enormous success, making Verdi "the first composer of the world," and became very popular in the following years in other opera houses throughout Europe. *Ernani* began the long collaboration between Piave and Verdi, producing some of Verdi's most popular operas, such as *Rigoletto* and *La traviata*. Today, *Ernani* is not exactly a repertory piece and is occasionally presented with great success.

Intolleranza 1960, *azione scenica* in two parts, April 13, 1961.
Luigi Nono (January 29, 1924, Venice—May 8, 1990, Venice)
Libretto by the composer, based on an idea by Angelo Maria Ripellino with texts by Ripellino, Henri Alleg, Bertolt Brecht, Aimé Césaire, Paul Eluard, Vladimir Mayakovsky, Julius Fucik, and Jean-Paul Sartre.

Intolleranza 1960 was written in three months after Nono received an invitation to present an opera at the prestigious Venice Biennale. Although the opera is overtly political, it contains some of the most lyrically impassioned vocal writing of the mid-twentieth century for both soloists and chorus. The premiere received a *stormy* reception, in part orchestrated by opposing political groups. Nono revised the opera to one act in 1974, calling it *Intolleranza 1970*. Nono's music is incredibly beautiful, but the opera's political content and perspective have kept the opera from most of the world's stages. The brave, trend-setting Sarah Caldwell presented *Intolleranza* in Boston in the late 1960s.

The Rake's Progress, *opera* in three acts, September 11, 1951.
Igor Stravinsky (between June 5 and 17, 1882, Oranienbaum, Russia—April 6, 1971, New York)
Libretto W. H. Auden and Chester Kallman, after William Hogarth's series of paintings (1732–33).

Stravinsky's one full-scale opera, *The Rake's Progress*, was premiered at Teatro La Fenice September 11, 1951, as part of the Venice Biennale. Stravinsky saw Hogarth's paintings—which depict the degeneration of a "rake" from his search for fortune to his demise in Bedlam—at the Chicago Art Institute on May 2, 1947, and they struck him as a series of scenes from an English drama of operatic nature. For some time he had wanted to write an opera in English. His California neighbor Aldous Huxley suggested W. H.

Auden as librettist, and Auden asked his friend Chester Kallman to collaborate as well. The premiere was a success, although Stravinsky received some criticism for "writing like Mozart with the wrong notes" (Act II is filled with licks from *Così fan tutte*). Elisabeth Schwarzkopf created the role of Anne Trulove. The opera is now a solid repertory opera throughout the world, having had more productions than any other opera written after 1924, the year marking Puccini's death.

Rigoletto, *melodramma* in three acts, March 11, 1851. Giuseppe Verdi (1813–1901)
Libretto Francesco Maria Piave, after Victor Hugo's play *Le roi s'amuse.*

Verdi called the period from 1839 to 1851, during which he wrote his first fifteen operas, his "years in jail," when he was unable to break from the musical conventions of the past. *Rigoletto* was the first of his three operas that released him from his artistic prison, the others being *Il trovatore* (January 1853) and *La traviata* (March 1853). Today they are known as Verdi's trilogy. Verdi called *Le roi s'amuse*, from which *Rigoletto* came, "one of the greatest creations of modern theatre." (The play was immediately banned from the stage in Paris because it portrayed King François I as a lecher and depicted an attempted assassination.) Francesco Piave, who had been named resident poet of Teatro La Fenice because of his previous successes with Verdi, encouraged the composer to fulfill a commission from the theatre with an operatic setting of the work. In November 1850, however, when Verdi got the libretto, the Venetian police and church censors began to intervene, saying the libretto contained "disgusting immorality and obscene triviality" and banned the performance. Piave then wrote a compromise libretto that Verdi rejected because it abandoned what to him were the dramatic essentials of the subject. Verdi stuck to his guns and insisted that the Duke of Mantua should have absolute power over his subjects; that the character of Rigoletto should remain a hunchback, and that he is beautiful because of his love for his daughter; that the body of Gilda should be in a sack (a curious sticking point with the censors); and that, in fact, the opera should fulfill the curse of Monterone. (Piave and Verdi had considered calling the opera *La maledizione,* or "The Curse," but surmised that church censors would really object if it were pointed out that the opera involved the carrying out of a curse.) Verdi agreed to change the tenor role from a king to a duke and acquiesced in several other minor changes, including renaming the protagonist: Tribolet became Rigoletto. Finally the Venetian censors agreed to the premiere at La Fenice. Verdi wrote the score in the first six weeks of 1851, and the premiere was an enormous success. Even though there were still problems with local censors, the opera immediately became part of the basic operatic repertory. To this day *Rigoletto* remains one of the most frequently performed operas in the international repertory.

Semiramide, *melodramma tragico* in two acts, February 3, 1823.
Gioacchino Rossini (1792–1868)
Libretto Gaetano Rossi, after Voltaire's *Sémiramis.*

The heroic drama *Semiramide* is the last opera that Rossini wrote in Italy. Changing his earlier custom, with this piece Rossini worked closely with his librettist. The premiere was very successful, even though the first act lasted two and a half hours. The title role was sung by Isabella Colbran, who had become Mrs. Rossini on March 16, 1822; it was the last of many roles he had written for her. The opera was very soon after staged in Milan, Vienna, Naples, London, and Paris and premiered in New York in 1835. Joan Sutherland and Marilyn Horne were responsible for the opera's comeback in the 1960s.

Simon Boccanegra, *opera* in a prologue and three acts, March 12, 1857.
Giuseppe Verdi (1813–1901)
Libretto Francesco Maria Piave, with additions by Giuseppe Montanelli, after Antonio Garcia Gutierrez's play *Simón Boccanegra.* The libretto was later further revised by Arrigo Boito.

Simon Boccanegra was a commission from La Fenice. Verdi was in Paris in the autumn of 1856 when he began to write the music to the opera, and so, although Piave was the opera's librettist, Verdi worked closely with another librettist, Giuseppe Montanelli, an exiled Italian revolutionary also living in Paris. The premiere was not a success and the libretto was harshly criticized. In fact, some called it a fiasco almost as great as that of the first performance of *La traviata* three years earlier. In 1879 Verdi completely revised the score and asked Arrigo Boito to revise the libretto, partially to "audition" him for future collaboration on *Otello.* This revised version was a resounding success at La Scala in 1881, and in its revised state, is considered one of his most compelling operas and contains some of his greatest dramatic music. Today it exists on the margins of the international repertory.

Tancredi, *melodramma eroico* in two acts, February 6, 1813.
Gioacchino Rossini (1792–1868)
Libretto Gaetano Rossi, after Voltaire's *Tancrède.*

Rossini wrote two versions of *Tancredi,* an opera seria, to suit the public at its first two performances: For the premiere in Venice, he wrote a happy ending; for a performance in Ferrara, a month later, he restored Voltaire's tragic conclusion. The opera is purely lyrical, demanding the greatest in singing technique from the performers. The principal protagonist is named for the character in Tasso's *Gerusalemme liberata,* but the story, although concerning Saracens and Christians, is completely different from that of Monteverdi's *Il combattimento di Tancredi e Clorinda.* Rumor has it that each of the opening nights of *Tancredi* was marred by an identical mishap; each leading lady fell ill in the middle of Act II and the performance had to be halted.

La traviata, *opera* in three acts, March 6, 1853.
Giuseppe Verdi (1813–1901)
Libretto Francesco Maria Piave, after Alexandre Dumas, fils, play *La Dame aux camélias.*

Verdi took a big risk in writing *La traviata,* the touching story of the ill-fated love between the mortally ill courtesan, Violetta Valery, and Alfredo Germont. After altruistically giving up Alfredo, Violetta dies of tuberculosis at the opera's end. Verdi said that others would not have used the subject for an opera because of traditional operatic conventions and for "a thousand other stupid scruples." Tuberculosis was a contemporary disease and Verdi wanted the singers in modern dress, but the censors made Verdi and Piave change the period to the beginning of the eighteenth century. Verdi wrote the opera in a record two months. The premiere turned into a highly celebrated disaster. First, the soprano singing Violetta was very heavy and looked nothing like the frail, tubercular demimondaine so expressively depicted in Verdi's music and Piave's script. Then, the baritone singing Germont, a notoriously high and difficult role (note the film of Zeffirelli!), was past his prime, although only two years before he had played a very convincing Rigoletto at that opera's premiere. As a consequence, Verdi canceled the rest of the run. Only after he had changed a great deal of Act II's music between Germont and Violetta and had found a more suitable cast did he allow further performances. These later productions, unequivocally successful, took place at Venice's Teatro San Benedetto. Today *La traviata* is perhaps Verdi's most loved opera.

The Turn of the Screw, *opera* in a prologue and two acts, September 14, 1954.
Benjamin Britten (November 22, 1913, Lowestoft, England—December 4, 1976, Aldeburgh, England)
Libretto Myfanwy Piper, after Henry James's tale of the same name.

The chamber opera *The Turn of the Screw* was a commission from the Venice Biennale of 1954. Britten composed the score in five months, rather an early-nineteenth-century kind of achievement. The opera is compact and full of musical inventivenes, highlighting the psychological turbulence of Henry James's terrifying tale of a governess and her unsuccessful attempts to protect her young charges from evil. The premiere received only mixed reviews, even though it was clear to many that this was Britten's finest work to date. The opera is presented relatively often throughout the world.

Details of Teatro San Benedetto premieres

Eduardo e Cristina, *dramma* in two acts, April 24, 1819.
Gioacchino Rossini (1792–1868)
Libretto Giovanni Schmidt, revised by Andrea Leone Tottola and
Gherardo Bevilacqua-Aldobrandini, after a libretto originally written for
an opera by Stefano Pavesi, *Odoardo e Cristina,* in 1810.

Eduardo e Cristina was written hastily by Rossini and, although he
composed a few new numbers, it is a pastiche of several of his earlier operas.
The premiere, which Rossini conducted from the harpsichord, was, according to the English poet Lord Byron, such a success that groupies ran after the
composer trying to cut off bits of his hair as a souvenir! The opera is not one
found in today's repertory.

L'italiana in Algeri (The Italian Girl in Algiers), *dramma giocoso* in two
acts, May 22, 1813.
    Gioacchino Rossini (1792–1868)
    Libretto mostly taken from Angelo Anelli's libretto for Luigi Mosca's
opera of the same title (presented at La Scala in Milan, 1808).

L'italiana in Algeri is Rossini's first masterpiece of a full-fledged opera buffa
in two acts, with one of Rossini's most brilliant and original scores, written in
twenty-seven days. The character of Isabella, the female lead, is fully
developed both musically and dramatically. Some of the large ensembles
contain a kind of delightful manic verbal onomatopoeia. It is a *very* funny
opera. The premiere, which Rossini conducted from the harpsichord, proved
a success. It quickly won popular acclaim throughout Italy and was the first of
his operas to be produced in Germany and in Paris. It remains in the
international repertory, and singers such as Teresa Berganza, Marilyn Horne,
Lucia Valentini Terrani, and Agnes Baltsa have been brilliant as Isabella.

Details of Rossini's farces at Teatro San Moisè

La cambiale di matrimonio (The Bill of Marriage), *farsa comica* in one
act, May 1810.
Gioacchino Rossini (1792–1868)
Libretto Gaetano Rossi, after Camillo Federici's play and Checcherini's
libretto for Coccia's opera *Il matrimonio per lettera di cambio* (1807,
Venice).

La cambiale di matrimonio was Rossini's first professional opera, written
when he was only eighteen. The opera already shows indications of his vivid
sense of invention, good technique, and unerring sense of timing.

L'inganno felice (The Happy Deception), *farsa* in one act, January 8,
1812.

Gioacchino Rossini (1792–1868)
Libretto Giuseppe Maria Foppa.

L'inganno felice, Rossini's third professional opera, was his first really popular hit and was played many times during his lifetime. It is not really a farce but rather a dramatic melodrama with buffo elements and contained Rossini's most original music to date.

La scala di seta (The Silk Ladder), *farsa comica* in one act, May 9, 1812.
Gioacchino Rossini (1792–1868)
Libretto Giuseppe Maria Foppa, after de Planard's libretto for Pierre Gaveaux's opera *L'échelle de soie* (1808, Paris).

La scala di seta is a youthful delight, Rossini's fifth opera written when he was twenty. Already he was spinning out beguiling musical lines.

L'occasione fa il ladro (Opportunity Makes a Thief), *burletta per musica* (a joke in music), in one act, November 24, 1812.
Gioacchino Rossini (1792–1868)
Libretto Luigi Prividali, after Eugène Scribe's play *Le Prétendu par hasard, ou L'occasion fait le non* (1810, Paris).

L'occasione fa il ladro, Rossini's seventh opera, is full of wild eccentrics. It is a disguise opera in which the female protagonist changes clothes with her maid to test her suitor's charms.

Il signor Bruschino *(Il signor Bruschino, ossia Il figlio per azzardo)* (Signor Bruschino, or The Son by Accident), *farsa giocosa* in one act, January 27, 1813.
Gioacchino Rossini (1792–1868)
Libretto Giuseppe Maria Foppa, after the play *Le fils par hasard, ou Ruse et folie* by Alissan de Chazet and E. T. Maurice Ourry.

Il signor Bruschino is the last one-act farce that Rossini wrote for Teatro San Moisè. It served Rossini well to have become expert in writing this acerbic kind of short farce, as he used the style in the first acts of some of his later comic operas such as *L'italiana in Algeri.* (All five of these farces can be heard today on one CD, Claves 50–9200.)

LODGING

Since Venice is often very crowded and frenetic, it is *very* important to find the right place to stay and to eat, where you can feel at home and not like a rushing tourist.

Hotel Paganelli, riva degli Schiavoni 4687
tel: (39–41) 522–4324   fax: (39–41) 523–9267
This is a lovely, reasonably priced, old-fashioned hotel with all

comforts (with the exception of an elevator), situated on the bank of the lagoon just to the east of San Marco. Ask for quiet and you will be placed in an interior room, or if you want to see the action, ask for a room facing the lagoon.

Hotel San Moisè, San Marco 2058
tel: (39–41) 520–3755
This hotel is reasonably priced and a stone's throw from La Fenice, as are:

Hotel Kette, San Marco–piscina San Moisè 2053
tel: (41) 520–7766   fax: (41) 522–8964

Hotel San Fantin, campiello de la Fenice 1930/a
tel: (39–41) 523–1401
Open mid-April to November.

Or, for luxury in a very central location, try one of the following hotels that feature prominently in the history of opera in Venice:

Hotel Danieli, riva degli Schiavoni 4196
tel: (39–41) 522–6480   fax: (39–41) 520–0208
The hotel is in the same building as the old Palazzo Dandolo. Most likely Claudio Monteverdi lived here while he was *maestro di cappella* at San Marco and the first performance of his *Il combattimento di Tancredi et Clorinda* most likely took place here as well. Who knows, you might sleep in the room where it was presented!

Hotel Metropole, riva degli Schiavoni 4149
tel: (39–41) 520–5044   fax: (39–41) 522–3679
The hotel is housed in the building of the Conservatorio of the Pietà where Antonio Vivaldi taught.

SNACKS

For an afternoon snack with a coffee, try *torta del doge* or *pan del doge* at any *pasticceria*. It is a rich and wonderful almond cake.

FOOD

Venice has always been famous for its cuisine. The Venetians were the first to use the fork at table and also the first to use fine glass stemware.
Some specialties of Venice are:

fegato alla veneziana (liver and onions Venetian style)
risi e bisi (a fine risotto with peas, butter, and Parmesan)

risotto di peoci (risotto with mussels)

seppie in nero (squid cooked in their ink)

polenta

Pesci alla griglia (grilled fish)

polenta alla griglia (grilled polenta)

baccalà mantecato (cod, mashed and creamed with olive oil; usually served with polenta)

coda di rospo alla griglia (grilled monkfish)

Ask for a Prosecco to drink. It is a simple, lightly effervescent, light white wine, great with all Venetian food.

Two honest, comfortably priced, and wonderful Venetian *trattorie* can be found between campiello Santo Stefano and salizada San Samuele on calle Botteghe:

Trattoria Da Fiore, Santo Stefano 3461, San Marco

tel: (39–41) 523–5310

Closed Tuesdays and the month of August.

And, on the same side of the street, two hundred feet further down on calle Botteghe stands:

Dal Bacharetto, Santo Stefano 3447, San Marco

tel: (39–41) 528–9336

Closed Saturday evening and Sundays and the month of August.

Both restaurants offer the Venetian specialties mentioned above.

Places near Venice of Operatic Interest

The Island of San Michele in the Venetian Lagoon

The Island of San Michele is a real necropolis, a "city" of the dead. In this city, some groups, such as children, or people of different religions, have their own "neighborhoods." In the Eastern Orthodox neighborhood, one finds the grave of Igor Stravinsky near that of Serge Diaghilev, his most famous choreographer (*Le Sacre du printemps, The Firebird, Petruska*).

My first visit to the grave took place on a hot, humid day in early September. I was awed by the enormity of this necropolis, so when I entered the Reparto Greci (Eastern Orthodox) section of the cemetery I was somewhat dazed. I started looking at all the Eastern European names and wondered how long it would take me to find Stravinsky. Then I saw a new pair of pink satin ballet slippers on a gravestone (I knew they were new because for weeks the mid-summer sun had been blasting down on Venice, but the slippers were neither faded nor dried out). It was Diaghilev's grave, engraved in Cyrillic. The marble

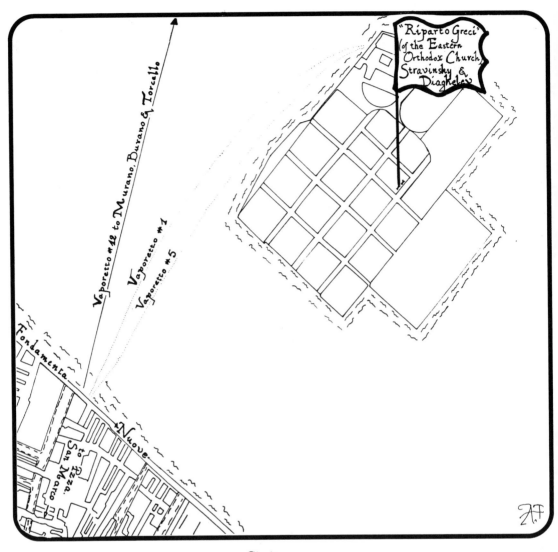

Cimitero

gravestone is carved to resemble a stage with a canopy over it. Then I looked to my right and saw that two nearby graves were swept clean of dust. The stones are simply inscribed Igor Stravinsky and Vera Stravinsky—no dates, no who he was, no what he did. But lying at the top of Igor Stravinsky's grave, held down by four small pebbles, was a scrap of music paper. In pencil someone had written *fagotto* (bassoon) and then the solo bassoon first line of *Le Sacre du printemps*.

A plaque at the entrance to the Reparto Greci says: Stravinsky and Diaghilev. Stravinsky's grave is number 36. Diaghilev's is unnumbered but unmistakable.

From Venice: Take a vaporetto from the Fondamenta Nuove to San Michele and ask the civil servant seated at the entrance of the cemetery for Igor Stravinsky. He will give you a map marking the Orthodox section of the cemetery and the approximate area of Stravinsky's and Diaghilev's graves. He will most likely also mark the grave of Ezra Pound in the Protestant section.

Cimitero (cemetery)
Open daily, 7:30 A.M.–4:00 P.M.

Murano

The island of Murano in the Venetian lagoon was the birthplace of the Venetian librettist Francesco Maria Piave (1810–76), with whom Giuseppe Verdi collaborated on some of his most famous operas between 1844 and 1862: *Ernani, I due Foscari, Macbeth, Il corsaro, Stiffelio (Araldo), Rigoletto, La traviata, Simon Boccanegra,* and *La forza del destino.* In 1859 Piave moved to Milan, where he taught and was stage director for La Scala. When Piave was paralyzed by a stroke in 1869, Verdi contributed to the support of his family, continuing to do so even after Piave's death.

Take the same vaporetto that goes to San Michele. Murano is the next stop.

Portogruaro

Today Portogruaro (forty miles northeast of Venice) is a rather ugly twentieth-century industrial town. Here Lorenzo Da Ponte (1749–1838) attended seminary to become a Catholic priest. Da Ponte was the great librettist with whom Wolfgang Amadeus Mozart collaborated for his best known and most popular "Italian" operas, *Le nozze di Figaro* (1786), *Così fan tutte* (1790), and *Don Giovanni* (1787).

Da Ponte, born a Jew in the nearby town of Ceneda (now called Vittorio Veneto), converted in 1763 and took the name of the bishop of Ceneda. In March 1773 he became a priest after training at the seminary at Portogruaro. In 1776 he was dismissed from the seminary and banned for fifteen years from the city of Venice for having shown a penchant for married women and liberal politics. (Giacomo Casanova, *the* Casanova, took holy orders at the same time at the same seminary!) Da Ponte proceeded to become a very cosmopolitan libertine. From 1781 to 1791 he lived in Vienna where, besides collaborating with Mozart, he also worked with the composers Salieri and Soler.

Da Ponte's librettos are characterized by the musical rhythm of his verses, the verbal depiction of very believable and sympathetic characters, and the rapid unveiling of plot that never allows the action to drop into dead points. His librettos allowed Mozart's genius the freedom to create drama through music. It is not simply by chance that of Mozart's operas these three are the most often performed today, with the possible exception of *Die Zauberflöte* (The Magic Flute).

Da Ponte left Vienna in 1791 and spent some years in Paris and London. In

1805 he moved to New York, establishing himself as a grocer. In 1819 he acquired American citizenship and then became professor of Italian at Columbia College in New York City. He was responsible for the first performance in the New World of Mozart's *Don Giovanni,* in 1827. He died in New York City in 1838.

VERONA

Although Verona presented no premieres of operas in today's standard repertory, the city hosts Italy's most famous summer festival. The Arena di Verona, built in the first century A.D., is second in size only to Rome's Colosseum. The summer festival performances have been going on since 1913, when it celebrated the centenary of Verdi's birth with a performance of *Aïda,* and, with the exception of the war years, 1914–18 and 1943–45, performances at this summer event have attracted thousands each year. Programming remains faithful to traditional operatic repertory. Given the spectacle required by *Aïda,* the Arena of Verona is the perfect place for this opera's presentation and it is almost always on the program. Contrary to what one might think, the acoustics are wonderful and really need no electronic enhancement, though the directors seem to think otherwise.

> **Verona Summer Festival of Opera,** Arena di Verona, Information Office, piazza Bra, 28, 37121 Verona
> tel: (39–45) 590–966 or 590–726 or 590–109
> Two-month season from July through August.

The Teatro Filarmonico, originally constructed from 1715 to 1729, was rebuilt after it burned in 1754, and reconstructed again from 1961 to 1975 after it was destroyed by Allied bombing, February 23, 1945. It has a regular spring and autumn season organized by the Ente Lirico Arena di Verona.

> **Teatro Filarmonico,** via Roma and piazza Bra, 37121 Verona
> tel: (39–45) 590–966

Chiesa dei Filippini, via dei Filippini, across from nos. 21 and 21B, down the street from the old slaughterhouse, on the east side of the Arena, is where Maria Callas married Giovanni Battista Meneghini at the end of 1948, just before she sailed from Genoa for performances in Argentina.

VICENZA

Although no important opera premieres took place here, it is worth a trip to this northern Italian city, situated between Verona and Venice, to see the famed Teatro Olimpico, the final work of the architect Andrea Palladio, born in

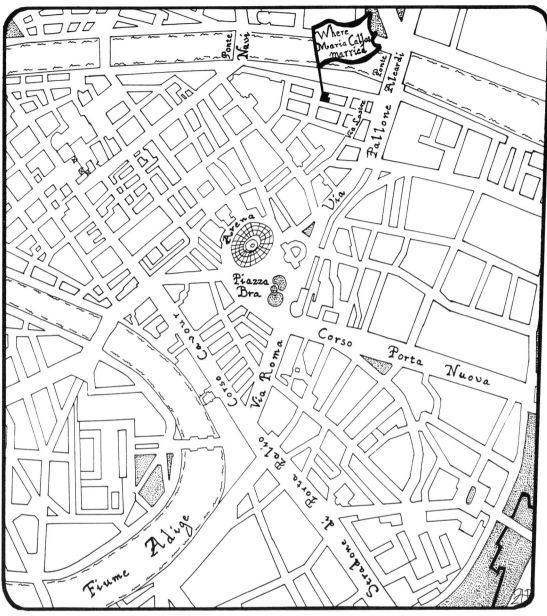

Operatic Verona

Vicenza in 1518. The theatre was inaugurated March 3, 1585. The stage is one of the finest in existence, with its superimposed niches, columns, and statues, and its amazing perspectives painted in trompe-l'oeil by Palladio's pupil Scamozzi. The acoustics are reputed to be the best in the world. The theatre seats 350.

Teatro Olimpico, largo Goethe 3
Open daily, May through October, 9:00 A.M.–noon and 3:00–5:30 P.M.;
November through April, 9:00 A.M.–noon and 3:00–4:00 P.M.

The theatre has only a short musical season during the first two weeks of September. For tickets and program information contact:

Aggenzia Viaggi "A. Palladio," contra Cavour 16, 36100 Vicenza
tel: (39–444) 546–111 or 543-615

AUSTRIA

❧ ❦

VIENNA (Wien)

Vienna, the seat of the Holy Roman Empire from 1558 to 1806, viewed itself as the defender of Christendom against the Ottoman Turks. The empire's boundaries extended south from the middle of the former Yugoslavia, well into Russia on the east, throughout the Czech Republic to the north, and deep into northern Italy and Switzerland on the west. Opera in Vienna was in Italian until the late 1700s when opera in German (*Singspiels*) became popular.

Italian opera was introduced to the Viennese court about 1630. In 1666–67 the Hoftheater auf der Cortina (Theater on the City Wall) was built for the 1668 performance of Antonio Cesti's *Pomo d'oro* (Golden Apple) in honor of the first marriage of Emperor Leopold I. Operas were also performed at court in various rooms in the Hofburg (Imperial Palace), in the city, and in the court's summer residences. The ballroom of the Hofburg, built in 1630, was quickly commandeered for use as an opera theatre, and the Italian architect Francesco Galli-Bibiena was called in to redo the space between 1698 and 1700.

During the Turkish siege of 1683 the Hoftheater auf der Cortina was torn down by the Viennese, who feared that its wooden structure presented too flammable a target for the approaching Turkish armies. The siege failed, leaving Vienna free at last of the Turkish menace and ready to flourish as a center of musical culture. (Viennese bakers celebrated the victory by creating a crescent-shaped roll in imitation of the crescent-shaped sword, a *Türkenschwert,* and the crescent moon of the Islamic flag. Thus was born the croissant, which became a veritable staple of the French diet.)

Actual Viennese opera scores are extant from about 1660 onward. In the early eighteenth century opera seria reigned supreme in Viennese public taste. Pietro Trapassi, known as Metastasio, resided at court. He was *the* librettist who influenced all librettos of opera seria.

151

Operatic Central Vienna

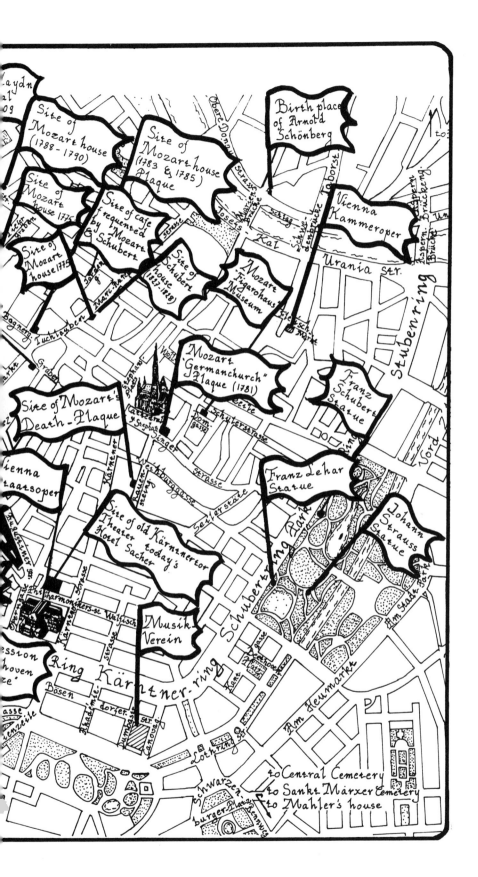

Site of Mozart house (1788-1790)

Site of Mozart house (1783 & 1785) Plaque

Birth place of Arnold Schönberg

Site of Mozart house 1775

Site of café frequented by Mozart & Schubert

Vienna Kammeroper

Site of Mozart house 1775

Site of Schubert house (1822-1818)

Mozart Figarohaus Museum

Urania str.

Stubenring

Mozart "Germanchurch" Plaque (1781)

Franz Schubert Statue

Site of Mozart's Death-Plaque

Vienna Staatsoper

Franz Lehar Statue

Johann Strauss Statue

Site of old Kärntnertor Theater today's Hotel Sacher

Schubertring Park

Musik-Verein

Ring Kärntner-ring

to Central Cemetery
to Sankt Märxer Cemetery
to Mahler's house

The audience of the imperial opera was restricted to members of the court, foreign dignitaries, ambassadors, and high-ranking visitors. But beginning in 1728, ordinary Viennese citizens were allowed to partake in intermezzos at the Kärntnertortheater, presentations that were really *adaptations* of operas—as if the court were bent on denying common citizens an experience identical to its own. After 1741 public opera was also performed at the Burgtheater.

In the late eighteenth century, under Archduke Joseph II, the Viennese public came to embrace opera totally. He hired the great Italian librettist Lorenzo Da Ponte, who, after working with some local composers and the Italian-born Antonio Salieri, successfully collaborated with Wolfgang Amadeus Mozart in three of the greatest operas ever written: *Le nozze di Figaro* (1786), *Don Giovanni* (1787), and *Così fan tutte* (1790). By the end of Joseph's life in 1790, Vienna possessed the finest opera company in Europe.

In 1857 Vienna undertook an enormous public works project designed to "straighten" the Danube where it flowed through the city. During the construction period, numerous canals were dug to bypass areas under renovation. This once-canal-filled region is now called the Prater (the forest), and where the Ferris wheel stands today was then known as "Venice in Vienna" (complete with a specially constructed "Doge's Palace"). A magnificent boulevard, the Ringstrasse, took the place of the medieval fortifications that surrounded the center of Vienna. The Ringstrasse was flanked by most of the important buildings in Vienna: the Parliament, the city hall, the university, major museums, and the opera house (though not the Konzerthaus or the Musikverein). The sumptuous architecture of the buildings that still stand today reflects the splendor of the Hapsburg Empire.

From 1741 to 1888 the first Burgtheater occupied the present site of the Michaeltor in the Michaelerplatz, right across from the Winterreitschule. Following in a grand French tradition, the theatre was originally a tennis court. In 1776 it became known as the Nationaltheater, marking the end of the court's monopoly on theatrical and operatic spectacles presented in Vienna. In 1888 the first Burgtheater was destroyed to make way for the Michaeltor, and the second and present Burgtheater was built. Allied bombing devastated the building in 1945 but after the city was freed from Soviet control in 1955, the theatre was rebuilt to look exactly as it had originally. It is an Italian-style theatre, today considered one of the most prestigious prose theatres in the German-speaking world.

Burgtheatre, Dr.-Karl-Luegger-Ring 2, A–1010 Vienna
tel: (43–1) 5144–42959
metro stop: Schottentor

The first Burgtheater presented the following premieres (full descriptions of some of these premieres are at the end of this chapter) *Il matrimonio segreto* (1792), Domenico Cimarosa; eleven operas by Johann Joseph Fux; sixteen operas

Burgtheater (1850)

by Christoph Willibald Gluck, including: *Alceste* (1767), *Iphigenie auf Tauris* (1781), *Orfeo ed Euridice* (1762); at least six operas by Johann Adolf Hasse; *Così fan tutte* (1790), Wolfgang Amadeus Mozart; *Die Entführung aus dem Serail* (1782), Wolfgang Amadeus Mozart; *Le nozze di Figaro* (1786), Wolfgang Amadeus Mozart; nineteen operas by Antonio Salieri.

The Kärntnertor Theater (also known as the Kaiserlich-Königliches Hofoperntheater nächst dem Kärntnertor) was built in 1709 where the Hotel Sacher now stands, just behind the present opera house. In 1785 Archduke Joseph II created a Deutsche Opéra Comique in the Kärntnertortheater to provide some healthy competition for the Italian opera so adored by the Viennese. Limiting the theatre's repertoire to opera sung only in German lasted just three years, however, after which a more varied bill included performances of both Italian and French opera.

In 1845–46, Hector Berlioz conducted four concerts in the Kärntnertorthea-

The Old Kärntnertortheater

ter, and in 1862–63, Richard Wagner conducted three concerts of excerpts from his operas. The theater avoided falling into bankruptcy in the mid-1860s by presenting the operettas of Jacques Offenbach and their classical Viennese progeny. Finally, the Kärntnertortheater was destroyed in 1870 to make way for the new Kaiserlich-Königliches Hofoperntheater im neuen Haus, which is the original name of today's Staatsoper.

The Kärntnertortheater presented the following premieres (full descriptions of some of these premieres are at the end of this chapter) four operas by Antonio Salieri; *Euryanthe* (1823), Carl Maria von Weber; *Fidelio*, final version, (1814), Ludwig von Beethoven; *Martha* (1847), Friedrich von Flotow; *Die Zwillingsbrüder* (1820), Franz Schubert.

Late in 1785 Mozart was asked by Emperor Joseph II to write a one-act *Singspiel* for presentation in the small theatre in the Orangerie of the Schönbrunn Palace. (A *Singspiel* is an opera in German in which the arias are sung and the dialogue is spoken. *Die Entführung aus dem Serail* and *Die Zauberflöte* are famous examples of the form.) The premiere of Mozart's *Der Schauspieldirektor* (The Impresario) took place February 7, 1786. Also premiered that same evening was Antonio Salieri's opera *Prima la musica e poi le parole* (First the Music, Then the Words).

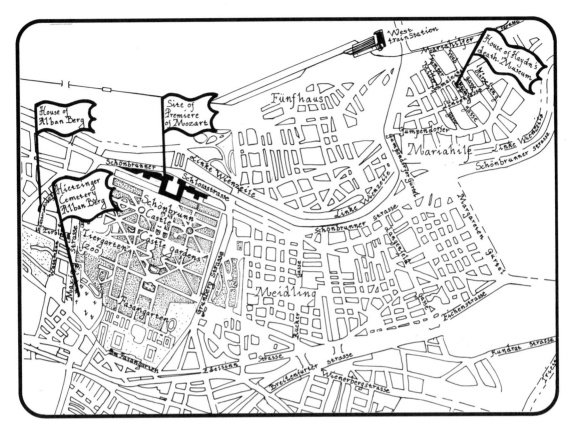

Operatic Vienna, near Schönbrunn Palace

Schönbrunn Palace, Schönbrunner Schloss Strasse 47, A–1130 Vienna
tel: (43–1) 811–130
metro stop: Schönbrunn or number 10 or 58 tram
Open April 1 through October 30, daily, 8:30 A.M.–5:00 P.M.; October
31 through March 31, daily, 8:30 A.M.–4:30 P.M.

Each summer Mozart operas are regularly performed in the
Schönbrunn Park.

The present-day Staatsoper, originally called the Hofoper because it was the
royal opera house, was built between 1861 and 1869. Modeled after Palais
Garnier, the Paris Opera, the building echoes the grandeur of the Hapsburg
Empire.

On May 25, 1869, the theater was inaugurated with *Don Giovanni* (sung in
German). By the end of the nineteenth century, it was one of the foremost
musical institutions in all of Europe. The works of Wagner and Verdi were
principal in the repertory and, in 1891, Pietro Mascagni came to conduct his
Cavalleria rusticana.

But Gustav Mahler, director of the theater from 1897 to 1907, made the
Vienna State Opera the finest in the world. Mahler enhanced the usual
repertoire—Wagner, Verdi, Mozart, and Beethoven—with works by Puccini,

Leoncavallo, Bizet, Saint-Saëns, Richard Strauss, Charpentier, and Tchaikovsky. This repertory Mahler championed has turned out to be, more or less, the standard repertory of the late twentieth century.

Just as Arturo Toscanini did a few years later in Milan, Mahler made radical procedural changes: He abolished the claque, banned seating latecomers after the beginning of an act, and forbade applause until an act's end. Like Toscanini, Mahler attempted to discipline the public, making audiences pay opera the respect the art form deserved. He was totally dedicated to the search for perfection and truthful interpretation, causing his orchestra to view him as something of a megalomaniac. He said his goal was to "frighten each musician into abandoning his little ego and to soar above himself." Also like Toscanini, Mahler had many enemies, but unlike the Italian master, Mahler was Jewish; the anti-Semitism that flourished inside and outside the company provided the final impetus that forced him to resign. Mahler was followed by a list of distinguished conductors: Felix Weingartner (1908–11); Richard Strauss (1919–24); Clemens Krauss (1929–34), who brought Alban Berg's *Wozzeck* to the theater in 1930; and Bruno Walter (1936–38).

After World War I the theatre changed its name from the Hofoper (Court Opera) to the Staatsoper (Vienna State Opera).

The Hofoper and the Staatsoper premiered (details of some of these premieres are at the end of this section) *Ariadne auf Naxos*, second version (1916), Richard Strauss (for first version, see Stuttgart, page 308); *Die Frau ohne Schatten* (1919), Richard Strauss; *Oedipus Rex*, staged version (1928), Igor Stravinsky; *Werther*, in German (1892), Jules Massenet.

Vienna Staatsoper

In March 1938, after the *Anschluss*, the Staatsoper was "Nazified" (*gleichgeschaltet*). About a month before the end of the war, on March 12, 1945, the building suffered a direct hit by Allied bombs, leaving only the façade, the loggia, and the great staircase. The theater was rebuilt and reopened in 1955 with a performance of Ludwig van Beethoven's *Fidelio*, conducted by Karl Böhm. Herbert von Karajan directed the Staatsoper from 1956 to 1964.

On afternoons when no rehearsals are in progress, conducted tours are offered to the Marmorsaal, the Schwind Foyer, which holds a bronze bust of Gustav Mahler by Auguste Rodin, and the Gobelinsaal, where Rudolf Eisenmenger's *Zauberflöte* tapestries are on display. The grand staircase is similar in style to that of the Paris Opera. A window for enquiries is located at the west side of the building.

The theatre holds 2,200 people (1,650 seated and 550 standing). The standing room on the ground floor includes some of the best space in the house! The opera season extends from September through June.

Vienna Staatsoper, Opernring 2, A–1010
metro stop: Karlsplatz
Staatsoper information:
Kärntner Strasse 40, A–1010 Vienna
tel: (43–1) 514–44–2960   tel, credit card sales: (43–1) 513–1513
Open 10:00 A.M. until one hour before the performance begins; Saturday, 10:00 A.M.–noon; and the first Saturday of each month and all Saturdays of Advent, 10:00 A.M.–5:00 P.M.

Advance booking by mail can be made no sooner than a month and no later than three weeks before the performance by writing to:

Osterreicher Bundestheaterverband, Bundestheaterkassen (ticket office), Hanuschgasse 3, A–1010 Vienna

Advance booking by telephone: tel: (43–1) 513–1513, Monday–Friday, 10:00 A.M.–6:00 P.M.; the first Saturday of each month and Saturdays during Advent, 10:00 A.M.–5:00 P.M.   Or call Wien-Ticket, tel: (43–1) 58–885. American Express, Visa, MasterCard, Diners Club accepted.

Since the operators of all the city's opera houses are quite often busy, the best way to be absolutely sure to get the tickets you want is to contact:

Austrobus, Opernpassage
tel: (43–1) 5341–1211
These tickets are slightly more expensive but worth it because Austrobus buys up blocks of good seats in advance.

The actor, librettist, singer, and impresario Emanuel Schikaneder became head of Theater auf der Weiden in 1789. One of his first acts was to commission

Wolfgang Amadeus Mozart to compose *Die Zauberflöte* (The Magic Flute) based on Schikaneder's own libretto. (Schikaneder also played the first Papageno, the *Magic Flute*'s birdcatcher.) When Mozart's wife Constanze fell ill and had to leave her young husband alone in Vienna, Schikaneder, a fellow Freemason, kept an eye on the composer and lent him his house near the theater where he could compose and relax with his circle of friends. This little dwelling, the Zauberflötenhäuschen, now nestles in the gardens behind the Mozarteum in Salzburg. (See Salzburg, page 186.)

Theater auf der Weiden burned down in 1801 and was replaced the same year by Theater an der Wien, destined to become the most congenial home for quintessential Viennese operetta. Operetta was first introduced to Vienna in 1864, when Jacques Offenbach's *Die Rheinnixen* (The Rhine Fairies) captured the hearts and minds of the music-loving Viennese. Johann Strauss II wrote *Die lustigen Weiber von Wien* (The Merry Wives of Vienna) in 1868, and the Viennese demonstrated their enthusiasm for operetta by embracing the tradition Offenbach had begun in Paris, carrying it on to make operetta synonymous with Vienna.

Theater an der Wien was used for Staatsoper productions from 1945 to 1955, during that theatre's postwar renovation. Theatre an der Wien was itself renovated in 1962. The theatre's original front door on Millöckergasse, at the intersection of Papagenogasse, is domed by a Papageno portal, a marble depiction of the *Magic Flute*'s birdcatcher.

A plaque on the wall also indicates that Beethoven lived above the theatre when completing the first version of *Fidelio* and other pieces:

Ludwig van Beethoven	Ludwig van Beethoven
Wohnte im Theater an	Lived in the Theater an
Der Wien 1803 und 1804.	Der Wien from 1803 to 1804.
Teile seiner Oper, der	Parts of his opera, the
Dritten Symphonie und	Third Symphony, and
Der Kreutzersonate	The Kreutzer Sonata
Sind hier entstanden	Were composed here.
Fidelio *und andere Werke*	*Fidelio* and other works
Erlebten in diesem Haus	Were premiered in
Ihre Uraufführung.	This house.

Theater auf der Weiden and Theater an der Wien premiered (details of some premieres at end of section) *Die Zauberflöte* (1791), Wolfgang Amadeus Mozart; *Fidelio*, first version (1805), Ludwig van Beethoven; *Fidelio*, second version (1806), Ludwig van Beethoven; thirteen operettas by Johann Strauss, including *Die Fledermaus* (1874), *Der Zigeunerbaron* (1885); eight operettas by Emmerich Kálmán, including *Gräfin Mariza* (1924); thirteen operettas by Franz Lehár, including *Die lustige Witwe* (1905); *Die Zauberharfe* (1820), Franz Schubert; one opera by Antonio Salieri (1804).

Today Theater an der Wien hosts a summer festival in May and June and presents musicals and occasional operettas during the rest of the year.

Theater an der Wien, Linke Wienzeile 6
tel: (43–1) 5883–0588   fax (43–1) 588–3033
metro stop: Kettenbrückengasse

The Volksoper stands on the Gürtel, the outer Ring, and opened in 1898 to perform popular repertory works, including the Viennese premieres of *Tosca* in 1907 and *Salome* in 1910, after both operas had been rejected by the censors of the Hofoper (present Staatsoper). It also presented the world premiere of Arnold Schoenberg's one-act opera *Die glücklische Hand* (The Lucky Hand), October 19, 1924.

Given the name Städtische Volksoper in 1938, the theater today is called the Wiener Volksoper. It is open ten months a year and presents Viennese operetta, American musicals, and an occasional standard repertory opera.

Wiener Volksoper, Währinger Strasse 78, A–1090 Vienna
tel: (43–1) 5144–43318
metro stop: Währinger Strasse or Volksoper

The original Theatre in der Josefstadt was built in 1788, then replaced in 1822. To celebrate this 1822 opening, Ludwig van Beethoven wrote an overture, *Weihe des Hauses* (The Consecration of the House). In 1857 the theatre hosted Vienna's first production of an opera by Richard Wagner: *Tannhäuser.* The famous Max Reinhardt directed the theatre from 1924 to 1935. Today Theater in der Josefstadt presents plays and light comedies.

Theater in der Josefstadt, Josefstädter Strasse, 26
tel: (43–1) 402–5127
metro stop: Rathaus

Vienna was birthplace or home to an astonishing roster of composers. Every place with some historic importance in the city and its surroundings has a red-and-white flag hanging out in front, usually just above the plaque identifying the house. Following are some places of particular operatic interest.

Ludwig van Beethoven (December 17, 1770, Bonn, Germany—March 26, 1827, Vienna) lived in Vienna from 1792 until his death in 1827. Beethoven's one opera, *Fidelio,* remains very much a part of the standard international repertory. The first version was premiered in 1805, the same year and month Napoleon's armies conquered Vienna. The poignancy of the plot—a woman who overcomes the tyrannical power of a despot to save the man she loves—is very much a story of its time. A plaque on the original front of Theater an der Wien, beneath the Papageno Portal, attests that Beethoven, watched over by Emanuel Schikaneder, lived in rooms over the theater while completing the first version of *Fidelio.* (See page 159.)

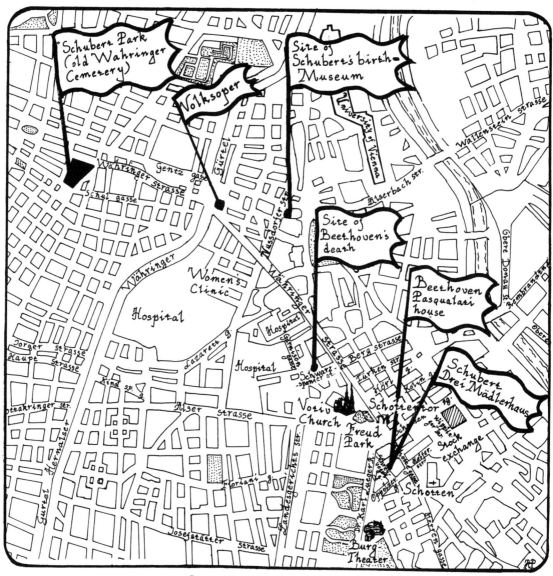

Operatic Northwestern Vienna

Theater an der Wien (original entrance), Millöckergasse at the corner of Papagenogasse

The Pasqualatihaus: Beethoven lived here off and on between 1804 and 1815. He composed at least some of *Fidelio*, and made all the opera's revisions, while residing here. His fourth-floor apartment now holds a small Beethoven Museum. Included in it is a life mask made in 1811–12 and a portrait of Beethoven's patron Andreas Razumovsky (the famous count to whom Beethoven's String Quartets opus 59 are dedicated). Especially moving is a Beethoven portrait by Willibord Joseph Mähler painted in 1804–05. The new Burgtheater stands nearby.

A plaque states that the Viennese playwright Franz Grillparzer also lived here in 1808.

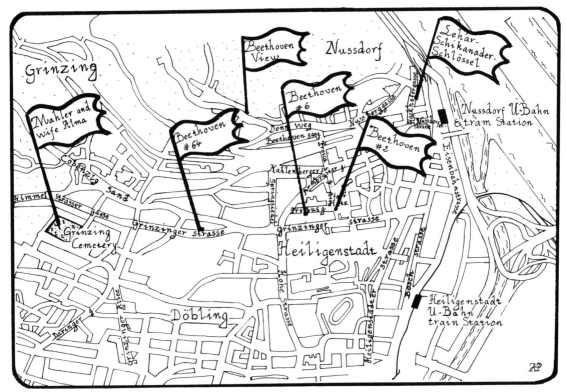

Operatic Heiligenstadt-Grinzing-Nussdorf

Pasqualatihaus Beethoven Museum, Mölker-Bastei 8 (at the top of the steps)
tel: (43–1) 535–8905
Open Tuesday–Sunday, 9:00 A.M.–12:15 P.M. and 1:00–4:30 P.M.
metro stop: Schottentor

In 1802 Beethoven lived in the village of Heiligenstadt, just northeast of Vienna, at Probusgasse 6. Here, suffering great despair over his increasing deafness, he wrote his *Heiligenstadt Testament* as a letter to his brothers and completed his Symphony no. 2. The house now hosts a small museum that exhibits rather ordinary things relating to the time that Beethoven spent in the village.

Heiligenstadt Testament House (Beethoven Museum), Probusgasse 6, Grinzing
Open Tuesday and Wednesday, Saturday and Sunday, 9:00 A.M.–noon and 1:30–4:30 P.M. (Call first to make sure it will be open!)
tel: (43–1) 318–8608
metro stop: Heiligenstadt, U4 from Vienna, then the 38A bus to the Grinzing Center stop.

Beethoven also lived a few hundred feet west at Grinzingerstrasse 64. In 1817, he again stayed in Heiligenstadt, adjacent to the Jacobkirche at Pfarrplatz 2,

163

during his vexing struggle to adopt his late brother's son Karl. Beethoven frequently walked in the surrounding woods, and to honor those walks a Beethovengasse and an Eroicagasse have been designated to the north of the village. Eroicagasse crosses the Schreiberbach, the north bank of which is called the Beethoven Gang, or Beethoven Ruhe (Beethoven's peace). A statue of the composer dating from 1863 distinguishes the site.

(To take a beautiful morning stroll, catch the D Tram from the Kärntner Ring/Oper to Nussdorf. See the Lehár/Schikaneder Haus on Hackhofergasse; walk down the Beethoven Gang along the stream; take Eroicagasse to Heiligenstadt to visit Beethoven's two houses there; then go on to his house on Grinzingerstrasse, finally stopping to visit Mahler's grave in the Grinzing Cemetery.)

March 26, 1827, Beethoven died in Vienna at Schwarzpannierstrasse 15, a house demolished in 1903. His body was carried to the Pfarrkirche in the Alserstrasse where his funeral was attended by a large crowd. He was buried in the Währinger Cemetery, but in 1888 his body was exhumed and transferred to the new Zentralfriedhof. The deconsecrated Währinger Cemetery is now called the Schubert Park.

A large Beethoven frieze, which some see as a testimonial to the composer's spirit, was painted by the Secessionist painter Gustav Klimt for the fourteenth exhibition of the Secession (the movement away from traditional artistic forms) in 1902. The Secession Building, on Operngasse, and the frieze in the basement were heavily damaged in World War II. Both were renovated and reinaugurated in January 1986.

Alban Berg (February 9, 1885, Vienna—December 24, 1935, Vienna), the composer of the twentieth-century operatic masterpiece *Wozzeck* (1925), lived in Heitzing at Trauttmannsdorffgasse 27. Heitzing, once a village, is now a part of Vienna just outside the western edge of the Schönbrunn Palace (see map, page 157).

Berg is buried in the Heitzingfriedhof, connected to the grounds of the Schönbrunn Palace. Other twentieth-century notables in the arts buried here are the painter Gustav Klimt; the dramatist Franz Grillparzer, and Otto Wagner of Secession fame.

Christoph Willibald Gluck conducted the private orchestra of Prince von Sachsen-Hildburghausen in the Auersperg Palace in Auerspergstrasse 1. He was married in the Ulrichskirche, which stands in Sankt-Ulrichs-Platz.

Joseph Haydn (March 31, 1732, Rohrau—May 31, 1809, Vienna) wrote twenty-five operas, most premiering in the opera house at the country residence of his employer, Prince Nikolaus I, in Eszterháza. Haydn and his brother Michael (1737–1806) were born in the nearby village of Rohrau, about five miles south of Vienna's airport. The house, now a Haydn Museum, was destroyed by fire in 1899 and has been completely rebuilt. Haydn's parents—his mother was the cook at the Schloss Rohrau—are buried in the village cemetery.

From the 1740s to 1755, while studying with the Italian composer Nicola Porpora (1686–1768), Haydn lived in a Viennese garret located at the corner of Kohlmarkt and Michaelerplatz. A plaque there states:

In diesem Hause wohnte	By 1750, Joseph Haydn
Joseph Haydn	Had been living in this house
Seit 1750 durch mehrere Jahre.	For several years.
Gewidmet von der geselschaft	Dedicated by the Society
Der Musik Freunde in Wien.	Of the Friends of Music, Vienna.

After the lucrative years Haydn spent in London composing for that city's first subscription concert series, he returned to Vienna. He was finally able to purchase a house, at Haydngasse 19, where he lived from 1797 until his death in 1809. The house is now a small but choice Haydn Museum, containing many interesting things from Haydn's life, including a wonderful depiction of the bombardment of Vienna on May 11 and 12, 1809, by Napoleon's troops. And, for reasons unexplained, one room of the museum is devoted to mementos belonging to Johannes Brahms (1833–97).

Haydn Museum, Haydngasse 19
tel: (43–1) 596–1307
Open Tuesday–Sunday, 9:00 A.M.–noon and 1:00–4:30 P.M.
metro stop: Zieglergasse

Although Haydn is buried at Eisenstadt, a memorial service was given for him on June 15, 1809, in Vienna's Schottenkirche (the Scottish Church), Freyung 6. Mozart's *Requiem* was performed and the French writer Stendhal was in attendance. The Schottenkirche is open daily, usually from 7:00 A.M. to 9:00 P.M. Call to make certain of hours.

Schottenkirche, Schottenstift, Freyung 6
tel: (43–1) 534–98
metro stop: Schottentor

The poet-librettist Pietro Trapassi, known to the world as Pietro Metastasio (January 3, 1698, Rome—April 12, 1782, Vienna), came to Vienna in 1730 to be court poet. From 1725 until well into the nineteenth century, more than *three hundred* composers made use of his twenty-seven opera seria librettos! He was buried in the crypt of the Michaelerkirche. A monument stands in the right (south) aisle of the Minoritenkirche, the national church of Italy in Vienna.

Minoritenkirche, Minoritenplatz 2
tel: (43–1) 533–4162
metro stop: Herrengasse

The great composer and conductor Gustav Mahler (July 7, 1860, Kaliste, Bohemia—May 18, 1911, Vienna) lived from 1898 to 1909 at Rennweg 5, near

Schwarzenbergerplatz, but no flag or plaque marks the building. Mahler is buried in the Grinzing Cemetery in the village of Grinzing. His grave can be found in group 7, row 2 (the first grave in the row between the signs saying *Gruppe* 6 and *Gruppe VII*). The tombstone was designed by the Secessionist sculptor Josef Hoffmann. Mahler's wife, Alma Mahler Werfel (1879–1964), is also buried here (group 6, row 6), right behind Mahler's tomb.

To get to Grinzing, Take the D Tram from in front of the Staatsoper, direction Nussdorf, to Heiligenstadt, or the U4 to Heiligenstadt and then the 38A bus, direction Kahlenberg (see map, page 163).

The town of Grinzing is most famous for its *Heurigen*, which celebrate the local white wine. An authentic *Heurige* is an unpretentious bistro run by vintners and offering a buffet. A pine branch hung on a pole at the door indicates that vintage wine is served. But beware, the wine is particularly deadly to those subject to hangovers!

Wolfgang Amadeus Mozart (January 27, 1756, Salzburg—December 5, 1791, Vienna). Six of his twenty operas received their premieres in Vienna *Bastien und Bastienne* (1768), Friedrich Anton Mesmer's house; *Die Entführung aus dem Serail* (1782), Burgtheater; *Der Schauspieldirektor* (1786), Orangerie, Schönbrunn Palace; *Le nozze di Figaro* (1786), Burgtheater; *Così fan tutte* (1790), Burgtheater; *Die Zauberflöte* (1791), Theater auf den Weiden.

(Four others were premiered in Salzburg; three in Milan; two in Munich; one, posthumously, in Frankfurt; two in Prague; and two are incomplete.)

From 1781 until his death in 1791, Mozart lived in twelve houses in Vienna. Only two are still standing. One is in the Deutschechordenskirche (Church of the Teutonic Order), at Singerstrasse 7. In the passageway on the right, before the courtyard, a plaque says that Mozart stayed here briefly in the spring of 1781.

Wolfgang Amadeus Mozart	Wolfgang Amadeus Mozart
Wohnte im Deutschen Hause	Lived in the German House
Vom 16 Marz bis zum 21 Mai	From March 16 to May 21
1781.	1781.

The other is the Figarohaus, where Mozart lived from 1784 to 1787 and composed *Le nozze di Figaro*. Today the house is a Mozart Museum containing manuscripts and drawings of several premieres of Mozart's operas.

Figarohaus Museum, Domgasse 5
tel: (43–1) 513–6294
Open daily, 9:00 A.M.–12:15 P.M. and 1:00–4:30 P.M.
metro stop: Stefansplatz

Mozart spent much of his life in Vienna in the small area framed by Wipplingerstrasse in the north, Kohlmarkt in the south, Tiefer Graben in the west, and Rauhensteingasse in the east.

In 1762 the Mozart family, Wolfgang, his older sister Maria Anna—

nicknamed Nannerl—and his father Leopold, made their first trip to Vienna from Salzburg so that the children could perform in the capital. By royal command they appeared in the Mirror Gallery of the Schönbrunn Palace, the summer palace, where they performed before Maria Theresa and the whole royal family. The story goes that after playing, Mozart flung himself into the lap of Maria Theresa and gave her a kiss. The whole court was beguiled by the confident little six-year-old. The story goes on: when he slipped on the floor, a little girl helped him up. He was heard to say, "When I grow up, I will marry you." The little girl was Maria Theresa's daughter Marie-Antoinette.

The home of Friedrich Anton Mesmer, near Stefansplatz, was the setting for the premiere of Mozart's *Bastien und Bastienne,* sometime between September and October of 1768. Mesmer was the Austrian doctor from whose name the term *mesmerism* derives. He purported—apparently very convincingly—that electricity in the form of magnetism could cure the sick; to achieve this end, he advised stroking the diseased person's body with magnets. By the 1780s his theories were all the rage throughout Europe. Think of how Mozart and Da Ponte playfully quote the good doctor's work in *Così fan tutte* when Despina uses a magnet to cure the sick lovers!

When Mozart and his father came to Vienna in 1775, they lived at Tiefer Graben 18.

In 1781 Mozart lived at Tuchlauben 6, in the family home of his future father-in-law Fridolin Weber, a music copyist and a member of the chorus at the court theatre. Initially Mozart had been enamored of Weber's daughter Aloysia, but she married and went off to pursue an excellent singing career. So Mozart transferred his affections to her sister Constanze.

In September 1781, after the first performances of *Die Entführung aus dem Serail,* he moved to a third-floor apartment on the site of nearby Graben 8, where he lived until July 1782, a month before his marriage to Constanze on August 4, 1782, in Vienna's Cathedral of St. Stephen.

A plaque attests to the fact that Mozart lived at both no. 3 and no. 4 Jordangasse in 1783 and 1785, respectively.

From mid–1788 to September 1790, Mozart resided at Wipplingerstrasse 16. Of an evening Mozart often performed casually at the Frauenhuber café, today the oldest coffeehouse in Vienna. It is in the city's center, just off Kärntnerstrasse. He also relaxed and played billiards at the café-billiard hall Zur ungarischen Krone (The Hungarian Crown), which then occupied the corner of Himmelpfortgasse and Seilerstätte. Some years later Franz Schubert enjoyed billiards there too.

Mozart lived from September 1790 until his death on December 5, 1791, at Rauhensteingasse 8. A plaque there states:

In dieser Stelle	At this site
Stand bis 1849	until 1849 stood
Das Haus im welchem	The house where

MOZART   MOZART
Am 5 Dezember 1791 On December 5, 1791
gestorben ist. Died.

In this apartment he composed much of *Die Zauberflöte* and *La clemenza di Tito*, and worked on a commissioned *Requiem* that turned out to be his own. When Mozart died, Constanze was too ill to attend his funeral. The family could not afford a private burial, so Mozart's remains were consigned to an unmarked communal grave in the tiny Sankt-Marxer-Friedhof (Cemetery of Saint Mark). A monument to the left of the cemetery's main walk pays late tribute to the great musician.

Sankt-Marxer-Friedhof, (just west of Rennweg at the Sankt-Marxer-Friedhof tram stop, on the way to the central cemetery), Leberstrasse, 6 Open 7:00 A.M.–6:00 P.M. (7:00 P.M. in the summer)

Since 1953 a statue of Mozart, completed in 1896 by the sculptor Viktor Tilgner, has graced the Burggarten, just inside the Ringstrasse entrance in back of the Staatsoper.

Mozart Memorial Sankt-Marxer-Friedhof

South of Vienna the spa town of Baden has a memorial museum to both Mozart and Beethoven.

Antonio Salieri (August 18, 1750, Legnano, Italy—May 7, 1825, Vienna; see Italy, page 71), who endures in infamy in the minds of those influenced by the 1984 film *Amadeus,* lived in Vienna from 1766 and was principal court composer from 1774 to 1804.

The village of Nussdorf, like Grinzing famed for its *Heurigen,* hosts a small museum at Hackhohergasse 18 in the baroque building where the librettist, actor, singer, director, composer Emanuel Schikaneder (September 1, 1751, Straubing, Austria—September 21, 1812, Vienna) lived in the early 1800s. Schikaneder, an extraordinarily versatile artist, wrote the libretto of *Die Zauberflöte,* performed as Papageno in the opera's premiere, and directed the theatre in which the tour de force took place. The composer Franz Lehár (*Die lustige Witwe*) lived in the same house in the late nineteenth century.

Lehár-Schikaneder-Schlössel, Hackhohergasse 19, Nussdorf
tel: 371–8213 (call to make sure it is open)
tram stop: from the Staatsoper take Tram D to Nussdorf

Arnold Schoenberg (September 13, 1874, Vienna—July 13, 1951, Los Angeles), considered the leader of the Second Viennese School and the inventor of the system of twelve-tone music, was born on Obere Donaustrasse 5. In the late nineteenth century, the area was called "Matzoh Island" because the quarter to the northeast of the Donau Kanal (Danube Canal) was predominantly Jewish.

The only composer of the First Viennese School born and bred in Vienna was Franz Schubert (January 31, 1797, Vienna—November 19, 1828, Vienna). He spent his entire short life in and around Vienna. Although most people do not know it, Schubert wrote over fifteen operas. Two were premiered in Vienna during his lifetime, but thirteen were performed only after his early death.

Schubert was born at Nussdorferstrasse 54 near the Volksoper, where a small museum now celebrates a Schuberts Geburtshaus at the sign of the Red Crayfish, or Haus zum roten Krebs.

Schubert Geburtshaus Museum, Nussdorferstrasse 54
Open daily 9:00 A.M.–noon and 1:30–4:30 P.M.

In 1801 the Schubert family moved to nearby Saulengasse 3.

From 1808 to 1813 while he was a member of the Vienna Boys Choir, Schubert boarded at the Universitätskirche (also called the Jesuitenkirche) on Dr-Ignaz-Seipel-Platz 1.

Schubert and his friends frequented the Anker Tavern in the Grünankergasse, which was named after the tavern. They also gathered at Caféhaus Bogner, which occupied the corner of Singerstrasse and Blutgasse.

Just around the corner from the Beethoven Pasqualatihaus at Mölker-Bastei 8 stands the Dreimäderlhaus, where, legend has it, Schubert had three sweethearts.

Dreimäderlhaus, Schreyvogelgasse 10

Schubert lived from mid-February 1827 until September 1828 on the second floor at Tuchlauben 16–18. He moved on to Kettenbrückegasse 6, near the Naschmarkt, only to die in his new home on November 19, 1828, at the age of thirty-one. His death was attributed to typhus. The apartment has been newly renovated and bears a plaque:

> *In diesem Hause starb am 19*   In this house, on the 19 of
> *November 1828 der Tondichter*   November 1828, died the composer
> *Franz Schubert.*   Franz Schubert.

Schubert's Todeshaus, Kettenbrückegasse 6 (second floor)
Open weekdays 9:00 A.M.–12:15 P.M. and 1:30–4:30 P.M.
    The Schubert Institute (Internationales Franz Schubert Institut) occupies the floor below.

Schubert was buried in the Währinger Friedhof (now called the Schubertpark). His body was exhumed and transferred to the Zentralfriedhof (Central Cemetery) after it opened in 1874.
    The Waltz King Johann Strauss II (October 25, 1825, Vienna—June 3, 1899, Vienna) lived in Prater on Praterstrasse 54.
    When he was sixty years old, Richard Strauss retired as music director of the Vienna Staatsoper, a position he had held from 1919 to 1924. At the retirement ceremony he received the keys to the city and a plot of land in the Belvedere, where he built a sumptuous villa.
    At the beginning of Kärntnerstrasse, just across from the Staatsoper, the Erzherzog Karl Hotel once stood. Both Carl Maria von Weber (for the premiere of his opera *Euryanthe*) and Richard Wagner stayed there while in Vienna.
    Finally, a stroll through the Zentralfriedhof offers anyone interested in operatic history a veritable Who-was-Who in Vienna:
    Enter the cemetery from the *Zweite Tur* (second door). The cemetery is laid out in groups. Many composers, performers, and other famous artists are in *Group 32A.*

Group 32A contains the graves of:

> Ludwig van Beethoven, no. 29 (1770, Bonn—1827, Vienna; his mortal
>   remains were moved to the Central Cemetery when it opened in 1874)
> Johannes Brahms, no. 26 (1833, Hamburg—1897, Vienna)
> Christoph Willibald Gluck—his other name, Ritter von Gluck, appears
>   on the gravestone no. 49 (1714, Erasbach, Upper Palatinate—1787,
>   Vienna)
> Franz Schubert, no. 28 (1797, Vienna—1828, Vienna)

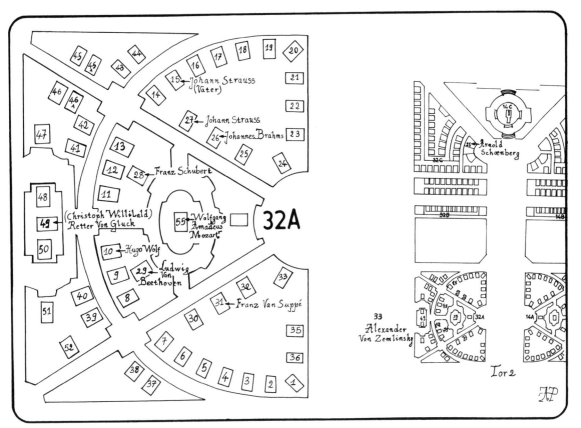

Musical Map of the Central Cemetery

Johann Strauss, father, no. 10 (1804, Vienna—1849, Vienna)

Johann Strauss, son, no. 27 (1825, Vienna—1899, Vienna)

Franz von Suppé, the first master of the Viennese operetta, no. 31 (1819, Split, Istria—1895, Vienna)

Hugo Wolf, no. 10 (1860, Windischgraz, now called Slovenj Gradec, Slovenia—1903, Vienna)

A monument to Wolfgang Amadeus Mozart, no. 55 (1756, Salzburg—1791, Vienna); although he was buried in the Sankt-Marxer Friedhof, the precise site is unknown

Arnold Schoenberg (1874, Vienna–1951, Los Angeles) is buried in *Group 32C*, no. 21A. His mortal remains were brought back to the city of his birth. Alexander Zemlinsky (1871, Vienna—1942, Larchmont, New York), Viennese composer of thirteen operas, was also brought back to his birthplace for burial in *Group 33G*.

Details of some Burgtheater premieres

Alceste, tragedia in three acts, December 26, 1767.
Christoph Willibald Gluck (July 2, 1714, Erasbach, Upper Palatinate—November 15, 1787, Vienna)
Libretto de' Calzabigi, based on Euripides.

Gluck attempted to reform opera by replacing the complicated story lines and excessively florid style of opera seria with plots and music of noble simplicity. *Alceste* was a great success, and its first Viennese run had more than sixty performances. Then for a 1770 revival of the opera in Vienna, Gluck rewrote the tenor role of Admeto, Alceste's husband, for a castrato. Today the role is usually sung by a tenor. As he often did, the cosmopolitan Gluck wrote one version of this opera in Italian for Vienna and another in French (*Alcestes*) for the Paris Opera (see page 196). This Italian version was written first, and although both are about the same subject, they are completely distinct operas.

Così fan tutte, *ossia la scuola degli amanti* (Women Are All the Same, or The School for Lovers), *opera buffa* in two acts, January 26, 1790.
Wolfgang Amadeus Mozart (January 27, 1756, Salzburg—December 5, 1791, Vienna)
Libretto Lorenzo Da Ponte.

Così fan tutte was a commission from Archduke Joseph II on a subject he chose himself, inspired by an anecdote then making the rounds of the salons of Vienna. In the story, a cynical and world-weary Don Alfonso wagers two young men deeply in love, Guglielmo and Ferrando, that Fiordiligi and Dorabella will not be faithful to them should they meet some charming "foreigners." Da Ponte rapidly put together a libretto and Mozart composed the music between August 1789 and the beginning of 1790. The premiere had a favorable reception, but the work seems to have been considered merely a light comedy. It is, however, the most complex drama of the Mozart–Da Ponte collaboration, with a subtly cruel text. Quite frequently the public regards it as amusing and fails to see it as a thought-provoking drama. Joseph II died two months after the premiere. He had been a reliable protector and his death was a blow to Mozart. The new emperor, Leopold II, retained Mozart's services but paid little actual attention to him. *Così* remains in the standard repertory to this day.

Die Entführung aus dem Serail, *Singspiel* in three acts, July 16, 1782.
Wolfgang Amadeus Mozart (1756–91)
Libretto Christoph Friedrich Bretzner, *Belmont und Constanze, oder Die Entführung aus dem Serail,* adapted and enlarged by Gottlieb Stephanie the Younger.

Die Entführung aus dem Serail was the first operatic commission Mozart received in Vienna after he had provoked the Archbishop of Salzburg into dismissing him from his position of organist and composer at the Salzburg Residenz earlier in the year. It was also his first opera in German and the one that made his operatic reputation outside Austria. Immediately after the premiere in Vienna, a new production was mounted in Prague, notwithstanding Joseph II's supposed remark, "Too many notes, my dear Mozart."

Prague took to the opera with a passion, and within the year there were productions in Warsaw, Bonn, Frankfurt, and Leipzig.

Through his sensational musical characterization Mozart turned the character of Osmin into a much more interesting and menacing character than he is in the libretto alone. The zany plot concerns young Belmonte's efforts to rescue his love, Konstanze, and her two servants, Blonde and Pedrillo, who have been captured by Osmin and taken to the seraglio of the Pasha Selim. The libretto, a serious comedy, cleverly touches on the Viennese interest in things Turkish (after Turkey's unsuccessful 1683 siege of Vienna) and general Western anxieties concerning certain Turkish customs. It contains sentiments basic to the Enlightenment, such as brotherly love, and presents a rather feminist point of view on the part of Konstanze and her maidservant, Blonde. The opera is delightful and contains some of Mozart's most inspired music. It is often performed today throughout the world.

Iphigenie auf Tauris, *tragédie* in four acts (Gluck's reworking of *Iphigénie en Tauride,* which had received its first premiere at the Paris Opera, May 18, 1779), October 23, 1781.
Christoph Willibald Gluck (1714–87)
Libretto Nicolas-François Guillard, based on Guymond de la Touche's *Iphigénie en Tauride,* itself based on Euripides, and translated into German by Johann Baptist von Alxinger.

After *Iphigénie en Tauride's* success at the Paris Opera (see Paris, page 241), Gluck altered the music of the opera to fit newly prepared German text. He also transposed the role of Orestes from baritone to tenor and replaced a dramatic recitative and chorus at the end of Act II with an instrumental sinfonia. In 1796 Lorenzo Da Ponte translated it into *Italian*—for London performances! In 1889 Richard Strauss made his own arrangement to present at Weimar. He rewrote many recitatives, altered other pieces, adding Wagner-like musical motifs of his own, joined Acts III and IV, and revised the end. This Strauss version was recorded in 1961 with Montserrat Caballé singing the title role.

Il matrimonio segreto (The Secret Marriage), *melodramma giocosa* in two acts, February 7, 1792.
Domenico Cimarosa (December 17, 1749, Aversa, Italy—January 11, 1801, Venice)
Libretto Giovanni Bertati, after David Garrick's play *The Clandestine Marriage.*

Cimarosa wrote more than sixty-eight operas. He was *maestro di cappella* (the Russian court liked to call things by foreign names) to the court of Catherine the Great in Saint Petersburg. He had very close ties to the Viennese court and in 1791 came to Vienna after the splendor of Catherine's court began to fade. Joseph II, who had planned to hire the composer, died just before Cimarosa arrived, but the new emperor Leopold II followed through by appointing him *Kapellmeister*.

Cimarosa did not disappoint. His first Viennese premiere, *Il matrimonio segreto*, was such a success that Leopold commanded another performance that very same evening in his chambers! Unlike many of the operas of the day, *Il matrimonio segreto* relies on an uncomplicated plot depicting a young couple who dare to go against established social codes and is, in fact, an expression of contemporary values. It is a beautiful opera, but because it lacks bite and freshness it is not so often produced.

Le nozze di Figaro, August 29, 1786.
Wolfgang Amadeus Mozart (1756–91)
Libretto Lorenzo Da Ponte, based on Pierre-Augustin Beaumarchais's play *La folle journée, ou le mariage de Figaro* (The Crazy Day, or The Marriage of Figaro.)

Beaumarchais's play was banned in Vienna, but in 1783 Giovanni Paisiello's opera *Le barbiere di Séville* had scored a triumph and went on to be one of the most popular operas in all of Europe. With the play still banned three years later, Mozart's opera *Le nozze di Figaro*, the continuation of the story, had a successful premiere and eight more performances in Vienna. However, in Prague six months later it generated far more public enthusiasm and achieved the smashing success it has enjoyed ever since. *Le nozze di Figaro* is the most nearly perfect and unproblematic of all Mozart's dramatic works, in large part because of Da Ponte's finely tuned plot and wonderfully witty libretto.

In the first part of the story (covered in *Il barbieri di Siviglia,* see Rome, page 14) Count Almaviva wooed Dr. Bartolo's ward, Rosina, with the aid of Figaro, who is now his valet. In *Le nozze di Figaro* the Count has just abolished the droit de seigneur, the nobleman's right to deflower every bride among his subjects. Almaviva is still a rogue, however, and is intent on luring Figaro's betrothed, Susanna, into his bed. But Susanna, the Countess, and Figaro together outsmart the Count.

The opera contains some of Mozart's most humorous and touching music. Its music, libretto, and depth put it light-years ahead of the typical opera buffa of the day. *Le nozze di Figaro* was revived successfully in Vienna in 1789, during which time it received twenty-six performances. It is, along with the other collaborations with Da Ponte, Mozart's second-most performed opera today (*Die Zauberflöte* is the first).

Orfeo ed Euridice, azione teatrale in three acts, October 5, 1762.
Christoph Willibald Gluck (1714–87)
Libretto Ranieri de'Calzabigi, after the classical myth.

This is the first of Gluck's reform operas, in which he broke with the tradition of opera seria's complicated plots and florid music. In *Orfeo ed*

Euridice he also attempts to return to the "purity" of the earliest operas by composing music of a noble simplicity befitting the universality of the mythological story. Because of the continuing popularity of the voice and persona of castrati in Vienna, in this version of the opera, the role of Orfeo is written for an *alto castrato*.

Today the role is sung by mezzo-sopranos, such as Marilyn Horne, who possess voices that are powerful, agile, and blessed with a vocal range of at least two-and-a-half octaves. *Orfeo ed Euridice* was an immediate success, and it is this first Italian version that remains in international repertory outside France. Gluck wrote a longer French version of *Orfeo* for L'Opéra, premiered August 2, 1774. (See Paris, page 243.)

Details of some Kärntnertortheater premieres

Euryanthe, *grosse heroisch-romantische Oper* in three acts, October 25, 1823.
Carl Maria von Weber (November 18, 1786, Eutin, Germany—June 5, 1826, London)
Libretto Helmina von Chezy, after the French romance *L'histoire du très-noble et chavalereux prince Gérard, comte de Nevers, et de la très-virtueuse et très chaste princess Euriant de Savoye, et sa mye* (The story of the very noble and chivalrous Prince Gérard, count of Nevers, and of the very virtuous and chaste Princess Euriant of Savoy and her conch shell).

Helmina von Chezy was a fellow member of the Dresden literary circle called the *Liederkreis* in which Weber moved. One of the few women librettists (and one of only two in this book), she protested her inexperience but Weber insisted that he wanted a libretto by her. The opera was only moderately successful. It was far too long, and even the always enthusiastic Schubert, who attended the rehearsals, was very critical, particularly about the form.

Fidelio, *Leonore, oder Der Triumph der ehelichen Liebe* (Leonore, or the Triumph of Married Love), third and final version, *Oper* in two acts, May 23, 1814.
Ludwig van Beethoven (1770, Bonn—1827, Vienna)
Libretto Joseph van Sonnleithner, after Jean-Nicolas Bouilly's French libretto *Léonore, ou L'amour conjugal,* with revisions by Georg Friedrich Treitschke.

The plot of *Fidelio* intertwines two stories, one domestic, the other heroic. Simpler music, such as strophic arias, characterizes the domestic story about Marzelline's love for Fidelio, who is really Leonore in disguise. Far more complicated and interesting music conveys the heroic tale about the nobility of Leonore's love for the imprisoned Florestan and the ultimate triumph of good over evil, and this music is what attracts audiences to this day. The chorus sung by the prisoners when released into the sunlight after years in a dungeon is one of the most moving pieces in all of opera. Nowadays *Fidelio* usually begins with the overture known as the *Leonore no. 4* (also called the *Fidelio Overture*). (See Theater an der Wien for the first and second versions, p. 178.) By the time of this third premiere, Beethoven had been working on *Fidelio*, its overtures, and its arias for more than ten years. The music is so uplifting that any deficiencies in plot can be easily disregarded. It is regularly performed today throughout the world.

Martha, *Martha, oder Der Markt zu Richmond* (Martha, or The Market at Richmond), *romantisch-komische-Oper* in four acts, November 25, 1847.
Friedrich von Flotow (April 27, 1812, Teutendorf estate, Mecklenberg—January 24, 1883, Darmstadt)
Libretto Wilhelm Friedrich, after an idea by Jules-Henri Vernay de Saint-Georges.

Set in England, *Martha* is a delightful romantic comedy of disguises and errors. Flotow incorporated the Irish folksong "The Last Rose of Summer" in his score. He is by no means a well-known composer today, but *Martha* is sometimes still performed. The tenor aria (translated into Italian) "M'appari tutt'amor" is one of *the* tenor staples (perhaps to be heard in the next Three Tenors concert?).

Die Zwillingsbrüder (The Twin Brothers), June 14, 1820.
Franz Schubert (January 31, 1797, Vienna—November 19, 1828, Vienna)
Libretto Georg von Hofmann.

This was the second of Schubert's operas to be performed during his lifetime, and also the last. His thirteen others were done only long after his death.

Details of some Staatsoper premieres

Ariadne auf Naxos, second version, *Oper* in a prologue and one act, October 4, 1916.
Richard Strauss (June 11, 1864, Munich—September 8, 1949, Garmisch-Partenkirchen)
Libretto Hugo von Hofmannsthal.

Vienna premiered this version of *Ariadne auf Naxos*, Strauss and von Hofmannsthal's revision of the 1912 production in Stuttgart (see Stuttgart, page 308), in the middle of World War I. The revision splits the opera into a prologue and one act. The prologue takes place backstage in an elegant Viennese house, where a young and very earnest composer of an opera seria is told that his masterpiece will be followed by a "vulgar" opera buffa, both of which must take place before fireworks go off at 9:00 P.M. The act following this prologue is "the opera." Characters from commedia dell'arte collide with operatic stereotypes from the eighteenth century in a wonderful mishmash of opera seria and opera buffa musical and dramatic styles. *Ariadne auf Naxos* may not rate as great opera, but the right singers can make it great fun, and it has always been situated on the edge of the repertory.

Die Frau ohne Schatten (The Woman Without a Shadow), *Oper* in three acts, October 10, 1919.
Richard Strauss (June 11, 1864, Munich—September 8, 1949, Garmisch-Partenkirchen)
Libretto Hugo von Hofmannsthal.

Die Frau ohne Schatten is a fairy tale that mixes a couple from another world with a poor earthly family. The other-world Empress attempts to buy the shadow of the poor wife of a Dyer. There's a wonderful moment when five fishes fly into a frying pan only to cry out in the voices of children pleading to be born. The opera contains few arias and much gloriously orchestrated recitative so that it is the most Wagner-like of all of Strauss's operas. *Die Frau ohne Schatten* is neither gripping like *Elektra* or *Salome,* nor seductively lush like *Der Rosenkavalier,* but has a compellingly noble and uplifting quality. Though a difficult dramatic work, it is often produced.

Oedipus Rex, *opera-oratorio,* staged version, February 23, 1928 (one year after the Paris premiere in concert version at Théâtre Sarah Bernhardt, page 235).
Igor Stravinsky (between June 5 and 17, 1882, Oranienbaum, now Lomonosov—April 6, 1971, New York)
Libretto Jean Cocteau, based on Sophocles.

Stravinsky was intrigued by the idea of writing a dramatic opera in a dead language, so the sung part of *Oedipus Rex* is in Latin but a narrator tells the story in the language of the host country. Stravinsky insisted that the main characters behave like statues. The musical language of the opera is set in a rigidly neoclassical idiom, with formal recitatives and triadic accompaniment, along the "Mozart-with-the-wrong-notes" lines of his later real opera, *The Rake's Progress.* The premiere was received by an uncomprehending audience, but it remains on the fringes of the repertory and has lately been given some excellent productions.

Werther, *drame lyrique* in four acts, in German, February 16, 1892.
Jules Massenet (May 12, 1842, Montaud, near St. Etienne—August 31, 1912, Paris)
Libretto E. Blau, Milliet, and Hartmann, based on Johann Wolfgang von Goethe's *Die Leiden des jungen Werthers.*

Massenet wrote *Werther* for a Paris Opéra Comique premiere in 1887, but the work's subject was judged too gloomy for production. A triumphant performance of Massenet's *Manon* in Vienna in 1890, however, inspired the Vienna Opera to commission a piece, and Massenet had *Werther* all ready. The work is passionately bleak, but it also contains Massenet's most inspired music. It remains on the fringes of standard repertory today.

Details of some operas premiered at Theater auf der Weiden and Theater an der Wien

Fidelio, Leonore, oder Der Triumph der ehelichen Liebe (Leonore, or the Triumph of Married Love), first version, *Opera* in three acts, November 20, 1805.
Ludwig van Beethoven (1770, Bonn—1827, Vienna)
Libretto Joseph von Sonnleithner, after Jean-Nicolas Bouilly's French libretto *Léonore, ou L'amour conjugal.*

The year 1805 boasted only three performances of *Fidelio.* Vienna was occupied by Napoleon's army, and many Viennese had left the city—not a good year to present an opera about tyranny! But Beethoven also felt the opera was too long and thus set about revising it. Beethoven preferred the title *Leonore,* and this version of the opera and the next are commonly called *Leonore.* The overture is known separately as *Leonore no. 2.* Because *Fidelio* remains in the repertory as one of the most passionately intense works on the deepest of subjects, it seems almost absurd that *Fidelio* was premiered in the same theatre as the comparatively frivolous operettas of Strauss and Lehár.

Fidelio, second version, *Opera* in two acts, March 29, 1806.
Ludwig van Beethoven (1770–1827)

This second version of the opera received only two performances, and its overture is known separately as the *Leonore no. 3.* Again Beethoven was displeased and worked on further revisions until the premiere of the third version at the Kärntnertortheater May 23, 1814 (see page 175). (The overture known as the *Leonore no. 1* was written in 1807 for a performance of the opera in Prague that did not take place.)

Die Fledermaus, komische *Operette* in three acts, April 5, 1874.
Johann Strauss (October 25, 1825, Vienna—June 3, 1899, Vienna).
Libretto Carl Haffner and Richard Genée, after Henri Meilhac and Ludovic Halévy's *Le réveillon* (The New Year's Eve Celebration).

Die Fledermaus is by far the most well-known Viennese operetta. The libretto is based on a witty story by Meilhac and Halévy, the pair who also furnished Offenbach with stories for some of his best operettas and provided the source for Bizet's *Carmen.* The plot concerns a husband, Gabriel von Eisenstein, his wife Rosalinde, and their maid Adele, who each want to attend a big party at the house of Prince Orlofsky *alone.* The opera is filled with a delightful combination of innocent and naughty sparkle and many of

Strauss's best-loved melodies. *Die Fledermaus* is often performed throughout the world on New Year's Eve.

Der Zigeunerbaron (The Gypsy Baron), *Operette* in three acts, October 24, 1885.
Johann Strauss (1825–99)
Libretto Ignaz Schnitzer.

Der Zigeunerbaron is a bona fide Mittel European story, complete with Gypsies, associations with Turks, and poetic depictions of the rural eastern countryside and peoples. Strauss felt that the subject matter brought him closer to writing a serious opera.

Die lustige Witwe (The Merry Widow), *Operette* in three acts, December 30, 1905.
Franz Lehár (April 30, 1870, Komáron, Hungary—October 24, 1948, Bad Ischl)
Libretto Victor Léon and Leo Stein after Herni Meilhac's *L'attaché d'ambassade* (The Embassy's Attaché).

Die lustige Witwe, the greatest commercial and popular success in the history of operetta, heralded a new era for Viennese operetta. The sophistication of the orchestral score reflects the richness of Italian verismo trends and the palette of Richard Strauss. The very light plot describes the rekindling of a passion between Danilo, a dashing cavalry officer, and Hanna, the merry widow herself. The waltz from *The Merry Widow* contains its most well-known melody, and the Vilja Song remains one of the most well-known arias in all of operetta. The operetta is regularly performed in German-speaking countries.

Die Zauberflöte, *Singspiel* in two acts, September 30, 1791.
Wolfgang Amadeus Mozart (1756–91)
Libretto Emanuel Schikaneder.

Mozart and Schikaneder intended *Die Zauberflöte* as a Masonic allegory expressing a coded commitment to Freemasonry. Early productions incorporated not only the "Egyptian" symbols used today but also many Islamic characters and motifs. Townspeople—the middle class rather than the nobility—packed the theatre for the premiere, and it was a triumph. Over the years, stage directors and designers have used the plot's imaginativeness as a jumping-off point to explore the limits of their own creativity. In particular, the appearance of the serpent in Act I has received ever new and ingenious productions with the aid of emergent stage technology. The story mixes the noble Tamino's search for truth and love (Masonic elements) with the wily actions of the bird catcher, Papageno. Because of its seemingly childlike simplicity and tunefulness, *Die Zauberflöte* is Mozart's best loved and most-often produced opera.

Details of a Volksoper premiere

Die glücklische Hand (The Lucky Hand), *Drama mit Musik* in one act,
October 14, 1924.
Arnold Schoenberg (September 13, 1874, Vienna—July 13, 1951, Los
Angeles)
Libretto by the composer.

Die glücklische Hand, although its title might suggest otherwise, is an
expressionistic representation of despair and pessimism. The premiere was a
success. Schoenberg wrote the opera as an autobiographical sketch discussing
the cold reception his music was receiving; his wife's brief departure with
another man; and the havoc the war had wreaked with his existence. The
composer's idea was that movements, forms, and colors should combine to
produce artistic effects just as notes of music do. The opera was written
during a period when Schoenberg was devoting much of his creative energy
to painting, and he developed a way to notate scenic effects and constantly
changing colored lighting. A complicated opera, it is not performed as often
as Schoenberg's other short opera, *Erwartung.*

For more information on specific operatic, musical, and theatrical events in
Austria, write to:

Osterreicher Bundestheaterverband, Goethegasse 1, A–1010 Vienna,
Austria

For more extensive information on Vienna and all it offers, contact:

Vienna Fremdenverkehrsbetriebe, Obere Augartenstrasse 40, 1025
Vienna, Austria

FOOD

Although the Viennese lived under the constant threat of conquest by the
Turks, Turkish proximity nevertheless afforded the city's inhabitants some lasting
benefits. One is coffee. Coffeehouses abound. When you order a coffee, it will
always be served along with a small glass of cool water. The Viennese feel that
any bad effects that might result from drinking their dark, strong brew can be
assuaged by downing a glass of water immediately thereafter! I find that the glass
of water certainly refreshes the mouth, whatever its other advantages. To order in
a café the following terms can be helpful: black coffee, a *Schwarzer*; black coffee
and whipped cream, an *Einspänner*; coffee with milk, a *Melange*; black coffee
with vanilla ice cream and whipped cream, an *Eiskaffee.*

Unlike the Italians, Viennese sit down to have their coffee and read the
paper, converse, or people-watch. Sweets: cookies and cakes are amazingly good
in Vienna.

Demel, Kohlmarkt 14, in the 1st district

This popular but tiny coffeehouse is in a blank-faced building with only a discreet display of cookie boxes in the windows facing the street— no sign nor a no. 14. But seek and ye shall find. Resist the fancy cakes and concentrate on the cookies. They are to die for!

Café Sacher, Philharmonikerstrasse 4, in the 1st district

When in Vienna, you must have a piece of the delectable chocolate cake called *Sachertorte,* first made in 1832 by Franz Sacher, chef to Prince Metternich. The secret of this light confection is the small amount of flour relative to the eggs, chocolate, and sugar. Each layer is covered with apricot jam and chocolate icing. A real *Sachertorte* will stay fresh for a good week. The restaurant and the hotel were built in 1876 by the original Sacher's son. Late in life, Johannes Brahms was known to breakfast on oysters in the restaurant!

Figlmüller, Wollzeile 5
tel: 512–6177

Figlmüller serves up the quintessential Wiener Schnitzel, which makes the restaurant quite a tourist attraction. Reservations are a must. The restaurant's owners have opened another branch in Grinzing near Beethoven's house on Grinzingerstrasse.

Ubl's Gasthaus, Pressgasse 26
tel: 587–6437
Open 11:00 A.M.–2:30 P.M. and 6:00–midnight.

Ubl's, a simple neighborhood restaurant, is a ten-minute walk from Theater an der Wien. The atmosphere is *echt* Viennese, all dark wood and glass, and few if any tourists will be there. The menu is handwritten and legible to few, but the waitress will say the names of the dishes for you. The food is simple and filling.

LODGING

Hotel-Pension Schneider, Getreidemarkt 5, A–1060 Vienna
tel: (43–1) 588–380   fax: (43–1) 5883–8212

Pension Schneider is a five-minute walk from the Staatsoper, standing directly across the Opernring and down two blocks. It is also right across the street from the Secession Building, around the corner from Theater an der Wien—a one-minute walk, door to door—and also from the Naschmarkt, Vienna's biggest open market. It is reasonably priced, immaculate, and the staff is very friendly.

Hotel zur Wiener Staatsoper, Krugerstrasse 11, A–1010 Vienna
tel: (43–1) 513–1274   fax: (43–1) 5131–27415

This small hotel (sixteen rooms) has a reputation for quiet elegance. The price range is *excellent,* and it is a three-minute walk to the Staatsoper.

Pension Beethoven, Millöckergasse 6, A–1060 Vienna
tel: (43–1) 5874–4820   fax: (43–1) 587–4442
Pension Beethoven stands right behind Pension Schneider, a five-minute walk to the Staatsoper and a one-minute walk to Theater an der Wien. Some of the hotel's windows look out on the theatre's Papageno Portal.

Hotel Römischer Kaiser, Annagasse 16, A–1010 Vienna
tel: (43–1) 5127–7510   fax: (43–1) 5127–75113
The Römischer Kaiser stands "within the Ring" in a palace built in 1684. It has been restored many times, has all modern conveniences, and is a two-minute walk across the famous Kärntnerstrasse to the Staatsoper. An amazing find in this part of Europe, the hotel is *exclusively* for nonsmoking guests!

Pension Am Operneck, Kärntnerstrasse 47, A–1010 Vienna
tel: (43–1) 512–9310
This inexpensive *pensione* is located on Kärntnerstrasse twenty feet from the Staatsoper.

Hotel Sacher, Philharmonikerstrasse 4, A–1010 Vienna
tel: (43–1) 51–456   fax: (43–1) 5145–7810
Hotel Sacher is a high-priced, first-class hotel evocative of the late nineteenth century. Built in 1876 on the original site of the Kärntnertortheater, the hotel is a two-minute walk to the entrance of the Staatsoper. Even those who stay elsewhere should visit the café for a piece of its signature *Sachertorte.*

Two Operatic Day Trips From Vienna

Eisenstadt

Eisenstadt occupies the low rolling hills about twenty-five miles due south of Vienna, twenty miles west of Sopron, very near the border between Austria and Hungary. The provincial capital of Burgenland, the small town's claim to fame stems from its favored status with the influential Esterházy family; Josef Haydn (1732–1809) was employed there as *Kapellmeister* for Prince Nikolaus Joseph Esterházy from 1762 to 1790.

From 1766 to 1778 Josef Haydn lived at Haydngasse 21, just east of the Schloss Esterháza (the Esterházy castle). The house burned in both 1768 and

1776, but was rebuilt each time by Esterházy. Today it is a Haydn Museum that also contains rooms dedicated to the pianist-composer-conductor Franz Liszt (October 22, 1811, Raiding, near Sopron, Hungary—July 31, 1886, Bayreuth). Liszt is famous in opera history for conducting several of Wagner's operas during his tenure at the Weimar Hofoper, his operatic transcriptions for the piano, the essays he wrote on behalf of contemporary opera, and—for a touch of scandal— because his daughter Cosima, after marrying the conductor and Wagner champion Hans von Bülow, ran off with Richard Wagner.

Two of Haydn's early operas (1763 and 1766) were premiered in Eisenstadt's Schloss Esterháza.

Esterháza (since 1950 it has been called Fertód)

The Esterházy palace at Fertód, former seat of this powerful family, is about twenty-five miles southeast of the Austrian border in today's Hungary. The palace was built by Prince Miklós Esterházy (Miklós the Magnificent), and remnants of its rococo splendor still tantalize the imagination. Nobility and peasants alike were invited to the operas staged here under the aegis of Prince Esterházy. The theater could once seat 400.

Maria Theresa remarked, "When I want to hear a decent opera I have to go to Esterháza." Haydn, on the other hand, felt very isolated in Esterháza and wrote many letters attesting to his misery. In one he plaintively recounts being awakened by the terrible north wind while dreaming of a thwarted performance of Mozart's *Le nozze di Figaro*. Many of the operas of Haydn are lost or exist only in fragments, and virtually none remain in today's standard repertory, a surprising state of affairs since his symphonic and chamber works are basic to the repertory of all concert-presenting organizations.

The premieres of fifteen operas by Haydn were presented at Schloss Esterháza from 1774 to 1784.

The palace has been restored, but the opera house on the grounds has burned down.

SALZBURG

Salzburg is known for its picturesque location in the foothills of the Dolomites. Long before it became a Roman municipality in A.D. 50, the city flourished as a junction of trade routes for the salt that came from nearby salt mines. The city was sacked by the barbarians in A.D. 477 and virtually abandoned. But in about 700 the town, first called Salzpurch, began to revive, building up around the abbey of St. Peter's and the Benedictine convent of Nonnberg. In 1598, the Italian architect Vincenzo Scamozzi, a student of Palladio, designed the Residenz

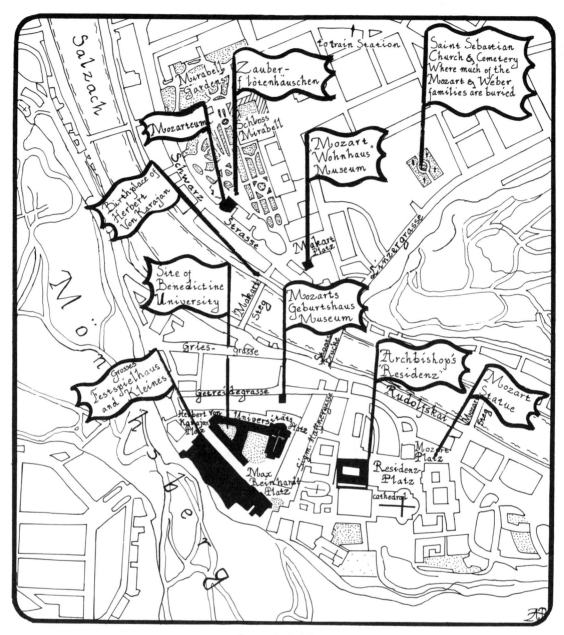

Operatic Salzburg

as well as several other Salzburg palaces and squares. The fortifications of the city withstood the terrible Thirty Years' War, and in 1622 the university was established.

Opera came quite early to Salzburg, with a 1615 performance of *L'Orfeo*, by Claudio Monteverdi, only eight years after its premiere in Mantua (page 55). The production took place in the Archbishop's Palace, the Residenz.

Leopold Mozart (1719–87) was born in Augsburg and came to live in Salzburg in 1737. A violinist and composer, he was appointed court composer in

Mozart's Geburtshaus

1757 and became deputy Kappellmeister in 1763. He lived in the city's center from 1747 to 1773. His son, Wolfgang Amadeus Mozart, was born at Getreidegasse 9, January 27, 1756, and baptized Johannes Chrysostom Wolfgang Theophilus Amadeus in the cathedral, Dom St. Rupert. Today it is a museum, Mozart's Geburtshaus. His hammerklavier (ca. 1780) and his clavichord (1760), as well as several other instruments, are on display. Family portraits were given to the Cathedral Musical Society by his wife Constanze in 1841.

Mozart's Geburtshaus, Getreidegasse 9 (third floor)
Open Tuesday through Sunday—July and August, 8:00 A.M.–8:00 P.M.; June and September, 9:00 A.M.–7:00 P.M.; October through May, 9:00 A.M.–6:00 P.M. Admission: öS 62

In the autumn of 1773 the Mozart family moved to the south side of the present Makartplatz and set up housekeeping in what is now called the

Tanzmeisterhaus. When he wasn't traveling, Mozart lived here until he left Salzburg for good in November 1780, claiming that Salzburg creates "no stimulus for my talent! When I play or when any of my compositions are performed, it is just as if the audience were all tables and chairs...." Most of the building was destroyed in an Allied air raid in October 1944. The rebuilt vestibule and music room contain a permanent exhibition of musical instruments of the late eighteenth century and autograph scores of Mozart's works. Today the room is used for recitals from June through September on weekdays at 5:00 P.M. The house faces the spacious Makartplatz and was renovated in 1995.

Mozart's Wohnhaus, Makartplatz 8

Just down the square, on the river, at Makartsteg 1 stands the birthplace of the conductor Herbert von Karajan (April 5, 1908, Salzburg—July 16, 1989, Anif).

And, of course, there is the Mozarteum, the Conservatory of Music, built in 1914 with an extension added in 1940. The Mozarteum has two concert halls and a library containing many of Mozart's letters and scores. In the gardens behind the Mozarteum you will find the *Zauberflötenhäuschen*, the little Magic Flute House, a rebuilt wooden summer house in which Mozart composed part of *Die Zauberflöte*. In 1874, the little house was dismantled and brought to Salzburg from outside Vienna.

Mozarteum, Schwarzstrasse 26

Zauberflötenhäuschen (in the rose garden behind the Mozarteum)
Open guided tours weekdays June through September, 9:00 A.M.–8:00 P.M.

Mozart's sister Nannerl (Marianne von Berchtold zu Sonnenburg, 1751–1829) is buried in a chapel in the Stiftskirche St. Peter. Mozart's C minor Mass was performed here in 1783 with his wife Constanze singing the soprano solos.

On Linzergasse on the east bank of the Salzach River is the Sebastianskirche. Southeast of the church are graves and monuments representing a panoply of the Mozart and Weber families: Leopold Mozart (1719–87); Nannerl's oldest daughter, Jeanette von Berchtold zu Sonnenburg (d. 1805); Constanze Weber Mozart, Wolfgang's wife (1762–1842); Constanze's second husband, George Nikolaus von Nissen (1761–1826); Constanze's aunt, Genoveva von Weber (d. 1798), mother of the composer Carl Maria von Weber; and two of Constanze's sisters, Aloysia and Sophie, who were transferred to the Mozart-Weber grave site in 1895.

In front of the Archbishop's Palace is Mozartplatz, with a statue of the composer in the center. The Archbishop's Palace (Residenz) hosted premieres of three of Mozart's early operas *La finta semplice*, (probably) May 1, 1769; *Il sogno di Scipione*, (probably) May 1772; *Il re pastore*, April 23, 1775.

Mozarteum

The Benedictine University hosted the premiere of Mozart's first opera, *Apollo et Hyacinthus,* May 13, 1767.

Mozart's life history can be traced by listing his works and the people for whom he wrote them. He spent a great deal of his youth traveling, composing, and performing for the great families of Europe. He sought a full-time position in one of Europe's large cities, and although he had many commissions and was regularly the toast of the cities where he performed, no offer of court composer, or *maestro di cappella,* was forthcoming. He was always accompanied by one of his parents, most often his very ambitious and well-connected father.

In 1778, however, on a trip to Paris to perform for the court of Louis XVI, his companion was his mother, who fell ill and died. On January 17, 1779, a day after he returned from burying his mother in Paris, the twenty-three-year-old musician took the post of official organist and composer to the Archbishop of Salzburg, a job whose routine he found tedious. In the summer of 1780, the Elector of Bavaria, Karl Theodor, asked Mozart to compose an opera seria for carnival season in Munich. Because Mozart based his composition on *Idomeneo, re di Creta* (Idomeneo, King of Crete), a libretto by the Salzburg court chaplain, the archbishop granted him a leave of absence. Although the opera was not particularly successful (indeed it shocked the Munich public because Mozart had given the protagonists uncommon individuality and asked them to express real emotion in music), Mozart was pleased to be free of the tedium of everyday life in Salzburg. When, shortly after the performances, the archbishop summoned Mozart to Vienna, Mozart provoked his employer into dismissing him from his service, thus finally breaking all but familial ties to Salzburg.

The Salzburg Festival originated in 1920 as a celebration of music and drama with a special emphasis on the works of Mozart. The Kleines Festspielhaus opened in 1925 as the Festspielhaus and was subsequently rebuilt in 1926, 1937, and 1939. The Grosses Festspielhaus was built in 1960. Originally the music festival was held in the Felsenreitschule and operas were performed in the small Stadttheater. Hugo von Hofmannsthal was the festival's first director, followed by Richard Strauss. Each year the festival presents new works, productions of rediscovered baroque operas, operas of Mozart, and works of standard repertory. The Festspielhaus stands on Herbert von Karajan Platz.

Some premieres at the Salzburg Festival were *Il re in ascolto* (1984), Luciano Berio; *The Bassarids* (1966), Hans Werner Henze.

Die Liebe der Danae, *heitere Mythologie* (cheerful mythology) in three acts, August 14, 1952.
Richard Strauss (June 11, 1864, Munich—September 8, 1949, Garmisch-Partenkirchen)
Libretto Joseph Gregor.

Strauss's penultimate opera, *Die Liebe der Danae,* begins the composer's swan song, and like many composers' late works, it goes on and on! Clearly Strauss saw himself as the opera's Zeus—old and losing his powers. But the music is elegant and vivid. The opera was first seen August 16, 1944, in the form of a public dress rehearsal. The scheduled premiere, meant to celebrate Strauss's eightieth birthday, had to be canceled because the Allied Second Front was threatening.

For more information write:

Salzburg City Fremdenverkehrsbetriebe, Auerspergstrasse 7, 5024 Salzburg (City), Austria

LODGING

Hotel Bristol, Makartplatz 4, A–5020 Salzburg
tel: (43–662) 873–557   fax: (43–662) 873–5576
An elegant hotel, the Bristol faces the Mozart Geburtshaus across Makartplatz.

Hotel Elephant, Sigmund-Haffnergasse 4, A–5020 Salzburg
tel: (43–662) 843–397   fax: (43–662) 8401–0928
This hotel occupies a typical sixteenth-century Salzburger townhouse. It is quiet, elegant, and right in the historic center of the city nearby all the Mozartiana.

Hotel Weisse Taube, Kaigasse 9, A–5020 Salzburg
tel: (43–662) 842–404   fax: (43–662) 841–783

Hotel Scherer, Plainstrasse 37, A–5020 Salzburg
tel: (43–662) 871–706   fax: (43–662) 876–568

BELGIUM

※ ·≪

BRUSSELS (Bruxelles)

Belgium's operatic history dates from 1650. The first Belgian public opera house opened in 1694, was destroyed by fire in 1695, then rebuilt on the site of the former Mint (La Monnaie). Thus the new theatre became Théâtre la Monnaie and was opened in 1700 with a performance of *Atys* by Jean-Baptiste Lully. Because of the danger posed by fire, only the foyer was heated but not the auditorium. During the eighteenth century the theatre's French repertory was identical to that being done in Paris. The tradition of presenting French repertory, often within months of an opera's Parisian premiere, continued until the 1940s.

When the French took over the city in 1745, Charles-Simon Favart was appointed to direct the theatre. (This is the same Favart after whom Salle Favart, Paris's Opéra Comique, was named.) In 1819 a new theatre was built on a site just behind the old opera house and again it was called Théâtre la Monnaie. During the Revolution of 1830, which led to the rise of the modern country of Belgium, the theatre was closed. It reopened in September that same year with heretofore banned performances of Daniel-François-Esprit Auber's *La Muette de Portici*. This opera became such an idée fixe in the minds of the Brussels public that it was given many times each year until 1906.

When the theatre reopened after World War I, *La Muette de Portici* was again the opera of choice. Then twenty-two performances marked the centenary celebration of the 1830 revolution and fourteen were given when the theatre reopened at the end of World War II. In 1963, in recognition that the population of Brussels was a mixture of French Walloons and Flemish-speaking Flemings, the theatre became Théâtre Royal de la Monnaie/Koninklijke Muntschouwberg.

Under its present direction Théâtre de la Monnaie appears to be a very forward-thinking theatre, a prototype for the twenty-first century. Today the opera house is enormously successful. Its season extends from September through June and usually includes twelve operas.

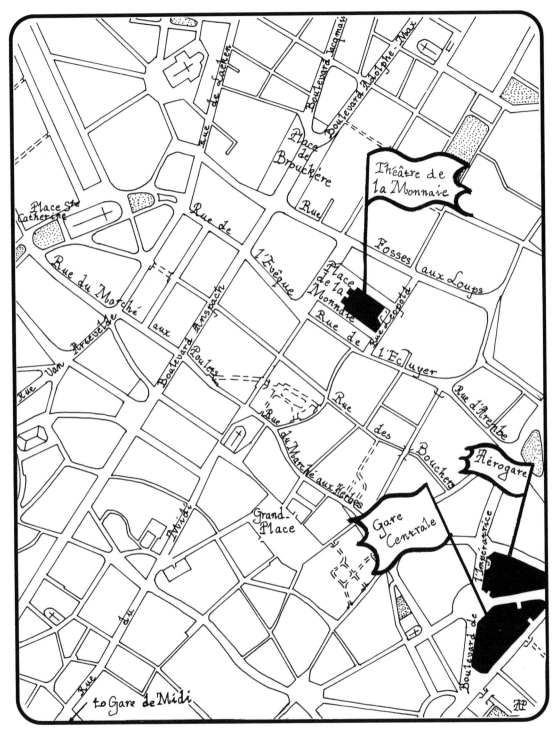

Operatic Brussels

191

Théâtre de la Monnaie, Place de la Monnaie/Muntplein, 1000 Brussels
tel: (32–2) 218–1211

Specific information on La Monnaie's season can be obtained by contacting:

The Belgian Tourist Office, rue du Marché aux Herbes 63, 1000
Brussels

or the Belgian tourist office in New York:

Belgian Tourist Office, 780 Third Avenue, New York, N.Y. 10017
tel: (212) 758–8130

    The tourist offices will also send the English-language monthly
magazine *What's On,* if asked.

Some of the premieres presented by Théâtre de la Monnaie include *Antigone*
(1927), Arthur Honegger; *The Death of Klinghoffer* (1991), John Adams; *The
Gambler* (1929), Sergei Prokofiev; *Gwendoline* (1886), Emanuel Chabrier; *Hérodiade* (1881), Jules Massenet; *Les Malheurs d'Orphée* (1926), Darius Milhaud; as
well as premieres by Chausson and Vincent d'Indy.

    Many operas in the European repertory received their premieres *in French* in
Brussels before being performed in Paris. Among them are Richard Wagner's
Lohengrin, Der fliegende Holländer, Die Walküre, Siegfried (1891), *Tristan und
Isolde;* Richard Strauss's *Salome, Elektra,* and *Ariadne aux Naxos;* Giacomo
Puccini's *Turandot;* Alban Berg's *Wozzeck;* Benjamin Britten's *Rape of Lucretia;*
and Igor Stravinsky's *Rake's Progress.* During World War I Richard Strauss
conducted performances of *Der Rosenkavalier* for the occupying German forces
here.

Details about some premieres at Théâtre de la Monnaie

The Death of Klinghoffer, March 19, 1991.
John Adams (born February 15, 1947, Worcester, Mass.)
Libretto Alice Goodman.

    The Death of Klinghoffer, based on the 1985 hijacking of the cruise ship
Achille Lauro, unfolds much like a Greek tragedy, through narratives and
meditations punctuated by comments from a chorus. The premiere was a
coproduction with Glyndebourne, Opéra Lyon (France), Houston Grand
Opera (which, incidentally, premiered Adams's first opera, *Nixon in China,*
October 22, 1987), the Brooklyn Academy of Music, the Los Angeles Opera,
and the San Francisco Opera.

Hérodiade, opéra in four acts, December 19, 1881.
Jules Massenet (May 12, 1842, Montaud, St. Etienne—August 31, 1912,
Paris)

Libretto Paul Milliet and Henri Grémont (Georges Hartmann), based on the 1877 story by Gustave Flaubert.

Hérodiade is about Massenet's favorite subject: erotic obsession. The premiere of the opera was rejected by the Paris Opera because the plot was deemed incoherent. It was only because of a chance meeting on the street between the director of Théâtre de la Monnaie and Massenet that the opera was premiered in Brussels. This lavish premiere began a fifty-five-performance run, and up until the turn of the century the opera was often performed throughout Europe and in the United States. Singers consider the five leading roles very rewarding, and *Hérodiade* was most recently revived as a vehicle for Montserrat Caballé and José Carreras.

FOOD

Belgium is justifiably noted for its seafood. In particular, diners should take advantage of the country's passion for mussels; they come prepared in *every* imaginable way. And *French* fries (*frittes*) in Belgium are raised to new heights!

Chez Leon, rue des Bouchers 18, 1000 Brussels
tel: (32–2) 511–1415
This moderately priced restaurant offers patrons a great opportunity to experience authentic and excellent Belgian food. Chez Leon is a five-minute walk from the opera.

Aux Armes de Bruxelles, rue de Bouchers 13 (off the Grand Place), 1000 Brussels
tel: (32–2) 511–2118
This elegant restaurant specializing in Belgian and French food is the perfect place for dinner after the opera, which is a six-minute walk away. Rue des Bouchers is known as the "street of restaurants."

LODGING

Hotel Ibis–Sainte-Catherine, rue Joseph Plateau 2 (Place Ste.-Catherine), 1000 Brussels
tel: (32–2) 513–7620   fax: (32-2) 514–2214
This large, centrally located, comfortable hotel is in the "fish market" area, a seven-minute walk from the opera.

Hotel Metropole, place de Brouckère 31, 1000 Brussels
tel: (32–2) 217–2300   fax: (32–2) 218–0220
This lovely hotel is a five-minute walk from the theatre.

Jolly Hotel Atlanta, boulevard Adolphe–Max 7, 1000 Brussels
tel: (32–2) 217–0120   fax: (32–2) 217–3758
This large chain hotel is a four-minute walk from the theatre.

CZECH REPUBLIC

※· ·※

PRAGUE (Praha)

In the mid-seventeenth century, the German-speaking nobility stopped using the Czech language and de facto the Czechs became a people of peasants, craftsmen, and servants. The nobility and bourgeoisie were German. In the eighteenth century, under the Hapsburg rule of Maria Theresa (1740–80), the Empress commanded that all judges and civil servants should know the "vulgar tongue," and Czech was again taught in schools. But by the middle of the nineteenth century the Austrian rulers were once more attempting to purge Prague and banned the Czech language from the civil service and the judiciary. Amazingly, the Czechs were nevertheless able to build a National Theatre in 1881 to present plays and operas by Czech writers and composers. In 1882 even the university split into Czech and German entities. German speakers retaliated against the National Theatre by building a newer and bigger Deutschetheater in 1888.

At the end of World War I, with the collapse of the Austrian and German monarchies, the Czechoslovak Republic was declared on October 28, 1918. The Czechs and Slovaks became equal partners in the new republic until March 15, 1939, when German troops marched into Prague and, meeting no resistance, took control of the country. Czechs were again defined as second-class citizens and the university was closed. Between 1939 and 1945, the Germans systematically exterminated the artists and the academics of Czechoslovakia in an effort to destroy these voices of national consciousness. They did not underestimate the power of the arts and *how* an idea is delivered (think of Verdi and *Nabucco*).

The development of opera in Prague is similar to that in most of northern Europe. A touring Italian opera company came to the court in November 1627 and presented an opera in Italian. The first Italian impresario began staging operas to a paying audience at the turn of the eighteenth century. Italian opera and Italian impresarios reigned until the late-eighteenth and early-nineteenth centuries, when German opera began to make inroads. Not until the middle of the nineteenth century were operas in Czech presented regularly.

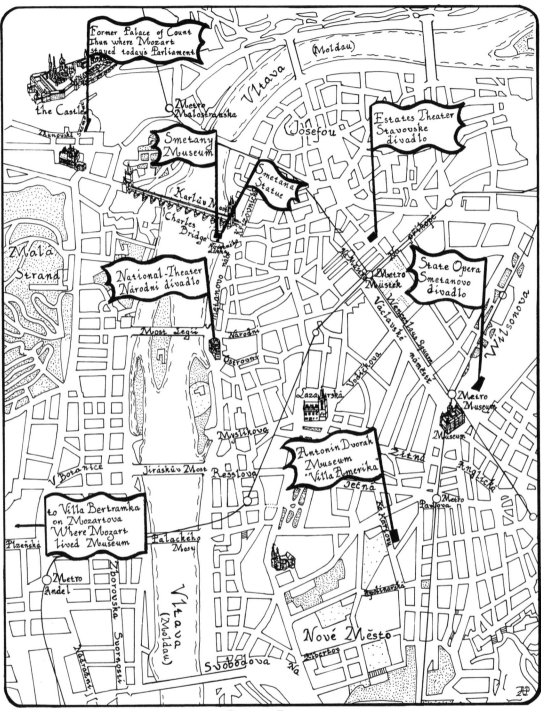

Operatic Prague

Because of the enormous success of performances of *Le nozze di Figaro* in Prague in December 1786, Mozart received a commission from Pasquale Bondini, the director of the new Prague National Theatre (Stavovské divadlo or Estates Theater), to write an opera. The preparations for this opera—*Don Giovanni*—went neither smoothly nor rapidly. Among other impediments was the death of

Mozart's father at the end of May 1787. Legend has it that the wonderfully evocative overture of *Don Giovanni* was not composed until two days before the opera's premiere.

Both Mozart and Da Ponte stayed at the Palace of Count Thun, which can now be found by going to the end of Tomásská Street, left into Thunovská Street, and right on to Snemovni Street. The Thun Palace occupies the whole length of the street's right side and today houses the Parliament of the Czech Republic.

Mozart also stayed at Villa Bertramka, in the slightly dilapidated Smichov quarter on the outskirts of the central city. When news of Mozart's death was received in Prague in December 1791, more than four thousand people gathered in the Saint Nicholas Church in Malà Strana, at the foot of the castle. Vienna did not accord such honors to the composer until well over fifty years after his death.

> **Mozart Museum Villa Bertramka** (Bertramka–Muzeum W. A. Mozart), Mozartova, 169 (just outside the city center), Smichov, Praha 5
> tel: 543–893
> Open daily, 9:30 A.M.–5:00 P.M.
> trams: 4, 6, 7, or 9 to Bertramka; metro, line B to Andel, and a short walk
> The museum occasionally presents concerts of Mozart's music.

Built in 1781, the Stavovské divadlo (Theatre of the Estates) was considered the most important theatre in Central Europe in the last quarter of the eighteenth century. Early in the next century the theatre belonged to the

Estates Theatre (Stavovské divadlo)

Bohemian Diet (Parliament) was made up of landed gentry, and thus in English it is called the Estates Theatre. In 1859 the structure was given an extra floor, and the whole theatre was restored again in 1983. In 1984 the Czech film director Miloš Forman filmed parts of *Amadeus* there. Since 1989 the theatre has been restored to its original appearance. It is a gem, set symmetrically at one end of a square with the present-day casino, once a theatre, at the other. Unfortunately, the operas presented at the Stavovské divadlo are performed by the National Theatre, Prague's lesser opera company. A performance can be quite trying, but seeing the theatre's interior and appreciating its wonderful acoustics are almost worth the experience.

The Stavovské divadlo (Theatre of the Estates) presented the premieres of:

Il dissoluto punito, ossia il Don Giovanni (The Libertine Punished, or Don Giovanni), *dramma giocoso* in two acts, October 29, 1787.
Wolfgang Amadeus Mozart (1756–91)
Libretto Lorenzo Da Ponte, based on Tirso de Molina's sixteenth-century play, *El burlador de Sevillia ed el convidao de piedra*.

Mozart called *Don Giovanni* a *dramma giocosa*, a comedy and a tragedy combined. The opera recounts a day in the life of the dissolute Don Giovanni, starting with his rape (attempted?) of Donna Anna and the murder of her father. After other amorous exploits, the Don invites the funerary statue of Donna Anna's father to dine with him, but when the Commendatore reciprocates, he pulls the Don, kicking and screaming, to Hell. Some of the opera's characters are straight out of opera seria, others from opera buffa. Leporello and even Donna Elvira derive from opera buffa, with their exaggerated emotions, patter songs, and flamboyant musical intervals. Zerlina and Masetto represent opera buffa's peasant element, the wise and wily servants.

On the other hand, the nobility of Don Ottavio and Donna Anna demand music directly from opera seria. Most of their recitatives are written in the seria style of *recitative accompagnato*. Don Giovanni himself is a chameleon, assuming the musical-dramatic qualities of whomever he accompanies, sometimes buffo and sometimes deadly seria. Today *Don Giovanni* is one of Mozart's most admired and most-often-produced operas.

La clemenza di Tito (The Clemency of Titus), *opera seria* in two acts, September 6, 1791.
Wolfgang Amadeus Mozart (1756–91)
Libretto Pietro Metastasio, revised by Caterino Mazzolà.

More than forty other composers had already set this libretto by Metastasio before Mozart did. Ill and near the end of his life, Mozart had his student Franz Xaver Süssmayr write the recitatives in order to complete the score by the commissioned date. As a consequence, the opera is uneven. It contains some ravishing solo pieces, such as "Non più di fiori," but many rather banal recitatives. The first few performances were only modestly successful, but the final night was a resounding triumph. Mozart missed this performance because he had left Prague on September 15 to return to Vienna for the premiere of *Die Zauberflöte*. News of this triumphal final performance of *La clemenza di Tito* was brought to Mozart at the premiere of *Die Zauberflöte*, which made that opera's success even sweeter to the composer. Although *La clemenza di Tito* is not one of Mozart's popular operas, it is occasionally produced today.

Stavovské divadlo (Estates Theatre), Ovocny trh 1, Praha 1
tel: 2491–4204   fax: 2491–1530
Open Monday–Friday, 10:00 A.M.–6:00 P.M.; Saturday and Sunday, noon–1:00 P.M. and 2:00–6:00 P.M.
   Tickets can be ordered from abroad by telephone or by fax. Someone always seems to speak English.
   Performances start at *7:00, 7:30, or 8:00. Check!*

By the mid-nineteenth century, Prague was finally able to take advantage of its national intellectual, linguistic, and artistic heritage—but not without overcoming numerous obstacles. In 1845 the wealthy and powerful German bourgeoisie of Prague turned down a plan for a large theatre presenting works in Czech. Finally in 1862, after seventeen years of discussion, the small (900 seats, with a thirty-foot-square stage) Royal Provincial Czech Theatre opened. The Czechs always called the hall The Provisional Theatre, for it was considered a provisional space until money could be raised to build a larger National Theatre. When the Czech National Theatre opened in 1881, the Provisional Theatre was incorporated into it.

   Among the Czech composers whose works were premiered at the National Theatre or the Provisional Theatre were Bedřich Smetana, Antonin Dvořák, and Leoš Janáček.

   Like many artists in the turbulent Europe of the early nineteenth century, Bedřich Smetana (March 2, 1824, Litomysl—May 12, 1884, Prague) was very involved in the nationalist movement of his country. A leader in the fight to obtain a national theater in Prague, he envisioned a theatre devoted to a Czech repertoire. Such a repertoire would sustain the patriotic ideas of the period in large part by freeing drama from prevailing Italian and German influences.

   With donations from all over the country, the Czech nationalist movement culminated in the building of the National Theatre. The site was purchased in 1852; the foundation stone was laid in 1868; and the large theatre (seating 1,500) opened June 11, 1881, with a performance of Smetana's opera *Libuše*, written for the occasion. Since then, the Czechs have reserved *Libuše* as a festival opera for presentation on days of special national celebration. Unfortunately, the theatre burned down a mere two months after its opening. But again, an outpouring of national sentiment in the form of cash donations enabled the theatre to reopen in 1883.

Antonin Dvořák (September 8, 1841, Nelahozeves, near Kralupy—May 1, 1904, Prague) was highly revered as an opera composer during his lifetime. From 1869 until his death, he was always involved in the composition of an opera. *Rusalka*, based on a fairy tale, stands apart from the naturalistic kind of operas being written at the beginning of the twentieth century. The music of *Rusalka* is of extraordinary sensual beauty, full of lively, personable leitmotivs. The harmonic language is rich and varied. After his death, Dvořák's eleven operas were virtually forgotten until recently. Now *Rusalka* is performed internationally, but Dvořák is far better remembered as a symphonist and composer of chamber music. Along with Smetana and Janáček, Dvořák is regarded as one of the greatest composers of the Czech nationalist movement. Leoš Janáček (July 3, 1854, Hukvaldy, Moravia—August 12, 1928, Ostrava) wrote some of the most interesting and exciting music of the late Romantic period, works only recently being rediscovered in the West.

The National Theatre was reconstructed between 1977 and 1983, and a new small theatre (Nová Scéna) was added for the performance of plays and chamber operas. The National Theatre presents prose theatre, ballet, and opera.

The National Theatre (or the Provisional Theatre) presented the following premieres: ten operas by Bedřich Smetana including four versions of *The Bartered Bride* premiered between May 30, 1866, and September 25, 1870; eight operas of Antonin Dvořák (1841–1904), between 1871 and 1904, including *Rusalka*, lyric fairy tale in three acts, March 31, 1901; Libretto Jaroslav Kvapil, based on Friedrich de la Motte Fouqué's *Undine*; as well as Hans Christian Andersen's *The Little Mermaid*.

The Excursions of Mr. Brouček (*Výlety páně Broučkovy*), opera of four acts in two parts: *The Excursion of Mr. Brouček to the Moon*; and *The Epoch-making Excursion of Mr. Brouček*, April 23, 1920.
Leoš Janáček (1854–1928)
Libretto by the composer with the help of F. Gellner, V. Dyk, F. S. Procházka, and others, after the novel *The True Excursion of Mr. Broucek to the Moon* by Svatopluk Čech.

The Excursions of Mr. Brouček places a slightly tipsy Prague landlord on the moon, a place of great artistic activity, where he has many experiences and falls in love. In Part 2 he finds himself back in Prague, but in the year 1420, with a Hussite twist. He returns to the right century by the end of the opera, stuck in a beer barrel in his apartment house courtyard.

The work is, needless to say, a comic opera, the only one Janáček wrote, but one unlikely to be staged in the West because of its many difficulties: a cast of thousands, fourteen singing roles, one mute part, two choruses, not to mention the knowledge of local history needed to understand the plot. (Janáček's other eight operas were premiered in Brno, at that city's National Theatre.)

National Theatre (Národní divadlo), Národní trida, 2, Praha
tel: (42–2) 2491–1675
Open Monday–Friday, 10:00 A.M.–6:00 P.M.; Saturday and Sunday,
10:00 A.M.–12:30 P.M. and 3:00 P.M.–6:00 P.M.
trams: 6, 9, 17, 18, or 22 to Národní divadlo
ticket office: Ostrovni 1
   Performances usually begin at 7:00 P.M.

The powerful resident German bourgeoisie, unwilling to limit German opera
performances to the small Estates Theatre, in 1888 built their own Deutschetheater on the ramparts now standing between the Wilson Station and the
National Museum. The Deutschetheater is the largest in Prague and an exact
copy of the Vienna Opera, though smaller. Over the years the theatre has had a
very distinguished list of musical directors, including Gustav Mahler, Richard
Strauss, Erich Kleiber, Bruno Walter, and George Szell.
   The Deutschetheater was partially destroyed in 1945. It reopened in 1948 as
the Smetana Theatre, and since 1992 has been called the Státni Opera Praha
(Prague State Opera). The Státni Opera is Prague's best, focused solely on opera.
This opera house continues to present standard international repertory as well as
the premieres of many new Czech operas.

A notable Deutschetheater premiere

Erwartung (Expectation), *monodrama* in one act, June 6, 1924.
Arnold Schoenberg (September 13, 1874, Vienna—July 13, 1951, Los
Angeles)
Libretto Marie Pappenheim.

   This expressionistic, dreamlike monodrama was written by Dr. Marie
Pappenheim, who was obviously very aware of contemporary psychological
and psychoanalytical thought. (A relative of hers was the famous Anna O. of
Sigmund Freud's *Studies in Hysteria.*) The single character, a woman in the
woods, is obsessed with erotic memories and her fruitless wait earlier in the
evening for her lover. Past and present are indistinguishable, memories of her
lover dead and lover alive confused. Schoenberg called the opera a "night-
mare, the slow-motion representation of everything that happens in a second
of great psychological stress." Schoenberg composed the opera's vast and
complex orchestral score in a remarkably short sixteen days!

Státni Opera Praha (The Prague State Opera), also known as
Smetanovo divadlo (the former German Opera House), Wilsonova 4,
Nové Mesto, Praha 1
tel: (42–2) 2426–5353
Open Monday–Friday, 10:00 A.M.–5:30 P.M.; Saturday and Sunday,
10:00 A.M.–noon and 1:00–5:30 P.M.
   Performances start at *7, 7:30, or 8:00. Check!*

In honor of the two internationally reknowned Czech composers who played important roles in Czech nationalism, Prague hosts a Dvořák Museum and a Smetana Museum.

Dvořák Museum, Villa Amerika (Muzeum Antonína Dvořáka), Ke Karlovu, 20, Praha 1
tel: (42–2) 298–214
Open Tuesday–Sunday, 10:00 A.M.–5:00 P.M.
trams: 4, 6, 16, or 22; metro to Pavlova
Closed Monday.

The Dvořák Museum is a baroque summer house, built between 1717 and 1720. In the early 1930s, the Prague Society for Building a Monument to Antonin Dvořák acquired the building, opening the museum on June 20, 1932. It contains wonderful Dvořák memorabilia, including photos of the composer receiving an honorary degree from Cambridge (England) and visiting Iowa and New York in the "New World." Uncirculated photos of the conductors Gustav Mahler, Arthur Nikisch, and even Hans von Bülow, who conducted the premiere of Dvořák's Fifth Symphony, are on exhibit. Outside Central Europe, Dvořák is known for his symphonies and his chamber music; in the Czech Republic, he is known for his operas and his choral and vocal music.

Smetana Museum (Muzeum Bedricha Smetany), Novotného Lávka, 1, Praha 1
tel: (42–2) 2422–9075
Open Wednesday–Monday, 10:00 A.M.–6:00 P.M.
The Smetana Museum is on the river's edge at the old city's end of the Charles Bridge. In 1995 it was closed, pending renovation. A statue of Smetana stands in front.

Each spring the city of Prague hosts a Spring Festival of music and art that begins with a May 12 performance of Bedřich Smetana's opera *Libuše* in commemoration of his death on that day in 1884. The festival always closes with Ludwig van Beethoven's Ninth Symphony which, of course, finishes with the "Ode to Joy."

Prague Spring International Music Festival, office: Hellichova, 18, Praha 1
tel: (42–2) 2451–0422   fax: (42–2) 536–040

As of 1995, the opera lover on the trail of Prague's famous operatic history is bound to encounter obstacles. The city is not yet set up to help tourists: Street signs are frequently lacking and maps are likely to be slightly misleading. Perseverance is required!

FOOD

Eating in Prague can be a bit of an ordeal—smoky, expensive, and not very tasty. A good rule to follow seems to be the simpler the restaurant, the better the food. We recommend

Hostinec Cern'y Orel, U luzického semináire 40, Prague 1
Go early and it is likely to be smoke-free! The goulash and dumplings are very good, perhaps accompanied by excellent "Budweiser" beer (the original!). The restaurant is five steps from Hotel U Páva.

LODGING

Stay in Malá Strana, across the river from the hustle and bustle of the old city. Faxing the hotel of your choice is the easiest way to reserve and gives you written confirmation of your reservation.

U Páva (The Peacock), U luzického semináire 32, Prague 1
tel: (42–2) 537–069   fax: (42–2) 533–379
The hotel is an elegantly restored house on a quiet, *gaslit* street in Malá Strana. The top floor (walk-up) offers a wonderful view of the old city across the river. The very efficient Prague subway stops only three minutes from the hotel and the Charles Bridge is a mere four-minute walk. The hotel has a restaurant and a bar.

U Trí Pstrosu, Drazického nám. 12, Prague 1
tel: (42–2) 2451–0779 or 2451–0782   fax: (42–2) 2451–0783
This beautifully renovated hotel is right at the Malá Strana end of the Charles Bridge. Most rooms have beamed ceilings and large windows. The hotel has a restaurant and a bar.

Hotel U Krále Karla (The King Charles Hotel), Nerudova/Uvoz, Prague 1
tel: (42–2) 598–805 or 531–880 or 533–618 or 530–636   fax: (42–2) 538–811
At the foot of the castle walls, this hotel is a beautifully renovated Gothic building offering some rooms with fireplaces. The hotel has two restaurants.

BRNO

Brno, the capital city of Moravia, was until the late eighteenth century no more than a village. Then in 1766 a single textile mill spawned an industry that soon caused the town to be dubbed the "Austrian Manchester." Brno's geographical position tied its cultural development very closely to that of Vienna. Now no more than an hour outside Vienna, even during the Hapsburg rule it was regarded as almost a Viennese suburb. If you come to Brno by train, do not be put off by the "neobrutalist" buildings on the city's outskirts. The city center is grand, and its opera house is the largest in all of Czechoslovakia. We suggest a quick visit to Brno betweens stays in Vienna and Prague.

Opera debuted in the castle nearby in the 1720s. In 1767 a German Singspiel was presented, arias sung in Czech and dialogue spoken in German. A permanent theatrical privilege was granted to the city by the Hapsburg Emperor Joseph II in 1786. At the beginning of the nineteenth century, most opera performances were in German. Italian and German opera began to be translated into Czech about 1840. Finally in the 1870s touring Czech companies brought Czech opera in Czech to Brno. From that time until 1918, Brno had two opera houses: a German and a Czech.

The Brno Stadttheater opened in 1882. As a Czech theatre from 1918 to 1945, it was called the National Theatre, or the Theatre on the Ramparts.

The National Theatre on the Ramparts presented the premieres of most of Leoš Janáček's eleven operas, including the internationally known *Kátya Kabanová*, November 23, 1921; *The Cunning Little Vixen*, November 6, 1924; *The Makropoulos Affair*, December 18, 1926; *From the House of the Dead*, April 12, 1930.

Leoš Janáček (July 3, 1854, Hukvaldy, Moravia—August 12, 1928, Ostrava) is Brno's claim to operatic fame. When he was eleven, Janáček was sent to Brno to be a chorister at the queen's monastery. He had his first operatic experience singing in the chorus of Meyerbeer's *Le Prophète*. He studied to be a teacher and taught from 1880 until he retired in 1904. During that period, he conducted many of the choral societies in Brno and, between 1884 and 1888, he founded and published a musical journal. In 1888 he became an avid collector of native Moravian folk music, which he used extensively in his own compositions.

In 1887 Janáček composed his first opera, *Šárka*, based on Czech mythology. The powerful German elite who ruled the operatic scene at that time disapproved, and the opera was not performed until 1925. A second opera met with audience approval, and when his third opera, *Jenůfa*, finally received its first Prague performance in 1916, it was a spectacular success. He wrote his next four operas and some of his most exciting instrumental music between the ages of sixty-four and seventy-four.

During this time it seems his creative life was stimulated by his long affair with a woman named Kamila Strösslová, for whom he appears to have had a very intense and fiery passion. He never left his wife but kept in daily contact with Kamila, either in person or in writing. His death, on August 12, 1928, came about because he caught pneumonia while searching for her son, who was lost in the woods in a storm.

His operas are famous for their directness and concision: most are over in two hours. All his music has superb vitality and driving force. The fact that his operas also have great plots adds to their powerful appeal. It is our good fortune that several of his operas have come into the standard repertory within the past ten years.

Today the Janáckovo Divadlo (Janáček Theatre) is the country's largest opera house. Built after the war, it is an unfortunately gray and unappealing building that opened in 1965 with a performance of Janáček's *Cunning Little Vixen.*

A Janáček Museum stands across the park on Kolinikova.

ENGLAND

❧ ❦

LONDON

The first thing an opera lover should do after arriving in London is buy *Opera Now* and *What's On in London*. *Opera Now* contains information on opera performances in Great Britain and throughout the world, whereas *What's On in London* is specific to that city, listing operatic, musical, theatrical, and cinematic offerings for the month.

The world's second public opera house (preceded only by Venice's Teatro San Cassiano) opened in London in 1639 to offer plays and "musical presentments." (In 1765 London also hosted the first public concerts.) The first English opera performed in London was probably an early 1640s production of *Lovers Made Men*, by Nicholas Lanier based on a Ben Jonson libretto. The opera was performed in the Italian "stylo recitativo" [sic].

Subsequent circumstances made this opera unique. Civil war from 1642 to 1649 brought Oliver Cromwell to power. His puritanical government prohibited theatre and musical entertainment including, of course, this Italianate style of opera. All theatres were closed.

When Charles II was reinstated in 1662, the Restoration gave birth to a different kind of English opera that had its roots in the *masque*, a creation of the late 1620s Stuart court. A masque is a kind of semi-opera, a half-spoken, half-sung type of musical theatre, in English. Masques were entertainments with quite elaborate costumes and scenery but not much in the way of coherent plots or characterizations.

Presenting these early semi-operas were the Dorset Garden Theatre (where the first proscenium arch was built in the early 1670s) and the Drury Lane Theatre. This musical form reached its zenith in the late 1680s and early 1690s in the works of Henry Purcell (1658 or 1659, London—November 21, 1695, London), such as *The Fairy Queen* and *King Arthur*.

The Dorset Garden Theatre opened on November 9, 1671, and was demolished in 1709. It premiered many semi-operas by Henry Purcell. Dorset

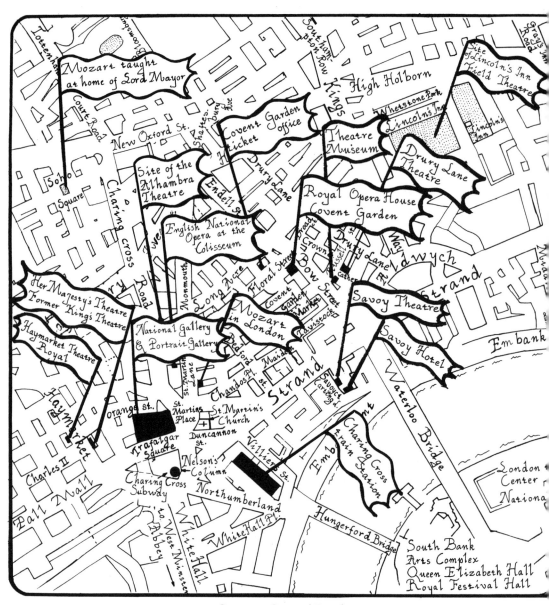

Operatic Central London

Garden Theatre stood near the river's edge, at the bottom of Dorset Rise (take Salisbury Court, off Fleet Street). The embankment has been widened over the years.

Drury Lane Theatre (now called the Theatre Royal, Drury Lane), which opened March 26, 1674, was destroyed by fire in 1791; it reopened in 1794, burned again in 1809, and was rebuilt in 1812. When Her Majesty's Theatre succumbed to fire in 1867, opera performances were transferred to the Drury Lane from 1868 to 1877. In 1870 the theatre presented *Der fliegende Holländer* (The Flying Dutchman), the first Wagner opera performed in England. The Opera Company of Sir Thomas Beecham used the theatre for its London seasons

in 1917–1919. Today the Theatre Royal, Drury Lane presents musicals. The foyer contains paintings, statues, and busts of the theatre's past owners, managers, and performers.

Theatre Royal, Drury Lane, Catherine Street, London WC2 B5JF
tel: (171) 494–5000
underground: Covent Garden

Two operas stand out from the period of the Restoration: *Venus and Adonis* and *Dido and Aeneas*.

Venus and Adonis, by John Blow (baptized February 23, 1649, Newark, Nottinghamshire—October 1, 1708, London), was probably performed at court in Oxford, sometime in 1681. Blow originally called *Venus and Adonis* "A Masque for the entertainment of the King," Charles II. Although the opera was a great success, Blow never wrote another stage work, instead devoting his compositional production to Anglican church anthems. Despite Blow's description of the work as a masque, it is all sung. The two protagonists are accompanied by a chorus whose role is to comment upon the action, amplify the drama, and reiterate the story (as in the earliest Florentine operas and the Greek tragedies after which they were modeled).

Henry Purcell's *Dido and Aeneas,* premiered sometime before 1689, is also all sung and is much like a miniature Venetian opera from the 1640s, albeit in English. Based on a classical subject, the opera is laid out in a few arias interspersed with very imaginative *recitar cantando*. Again, the chorus amplifies the drama.

Dido and Aeneas was written to be performed in Josias Priest's boarding school for young women in Chelsea, then a suburb of London. Priest was a well-known dancer and choreographer. The first performance probably took place in the spring as part of May Day festivities. *Dido* is a very popular operatic subject and was set no fewer than ten times, starting with a version in 1641 by the Venetian composer and student of Claudio Monteverdi, Francesco Cavalli.

The tombs of both Henry Purcell and John Blow are in the pavement of the North Choir Aisle in Westminster Abbey. Diamond-shaped stones in the pavement nearby honor other men of music. Of particular interest to opera lovers are those commemorating the composers Benjamin Britten and Sir William

207

Theatre Royal, Drury Lane

Walton. There is also a memorial to Dr. Charles Burney, the eighteenth-century music historian who traveled throughout continental Europe and recorded musical and operatic trends. Burney, organist at the Royal Hospital, is buried in the closed graveyard on Royal Hospital Road.

The organ of the choir in Saint Paul's Cathedral was built under the direction of John Blow and was played by Jeremiah Clarke, who composed the very famous trumpet voluntary often attributed to Purcell. The north transept of Saint Paul's Cathedral contains a memorial to the composer Sir Arthur Sullivan, of the famous team Gilbert and Sullivan.

Queen Elizabeth Hall in the South Bank Theatre Complex contains a Purcell Room.

In 1703 the Queen's Theatre in the Haymarket (now Her Majesty's Theatre) was built specifically to put on performances of Italian opera. (During the course of history, the theatre would also be called The King's Theatre or His Majesty's Theatre, depending on the sex of the current ruler. Sometimes the theatre is also called Larger Haymarket Theatre, which seems an expedient title to use here.) The theatre was designed as a money-making enterprise and catered to an admission-paying audience. Italian opera took London by storm in the early eighteenth century. The English audiences were particular aficionados of the castrato voice. Larger Haymarket Theatre was London's principal Italian Opera House from 1703 until the 1840s. It burned down several times and was always rebuilt, the fourth and last time in 1897. The theatre joined forces with Covent Garden Theatre in 1847.

Larger Haymarket Theatre presented the first Italian-style opera to receive its premiere in London: *Rinaldo* (February 24, 1711), written by the newly arrived George Frideric Handel (February 25, 1685, Halle—April 14, 1759, London).

Handel was twenty-five years old and had already had five successful operas performed in Hamburg, Florence, and Venice. He had come to London in the autumn of 1710, and devoted most of his compositional focus to opera until 1741.

The list of the thirty operas by George Frideric Handel premiered in Larger Haymarket Theatre should give a clear idea of the role of "Italian" opera in the early eighteenth century. Although Naples was the city from which eighteenth-century Italian opera emanated, the most lasting examples of this genre were written by distinctly non-Neapolitan Germans, such as George Frideric Handel and Christoph Willibald Gluck (July 2, 1714, Erasbach, Upper Palatinate— November 15, 1787, Vienna), to name only two. Handel and Gluck wrote bel canto opera, "singer's opera" (also called "number opera"), works that showed off vocal prowess, agility, and musical imagination.

These operas are characterized by beautiful, flamboyant, and lyrical arias, more than half of which were written in an ABA, or da capo, form. The style of the early eighteenth century demanded that a performer of a da capo aria improvise, often flamboyantly, when returning to the second A section. It was this unique moment, a performer could really demonstrate his artistic (and gymnastic) prowess, that audiences waited for. Here the unnatural beauty, power, and agility of the castrato voice showed to its best advantage. These bel canto operas are basically a series of beautiful arias strung together with dialogue set in recitative (from whence comes the name "number" or "singer's" opera).

Today only two operas by Handel, *Serse* (or *Xerxes*) and *Giulio Cesare*, and one opera by Gluck, *Orfeo ed Euridice*, are performed internationally with any regularity. Although the actual librettos for these operas were written by Italian poets from the early eighteenth century, most of the texts have as their basis classical history, or classical mythology. They draw, for example, from Ovid's *Metamorphoses*, from the great Italian epic poets— Ludovico Ariosto's *Orlando Furioso*, and Torquato Tasso's *Gerusalemme liberata*—or from the Italian pastoral poet Giovanni Battista Guarini's *Il pastor fido*.

Thirty operas by Handel premiered in Larger Haymarket Theatre, including *Giulio Cesare* and *Serse* (*Xerxes*).

Larger Haymarket Theatre also premiered three operas by Luigi Cherubini between 1785 and 1786; *I masnadieri*, July 22, 1847, a commission by Giuseppe Verdi, as well as the English premieres, from 1842 to 1858, of *Ernani*, *I lombardi*, *I due Foscari*, *Attila*, *Luisa Miller*, *Nabucco*, *La traviata*, and *Il trovatore*.

Larger Haymarket Theatre is at present Her Majesty's Theatre and devotes its stage to musicals by Andrew Lloyd Webber.

Her Majesty's Theatre, Haymarket, London SW1
tel: (44–171) 494–5400
underground: Piccadilly Circus

Her Majesty's Theatre (Larger Haymarket Market Theatre)

The Little Theatre in the Haymarket, on the Haymarket's east side and opposite Larger Haymarket Theatre, was built in 1720 and hosted many ballad operas and a few Italian operas. The theatre was demolished in 1820. The present Theatre Royal Haymarket, which opened in 1821, stands on the site of the original theatre.

Theatre Royal Haymarket, Haymarket, London SW1
tel: (44–171) 930–8800   fax: (44–171) 839–3798
underground: Piccadilly Circus

Almost all of Handel's scores are in the British Library, and most of them are complete.

British Library, Great Russell Street, London WC1
tel: (44–171) 323–7222

Open Monday–Saturday, 10:00 A.M.–5:00 P.M.
underground: Russell Square or Holborn

George Frideric Handel lived at 25 Brook Street from 1725 until his death in 1759.

Handel appears to have been a very charitable human being. He supported the Foundling Hospital (today called the Thomas Coram Foundation for Children), located at 40 Brunswick Square, with an annual presentation of the *Messiah*. When Handel died, he left many mementos to the organization, including the manuscript score of the *Messiah*. Each year, to celebrate his February 23rd birthday, a concert is given in the hall of the old building.

Handel regularly played the 1612 harpsichord in Fenton House, where concerts are now given on summer evenings.

Fenton House, Hampstead Grove, London, NW3 6RT
tel: (44–171) 435–3471
Open April through October, Saturday–Wednesday, 11:00 A.M.–6:00 P.M.; March, only Saturday and Sunday, 2:00–6:00 P.M.
underground: Hampstead

In Westminster Abbey's Chapel of Saint Faith, on the right-hand side on the west wall, is a statue of Handel holding the score of the *Messiah* opened to "I know that my Redeemer Liveth."

A splendid 1756 portrait of Handel by the early Georgian painter Thomas Hudson hangs in the National Portrait Gallery.

National Portrait Gallery, Trafalgar Square (directly across from St. Martin in the Fields)
tel: (44–171) 306–0055
underground: Charing Cross

Wolfgang Amadeus Mozart stayed in nearby Covent Garden when he visited London in 1764. The Mozart family lived at several addresses during this visit:

180 Ebury Street
Cecil Court, off of Saint Martin's Street
20 Firth Street.

The eight-year-old Mozart taught music at the 22 Soho Square residence of London's Lord Mayor.

Lincoln's Inn Fields Theatre, built in 1695 by converting a tennis court (an idea already executed by the French for Paris's first opera house), was also called the Duke's Theatre and vied with Larger Haymarket Theatre for a prominent role in the presentation of Italian opera in London. The theatre took the name of its site, the largest square in central London, called Lincoln's Inn Fields. Before the gardens were enclosed, they were the haunt of thieves and a place where duels were regularly fought. The square was laid out as a whole in 1618 by Inigo Jones, one of the seventeenth-century's most famous English architects. Lincoln's Inn

Fields Theatre, which stood on the south side of the square, was demolished in 1848 and the Royal College of Surgeons now occupies the site.

Lincoln's Inn Fields Theatre presented the first paid *public* presentations of *Dido and Aeneas* (1700) Henry Purcell; premieres of Handel's final two operas: *Imeneo*, November 22, 1740, *Deidamia*, January 10, 1741; and, most important, *The Beggar's Opera*, ballad opera in three acts (January 29, 1728), based on popular songs arranged by Johann Christoph Pepusch, libretto by John Gay.

The Beggar's Opera is always attributed to John Gay while the contribution of Pepusch is largely ignored. Gay changed the words of sixty-nine well-known songs and contextualized these with dialogue. In the story, a highwayman (Macheath) falls in love with the daughter of Peachum, the equivalent of a Mafioso chief. For fear she will betray his secrets to Macheath, Peachum has the highwayman arrested and almost hanged—but all ends happily.

The extraordinary success of *The Beggar's Opera* resulted from audience reaction against the prevailing passion for Italian opera evinced by many Englishmen. It was performed sixty-two consecutive times and gave birth to the *ballad opera*, opera in English made up of spoken dialogue and songs that were the popular ditties of the day. Many opera theatres present this piece today, but most come to grief. The popular songs Pepusch arranged had meaning for the public of his day, but now they usually seem rather silly and shallow. Bertolt Brecht based his text of *Die Dreigroschenoper* on Gay's story. The Brecht–Kurt Weill version of the story premiered in Berlin in 1928 is much more compelling (Berlin, Theater an Schiffbauerdamm, page 266).

Covent Garden, also called the Royal Opera House, opened on December 7, 1732, as the Theatre Royal at Covent Garden. The financial success of *The Beggar's Opera* provided the capital to build the theatre. It is named after the area that was once the *convent garden* of the monks of Westminster Abbey. A royal decree early in the eighteenth century granted the Theatre Royal at Covent Garden and the Drury Lane Theatre almost sole rights to spoken theatre in London. Thus, for at least the first one hundred years of its existence, Theatre Royal at Covent Garden was devoted primarily to this type of drama. However, on several notable occasions, lyric theatre took precedence.

During the second half of the eighteenth century, Theatre Royal at Covent Garden and Larger Haymarket Theatre were the leading playhouses in London, open more than two hundred nights per season. The first Covent Garden theatre was destroyed by fire in 1808 but was rebuilt and reopened in 1809 with a performance of Shakespeare's *Macbeth*.

The political and artistic climate that accompanied the beginning of the decline of the British Empire during the first third of the nineteenth century caused Covent Garden's reputation as a first-rate opera theatre to decline. Operas presented by the theatre were mainly free adaptations (in English) of pieces by Mozart and Rossini, to which rather mediocre contemporary English composers added their own work. Finally, in 1826, in an attempt to get on course again, the theatre hired Carl Maria von Weber (November 18[?], 1786, Eutin—June 5, 1826, London) as musical director. Weber had had great success as musical director of Dresden's Deutsche Opera (see Dresden, page 279). However, he died only two months after the London premiere of his last opera, *Oberon*, April 12, 1826. He had had tuberculosis since his youth, and London's foggy, smoke-filled air finally put an end to him.

The theatre was destroyed by fire a second time on March 5, 1856, and after a financial crisis, it reopened on May 15, 1858, with a performance of Meyerbeer's *Les Huguenots*. In 1892, during the reign of Queen Victoria, the theatre was renamed the Royal Opera House.

Some Covent Garden premieres (details of some at chapter's end):

In the eighteenth century: nineteen operas, including *Artaxerxes* (1762), by Thomas Arne; *Oreste* (December 18, 1734), George Frideric Handel; *Ariodante* (January 8, 1735), George Frideric Handel; *Alcina* (April 16, 1735), George Frideric Handel; *Atalanta* (May 12, 1736), George Frideric Handel; *Arminio* (January 12, 1737), George Frideric Handel; *Giustino* (February 16, 1737), George Frideric Handel; *Berenice* (May 18, 1737), George Frideric Handel.

Many of Handel's oratorios were premiered in the theatre from 1738 to 1759, including: *Semele*, a musical drama (February 10, 1744), with a libretto by William Congreve.

In the nineteenth century: Ivanhoe (1891), Sir Arthur Sullivan; *La Navarraise* (1894), Jules Massenet.

Covent Garden also presented the English premieres of many operas that had proven themselves elsewhere: all of Verdi's operas from *Rigoletto* to *Falstaff,* Wagner's *Lohengrin* (in Italian!), and finally the great verismo operas of Mascagni, Puccini, and Leoncavallo.

In the twentieth century: Arianna (1995), (lost opera by Monteverdi) completely reconstructed by Alexander Goehr; *Billy Budd* (1951), Benjamin Britten; *Gawain* (1991), Sir Harrison Birtwistle; *Gloriana* (1953), Benjamin Britten; *The Ice Break* (1977), Sir Michael Tippett; *King Priam* (1962), Sir Michael Tippett; *The Knot Garden* (1970), Sir Michael Tippett; *Midsummer Marriage* (1955), Sir Michael Tippett; *Owen Wingrave*, first staged version (1973), Benjamin Britten; *The Perfect Fool* (1923), Gustav Holst; *Taverner* (1972), Sir Peter Maxwell Davies; *Troilus and Cressida* (1954), Sir William Walton; *Victory* (1970), Richard Rodney Bennett; *We Come to the River* (1976), Hans Werner Henze; among others.

During World War I the Royal Opera House, Covent Garden was requisitioned by the Ministry of Works as a furniture repository, and during World War II it became a dance hall! It would have remained a dance hall had the music publishers Boosey & Hawkes not intervened. The theatre reopened on February 20, 1946, with a performance of the ballet *The Sleeping Beauty*. With the appointment of the brilliant director Peter Brook in 1948, the house began to be more artistically adventuresome.

Today the Royal Opera House is considered the foremost opera-presenting organization in London. The theatre seats 2,011 and is located on Bow Street, which gets its name from its bent-bow shape. The house will close in 1996 to undergo major renovations.

The Royal Opera House, Covent Garden, Bow Street, London WC2E 9DD
tel: (44–171) 304–4000

Royal Opera House, Covent Garden

Royal Opera House Advance Ticket Box Office, 48 Floral Street,
London WC2E 7QA
Open Monday–Saturday, 10:00 A.M.–8:00 P.M.
tel: (44–171) 304–4000   fax: (44–171) 497–1256
underground: Covent Garden

Just down the street from the Royal Opera House, Covent Garden stands the
Theatre Museum, which boasts an excellent library and several changing
exhibits. (In 1995 a large exhibit dealing with contemporary performances of
Henry Purcell's operas commemorated the tercentenary of his death.) Besides
items appealing to adult theatre lovers, a number of hands-on exhibits and classes
are geared to children's tastes. There is also a shop full of operatic and theatrical
goodies, and a café.

Theatre Museum, Russell Street, Covent Garden, London, WC2
tel: (44–171) 836–7891
Open Tuesday–Sunday, 11:00 A.M.–7:00 P.M.
admission: £3
underground stop: Covent Garden

The Sadler's Wells Theatre opened in 1753 as a music hall offering various
kinds of "spectacles," ranging from Shakespeare's plays to "aquatic drama." (The
theatre was built over a medicinal well covered by a trap door; hence its name.)
The theatre closed in 1906 and reopened in 1931 as a legitimate opera theatre.
Closed again during World War II, it reopened on June 7, 1945, with the world
premiere of Benjamin Britten's gripping *Peter Grimes*.

Since 1945 the theatre has presented the premieres of operas by several
distinguished English composers, including *Infidelio* (1973), Elisabeth Lutyens;
Peter Grimes (1945), Benjamin Britten; *Time Off?—Not a Ghost of a Chance!*
(1972), Elisabeth Lutyens.

The British government at one time promised the Sadler's Wells Opera
Company a new theatre on the South Bank but abandoned the project in 1968.
That same year the company left the Sadler's Wells Theatre and moved to the
Coliseum, a theatre built in 1904. In 1974 the company changed its name to the
English National Opera Company (ENO) and has owned the freehold of the
Coliseum since 1992.

The ENO is exemplary in promoting opera in today's society. The company
performs all operas in English, each year commissioning and performing a work
from a British composer. It also supports a Contemporary Opera Studio to
encourage the creation of smaller-scale works and funds and operates an
educational outreach program.

English National Opera (box office), London Coliseum, Saint Martin's
Lane, London WC2N 4ES
Open twenty-four hours a day
tel: (44–171) 632–8300   fax: (44–171) 379–1264

Today the Sadler's Wells Theatre mainly presents ballets.

Sadler's Wells, Rosebery Avenue, London EC1R 4TN
tel: (44–171) 278–8916
underground: Angel

The Lyceum, opened in 1772, presented many English premieres of popular Continental operas, including Carl Maria von Weber's *Der Freischütz* in 1824 and Wolfgang Amadeus Mozart's *Così fan tutte* (done *in English* as *Tit for Tat, or The Tables Turned*). The flamboyant impresario James Henry Mapleson (1830–1901), who tendered opera throughout the United States in the 1880s, was briefly impresario at the Lyceum. In 1861 he presented the English premiere of Giuseppe Verdi's *Un ballo in maschera* as well as that of Verdi's *Otello* in 1889, which was given by the touring company of Milan's La Scala. Closed during World War II, the theatre today is a tavern and dance hall.

Lyceum Tavern, The Strand, London WC2
tel: (44–171) 240–1663

In 1875 the impresario Richard D'Oyly Carte needed a companion piece to complete a program starting with Offenbach's *La Périchole*, scheduled at the Royalty Theatre. He commissioned a short (half-hour) opera from the librettist W. S. (William Schwenck) Gilbert (November 18, 1836, London—May 29, 1911, Grim's Dyke, Harrow Weald) and the composer Arthur Sullivan (May 13, 1842, London—November 22, 1900, London). The piece was *Trial by Jury* (1875), and its success motivated the Gilbert and Sullivan team and D'Oyly Carte to pursue their theatrical relationship. Between 1875 and 1881 at various London theatres, five of the team's operettas, including *The Sorcerer* (1877), *HMS Pinafore* (1878), and *The Pirates of Penzance* (1879), were smash hits.

Gilbert and Sullivan's operettas so captured New York audiences that unauthorized productions proliferated. But D'Oyly Carte, ever the clever businessman, retaliated by staging the New York premiere of *The Pirates of Penzance* on December 31, 1879, only one day after its London premiere, thus beating would-be pirate producers out of a chance at first-run proceeds.

In 1881 D'Oyly Carte built the Savoy Theatre specifically for producing Gilbert and Sullivan operettas. The theatre was posh, the first in London to be lit entirely by electricity. Beginning with *Iolanthe* (1882), eight of the fourteen operettas by Gilbert and Sullivan were premiered here, becoming known as the Savoy Operettas. The 1885 production of *The Mikado* was the most popular in its time.

Although five operettas by Sullivan with other librettists also premiered at the Savoy, only those by Gilbert and Sullivan remain popular today. Indeed, until recently English light opera, or operetta, was synonymous with Gilbert and Sullivan. The D'Oyly Carte Company held a monopoly on all professional productions of Gilbert and Sullivan operettas until 1961, when the copyright expired. The Savoy, gutted by fire on February 12, 1990, was rebuilt in flamboyant 1930s art deco style and reopened July 19, 1993. Today the Savoy presents musicals.

Savoy Theatre, Savoy Court, The Strand, London WC27 0ET
tel: (44–171) 836–8888   fax: (44–171) 379–7322

The Savoy Theatre is connected to the Savoy Hotel, which, owing to its central location, has housed many guests pivotal in opera history, from Giuseppe Verdi to Maria Callas.

The Alhambra Theatre commissioned and presented the premiere of Jacques Offenbach's *Whittington* in 1874. Offenbach had suffered severe financial reverses in his Parisian theatres and wrote *Whittington* simply for the money. He then went on to the United States, where he gave over forty concerts to rave reviews. The Alhambra Theatre stood in Leicester Square but was torn down after World War I.

Details of some operas premiered at Larger Haymarket Theatre

Giulio Cesare in Egitto (Julius Caesar in Egypt), *opera* in three acts, London Larger Haymarket Theatre, February 20, 1724.
George Frideric Handel (1685–1759)
Libretto Nicola Francesco Haym, based on Giacomo Bussani's libretto of the same title.

Giulio Cesare scored a big success at the premiere and at many subsequent performances, and Handel revised and revived the opera three times between 1725 and 1732. The story is a fictional rendering of Julius Caesar's visit to Egypt between 48 and 47 B.C. The roles of Caesar, Ptolemy, and Nirenus, written for castrati, are today sung by mezzo-sopranos. The orchestral writing is rich and elegant; the musical painting of the character of Cleopatra, who shifts from seductive to grief-stricken in between her two well-known ABA arias—"V'adoro pupile," with its provocative and lush instrumental sonorities, and "Piangerò la sorte mia," a fabulously extravagant grief-revenge da capo aria—is very moving. *Giulio Cesare* is a mainstay in the repertory of many of today's opera houses. Joan Sutherland, Montserrat Caballé, and Beverly Sills have recorded the role of Cleopatra, and the late Tatiana Troyanos was a particularly memorable Caesar.

Serse (Xerxes), opera in three acts, London King's Theatre, April 15, 1738.
George Frideric Handel (1685–1759)
Libretto, an anonymous revision of Silvio Stampiglia's *Il Xerse* (which the composer Bononcini set as an opera), in its turn based on Nicolo Minato's *Il Xerse*.

Xerxes, an opera buffa full of intrigue, treads the fine line between farce and tragedy. Xerxes, the king of Persia, is betrothed to Amastre but madly in love with Atalanta. Atalanta, however, is in love with the king's brother, Arsamene, as is her sister Romilda. *Xerxes* is very different in style from Handel's *opere serie* in that the arias are short and few are da capo in form. The opera's most famous aria, "Ombra mai fù'," is often called Handel's "Largo." Presumably the aria, sung in praise of a plane tree, is satirical; be that as it may, today the "Largo" is often played for very serious occasions, such as weddings or funerals.

Xerxes is Handel's greatest comic opera and was his last operatic success written for the King's Theatre. The premiere cast included the famous castrato Caffarelli (whose real name was Gaetano Marjorano) in the title role of Xerxes. The opera was revived in the 1980s and since then has often been performed throughout the world.

Details of a premiere at Sadler's Wells

Peter Grimes, opera in a prologue and three acts, June 7, 1945.
Benjamin Britten (November 22, 1913, Lowestoft—December 4, 1976, Aldeburgh)
Libretto Montagu Slater, after George Crabbe's poem, *The Borough*.

Peter Grimes is dedicated to the great conductor Sergey Koussevitsky, who commissioned the work. Britten and his companion, the tenor Peter Pears, wrote the scenario for *Peter Grimes* after reading Crabbe's poem, *The Borough*. They altered the character of the protagonist from a truly bad guy to someone who is the victim of both society and his own instability and weaknesses. Grimes is an ambiguous character, and Britten set him in music with the utmost compassion. At the end of the opera, the audience is left to decide whether Grimes should be blamed or pitied. The music, which includes four "Sea Interludes," is some of the most theatrically potent ever written. *Peter Grimes* is one of the most successful twentieth-century operas.

Details of some Covent Garden premieres

Artaxerxes, opera in three acts, February 2, 1762.
Thomas Arne (March 12, 1710, London—March 5, 1778, London)
Libretto probably by the composer.

Nineteen of Thomas Arne's fifty-five operas were premiered at Covent Garden. (Another twenty-two were premiered at the Drury Lane Theatre, two at Larger Haymarket Theatre, one at Lincoln's Inn Field Theatre, and six at the Little Theatre in the Haymarket.) A plaque nearby Covent Garden Opera informs that Arne was born in the Covent Garden area and spent all his life there. *Artaxerxes* is an Italian-style opera. It has arias and recitatives like all other eighteenth-century operas, is entirely sung, and is remembered today because of the flamboyant bel canto aria "A Soldier Tired of War's Alarms," performed by Joan Sutherland in the late 1950s on her first solo record, *The Art of the Prima Donna*. In its day *Artaxerxes* was a fabulous success.

Billy Budd, opera in a prologue and two acts, December 1, 1951.
Benjamin Britten (1913–76)
Libretto E. M. Forster and Eric Crozier, after Herman Melville's story.

Billy Budd is a painfully touching story of a good and beautiful young sailor who is loved by all but one of his shipmates. This intensely jealous fellow seaman falsely accuses Budd of instigating a mutiny. The accusation makes Budd stammer, as he is known to do when nervous. Goaded by the evil shipmate, Budd hits him and accidentally kills him. He is tried for murder and finally executed. The opera's music enhances the story, making it almost unbearably beautiful. *Billy Budd* originally had four acts, but after the premiere Britten revised the score so that when the opera was performed again at Covent Garden in 1964, it had two acts. Today it is known in this two-act version.

FOOD

One can grab a quick bite before the opera in the Crypt of Saint Martin's in the Fields. It is a pleasant cafeteria with good, inexpensive food and wine—and a great place to observe Londoners of all ages.

Covent Garden itself is full of eating places with both indoor and outdoor seating. It offers excellent people-watching possibilities also.

In England, in general, Indian or Italian food seems the best buy and the tastiest fare, as well as supplying the most balanced diet.

LODGING

Savoy Hotel, The Strand, London WC2R 0EU
tel: (44–171) 836–4343   fax: (44–171) 240–6040

For a hotel so steeped in operatic history—not to mention its convenient location, only a five-minute walk from Covent Garden and eight minutes from the ENO—the Savoy is not *that* expensive.

Howard Hotel, 12 Temple Place, London WC2R 2PR
tel: (44–171) 836–3555   fax: (44–171) 379–4547

This lovely hotel is about as close as you can stay to the opera houses without actually taking up residence in them.

Pastoria Hotel, 3–6 Saint Martin's Street (off Leicester Square), London WC2H 7HL
tel: (44–171) 930–8641   fax: (44–171) 925–0551

The Pastoria is conveniently near the Charing Cross underground station, a ten-minute walk from Covent Garden, five minutes from the ENO, and two minutes from the National Portrait Gallery.

Royal Trafalgar Thistle Hotel, Whitcomb Street, London WC2H 7HG
tel: (44–171) 930–4477   fax: (44–171) 925–2149

This hotel is also near the Charing Cross underground station, a ten-minute walk from Covent Garden, and five minutes from the ENO.

Two Summer Opera Festivals Near London

Glyndebourne

Glyndebourne, about seventy miles south of London, was the country home of John Christie, who built a small opera house there in 1934 and began the Glyndebourne Festival Opera. A new, larger theatre was christened in 1994 with a gala performance of *Le nozze di Figaro*. The tradition is that one dresses formally, brings an elegant picnic dinner, dines on the grass, and then attends an opera in an intimate setting. Five or six operas are presented each season, one of which is always by Mozart.

Glyndebourne premiered *The Rape of Lucretia* (July 12, 1946), Benjamin Britten; *Albert Herring* (June 20, 1947), Benjamin Britten; premieres of the English composers Oliver Knussen, Nicholas Maw, Nigel Osborne, Sir Michael Tippett.

For tickets:

Glyndebourne Festival Opera, Glyndebourne, Lewes, Sussex BN8 5UU
tel: (44–1273) 813–813   fax: (44–1273) 812–783

Aldeburgh

Aldeburgh is a small town on the Suffolk coast eighty miles from London. Benjamin Britten lived there from 1947 until his death in 1976, and the town is the actual setting for his "sea opera," *Peter Grimes* (1945). At the suggestion of his longtime companion, the tenor Peter Pears, Britten established a festival that gives a cultural focus to the area. The festival takes place in Aldeburgh's Jubilee Hall each June and lasts two and a half weeks. Six operas are presented each season, on average.

Aldeburgh premieres of Benjamin Britten include *The Little Sweep* (a children's opera), June 14, 1949; *Noyes Fludde*, June 18, 1958; *A Midsummer Night's Dream*, June 11, 1960; *Curlew River*, June 12, 1964; *The Burning Fiery Furnace*, June 9, 1966; *The Prodigal Son*, June 10, 1968; *Death in Venice*, June 16, 1973; *Paul Bunyan* (1941), the first British production, June 4, 1976.

Aldeburgh also presented premieres of works by the English composers Sir William Walton, Sir Lennox Berkeley, and Sir Harrison Birtwistle.

For tickets:

Aldeburgh Foundation, High Street, Aldeburgh, Suffolk IP15 5AX, Great Britain
tel: information and twenty-four–hour box office: (44–1728) 453–543

FRANCE

>≫ ≪

PARIS

Upon arriving in Paris, an opera lover should buy three magazines:

> *Pariscope*, a week's review of all events taking place in the city, with telephone numbers, addresses, and metro directions to all theatres (and museums, cinemas, restaurants, etc.);
>
> *Le Monde de la Musique*, a monthly magazine encompassing that month's musical offerings in France and containing advertisements for many future events throughout France;
>
> *Opéra International*, a monthly magazine devoted to opera, including many advertisements of *l'art lyrique* in France.

Through the ages, every development in French opera came to pass in the city of Paris. Whatever "it" might be, if it didn't take place in Paris, it wasn't considered important. Opera developed in France in the late seventeenth century, influenced by imports from Italy. French opera quickly distinguished itself from Italian by its emphasis on ballet and use of the French language. Some early French operas are, in fact, called *opéra ballets*. The composition and performance of French opera were subject to strict royal regulation and licensing.

On February 7, 1662, to celebrate the marriage of Louis XIV to Maria Theresa, daughter of the King of Spain, the court put on the premiere of the opera *Ercole amante* by the Venetian composer Francesco Cavalli. The event took place in the palace of the Tuileries in a newly constructed theatre notorious for its bad acoustics. (The palace and the theatre were destroyed during the Revolution of 1848.)

By the end of the decade, Italian opera had gone out of fashion in the court, and in 1669 Louis XIV gave exclusive rights for performing opera in Paris to the librettist Abbé Pierre Perrin and the composer Robert Cambert. These two had collaborated in 1659 to write a *comédie française en musique*, the first French pastoral lyric drama. Perrin and Cambert were colorful figures: Perrin spent a good portion of his life in debtor's prison, and Cambert was murdered by his own valet while in London in 1677.

Perrin opened the Academie Royale de Musique on March 16, 1671, but soon suffered financial difficulties, thanks to his unscrupulous business partners. In 1672, while Perrin languished in prison, Jean-Baptiste Lully offered to extricate him by paying his debts in exchange for the monopoly on performing opera. Thus, today it is Lully who is considered the "father of French opera."

The Academie Royale de Musique stood at the corner of rue Mazarine and rue Jacques Callot (a long "square" hemmed on both ends by eating places with outdoor seating). A plaque on the northeast corner of rue Callot says:

Ici s'élevait la salle du Jeu de	Here stood the Tennis Court
Paume de la Bouteille où fut	called la Bouteille in which the
ouvert Le Premier Opéra de Paris	first opera house of Paris opened
le 16 Mars 1671	March 16, 1671

(While learning about opera in Paris, I also aquired some tennis tidbits: Tennis was very popular among Parisian royalty in the sixteenth century. By the late seventeenth century, it had gone out of style among the French but had become very fashionable in England. The name of the game is English, derived from the French service term *tenez* [take that]; the tennis term "love," which means "zero," comes from French sixteenth-century slang for zero, *l'oeuf* [the egg!].)

The area in which the earliest opera house was situated is in the sixth arrondissement. It is full of other bits of opera lore.

At no. 14 rue Jacob, a plaque states that:

Richard Wagner a vécu ici	Richard Wagner lived here
du 30 Ottobre 1841 au	from October 30, 1841, to
7 Avril 1842	April 7, 1842

The house of Adrienne Lecouvreur stands between rue Bonaparte and rue de Seine at no. 16 rue Visconti. Lecouvreur's life inspired the playwright Eugène Scribe, and in 1902 the Italian composer Francesco Cilea wrote the opera *Adriana Lecouvreur* based on Scribe's play. Rue Visconti is rich in fame: Racine died at no. 24 and Balzac founded his print shop at no. 17.

Because of the aforementioned monopoly, the need to obtain a royal license to present opera, and later laws that governed its performance, Paris (and all of France) developed its own kinds of opera: *opéra-ballet*, opéra comique, *tragédie lyrique*, etc. Whereas Italian composers often based new works on the same or similar librettos, French composers wrote operas solely on the basis of newly written librettos that had first been approved by the Directorate of the Opéra.

In both its composition and performance, opera was very much under control of the King until the Revolution in 1789. In fact until the Revolution the

Operatic Paris (detailed maps head each section)

Théâtre des Bouffes Parisiens

L'Opéra Comique

Théâtre des Variétés

Théâtre du Châtelet

Théâtre de la Ville

Opéra Bastille

Bld. Ney

Rue Jean Jaurès

Bd. Stalingrard

Rue de Belleville

Rue

Rue la Fayette

Rue la Opéra

Rue de l'Opéra

R. St. Honoré

Q. du Louvre

Rue de Sébas.

Rue du Temple

Place du Châtelet

Rivoli

Av. de l'Hôtel de ville

Notre Dame St. Louis

St. Germain

Place Bastille

Bld. Voltaire

Didérot

Pl. de la Nation

Rue Daumesnil

Vaugirard

Jardin du Luxembourg

Bld. de l'Hôpital

Quai d'Austerlitz

Boula.

Quai de Bercy

Montparnasse Bld. Diderot Royet

Pl. Denfert Rochereau

Bd. D'Italie

Rue d'Italie

Boulevard Poniatowski

Rue de Tolbiac

Masséna

Bld. Jourdan

Bld. Kellermann Boulevard

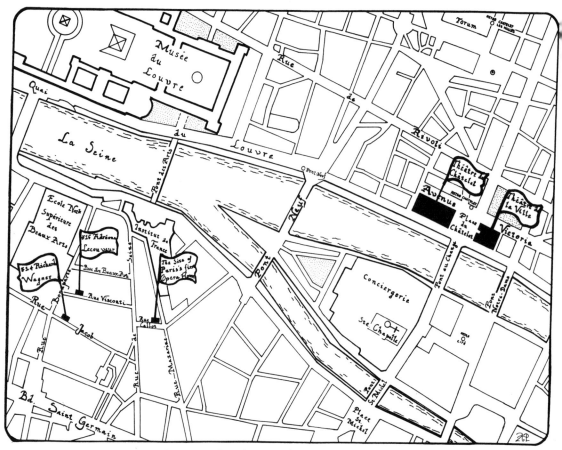

The map contains the following labels: Musée du Louvre, Rue, de, Rivoli, Quai, du, La Seine, Louvre, Pont-Neuf, Théâtre Châtelet, METRO CHÂTELET, Avenue, Place du Châtelet, Théâtre la Ville, École Nat. Supérieure des Beaux Arts, Institut de France, Forum, METRO CHÂTELET LES HALLES, Victoria, #16 Adriana Lecouvreur, The Site of Paris's first Opera, #3 t Richard Wagner, Rue des Beaux-Arts, Seine, Rue, Pont Neuf, Rue Visconti, Rue Jacob, Rue de l'Échaudé, Rue Bonaparte, Rue des Saints-Pères, Rue de Lille, Rue Mazarine, Rue Dauphine, Conciergerie, Pont au Change, Pont Notre Dame, Ste. Chapelle, Île de la Cité, Rue St. Michel, Place St. Michel, Bd. Saint Germain.

6th, 1st, and 2nd Arrondissements (Detail)

monarchy dominated virtually all aspects of French cultural life. Then laws passed in 1791 granted anyone the right to open a public theatre, resulting in an enormous proliferation of opera companies between 1791 and 1807. But in 1806 and 1807, Napoleon issued decrees that not only revoked this right but also dictated the repertory of each company and limited the total number of theatres in Paris to eight. Thus the primacy of L'Opéra was established. (The organization, wherever housed, was called L'Opéra and also held the name Académie National de Musique, harkening back to the birth of opera in Paris.)

By the end of the first third of the nineteenth century, Giacomo Meyerbeer had fully formulated a new French style of opera, called "grand opéra," by using elements found in the late operas of Christoph Willibald von Gluck (July 2, 1714, Erasbach, Upper Palatinate—November 15, 1787, Vienna) as his model. His 1831 opera *Robert le diable* is the first true grand opera. (Meyerbeer, the most French of French composers in the nineteenth century, was born Jakob Liebmann Meyer Beer, near Berlin. Not only was he German but also Jewish.) By 1831 grand opera described a very particular kind of work written for L'Opéra. Grand opera requires enormous forces, with many leading characters, numerous secondary roles, large choruses, ballet, and a vast orchestra, as well as special musical effects—such as a separate off-stage orchestra. A grand opera had to meet certain requirements. For example,

> it had to be based on an ennobling subject of history or mythology;
> it had to have five acts;
> it had to contain at least one ballet (note the Paris versions of Giuseppe Verdi's *Don Carlos* and Richard Wagner's *Tannhäuser* and their ballets).

Great pagentry and inventive staging were de rigueur. To get the picture, consider the titles of some of the operas Rossini wrote for L'Opéra: *Le Siège de Corinthe, Moïse et Pharaon,* and *Guillaume Tell.* New stage machinery contributed to making these productions spectacular: for example, an *erupting volcano* embellished Daniel-François-Esprit Auber's *La Muette de Portici.* In fact, many future developments in orchestral music, staging, and lighting had their origins in the spectacle required by grand opera. The need to balance so many demanding elements gave birth to the role of the stage manager. For the first time, an a priori plan was necessary in order to produce opera successfully.

Production books were published for each new opera to allow the production to be copied in the provinces. (These books are on view at the Museum de L'Opéra, in the Opéra Garnier.) Of course, few provinces—or even other countries, for that matter—had the theatrical infrastructure or economic resources to stage grand opera in the manner it was intended to be performed. As a consequence, the style did not flourish outside Paris, but some aspects of grand opera nevertheless influenced many composers throughout Europe.

The greatest composers of grand opera are considered to be Luigi Cherubini (September 8, 1760, Florence—March 15, 1842, Paris), Gaspare Spontini (November 14, 1774, Maiolati, near Iesi, Italy—January 24, 1851, Maiolati), and Giacomo Meyerbeer (born Jacob Liebmann Meyer Beer, September 5, 1791, Vogelsdorf, near Berlin—May 2, 1864, Paris). *All* were distinctly not French-born.

The principal rule governing opera performed at L'Opéra from the late eighteenth until well into the twentieth century was that the whole work had to be sung. Spoken dialogue, considered frivolous, was forbidden on the stage of L'Opéra. The most popular French opera, Georges Bizet's *Carmen,* was commissioned by L'Opéra Comique, which allowed spoken dialogue. After the opera's premiere and Bizet's premature death, the dialogue was set in recitative by Bizet's friend Ernest Guiraud. (Guiraud's sole claim to fame came through his association with other composers; in 1881, after the death of Offenbach, he completed and orchestrated *Les Contes d'Hoffmann.*) *Carmen,* the Guiraud version, was first performed on the stage of L'Opéra in 1883, eight years after its premiere at L'Opéra Comique.

During the urban renewal of Napoleon III's Second Empire, the city of Paris held an architectural competition to design a new opera house. One hundred seventy-one proposals were submitted, and the architect Charles Garnier won.

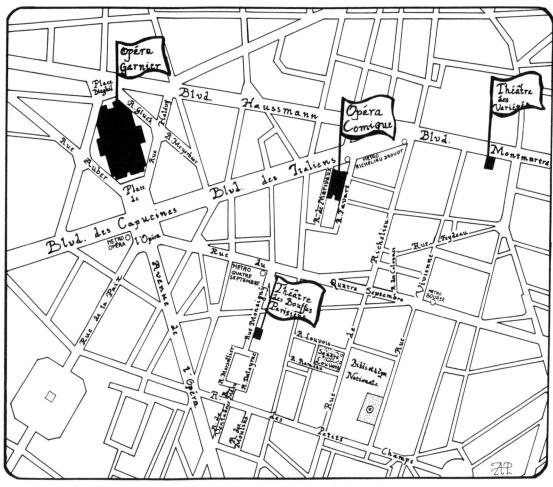

2nd and 9th Arrondissements (Detail)

For each proposal, the architect also had to supply a motto. Garnier's motto, in Italian, was "Bramo assai, spero poco" (I desire a great deal, I hope for little). L'Opéra Garnier, or Palais Garnier, opened in January 1875 and housed the Paris Opera until 1989. This elegant building is the quintessential opera house. It is huge, beautiful, acoustically superb, and welcoming. Every aspect conspires to make what you are seeing something very special.

The actual construction of the opera house was fraught with difficulties. The ground was so marshy that Garnier had to pump water from the swamp twenty-four hours a day for seven months! Because of the care he took in the basic construction, the basements of the building are uniquely dry. During the Paris Commune of 1869–70, they provided the only place in the city center dry enough to store provisions.

Garnier's architectural philosophy blended utilitarian ideals with classically influenced Italian art. The grand staircase is a masterpiece of utility and, as Garnier pointed out, when occupied by people, it resembles a Veronese painting. Electric lighting was installed in the whole house in 1881. The hall seats 1,991 people, but some seats have slightly limited sight lines.

L'Opéra, as an entity but not necessarily in Opéra Garnier, presented the following premieres (a full description of some of the premieres is at end of the chapter) twelve operas by Daniel-François-Esprit Auber including: *La Muette de Portici* (February 29, 1828), *Le Philtre* (June 15, 1831); *Lulu* (completed version, January 24, 1979), Alban Berg; *Benvenuto Cellini* (September 10, 1838), Hector Berlioz; three operas by Luigi Cherubini; four operas by Gaetano Donizetti including *La favorite* (December 2, 1840); seven operas by Christoph Willibald Gluck including *Alcestes* (April 23, 1776), *Iphigénie en Tauride* (May 18, 1779), *Orphée et Eurydice* (August 2, 1774); five operas by Charles Gounod; four operas by Jules Massenet including *Le Cid* (November 30, 1885), *Thaïs* (March 16, 1894); *L'Africaine* (April 28, 1865), Giacomo Meyerbeer; *Les Huguenots* (February 29, 1836), Giacomo Meyerbeer; *Le Prophète* (April 16, 1849), Giacomo Meyerbeer; *Robert le diable* (November 21, 1831), Giacomo Meyerbeer; *Le Siège de Corinthe* (October 9, 1826), Gioacchino Rossini; *Moïse et Pharaon* (March 26, 1827), Gioacchino Rossini; *Le Comte Ory* (August 20, 1828), Gioacchino Rossini; *Guillaume Tell* (August 3, 1829), Gioacchino Rossini; two operas by Antonio Salieri; five operas by Gaspare Spontini including *La vestale* (December 15, 1807); *Le Rossignol*, The Nightingale (May 26, 1914), Igor Stravinsky; *Renard*, The Fox (May 18, 1922), Igor Stravinsky; *Mavra* (June 3, 1922), Igor Stravinsky; *Persephone* (April 30, 1934), Igor Stravinsky; *Les vêspres siciliennes* (June 13, 1855), Giuseppe Verdi; *Don Carlos* (March 11, 1867), Giuseppe Verdi; *Tannhäuser*, third version, with Venusberg ballet music (March 13, 1861), Richard Wagner.

Opera Garnier, Place de l'Opéra, 2nd arr., 75009 Paris
tel: (33–1) 4742–5371

Museum de l'Opéra, the museum of Opéra Garnier, has a fantastic collection of operatic treasures: costumes and masks galore as well as drawings for the costumes and sets of operas and ballets. It also contains an archive run by the Bibliothèque Nationale with a reading room that offers thousands of operatic scores as well as small mock-ups of sets, including those for a 1875 production of Mozart's *Don Giovanni,* and marble busts of singers, librettists, and composers. Numerous paintings illustrate other halls that hosted L'Opéra, such as Salle Le Peletier and Salle Louvois, before Salle Garnier was built in 1875.

During visiting hours, music from the great operas presented at L'Opéra surges through the halls. The museum is always full of opera buffs and curious-minded people. This is a fabulous place for an opera lover or a balletomane! The museum spills over into the hallways and foyers of the elegant marble building. This imposing edifice has so many dark nooks and crannies that even the least imaginative person cannot doubt its role in inspiring the drama of *Phantom of the Opera.*

A marvelous gift shop (with, among other things, many excellent and rare photo-postcards of composers and singers) is set up in the front foyer.

Opéra Garnier

Grand Staircase of Palais Garnier

Museum de L'Opéra Garnier
Open Monday–Saturday, 10:00 A.M.–5:00 P.M. (The last ticket is sold at 4:30.)

In 1989 Opéra Bastille, built to replace the glorious Opéra Garnier, opened its doors. Located in Place de la Bastille, it is billed as the "people's opera," although seats are very expensive. Its uninviting exterior suggests a factory rather than a place to enjoy yourself, but all four of its halls are quite comfortable inside. The halls, from the large Grande Salle to the Salle Modulable, the Amphithéâtre, and the Studio, have surprisingly good acoustics. The Grande Salle has 2,700 seats.

On March 1, 1996, after extensive remodeling, L'Opéra Garnier reopened with performances of *Don Giovanni* and *Così fan tutte.* Happily for opera lovers, the Paris Opera, which manages both L'Opéra Garnier and L'Opéra Bastille, has decided to present mixed programs of opera and ballet in both.

Opéra Bastille, Place de la Bastille, 75011 Paris
Ticket office open: Monday–Saturday, 11:00 A.M.–6:30 P.M.
tel, taped information: (33–1) 4343–9696
tel, ticket office: (33–1) 4473–1300
The ticket office is located in the street-level hallway in front of the theatre. Tickets are also available at the department store FNAC.

For tickets by mail:

Opéra Bastille, Service Développement Public, 120, rue de Lyon, 75012 Paris

In the eighteenth century opéras comiques evolved as popular antitheses of the stately operas that preceded grand opéra. By the nineteenth century, L'Opéra Comique presented operas based on librettos that today might be labeled "fit for family consumption," encompassing a broad range of subjects germane to "the human comedy." The arias and ensembles were separated by *spoken* dialogue. Théâtre des Italiens presented Italian operas, both opera seria with accompanied and secco recitative as well as opera buffa with secco recitative or spoken dialogue. The Italian opera that had the greatest impact on French opéra comique was *La serva padrona* (1733) by Giovanni Battista Pergolesi (1710–36). (See Naples, page 102).

The development of opéra comique as a genre was spurred on by the performances of opera buffa put on by the Théâtre des Italiens. Opera buffa and opéra comique were generally farcical works written in short rhyming couplets. Quite often opéras comiques parodied arias and situations taken from *opéra tragique.* From 1789 to 1870 L'Opéra Comique and Théâtre des Italiens, although completely separate entities, often shared the same theatrical space. The theatre was moved from space to space depending on politics, finances, or whether a hall had burnt down (as halls did with some regularity).

The nearby boulevard des Italiens takes its name from the Théâtre des Italiens, which finally folded in 1878. On and off since 1783, L'Opéra Comique has performed in Salle Favart.

Salle Favart was built in 1783, burned down in 1838, and was rebuilt in 1840. In 1887, this second hall also burned, only to be rebuilt again on the same spot and reopened in December 1898. The 1887 fire claimed many victims, and there is a monument to them in Père-Lachaise cemetery. The Museum of Opéra Garnier has a dramatic painting of L'Opéra Comique in flames that fateful night in May 1887. Salle Favart is named after the most highly regarded librettist of L'Opéra Comique during the mid-eighteenth century, Charles-Simon Favart (1710–92).

L'Opéra Comique presented premieres of (details of some premieres at the end of the chapter) thirty-two operas by Daniel-François-Esprit Auber, including *Fra Diavolo* (January 28, 1830); *La Damnation de Faust*, concert performance (December 6, 1846), Hector Berlioz; *Djamileh* (May 22, 1872), Georges Bizet; *Carmen* (March 3, 1875), Georges Bizet; twenty operas by Adrien Boieldieu, including *La Dame blanche* (December 10, 1825); *Louise* (February 2, 1900), Gustave Charpentier; *Julien* (June 4, 1913), Gustave Charpentier; twelve operas by Luigi Cherubini, including *Médée* (March 13, 1797); *La Fille du régiment* (February 11, 1840), Gaetano Donizetti; *Rita* (posthumously, May 7, 1860), Gaetano Donizetti; *Cinq-Mars* (April 5, 1877), Charles Gounod; eight operas by Jules Massenet, including *Manon* (January 19, 1884); five operas by Jacques Offenbach, including *Les Contes d'Hoffmann*, (February 10, 1881).

During the first decade of the nineteenth century, Salle Favart (then called Théâtre des Italiens), under the musical direction of the composer Ferdinando Paer (Parma, 1771–Paris, 1839), presented Mozart's great collaborations with Da Ponte in Italian: *Le nozze di Figaro* in 1807; *Così fan tutte* in 1809; *Don Giovanni* in 1811. Paer was a limited composer and felt intensely jealous when the extraordinarily gifted Gioacchino Rossini became the toast of Paris. Paer attempted to sabotage Rossini's initial reputation in Paris by mounting inferior productions of his operas, beginning with *L'italiana in Algeri* in 1817.

But things changed dramatically when Rossini himself became director of the theatre, a position he held from 1824 to 1826. Rossini wrote his last Italian-style opera, *Il viaggio a Reims*, premiered in 1825, for the theatre's troupe, which was made up of some of the day's greatest singers, including Giuditta Pasta. Rossini was very supportive of fellow composers, no matter what their nationality. He launched Giacomo Meyerbeer's career in Paris by producing his *Il crociato in Egitto*. In 1827, the management of the theatre reverted to entrepreneurs, but Rossini continued as a kind of directorial consultant. He assisted in recruiting such fine singers as Maria Malibran and Giovanni Battista Rubini and helped commission operas such as Vincenzo Bellini's *I puritani* and Gaetano Donizetti's *Mariano Faliero*.

As the Théâtre des Italiens, Salle Favart presented premieres by (details of some premieres at end of chapter) *Don Pasquale* (January 3, 1843), Gaetano Donizetti; *Mariano Faliero* (March 12, 1835), Gaetano Donizetti; *I puritani* (January 24, 1835), Vincenzo Bellini; *Il viaggio a Reims* (June 19, 1825), Gioacchino Rossini.

Today Théâtre des Italiens no longer exists and Salle Favart is only L'Opéra Comique. It is located just off boulevard des Italiens and seats 1,300 people.

Opéra Comique (Salle Favart), Rue de Marivaux, 75002 Paris
Ticket office open: Sunday–Friday, 11:00 A.M.–7:00 P.M.
tel: (33–1) 4286–8883
    One enters from the side of the theatre.

The area south between Salle Favart, L'Opéra Comique, and rue des Petits Champs, and north to the metro stop Le Peletier, contains remnants of the neighborhood's illustrious operatic past.
    Salle Louvois, once the home of L'Opéra, stood where rue Louvois meets Square Rameau, across from the Bibliothèque Nationale. Salle Louvois burned in 1821.
    Théâtre Feydeau served L'Opéra Comique almost exclusively between 1791 and 1829. The theatre stood at nos. 19–21 rue Feydeau. Rue des Colonnes was built to make the theatre more easily accessible.
    Salle Ventadour, which also housed L'Opéra Comique and Théâtre des Italiens, is now home to the social services offices of the Banque de France. It stands in the square that forms at the end of the very short rue de Méhul, off rue des Petis Champs, before forking into rue Marsollier and rue Dalayrac. (The streets again merge into rue Mosigny where Théâtre Bouffes Parisiens is located; see below.)
    Salle Le Peletier housed L'Opéra from 1821 until the hall burned down in 1873. Salle Le Peletier was near the metro stop on rue Le Peletier. The theatre, street, and metro stop are named after Louis Michel Le Peletier (1760–93), the nobleman who cast *the* decisive vote for the decapitation of Louis XVI and the royal family in 1792. As a member of the nobility, Le Peletier himself was guillotined a year later!
    Théâtre Lyrique in boulevard du Temple was started in 1847 as a third opera-presenting organization to present French opera, and for one year this company posed the greatest competition to L'Opéra. Then came the disastrous Revolution of 1848. Also called the "revolution of the intellectuals," the 1848 uprising was motivated by Parisian idealists who, when push came to shove, did not know how to extend their rebellion to change the social and economic systems of France. Losing control of the revolution, they turned to Louis Napoleon Bonaparte to save the day.
    Théâtre Lyrique was destroyed during the upheaval, and a new one was built

in 1851 in Place du Châtelet. In 1899, the theatre was christened with its present name, Théâtre Sarah Bernhardt, after the great actress herself bought it late in her life in order to play some roles she was clearly too old to perform. Today it is called either Théâtre Sarah Bernhardt or Théâtre de la Ville. From 1887 to 1898, after L'Opéra Comique in Salle Favart burned down, performances of L'Opéra Comique were presented at Théâtre Lyrique.

Théâtre Lyrique premiered (details of premieres at chapter's end) five operas by Charles Gounod, including *Faust* (March 19, 1859); two operas by Georges Bizet, including *Les Pêcheurs de perles* (September 30, 1863); *Les Troyens*, the final three acts (Carthage), (November 4, 1863), Hector Berlioz; and premieres by many others including Fromental Halévy, Adolphe Adam, Léo Delibes.

Today Place du Châtelet is the geographical center of Paris, sporting two almost matching theatres that flank the square like bookends. The exterior of Théâtre de la Ville still looks much as it did when it was first built. The inside was completely renovated in 1968. Today Théâtre de la Ville is one of Paris's finest theatres, presenting the most diverse artistic events, from the cutting edge in contemporary music, ballet, and theatre to seventeenth- and eighteenth-century opera, concerts of classical music, and prestigious solo recitals. The theatre seats 1,000. The present-day Théâtre du Châtelet, also called the Théâtre Musical de Paris, replaced the Théâtre Imperial in Boulevard du Temple, which presented operetta. Lately, Théâtre Musical de Paris has begun to present very interesting opera performances along with its usual musicals. (If you face Place du Châtelet with your back to the Seine, Théâtre de la Ville is to the right.)

Théâtre de la Ville

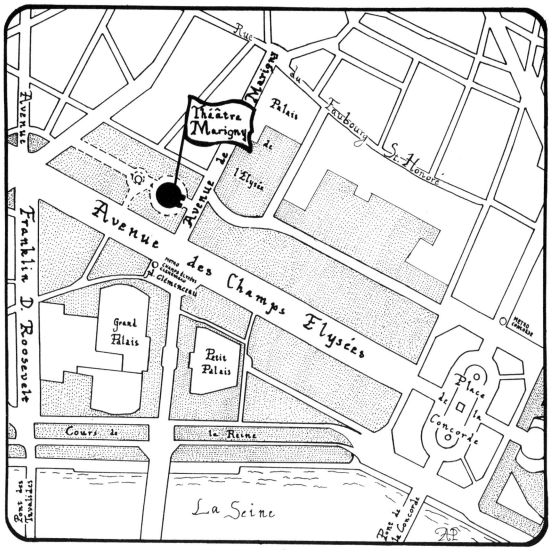

Detail of 8th Arrondissement

Premiere at Théâtre Sarah Bernhardt *Oedipus Rex*, concert version, May 20, 1927, Igor Stravinsky (See Vienna, Staatsoper for staged premiere, page 177).

Théâtre de la Ville (Théâtre Sarah Bernhardt), Place du Châtelet, 75002 Paris
Ticket office open: Tuesday through Saturday, 9:00 A.M.–8:00 P.M.; Sunday and Monday, 11:00 A.M.–6:00 P.M.
tel: (33–1) 4274–2277

Théâtre Musical de Paris, Place du Châtelet, 75002 Paris
tel: (33–1) 4028–2840

The components of opéra bouffe (comic opera) are very singable short melodies, exhuberant instrumental music, and witty, often satirical, spoken dialogue. As a specific art form it developed in the mid-nineteenth century, countering the rather tamer contributions of L'Opéra Comique. Early on, opéra bouffe often distinguished itself from opéra comique by its biting, satirical librettos. Jacques Offenbach is, without doubt, the greatest composer of nineteenth-century opéra bouffe. Under the influence of his sparkling, memorable melodies and witty charm, operetta became the rage in Paris, Vienna, and Berlin throughout the second half of the nineteenth century.

The next three theatres are on the operatic map because of Jacques Offenbach (June 19, 1819, Cologne, Germany—October 5, 1880, Paris). Offenbach, whom we remember today for his lyric drama *Les Contes d'Hoffmann* and his extraordinarily catchy melodies (such as *the* cancan tune), was responsible for the worldwide popularity of operetta in the late nineteenth and early twentieth century. Offenbach was gifted with not only musical talent but also a winning personality and a consuming desire to create the kind of music he wanted, which turned out to be trend-setting.

Offenbach had been trained by his father as a cellist, and after a year at the Paris Conservatoire, he played cello in the orchestra of L'Opéra Comique. He converted to Catholicism in 1845, which gave him many more professional opportunities than he had had as a Jew. In 1850, he was appointed conductor of the Théâtre Français.

Then, in 1855, he opened a summer theatre he called Les Bouffes-Parisiens in the Salle Lacaze, which was then replaced by Théâtre Marigny. When Offenbach was in residence, he called the theatre Théâtre Bouffes-Parisiens. As Théâtre Bouffes-Parisiens Salle Lacaze presented premieres of ten of his operettas between July 5, 1855, and July 31, 1856. Today the names of Offenbach and (Ludovic) Halévy emblazon the top of the theatre on the corner of avenue de Marigny and boulevard des Champs Elysées, directly across the Champs Elysées from the Grand Palais. Today the theatre holds 1,000 and presents plays.

Théâtre Marigny, avenue (Carré) Marigny, 75008 Paris
Ticket office open: 11:00 A.M.–6:30 P.M.
tel: (33–1) 4256–0441

In the winter season of 1856, Offenbach settled in Salle Choiseul, today's Théâtre les Bouffes-Parisiens, and opened the theatre with a competition for young opera composers. Seventy-eight entered, and the contest was jointly won by Georges Bizet (1838–75) and Charles Lecoq (1832–1918) for their separate settings of *Le Docteur Miracle.* Bizet, of course, is remembered for *Carmen* and *Les Pêcheurs de perles,* and Lecoq might be remembered for the overture to his operetta *La Fille de Madame Angot,* which is full of rousing Offenbach-like tunes.

In 1860 Offenbach became a naturalized French citizen and in 1861 a Chevalier of the Légion d'honneur. He resigned as director of Les Bouffes-Parisiens in 1862 but continued to have his works premiered there and in the nearby Theatre des Variétés. Offenbach wrote ninety-seven operettas and one opera. The opera, which he called an *opéra fantastique,* is *Les Contes d'Hoffmann,* regularly produced today as part of the international repertory.

Théâtre Marigny

Of his ninety-seven operettas, *La Périchole* and *Orphée aux enfers* are found frequently in contemporary repertory; *La Belle Hélène* (his biggest Parisian success), *Barbe-bleue* (Bluebeard), *La Vie parisienne,* and *La Grand-Duchesse de Gérolstein* are known to connoisseurs because of the wonderful recordings made in the 1950s by the great mezzo-soprano Régine Crespin. In 1876 Offenbach came to the United States and gave more than forty concerts in New York and Philadelphia.

Théâtre les Bouffes-Parisiens premiered (details at section's end) *Le Docteur Miracle* (April 9, 1857), Georges Bizet; forty-four operas by Jacques Offenbach, including *Orphée aux enfers* (October 21, 1858).

Today the theatre usually presents light comedies. It seats 690 people.

Théâtre Bouffes-Parisiens, 4, rue Monsigny, 75002 Paris
Ticket office open: daily 11:00 A.M.–7:00 P.M.
tel: (33–1) 4296–6024

Although built in 1807, Théâtre des Variétés experienced its heyday in the Offenbach period of the 1860s. All Offenbach's operas and operettas that premiered in this theatre were written for and performed by Offenbach's favorite performer, Hortense Schneider.

Théâtre des Variétés premiered (details at chapter's end) eight operas by Jacques Offenbach, including *La Belle Hélène* (December 17, 1864), *Barbe-bleue*

(February 6, 1866), *La Grande-Duchesse de Gérolstein* (April 12, 1867), *La Périchole* (October 6, 1868).

Théâtre des Variétés, 7, boulevard Montmartre, 75002 Paris
Ticket office open: daily 11:00 A.M.–7:00 P.M.
tel: (33–1) 4233–0992

Originally called Théâtre de la Popelinière, Théâtre Ranelagh was built by a retired general and farmer named Popelinière in the gardens of his Château de Boulainvilliers. From its exterior, which barely resembles that of a theatre, to its beautiful but tiny interior, Théâtre Ranelagh hardly seems likely to have hosted the French premiere of Richard Wagner's *Das Rheingold,* April 26, 1900. Most incredible is the minuscule size of the orchestra pit; two grand pianos could fill it! The theatre was built in 1747 in the village of Passy that stood in the forest outside the gates of Paris. In 1755 Jean-Philippe Rameau (1683–1764) organized musical events for the royal court in the theatre. Today it is an experimental cinema.

Théâtre Ranelagh, 5, rue des Vignes (Passy), 75016 Paris
Ticket office open daily, 11:00 A.M.–6:00 P.M.; Sundays, 11:00 A.M.–3:00 P.M.
tel: (33–1) 4288–6444

Two hundred feet further down rue des Vignes from Théâtre Ranelagh, at no. 32, a wall plaque, slightly obscured by ivy, attests to the fact that Gabriel Fauré,

Interior of Théâtre Ranelagh

composer of the opera *Pénélope* (premiered in Monte-Carlo in 1913), lived in the house from 1912 until his death on November 4, 1924.

In the nearby Ranelagh Gardens, which until the early twentieth century lay in open country, is avenue Ingres. The avenue was once lined with villas, and Gioacchino Rossini (February 29, 1792, Pesaro, Italy—November 13, 1868, Paris) lived in one at the site now occupied by an office building at no. 5, avenue Ingres. He died there in 1868. Today the buildings of avenue Ingres reflect that unfortunate neobrutalism characteristeric of post–World War II apartment construction. At the time of Rossini's death, however, Passy was a country village and this area was on its western edge.

After creating thirty-nine operas in nineteen years, Rossini stopped composing following the extraordinary success of his grand opéra *Guillaume Tell*. Rossini spent the rest of his life helping young singers and advancing the cause of music in Italy and France. Most of his work had been successful, and several of his operas—including *Il barbiere di Siviglia*, *L'italiana in Algeri*, and *La Cenerentola*, as well as many of his opera overtures, most notably *Guillaume Tell*, *La gazza ladra*, and *Il barbiere di Siviglia*—remain as favorites today. Although he returned to Bologna several times over the course of his career, he came back to Paris in 1855 and spent the rest of his life there.

Maria Callas (December 2, 1923, New York—September 16, 1977, Paris) also spent the last years of her life in Paris. Of all the singers of her generation, she had the greatest musical-dramatic instincts, the most intelligent approach to her art, and the most profound comprehension of operatic musical style. Everything she did and every phrase she uttered on the stage had a profound impact on the performance of opera from the 1950s through the present. Almost every soprano copies at least some of her extraordinary vocalisms. Unfortunately, most fail to achieve results anywhere near so interesting. One of her greatest triumphs in Paris was the title role of Luigi Cherubini's *Médée* (see L'Opéra Comique, page 248). The apartment in which she died is at 36, avenue Georges Mandel (on the corner of rue des Sablons) and has a plaque on the front wall. The tree-lined street gives one the feeling of being in the country, belying the proximity of busy place Trocadero.

Gaetano Donizetti (November 29, 1797, Bergamo—April 8, 1848, Bergamo page 22) was acclaimed by all Paris in 1835 with the first performances of *Mariano Faliero* at the Théâtre des Italiens, after which he immediately returned to Naples for the premiere of *Lucia di Lammermoor*. Within weeks, both of his parents and his wife died. In 1838 he abandoned Naples for Paris and in 1840 scored his greatest success with *La Fille du régiment*. Suffering from the effects of spinal-cerebral syphilis, he became paralyzed and spent from 1844 to 1847 in a sanitorium in Ivry, in what is now the thirteenth arrondissement, where Giuseppe Verdi visited him. In 1847 he returned to his birthplace, Bergamo. There, under the care of a nephew and the Baronessa Scotti, an admirer, he died in April 1848.

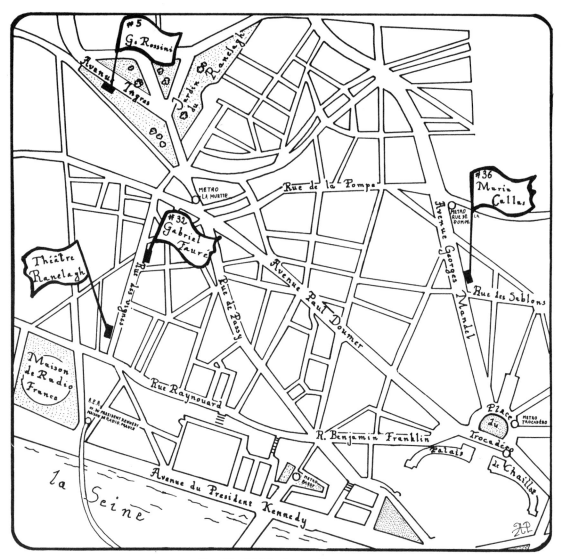

Detail of 16th Arrondissement

After successful performances of his first nine operas in Italy, Vincenzo Bellini (November 3, 1801, Catania—September 23, 1835, Puteaux) came to Paris in August 1833 at the age of thirty-one. He became close friends with Gioacchino Rossini and was very much part of the Parisian cultural scene of the 1830s. In early 1834 he received almost simultaneous commissions from Naples's Teatro San Carlo and Paris's Théâtre des Italiens. He turned down the San Carlo offer and began work on what turned out to be his last opera. On January 24, 1835, *I puritani* was premiered to great acclaim at the Théâtre des Italiens, after which Bellini was appointed Chevalier of the Légion d'honneur.

When he fell ill at the end of August, he was thought to have cholera and thus was moved from Paris to the country village of Puteaux, where he was put into isolation. (Puteaux lies just beyond the present-day suburb of Neuilly and across the Seine, west of Paris.) He died alone on September 23, 1835, age thirty-four. A postmortem identified the cause of death as "an inflamed intestine and an abscess on the liver."

His funeral at the Church of the Invalides was attended by all the Parisian notables, and Rossini, Cherubini, and Paer each held a corner of the shroud that covered his casket. He was buried in Paris's Père Lachaise Cemetery, but in 1876 his mortal remains were moved to the cathedral of Catania, his home town. (See Catania, page 40.)

Details about some L'Opéra premieres

Don Carlos, opéra in five acts, French version, March 11, 1867.
Giuseppe Verdi (1813, Le Roncole—1901, Milan)
Libretto Joseph Méry and Camille Du Locle, after Friedrich von Schiller's dramatic poem *Don Carlos, Infant von Spanien.*

The five-act *Don Carlos* is Verdi's longest opera, even after he made drastic cuts during rehearsals for the premiere. As was the tradition in Paris, the premiere relied on great spectacle and theatrical effects, and Verdi was daunted by the enormity of the task. Implicitly he knew that the special effects diminished the work *he* had written. And indeed, though *Don Carlos* has some of Verdi's greatest music, the considerable pageantry he had to allow to make it a grand opera ultimately detracts from the opera's dramatic thrust. *Don Carlos* was dropped from the repertory of L'Opéra only two years after its premiere.

Don Carlos is the story of the unrequited love between Don Carlos, the Infante of Spain, and his stepmother Elisabeth de Valois. It is complete with a jealous mezzo-soprano, a baritone who dies for Carlos, and an oppressive Grand Inquisitor, who is, naturally, a bass. Recent performances of the opera in its original five-act French version have made it one of the late-twentieth-century public's favorite Verdi operas. In the United States, we mostly hear the four-act Italian translation premiered at La Scala January 10, 1884 (see Milan, page 83). A fabulous recording of the full French *Don Carlos*, conducted by Claudio Abbado, is now available on CD.

Iphigénie en Tauride, tragédie in four acts, May 18, 1779.
Christoph Willibald Gluck (July 2, 1714, Erasbach [Upper Palatinate]—
November 15, 1787, Vienna)
Libretto Nicolas-François Guillard, based on Guymond de la Touche's
Iphigénie en Tauride.

Iphigénie en Tauride is without doubt Gluck's greatest dramatic work, the one in which his ideas about operatic reform are most successful. He achieves a stunning balance between music and drama: In portraying Agamemnon's sacrifice of his daughter, the musical structure always serves to promote the drama's development and every detail is subordinate to the whole. Gluck's operas have long been favorites of musicians and composers. Richard Wagner produced his own arrangement of *Iphigénie en Aulide,* in German, for performances in Dresden's 1847 season. Richard Strauss followed with an arrangement of the opera in late nineteenth-century style for Weimar in 1889. *Iphigénie en Tauride* and *Orfeo ed Euridice* (the Italian, Viennese version) have always been Gluck's most popular operas.

Les Huguenots, *grand opéra* in five acts, February 29, 1836.
Giacomo Meyerbeer (September 5, 1791, Vogelsdorf, near Berlin—May 2, 1864, Paris)
Libretto Eugène Scribe and Emile Deschamps.

The late sixteenth-century confrontation in France between Catholics and Protestants, which led to the Edict of Nantes under Henry IV in 1598, was popular subject matter for early nineteenth-century Paris. *Les Huguenots* was preceded by several plays, a comic opera, and a book by the popular novelist Prosper Mérimée, who also wrote the novel on which *Carmen* was based. Meyerbeer knew he had a good subject for a successful opera. *Les Huguenots* was performed over a thousand times at L'Opéra, the first work to achieve this distinction. The opera is action-packed, reflecting the public turmoil of the period, and was admired even by Meyerbeer's detractors. As with most grand opera, *Les Huguenots* has never entered the international standard repertory but is still sometimes produced in France.

Lulu, opera in a prologue and three acts, completed by Friedrich Cerha, February 24, 1979.
Alban Berg (February 9, 1885, Vienna—December 24, 1935, Vienna)
Libretto by the composer, after Frank Wedekind's plays *Erdgeist* (Earth Spirit), and *Die Büsche der Pandora* (Pandora's Box).

Berg had finished the short score (sketches in piano score) for *Lulu* by 1934, but under the Nazi regime a German or Austrian performance of so daring an opera was impossible. To circumvent this difficulty, Berg wrote, and orchestrated, a concert suite called *Symphonische Stücke aus der Oper "Lulu"* so that at least parts of the opera might be performed somewhere. Erich Kleiber conducted the first performance of this suite in Berlin on November 30, 1934. Acts I and II of the opera *Lulu* were premiered by the Zurich Stadttheater June 2, 1937, a year and a half after the death of the composer.

Berg's widow had prohibited anyone from completing the score, but in the early 1960s, the opera's publisher, Universal Edition, allowed the Austrian composer Friedrich Cerha access to the sketches of Act III. Although the Alban Berg Foundation took legal action to stop it, the completed opera received its premiere in Paris in 1979, the American premiere in Santa Fe in the summer of 1979, and the British premiere at Covent Garden in 1981.

Since then it has received regular performances throughout the operatic world.

L'Orphée et Eurydice, *tragédie* in three acts, August 2, 1774.
Christoph Willibald Gluck (1714–87)
Libretto Pierre Louis Moline, after the libretto of *Orfeo ed Euridice* by Ranieri de' Calzabigi (see Vienna, Burgtheater, page 175).

Countertenors, not castrati, usually sang heroic roles in Paris, so for the French premiere, Gluck changed the role of Orpheus from an *alto castrato* to a countertenor to suit Parisian taste. Unlike the rest of Europe, the French took a dim view of castrati and found the "unnatural" voice downright freaky, not suited for serious operatic endeavors. Gluck also added both vocal and instrumental pieces to make the opera longer and grander. The Parisian success was clamorous, and *L'Orphée et Eurydice* has remained prominent in the repertory of L'Opéra. The Italian version, premiered in Vienna's Burgtheater, October 5, 1762, is performed regularly outside France.

Le Prophète, *grand opéra* in five acts, April 16, 1849.
Giacomo Meyerbeer (1791–1864)
Libretto Eugène Scribe.

Unlikely as it might seem today, the premiere of *Le Prophète* was a resounding success. This was probably as much due to the plot, which bears some resemblance to story lines of the hugely popular biblical films made in the 1950s, as to the novel stage effects made possible by the first-ever use of electric lighting for this purpose.

The prophet is a young man who has dreamed he is the Messiah and is used by some Anabaptists in their seditious activities. He not only comes to believe he is the son of God but also gets crowned Emperor. Rousing choruses and crowd scenes abound. A love interest, mother-son hostility, and an unjust ruler are integral to the action, not to mention an *ice-skating* ballet, musically represented by a rapid diminuendo on a series of sustained chords. The whole opera, five acts and nine *long* scenes, ends with an explosion that kills everyone onstage. The work was premiered only a year after the violent Revolution of 1848, and the authorities promoted it as a piece about popular sedition ignited by demagoguery.

Robert le diable, *grand opéra* in five acts, November 21, 1831.
Giacomo Meyerbeer (1791–1864)
Libretto Eugène Scribe and Germain Delavigne.

The increasing extravagance that came to characterize grand opera is illustrated by the budget for the premiere of *Robert le diable,* which allocated even more money for its spectacular sets than for its lavish costumes. One can see lithographs of these amazing sets in the Museum de l'Opéra. And the opera pushed the limits of musical demands, too, the title role containing some of the most difficult vocal music of the early nineteenth century. The opera comes to a grandiose climax: one of the principals is swallowed up by Hell while Robert, the hero, ascends to a Heaven populated by a full chorus of angels and his beloved. *Robert le diable* is not an opera one generally sees outside of France.

Tannhäuse (third version), *grosse romantische Oper* in three acts, March 13, 1861.
Richard Wagner (1813, Leipzig—1883, Venice)
Libretto by the composer.

Giacomo Meyerbeer, indisputably the most important composer in mid-nineteenth-century France, convinced the Emperor Napoleon III of Richard Wagner's operatic importance. L'Opéra invited Wagner to mount the French premiere of *Tannhäuser*. After a rather unsuccessful premiere in Dresden (see Dresden, page 283) in 1845 and a better received revision in 1847, also in Dresden, *Tannhäuser* had established itself as part of the repertory in Germany.

To meet the requirements of L'Opéra, Wagner wrote a ballet for the Paris premiere, placing it in the opening scene, the Venusberg. Although Paris management expected the ballet to fall in the traditional second act, it allowed this departure from custom. The ballet is a riotous bacchanal filled with the sound of castanets, intended to portray the sensual pleasures of the home of Venus.

The Paris premiere of *Tannhäuser* was one of the most celebrated debacles in operatic history. Germans and German music were viewed with great suspicion in the Paris of the 1860s. Incensed members of the Jockey Club interrupted the premiere and the following two performances by blowing on whistles and howling like dogs. Wagner withdrew the opera after three performances.

Meyerbeer's championing of Wagner is particularly poignant in view of Wagner's published anti-Semitism. In his 1850 treatise *Das Judentum in der Musik* (Jewishness in Music), Wagner equates the fake, flashy charms of most contemporary art with the work of Jewish musicians, asserting that the Jews' historical role as moneylenders led to this cultural sterility. Many historians feel that Meyerbeer's influence on grand opera played an important role in Wagner's development of *Musik Drama* and that Wagner could not bear to owe this debt, especially to a Jew. It is certainly well documented that Wagner seemed forced to bite the hand of those who believed in him. Consider, for example, the case of the conductor Hans von Bülow, one of Wagner's most important champions. Wagner seduced von Bülow's wife Cosima and had three children with her before she was divorced from von Bülow. (See Munich, page 299.)

Thaïs, *comédie lyrique* in three acts and seven scenes, March 16, 1894.
Jules Massenet (May 12, 1842, Montaud, St. Etienne—August 31, 1912, Paris)
Libretto Louis Gallet, after the novel of the same title by Anatole France.

As a *comédie lyrique, Thaïs* was originally slated to premiere at L'Opéra Comique, but just before the scheduled event, Sibyl Sanderson, for whom Massenet had written the title role, was hired by the much more prestigious L'Opéra. It is crucial that the singer of the title role *look* the part because of her character as a temptress. In this unlikely legend, Thaïs is a courtesan desired by a monk who transforms his lust into zeal to save Thaïs's soul, and finally she becomes a saint.

The original story was recorded by a tenth-century German nun, Hrostwitha, and France's novel was published as a lurid anticlerical satire in serial form in 1889. It has just the kind of libidinous plot line Massenet loved to set. Its controversial subject proved open to quite theatrical interpretation. In the premiere, Sanderson "accidentally" exposed her breast, and in a famous 1973 production in New Orleans, the beautiful, voluptuous soprano Carol Neblett became the first frontally nude opera singer. In spite of its racy aspect, the Parisian premiere was not a success, and *Thaïs* has never become part of standard repertory, unlike Massenet's *Manon* and *Werther.*

Les Vêpres siciliennes, *opéra* in five acts, June, 13, 1855.
Giuseppe Verdi (1813–1901)
Libretto Eugène Scribe and Charles Duveyrier, based on their libretto *Le Duc d'Albe.*

Verdi wrote *Les Vêpres siciliennes* in 1854, just after making the dramatic and compositional breakthroughs that characterize *Rigoletto, Il trovatore,* and *La traviata.* Unlike those operas, however, *Les Vêpres siciliennes* has not remained in the standard repertory. Once again, the excessive demands of a Paris premiere resulted in an opera that was too long and hampered by gratuitous pageantry. Nevertheless, this was a crossover period for Verdi; all his subsequent operas reflect the musical and dramatic strides he made while writing *Les Vêpres.* The Italian premiere was delayed because of the revolutionary nature of the opera's subject (the Sicilian uprising against the tyrannical French occupying forces). It finally received its Italian premiere at Parma's Teatro Regio.

Details about some premieres at L'Opéra Comique

Carmen, *opéra comique* in four acts, March 3, 1875.
Georges Bizet (1838–75)
Libretto Henri Meilhac and Ludovic Halévy, after Prosper Mérimée's novel, *L'Histoire de Carmen.*

Carmen, the story of the volatile Gypsy who seduces the simple soldier Don José, then goes off with Escamillo the toreador, and in the end is killed by a deranged José, is undoubtedly the most popular opera in the world. Since its unsuccessful premiere 120 years ago, L'Opéra Comique (Salle Favart) alone has given it over four thousand performances.

The premiere failed because L'Opéra Comique was a "family" theatre. Never before had there been such a realistically sexy woman or a violent death in any opera presented there. The singers complained about the "unsingable" melodies! The chorus complained at having to act as individuals and not as a proper chorus. The orchestra complained about the "cacophonous" score. Applause met the end of the first act; the audience evinced less enthusiasm after Acts II and III; and total *silence* greeted the opera's end! This is *truly* unbelievable, considering how popular *Carmen* has become.

Then, Bizet had the misfortune to die on the night of the opera's thirty-third performance, three months after its premiere. He was only thirty-seven. *Carmen* was his sixteenth opera and the first to manifest his compositional genius: some of the other operas are interesting, but none has the compositional élan of *Carmen.*

In October of 1875, Bizet's friend, the composer Ernest Guiraud, set the spoken dialogue in recitative. In this form *Carmen* took Vienna by storm late in the year, going on to capture a worldwide audience. It became the favorite opera of Brahms, Wagner, and Tchaikovsky, who immediately recognized the opera's brilliance. Only in 1883, after it had become an international hit, was it performed at Paris's L'Opéra. Since then, in the fully sung Guiraud version, L'Opéra has staged *Carmen many* times.

I prefer *Carmen* in its original version with spoken dialogue because of its stronger dramatic impact, so I'm sorry the Guiraud version is that most often performed today. My explanation is that it is easier for non-French speakers to *sing* in French, with the music suggesting the proper cadence and stress to the words, than it is to sound convincing *speaking* French!

Over the years *Carmen* has also inspired several films, including one in which Charlie Chaplin plays a character named "Don Hosiery" (Don José), and *Carmen Jones,* which takes place largely in Harlem. Even Spike Jones recorded his own version of the opera.

Les Contes d'Hoffmann, *opéra fantastique* in five acts, February 10, 1881.
Jacques Offenbach (June 20, 1819, Cologne—October 5, 1880)
Libretto Jules Barbier, after the play by Barbier and Michel Carré based on stories of E. T. A. Hoffmann.

The opera's three acts portray the spiritual and moral decline of Hoffmann, who appears as himself, through a succession of fantastic love affairs and infatuations. *Les Contes d'Hoffmann* is Offenbach's last work and his only "serious" opera, one he did not live to see premiered. In fact, some of the orchestration was completed by Albert Guiraud, the same composer who orchestrated the dialogue in *Carmen* after Bizet's death. E. T. A. Hoffmann's stories make up part of today's collective unconscious. *The Nutcracker*, which is based on his stories, taps the anxieties and desires of children with its fantasy.

La Damnation de Faust, *légende dramatique* in four parts, concert performance, December 6, 1846 (fully staged premiere, Monte-Carlo, in 1893).
Hector Berlioz (1803–69)
Libretto by the composer and Almire Gandonnière, after Goethe's *Faust* (see Weimar, page 310).

Berlioz wrote *La Damnation de Faust* as an *opéra de concert*. The premiere at L'Opéra Comique was considered an artistic success even though it was a dismal failure at the box office. The opera contains some of the most dramatic music ever written, and some opera lovers, myself included, find it ever more appealing, musically and dramatically, than Gounod's *Faust*. The opera was finally given its staged premiere February 18, 1893, in Monte-Carlo (see Monte Carlo, page 275). The opera has proved unwieldy to stage, however, and today it is generally presented in its original concert version.

La Fille du régiment, *opéra comique* in two acts, February 11, 1840.
Gaetano Donizetti (1797–1847)
Libretto Jules-Henri Vernoy de Saint-Georges and Jean-François-Alfred Bayard.

La Fille du régiment is Donizetti's fifty-third opera, his second written in French. The score is full of real military tunes that become irresistible in the opera's context. The role of Marie must be played by a soprano of great vocal agility and charming deportment. The tenor role of Tonio, well-known for the aria "Pour mon âme" and its stratospheric line of nine (!) high C's, demands a light but heroic tenor. (Remember the 1995 Pavarotti *scandale* when he flubbed the notes even though he sang the aria transposed down a whole step!) The tale of young love overcoming many obstacles, *La Fille du régiment* is such a delight and such a wonderful opera for fine singers that between its premiere in 1840 and 1914, L'Opéra Comique presented it more than one thousand times. Joan Sutherland revived the opera, in its Italian version, in 1965. Today, outside France, it is the Italian version, *La figlia del reggimento,* that is generally heard (see Milan, La Scala, page 83).

Fra Diavolo, *opéra comique* in three acts, January 28, 1830.
Daniel-François-Esprit Auber (January 29, 1782, Caen—May 12, 1871, Paris)
Libretto Eugène Scribe.

Fra Diavolo is supposedly based on the life of a bandit who, Robin Hood–like, embodied the qualities of both monk and criminal, and who ravaged southern Italy around 1800. Because of the political atmosphere in Paris in the 1830s, Scribe could not expect a libretto about a moral and charitable robber fighting the rich and powerful to be performed at any Parisean theatre. As a result the opera is a cheerfully ironic tale. Auber wrote forty-eight opéras comiques and of them, *Fra Diavolo* is the best. It was one of the most frequently performed operas in the nineteenth century, presented in Paris alone over nine hundred times by 1900. Today the overture of *Fra Diavolo* is performed regularly, but the opera itself only rarely.

Louise, *roman musical* in four acts, February 2, 1900.
Gustave Charpentier (June 25, 1860, Dieuze, Lorraine—June 25, 1956, Paris)
Libretto by the composer or (heatedly denied by the composer) by Saint-Pol-Roux.

Charpentier began work on *Louise* in 1887 but did not finish it until 1896; he completed only one other opera. *Louise* is a "naturalistic" drama about free love with the sordid realism of a Zola novel. The soprano Mary Garden was celebrated for her interpretation of the title role. The one piece that remains in the repertory today is the lovely soprano aria "Depuis le jour."

Médée, *opéra comique* in three acts (March 13, 1797).
Luigi Cherubini (September 8, 1760, Florence, Italy—March 15, 1842, Paris)
Libretto François-Benoit Hoffman.

Between 1788 and 1833, eighteen operas by Cherubini were premiered in Paris. Although Cherubini called *Médée* an opéra comique, the work has few equals in its representation of unmitigated horror. Its spoken dialogue is the *only* reason it is called an opéra comique. The librettist, Hoffmann, filled three hours with one unrestrained emotion, revenge, and one action, murder. Cherubini wrote some of the most dramatic music of the period. Despite critical approval, *Médée* disappeared from the stage after only twenty performances. Paris did not mount another production until the 1950s, when Maria Callas, after singing the opera in Florence, was responsible for its return to the French operatic stage.

The title role is *extremely* demanding. The soprano must have a voice at once both dramatic and agile. When the opera premiered in 1797, the title role was sung by Julie-Angélique Scio, famous for her dramatic vocal agility. Her early death from tuberculosis was attributed to her frequent perform- ances of roles demanding displays of vocal gymnastics, like that of Médée.

Although the opera is not really part of today's standard repertory, its spirit surely is. The famous pictures of Callas on the stage of L'Opéra with her lover Aristotle Onassis applauding her from a box evoke the persistent power of the work.

Manon, *opéra comique* in five acts, January 19, 1884.
Jules Massenet (May 12, 1842, Montaud, St. Etienne—August 31, 1912, Paris)
Libretto Henri Meilhac and Philippe Gille, after Antoine-François Prévost's novel, *L'histoire du chevalier des Grieux et de Manon Lescaut.*

Abbé Prévost's text was made into three operas, the first by Auber in 1856 (*Manon Lescaut*), then Massenet in 1884 (*Manon*), and finally Puccini in 1893 (*Manon Lescaut*). Manon is the stereotypical seductive woman, the eternal female, and the erotic subject matter was a great favorite of Massenet. *Manon* has always been Massenet's most popular opera. A good-time girl with a big heart, shy yet ambitious, Manon is unable to choose between love and riches, and her indecision sets her up for tragedy. As an opéra comique, *Manon* has very little freely spoken text. Instead, Massenet wrote most of the dialogue as *mélodrame,* that is, the text is spoken over the orchestra. Massenet was a master of this style. The premiere was a great success, and the opera has remained in the repertory of L'Opéra Comique, having received over two thousand performances to date. Although Puccini's *Manon Lescaut* is done more often today, *Manon* is still part of the international repertory.

Details about some premieres at Théâtre des Italiens

Don Pasquale, *dramma buffo* in three acts, January 3, 1843.
Gaetano Donizetti (November 29, 1797, Bergamo—April 8, 1848, Bergamo)
Libretto Giovanni Ruffini and the composer.

Don Pasquale is among Donizetti's best operas, and its premiere was an instant success. Only three months later, on April 17, 1843, Milan's La Scala staged the Italian premiere, and by the end of 1843 the opera had been performed in Vienna and London. In 1846 it reached New York, where it was presented in English. The plot has elements of a good Da Ponte libretto—lots of wit, humor, wry tenderness, and humanity—and Donizetti is at his melodious best. It is the tale of young love overcoming many obstacles, including a May–December "marriage" and a very amusingly shrewish "wife." Although it is an opera buffa, Donizetti accompanies the recitatives not with the harpsichord but with the strings, which gives the work more breadth.

I puritani, *melodramma serio* in three acts, January 24, 1835.
Vincenzo Bellini (November 3, 1801, Catania—September 23, 1835, Puteaux)
Libretto Carlo Pepoli, after the play *Têtes Rondes et Cavaliers* by Ancelot and Xavier.

Because Bellini was writing for the highly erudite, Italian-opera-loving Parisian public, *I puritani* is his most sophisticated opera. By the end of 1835 it had been produced in London, Milan, and Palermo, where its title had to be changed to satisfy the religious censors (the setting is the seventeenth-century English Civil War between the Puritan Roundheads and the Anglican Cavaliers).

At Venice's La Fenice, Giuseppina Strepponi (who later married Giuseppe Verdi) gave the first performance as the female lead, a role she subsequently played often and for which she became famous. Some of the music, in particular, "Suoni la tromba intrepida," is unforgettably rousing, and Arturo's last aria is sublime. This aria, "Ella è tremante," contains a written high F-sharp in the soprano range, which gives us an idea of early nineteenth-century vocal technique. Of all the recordings of *I puritani*, the best is a 1975 version with Joan Sutherland and a young, vibrant-voiced Luciano Pavarotti, who makes the high F-sharp shine heroically.

Il viaggio a Reims, ossia L'albergo del giglio d'oro (The Journey to Reims, or the Hotel of the Golden Lily), *dramma giocoso* in one act, June 19, 1825.
Gioacchino Rossini (February 29, 1792, Pesaro, Italy—November 13, 1868, Paris)
Libretto Luiggi Balocchi, derived in part from Mme. de Staël's novel *Corinne, ou L'Italie.*

Il viaggio a Reims was written as a scenic cantata to celebrate the coronation of Charles X, so although it contains some of Rossini's most inspired vocal music, it is rarely performed. He reused some of the music in *Le Comte Ory*, which premiered at L'Opéra in 1828. A gala performance of *Il viaggio a Reims*, coproduced by Pesaro and L'Opéra Comique, and starring, among others, Samuel Ramey, was carried by PBS in 1985.

Details about premieres at Théâtre Lyrique

Faust, opéra in five acts, March 19, 1859
Charles Gounod (June 17, 1818, Paris—October 18, 1893, Saint Cloud, outside of Paris)
Libretto Jules Barbier and Michel Carré after Goethe's *Faust*, Part I.

Faust is Gounod's most famous work, though many critics find it wanting in musical style, calling the opera saccharine, mere fluff, and complaining that the role of Méphistophélés has more than a bit of Leporello in it. It is true that many performances of *Faust* lack singers of the caliber needed to pull it all off, but most people nevertheless find the opera very moving. Certainly Marguerite's heroic final call for divine protection, "Anges purs, anges radieux," culminating in "Christ est ressucité," raises the roof. With

Faust Gounod surpassed Meyerbeer in popularity and established a new kind of French opera. Although he wrote twelve operas, only *Faust* is part of the international repertory.

Les Pêcheurs de perles, *opéra* in three acts, September 30, 1863.
Georges Bizet (1838–75)
Libretto Eugène Cormon and Michel Carré.

Bizet wrote his sixth opera, *Les Pêcheurs de perles*, when he was twenty-four. It was his second to be performed. Like *Carmen*, the libretto reflects the mid-nineteenth-century fascination with the exotic and takes place in Ceylon. The beautiful tenor-baritone duet, "Au fond du temple saint," is only one reason to see the opera. The work abounds with melodies, colorful orchestration, and wonderful choruses.

Les Troyens, *opéra* in five acts, Acts III through V (Carthage), November 4, 1863.
Hector Berlioz (December 11, 1803, La Côte-St. André, Isère—March 8, 1869, Paris)
Libretto by the composer, after Virgil's *Aeneid.*

Les Troyens, a monumental work, is in fact really two separate operas. Acts I and II are about Aeneas in Troy and the Trojan War, and Acts III through V are about Carthage and Dido and Aeneas. The opera's enormous scope—for example, twenty singing roles, many of them quite lengthy—prevents it from being performed more often. Even though both Cassandra and Dido are mezzo-soprano roles, it is virtually impossible for one singer to perform both parts. Berlioz used his knowledge of the sonority of the orchestra and the voice to shape a truly profound operatic work. Like the composers of early opera, Berlioz felt that the union of music and poetry possessed much greater power than either art alone.

Details about a premiere at Théâtre les Bouffes-Parisiens

Orphée aux enfers, *opéra bouffon* in two acts, February 7, 1858.
Jacques Offenbach (1819–80)
Libretto Hector-Jonathan Crémieux and Ludovic Halévy, loosely based on classical mythology.

Orphée aux enfers, Offenbach's thirty-second opera, is a spoof of classical mythology. Orpheus and Euridice cannot abide each other; Euridice hates Orpheus's violin playing (ideally, the role of Orpheus should be sung by a tenor who also plays the violin!); Euridice has a lover for whom Orpheus has laid a trap of poisonous snakes; Euridice goes to warn him and is bitten; Jupiter (who has, of course, seduced beauties in the form of a swan, a bull, a cloud) appears to Euridice in the form of a fly, at which point a wonderful fly "buzzzzzing" duet ensues. The opera is full of memorable melodies, including the famous cancan tune.

Details about a premiere at Théâtre des Variétés

La Périchole, opéra bouffe in two acts, October 6, 1868.
Jacques Offenbach (1819–80)
Libretto Henri Meilhac and Ludovic Halévy, after Prosper Mérimée's comedy, *Le Carrosse du Saint-Sacrement.*

Of all Offenbach's operettas, *La Périchole* is his most charming and most likely to be seen today. It contains only a bit of the topical, biting satire of his other comedies. Several of the protagonist's arias are often performed outside opera: for example, the wistful Letter Song, "Oh mon cher amant, je te jure," the tipsy "Ah, quel diner," and the wonderfully sensuous "Tu n'es pas beau."

FOOD

In Paris one can eat very well almost everywhere. A few traditional places not to miss are:

Balzar, 49, rue des Ecoles, 75005 Paris
tel: (33–1) 4354–1367   fax: (33–1) 4407–1491
Closed in August and on Christmas to January 1.
Right in the city center, this traditional Parisian favorite has an excellent small menu. Especially in winter months, don't miss the spinach or the liver!

Le Procope, 13, rue de l'Ancienne Comédie, 75006 Paris
tel: (33–1) 4326–9920   fax: (33–1) 4954–4600
This is one of the oldest continuously operating restaurants in Paris. It is definitely worth a visit.

Les Beaux Arts, 11, rue Bonaparte, 75006 Paris
tel: (33–1) 4326–9264
This small, homey restaurant serves one of the best meals available in Paris at a modest price. It is always filled with artistic Left Bank types.

LODGING

Le Relais du Louvre, 19, rue des Prêtres-St.-Germain-l'Auxerrois, 75001 Paris
tel: (33–1) 4041–9642   fax: (33–1) 4041–9644
This elegant old hotel is said to be the setting for Giacomo Puccini's *La bohème.* It is right across Pont Neuf from all the opera sites in the

sixth arrondissement and a five-minute walk from Théâtre de la Ville in Place du Châtelet.

Hôtel des deux Continents, 25, rue Jacob, 75006 Paris
tel: (33–1) 4326–7246   fax: (33–1) 4325–6780
    This lovely old hotel stands across the street from where Wagner stayed in Paris in 1842 and is a five-minute walk from the site of Paris's first opera house.

Hôtel d'Angleterre, 44, rue Jacob, 75006 Paris
tel: (33–1) 4260–3472   fax: (33–1) 4260–1693
    This is another beautiful and venerable hotel right down the street from where Richard Wagner stayed in 1842. The building once housed the British embassy and has some lovely large rooms, many of which look out on a quiet courtyard. The hotel has a slightly rundown, comfortable feeling to it.

Le Madison, 143, boulevard Saint-Germain, 75006 Paris
tel: (33–1) 4051–6000   fax: (33–1) 4051–6001
    Directly across the street from the church of St. Germain, Le Drugstore, Café Flore, Brasserie Lipp, and other hot spots of the sixth arrondissement, this hotel is a ten-minute walk from Paris's first opera house.

Hôtel de Seine, 52, rue de Seine, 75006 Paris
tel: (33–1) 4634–2280   fax: (33–1) 4634–0474
    Right on the corner of rue Jacob, Hôtel de Seine is a three-minute walk from the first opera house and only a minute from where Wagner stayed in Paris. This is the artistic center of Paris, an area filled with art galleries and good restaurants.

Hôtel Caron de Beaumarchais, 12, rue de Vieille Temple, 75004 Paris
tel: (33–1) 4272–3412   fax: (33–1) 4272–3463
    This cozy hotel is named after Pierre-Augustin Beaumarchais, author of *La Folle journée, ou Le Mariage de Figaro,* on which such operas as *Le nozze di Figaro, Il barbiere di Siviglia,* and *The Ghosts of Versailles* are based. It is a five-minute walk from Théâtre de la Ville in Place du Châtelet.

L'Hôtel à L'Hôpital de l'Hôtel Dieu, 1, Place du Parvis Nôtre Dame, 75004 Paris
tel: (33–1) 4432–0100   fax: (33–1) 4432–0116
    This quirky "hotel" offers a good price, a great quiet location, and a grand adventure! It is situated on the top floor of the hospital Hôtel Dieu (Hotel of God), on Ile de la Cité, right behind the cathedral of Nôtre

Dame. The rooms were originally set aside for the families of patients and they are now rather charming, very clean hotel rooms. The adventure consists of walking through the hospital to get to the rooms. It is a ten-minute walk from the first opera house and three minutes from Théâtre de la Ville.

GERMANY

G erman cities host the most famous repertory opera companies in the world. If you have the opportunity to get into an opera performance in *any* town (large or small), you are more than likely to be very pleased. As a general rule, you can purchase tickets at reduced price the day of the performance. The only theatres that might disappoint are those that are *not* repertory companies, like Berlin's Deutscheoper, where international stars regularly perform. Theatres *not to miss* are Berlin's Staatsoper and Komische Oper, Hamburg's Staatsoper, Frankfurt's Opera, and Cologne's Opera. These have at least ten-month seasons and stage some of the finest opera productions of the late twentieth century.

All the hotels mentioned in this book provide guests with a detailed map of the city's center, where most points of operatic interest lie. With these maps and the maps in this book, you should have absolutely no trouble finding your way around.

Most of the hotels mentioned here are *relatively* inexpensive (given the exchange rate and cost of living in Germany). They have been chosen to provide the guest the most pleasant stay no matter what the season. All have light and airy rooms and are located near present-day opera houses and points of operatic interest.

Because all hotels serve copious buffet breakfasts, we suggest you make a sandwich with the extra rolls, meats, vegetables, and cheeses supplied, and have a lunch on the go.

Cafés in Germany serve wonderful afternoon tea (or coffee) and pastries, and many serve light lunches of soup and sandwiches.

Restaurants in general are pricey and the food *quite* heavy. Because of the more-than-ample breakfasts, a dinner of soup and salad is usually sufficient—and you will not be so full you cannot stay awake for the evening's opera.

Through the nineteenth century, Germany, like Italy, was a geographical term, not a political entity; it was a country of principalities, dukedoms, and margravates. In Germany, artists and the works they performed were viewed largely as commodities, foreign products for the most part. Unlike in Italy, where public taste determined the status of a musician or an opera, in Germany a prince, margrave, duke, or elector chose—and paid for—who performed and what they performed. By the mid-eighteenth century, fully half the most famous singers in all of Europe were in the employ of the Electors of Saxony, at the court of Dresden. These artists, no matter how talented, had to be politically astute. If they offended their employers, they could be dismissed arbitrarily and condemned to a nomadic life of financial uncertainty.

Under this system where the local ruler both dictated and subsidized the cultural pleasures of the well-to-do, the general populace was allowed to reap the benefits of trickle-down cultural appreciation: less-well-off citizens were allowed to attend the opera *free*, provided they were decently dressed.

Throughout Germany, each city's operatic history demonstrates that the names of the opera houses changed according to who was in charge and paying for production costs. Early on, when the houses were often part of the palace (Hof) and subsidized by a prince (*Fürst*), king (*König*), or duke (*Graf*), they were called *Hof*oper, or, more specifically, *König*liches Hofoper, *Markgräf*liches Opernhaus, or *Kurfürst*liches Theater.

When opera became a state entertainment in the nineteenth century, the names of theatres were often changed to Nationaltheatre or Staatsoper. A *city*-supported theatre was a Stadtstheater. Of course, in a Free City governed by a Confederation of Burghers, such as Hamburg, theatres were usually named after the square in which they stood, as was the case with the popularly run Theater am Gänsemarkt, which retained that name until after World War II, when it became the Staatsoper.

Not until well into the nineteenth century did German opera—that is, opera in German by German composers—flower, encouraged by the rise of nationalism and the loosening of religious strictures. Much of Germany in the seventeenth and eighteenth centuries was Protestant, principally Lutheran. The moral imperative of Protestantism emphasizes denial, whereas the ritual of opera underscores pleasure. It is no accident that the great Lutheran composer Johann Sebastian Bach did not write in the most popular musical style of his day: the margraves and princes who paid him to write music were Lutherans.

The first moves toward a united Germany began in 1834 with the development of the German Customs Union and the Railway, and in 1918, the rulers of both Austria and Germany lost their thrones and each country was united.

Under Hitler, Germany took over Austria, Czechoslovakia, and Poland, lands once ruled by the Holy Roman Emperor. In 1945, at the end of the war, Germany was divided into two provisional entities with an Iron Curtain between them, the Bundes Republic of Germany and the German Democratic Republic. Each maintained an extraordinary level of operatic sophistication and commitment. Only since 1989 have the two been reunited, and the first free elections in the reunited Germany took place in December 1990. Under one government even German opera houses are feeling economically pinched. The now united city of Berlin with its three world-class opera houses is, rumor has it, even considering closing one.

Following World War II, German cities invariably struggled to support and present opera in whatever space was available. As performances of opera have throughout its history, these productions gave people comfort, social contact, accord, and a means to shape their future by providing a metaphor for their lives. In some cities, opera houses were rebuilt within two years after the war. In others, the task took forty years.

BERLIN

Opera came to Berlin relatively late. The city's first opera house was begun in 1740, when Frederick the Great became elector and made its construction a priority. Called the Königliches Opernhaus, or Hofoper (Royal Opera House), it opened on December 7, 1742, on Unter den Linden, where the present Staatsoper, a replica of the original theatre, now stands. Frederick exercised complete control over *every aspect* of the theatre's operatic production. He largely preferred Italian opera but occasionally enjoyed French as well. Admission was free and limited to members of the court, army officers, and the elite of Berlin society.

By the time Frederick died in 1786, impresarios had taken control of opera presentations in Berlin and court-supported opera was on the wane. For a while the Hofoper was used to store bread! By 1806, when Napoleon's armies occupied Berlin, the city had several public theaters, a trend that was to continue. Throughout the nineteenth and early twentieth centuries, Berlin made up for its late start and opera flourished in many theatres, including the Schauspielhaus am Gendarmen Markt.

The Schauspielhaus am Gendarmenmarkt premiered *Der Freischütz* (The Freeshooter), June 18, 1821, by Carl Maria von Weber (details at end of the section). Today the Schauspielhaus, rebuilt in the 1980s and now called the Konzerthaus, is home to the Berlin Symphony Orchestra. An elaborate statue of Friedrich von Schiller, seated and surrounded by four Muses representing drama, poetry, history, and philosophy, commands the front of the hall. Figures of Bacchus and Ariadne grace the northern portal, Orpheus and Eurydice the southern.

Konzerthaus, Gendarmenmarkt 2, 10117 Berlin
tel: (49–30) 203–090

Richard Strauss was principal conductor of the Hofoper from 1908 to 1913, when he was promoted to music director. He remained in that position until November 1919, when he became director of the newly created Staatsoper (court opera and the German monarchy both ended after World War I, and the Hofoper

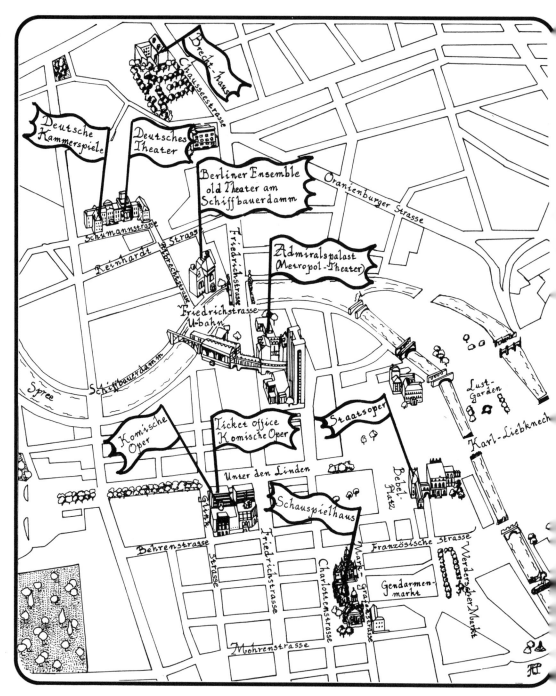

Operatic Berlin East of the Tiergarten

became the Staatsoper), a position he held for one year before becoming director of the Vienna Staatsoper.

By 1933 the Nazis' suppression of political dissent and their systematic rooting out of Jews from all public and private institutions drove most of Berlin's leading performers, conductors, and composers into exile. The Staatsoper

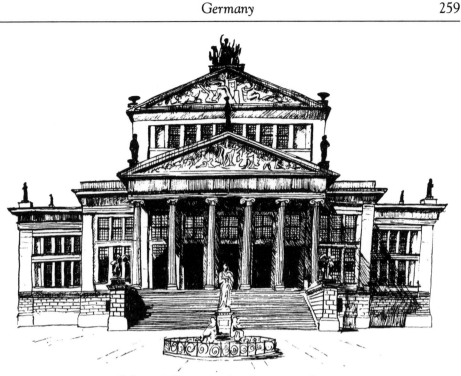

Schauspielhaus am Gendarmenmarkt

continued to present productions of traditional opera, sung and conducted by the "finest Aryan performers." The Staatsoper was bombed and destroyed on April 9, 1941, in an early Royal Air Force bombing raid carried out in retaliation for Germany's ceaseless bombing of London. As the theatre was the foremost in the Reich, it was immediately rebuilt and reopened on December 7, 1941, with a performance of Hitler's favorite opera, Wagner's *Die Meistersinger von Nürnberg*. In 1944 Joseph Goebbels ordered all theatres closed so that their manpower could be used in the war effort.

The Staatsoper was bombed again and completely destroyed on February 3, 1945. At the end of the war, even though the city was almost totally in ruins and its eastern sector even more impoverished than its western, opera performances were resumed in the Admiralpalast on December 8, 1945. By the time the Staatsoper was rebuilt and reopened on September 4, 1955, tensions between the eastern and western sections of the city were mounting, and by August 13, 1961, when the Berlin Wall went up overnight, a majority of the Staatsoper's most prominent artists were already in residence in the western sector's Deutsche Oper. The Staatsoper retained some major singers, however, such as Theo Adam and Peter Schreier, who had outstanding international careers while remaining citizens of the DDR (Deutsche Democratische Republic). Today the Staatsoper is one of the finest repertory companies in the world.

Premieres by distinguished composers presented by the Königliche Opernhaus (then the Hofoper and finally the Staatsoper) include (some details at

Staatsoper

chapter's end) *Die Bürgschaft* (March 10, 1932), Kurt Weill; *Christophe Colombe* (May 5, 1930), Darius Milhaud; *Die lustigen Weiber von Windsor* (March 9, 1849), Otto Nicolai; *Royal Palace* (March 2, 1927), Kurt Weill; *Wozzeck* (December 14, 1925), Alban Berg.

Staatsoper, Unter den Linden 7, 10117 Berlin (Mitte)
tel: (49–30) 2035–4466   fax: (49–30) 2035–4483
   By going to the box office to buy your tickets after 11:00 A.M. the day of the performance, you can get a 50 percent price reduction, and if you wait until one hour before the performance, your ticket will cost DM 10!

The Admiralspalast (today called the Metropol-Theater) is the theatre that gave a home to today's Deutsche Oper when the theatre was destroyed in 1943. It also served as home to the Staatsoper in 1945 until that theatre was rebuilt on Unter den Linden. The elegant building with its byzantine façade still stands near the Friedrichstrasse subway station and presents musicals such as *West Side Story.*

Admiralspalast, Friedrichstrasse 101–102, 10117 Berlin (Mitte)
tel: (49–30) 204–4704   fax: (49–30) 208–4236

The Kroll Theater opened in 1924 when the old Königliches Operettenthea-ter was rebuilt and enlarged to a seating capicity of 2,100. The theatre became incredibly popular; its ticket prices were low and, under the brilliant directorship of Otto Klemperer, it produced both bold reinterpretations of the classics (a 1927 production of Beethoven's *Fidelio* caused a *scandale* by paralleling contemporary

repression) and daring German premieres of such twentieth-century masterpieces as Igor Stravinsky's *Oedipus Rex,* Arnold Schoenberg's *Erwartung,* and the
world premiere of *Neues vom Tage* (1929) by Paul Hindemith. By the early 1930s
the theatre was considered a hotbed of left-wing ideas, and the rising political
right wing closed it after a particularly "political" production of Mozart's *Le nozze
di Figaro* that stressed the political issue of class in a manner distasteful to the
Nazis.

During the Third Reich, in order to survive, theatres and publishers tried to
accommodate to the philosophy of the dominant political system. In 1936,
several years after "degenerate" art had been banned from Germany's theatres,
Joseph Goebbels outlawed art criticism by dictating that newspapers hire "art
writers" who "evaluate less, and praise more." This sounded an artistic death
knell in a city that had presented some of the most provocative music of the
twentieth century.

The Komische Oper was opened in 1947 as a postwar realization of the Kroll
Oper. Directed by Walter Felsenstein, it was to be a radical extension of the
Volksoper concept, a "people's theatre" where smaller scale operas would be
produced as *realistisches Musiktheater* (realistic music theatre). Felsenstein established a "school" of East German opera production from which directors such as
Götz Friedrich have come. Like the Staatsoper, the Komische Oper is an
excellent repertory company. The stark modernism of the theatre's exterior belies
its sumptuous and welcoming interior.

Komische Oper, Behrenstrasse 55–57, 10117 Berlin (Mitte)
tel: (49–30) 202–600
Daytime ticket office: Unter den Linden 41 (just behind the theatre),
10117 Berlin (Mitte)
Open daily, 11:00 A.M.–5:30 P.M.
tel: (49–30) 2026–0360   fax: (49–30) 2026–0260

Originally called the Neues Theater, the Theater am Schiffbauerdamm
opened November 19, 1892. The great director Max Reinhardt was manager from
1903 to 1905 and gave the hall a revolving stage and an orchestra pit. New
management took over in 1928 and the theatre's name was changed to Theater
am Schiffbauerdamm.

In a wry historical twist, the operettas of the Jewish, German-born, but
naturalized and fanatically patriotic French citizen Jacques Offenbach (1819–80)
led directly to the development of the "cabaret-opera," unique to Berlin. By the
twentieth century, Offenbach's satirical operettas had influenced such theatres
as Theater am Schiffbauerdamm and the Komische Oper, and by the 1920s
Berlin totally embraced cabaret-operas, distinguished by their political satire and
their sweet-sour musical flavor derived from jazz. Of all these "operas" of the
1920s, Kurt Weill's (March 2, 1900, Dessau—April 3, 1950, New York City) *Die
Dreigroschenoper* is the most famous.

Theater am Schiffbauerdamm

In 1928 the new management of Theater am Schiffbauerdamm, determined to open with a hit, commissioned *Die Dreigroschenoper,* one of the great theatrical events of the early twentieth century. The premiere took place on August 31, 1928 (details about the premiere at section's end), and began the theatre's long association with Bertolt Brecht. The building suffered only minimal damage during the war and since 1954 has housed the Berliner Ensemble, giving the theatre yet another name—Berliner Ensemble. A large statue of Bertolt Brecht was placed in a small park at the theatre's entrance in 1988 to commemorate the ninetieth anniversary of his birth. The tiny theatre (seating 175), which today presents only prose drama, is well worth a visit. Its neoclassical lobby, lavish neorococo interior, and handmade dark wooden staircase and upstairs foyer (often used today for poetry readings and meetings) are stunning.

Berliner Ensemble (Theater am Schiffbauerdamm), Bertolt-Brecht-Platz 1, 10117 Berlin (Mitte)
Open Monday–Saturday, 11:00 A.M.–6:00 P.M.; Sunday, 3:00–6:00 P.M.

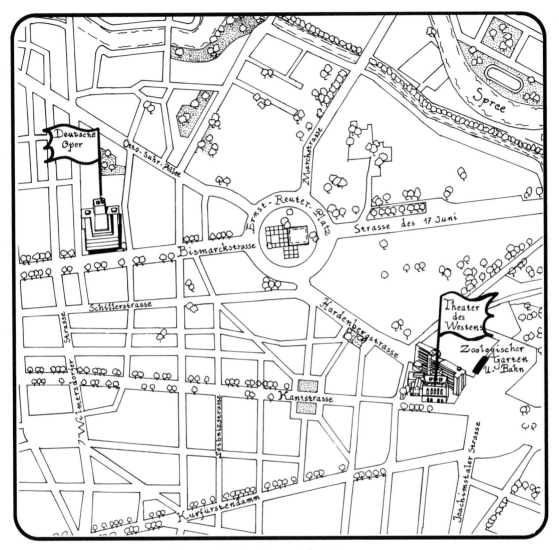

Operatic Berlin West of the Tiergarten

tel, box office: (49–30) 282–3160 tel, information: (49–30) 28–880   fax: (49–30) 2888–0162

Bertolt Brecht's home stands nearby. He spent the war years in exile in America, returned to Berlin in 1948, and lived here until his death in 1954. The house is open for guided tours.

Bertolt Brecht Haus, Chauseestrasse 125
tour hours: every thirty minutes—Tuesday–Friday, 10:00–11:30 A.M.; Thursday, 10:00–11:30 A.M. and 5:00–6:30 P.M.; Saturday, 9:30 A.M.–1:ʹɔ P.M.
tel: (49–30) 282–9916 to book an English-speaking guide

You must phone ahead to arrange for tours in English. The tours are restricted to eight people and offer a fascinating view into Brecht's life.

The Städtische Oper (today's Deutsche Oper) opened in the newly urbanized Charlottenburg neighborhood in 1912. Unlike the Royal Opera House (Hofoper) in Unter den Linden, it was planned as a "people's opera." After 1933 the theatre became known as the Deutsches Opernhaus, and on November 23, 1943, it was destroyed in an Allied bombing raid. Performances continued to be staged in the Admiralspalast until the autumn of 1944, when all German theatres were closed. After the war, the theatre, as the opera house of the western sector, reclaimed the name Städtische Oper, and on September 4, 1945, opened in the relatively undamaged Theater des Westens with a performance of *Fidelio*.

On May 24, 1961, the renamed Deutsche Oper (1,885 seats) inaugurated its own newly built theater with Mozart's *Don Giovanni*. Since 1961, it has presented premieres of Hans Werner Henze's *Der junge Lord* (1965) and *Das verratene Meer* (1990). (In 1956, during its stay in Theater des Westens, the theatre premiered Henze's *König Hirsch*.) The Deutsche Oper has always had great conductors: Bruno Walter before the war and, since its reopening, Lorin Maazel, Daniel Barenboim, Giuseppe Sinopoli, and Jesus López-Corbos.

Deutsche Oper, Bismarckstrasse 33, 10627 Berlin (Charlottenburg)
tel: (49–30) 341–8401
    By going to the box office to buy your tickets after 11:00 A.M. the day of the performance, you can get a 50 percent price reduction, and if you wait until one hour before the performance, your ticket will cost DM 10!

Theater des Westens still stands, a block and a half from the Zoo-Station of the subway, and presents musicals such as *Hello, Dolly!* and satirical musicals such as Kurt Weill's *Johnny Johnson*. The theatre's foyer is decorated in splendid *Jugendstil*.

Theater des Westens, Kantstrasse 12, 10623 Berlin
Open daily, 10:00 A.M.–6:00 P.M.
tel: (49–30) 882–2888   fax: (49–30) 3190–3118 or 3190–3137

Note: In Berlin, posters advertising opera and concert performances give *both* the starting and the finishing times; for example, 19:00–21:45 (starting at 7:00 P.M. and finishing at 9:45 P.M.)

Berlin probably has more theatres and cabarets than any other city in the world. Theatre, whether sung or spoken, has always afforded an opportunity to express dissent and passionate opinions.

Details of a premiere at the Schauspielhaus

Der Freischütz (The Freeshooter), *romantische Oper* in four acts, June 18, 1821.
Carl Maria von Weber (November 18, 1786, Eutin—June 5, 1826, London)

Libretto Johann Friedrich Kind, after *Gespensterbuch* by August Apel and Friedrich Laun.

Weber spent much of his short life struggling to bring German opera to greatness. The typical *Singspiel* of the beginning of the nineteenth century had too light a plot: witness Mozart's *Zauberflöte* and *Entführung aus dem Serail.* So Weber built *Der Freischütz* around concepts, subject matter, and spectacle found in grand opera. In this work he attempted to create a total balance between music, drama, and spectacle and to incorporate much of the drama into the music itself. His setting for the Wolf's Glen scene and musical depictions of the preternatural—flapping nightbirds, a hurricane, cracking whips, thundering horses, and wheels of fire—are simply breathtaking.

Weber himself conducted the premiere of *Der Freischütz*, which was the first opera staged in the newly rebuilt Schauspielhaus. The highly successful premiere was attended by the wealthy and artistically minded citizens of Berlin (the poet Heinrich Heine and the composer Felix Mendelssohn, for example), but not the nobility, who preferred Italian opera. *Der Freischütz* is really *the* seminal German Romantic opera, and Weber's struggle to advance German opera finally came to fruition in the late works of Richard Wagner. *Der Freischütz* is not really part of the international standard repertory, but when it is performed it still speaks to contemporary audiences.

Premieres presented by the Königliche Opernhaus (also known as the Hofoper and, finally, the Staatsoper)

Die lustigen Weiber von Windsor, *komische-fantastische Oper* (a fantastic comic opera) in three acts, March 9, 1849.
Otto Nicolai (June 9, 1810, Königsberg, now Kaliningrad—May 11, 1849, Berlin)
Libretto Salomon Hermann Mosenthal, after *The Merry Wives of Windsor* by William Shakespeare.

Nicolai was *Kapellmeister* at the Vienna Hofoper when he wrote *Die lustigen Weiber von Windsor* and fully expected it to be premiered in Vienna, where he had encountered some success with his first four Italian-style operas. When the Hofoper declined to produce it, he quit and took a post in Berlin at the cathedral and at the Royal Opera House. *Die lustigen Weiber* was premiered there with great success. Nicolai died of a stroke only two months after conducting the premiere. Although the opera is not often performed, its lively overture is to be heard at many orchestra concerts.

Wozzeck, *Opera* in three acts, December 14, 1925.
Alban Berg (1885–1935)
Libretto by the composer, after Georg Büchner's play *Woyzeck* (written sometime before his death in 1837).

After seeing Büchner's play in May of 1914, Berg at once began an operatic treatment. The horrors of World War I further motivated him to complete the work. Wozzeck is an army private powerless over his own life and fate, and abused by all those in power over him. The play has twenty-five scenes, of which Berg uses fifteen divided evenly into three acts. Each scene is musically self-contained and connected by dramatic thematic musical material. Berg changed the protagonist's name to Wozzeck on the grounds that it had more impact than the softer-sounding diphthong in Woyzeck.

The vocal parts are rife with Berg's expressive inventiveness. He makes use of *Sprechstimme*, a highly declamatory manner of delivering text, as well as transmuting coughing, whistling, and laughter into music. Erich Kleiber conducted the triumphant Berlin premiere, and a second Berlin production was mounted in 1932. After that Berg was officially proscribed by the Nazi regime and the opera was not performed again in Germany until 1948. Leopold Stokowski conducted the American premiere in Philadelphia in March 1931.

Wozzeck is a tightly constructed opera and speaks powerfully about man's inhumanity to man. Büchner, who died in 1837, based the drama on fact, and even though it was written over 150 years ago, it speaks to today's audiences with great passion. Notwithstanding its modernist musical idiom, *Wozzeck* is very much a part of today's repertory.

Premiere presented by the Theater an Schiffbauerdamm

Die Dreigroschenoper (The Threepenny Opera), play with music in a prologue and three acts, August 31, 1928.
Kurt Weill (March 2, 1900, Dessau—April 3, 1950, New York City)
Libretto Bertolt Brecht, after John Gay's eighteenth-century *The Beggar's Opera*.

Die Dreigroschenoper was commissioned to open the new Theater am Schiffbauerdamm and with 350 performances in two years became the biggest theatrical success of the Weimar Republic. The great singing actress Lotte Lenya, who was also married to the composer Kurt Weill, played the role of Jenny. By 1933, over 133 new productions had taken place throughout the world. The text has been translated into all the major languages, with no fewer than eight versions in English. In a translation by Marc Blitzstein, *Die Dreigroschenoper* was performed 2,611 consecutive times in New York City in the 1950s. Brecht worked from a translation by Elisabeth Hauptmann of Gay's *Beggar's Opera* (1728), to which he added poems (in translation) by François Villon and Rudyard Kipling. After World War II, he added references to the Nazi atrocities.

Weill wrote the music as a "reform opera" in reaction to the passion for emulating Wagner's music dramas (just as Gay had written the original in reaction to the passion for Italian opera in England in the eighteenth century; see London, Lincoln's Inn Fields Theatre, page 211). Weill wrote that the "charm of the piece is in the fact that the risqué text is set to music in a gentle and pleasant way." Many of the melodies and textual phrases such as "Mack the Knife" and the song that accompanies the phrase are part of today's common language. The pervading tone of the piece is a deliberately off-balance mixture of sentimentality and caustic social comment.

For more Berlin information write:

Berlin Fremdenverkehrsbetriebe, Martin-Luther-Strasse 105, 13467 Berlin, Germany

FOOD

Do try Berlinerweisse Beer!

LODGING

Staying in the old eastern sector near the Staatsoper, Komische Oper, and the old Schauspielhaus (today's Konzerthaus) puts you near many of the city's cultural events as well as close to several very convenient subway stops. The atmosphere here is also much more pleasing than that in the old western sector.

Albrechtshof, Albrechtstrasse 8, 10117 Berlin (Mitte)
tel: (49–30) 284–030   fax: (49–30) 284–3100
This hotel is a haven of tranquillity, even though it stands in the middle of a very bustling area, surrounded by theatres and small restaurants. It is also run by very nice people! It is a ten-minute walk to both the Staatsoper and the Komische Oper, two minutes from the old Theater am Schiffbauerdamm, and three minutes from the old Admiralpalast. The Deutsche Theater, Friedrichstrasse Palast, and Pergamon Museum are all nearby. Five minutes away is the Friedrichstrasse subway station for going quickly to the Deutsche Oper, Theater den Westens, and everything else in the old western sector.

Maritim Grand Hotel, Friedrichstrasse 158–164, 10117 Berlin (Mitte)
tel: (49–30) 23–270   fax: (49–30) 2327–3362
This is truly a "grand" hotel, with a lobby almost like a theater. It is in the same block as the Komische Oper and two short blocks from the Staatsoper. At the time of this writing, new owners were being sought; we can only hope the new owners will maintain it in the pristine manner of the Maritim chain!

Hotel Kubrat, Leipziger Strasse 19, 10117 Berlin (Mitte)
tel: (49–30) 201–2054   fax: (49–30) 201–2057
   This hotel is just off Friedrichstrasse, which at this point appears to be a Berlin version of Rodeo Drive in Beverly Hills. The bustling area is a ten-minute walk from the Komische Oper and the Staatsoper.

BAYREUTH

If you can choose only one operatic place to visit in Germany, make it Bayreuth. Bayreuth hosted its first opera performance in 1661, and by 1735 opera in the city had achieved major importance. Frederick the Great's sister, Wilhelmine, the consort of Margrave Friedrich of Bayreuth and herself a composer of operas, had excellent relations with her brother and thus was in constant contact with his court and all the composers and performers therein. In 1745 Wilhelmine oversaw the construction of the Markgräfliches Opernhaus, a magnificent Italian-style theatre by the eminent Italian theatre designer Giuseppe Galli-Bibiena and his son Carlo. The foyer is somewhat subdued, reflecting eighteenth-century Lutheran taste. The stage is particularly deep, a feature that attracted Richard Wagner to Bayreuth in the hope that the theatre would be suitable to stage his *Ring* cycle. (It wasn't. See Festspielhaus, below.)

   The interior of the Markgräfliches Opernhaus, in jarring contrast to its stark foyer, is a sumptuous excercise in eighteenth-century excess, all blue and gold, decorated with bare-bosomed goddesses, naked putti, angels playing instruments, columns, and painted trompe-l'oeil effects. Undamaged in the war, the theatre is still in mint condition. Acoustics are excellent as the house is full of reflective surfaces. The theatre hosts the Bayerisches Festwochen each May and June, presenting early operas and ballets in productions by the Bavarian Staatsoper, Munich. During the Wagner Festival in August, it offers concerts on days the Festspielhaus is closed.

Markgräfliches Opernhaus, Opernstrasse
tel, information: (49–921) 65–313
Open Tuesday through Sunday—April through September, 9:00 A.M.–noon and 1:20–5:00 P.M.; October through March, 1:00 A.M.–noon and 1:30–3:30 P.M.
admission: DM 2

In 1863, Richard Wagner described his ideal theatre for his *Ring* cycle: It should be in "one of the less large towns in Germany"; a town "capable of accommodating an unusual number of guests"; a town "where one would not have to compete with large-city audiences and their established customs"; and in a theatre "built in the shape of an amphitheatre with the orchestra invisible to the audience." In addition, performers would be "singers from German opera houses,

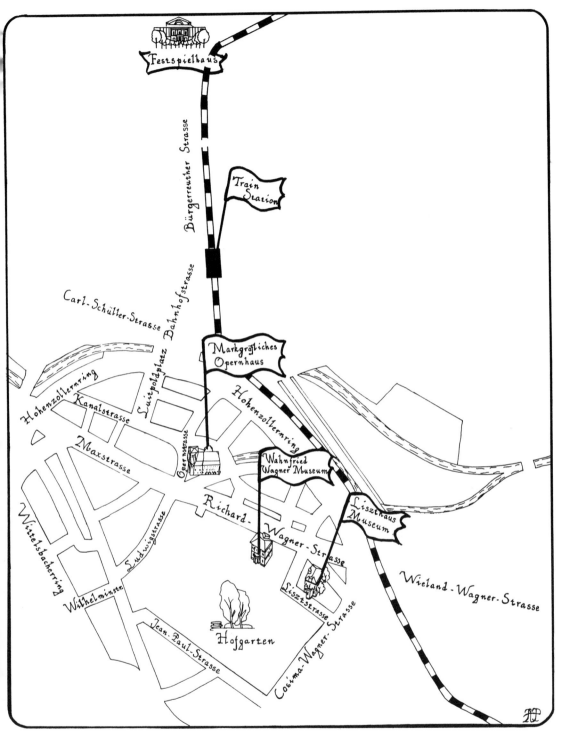

Operatic Bayreuth

chosen for their outstanding acting skills, who would be summoned in the early spring to rehearse several parts of my work, uninterrupted by any other artistic activity. Performances of the complete cycle would be given at the height of summer on four successive evenings." He also stipulated that the hall should be used exclusively for the presentation of his operas and called a *Festpielhaus* (festival hall).

The mayor and civic authorities obviously believed that Wagner's vision could put Bayreuth on the world's artistic map. They offered him—free of charge—a site on a hill on the town's northern edge. (Bayreuth had the added advantage of being within the territories of Wagner's patron, King Ludwig.) The foundation stone for the theatre was laid on May 22, 1872, an event for which Wagner himself conducted Beethoven's Ninth Symphony in the Markgräfliches Opernhaus. Once the Festspielhaus was built, paid for by King Ludwig and the city, its acoustics were tested by filling it with soldiers from nearby army barracks!

The foyer of the Festspielhaus is timbered with natural, unvarnished wood and greatly resembles a sauna. The interior of the theatre is built on a single, fan-shaped, sharply raked level. The shape is that of a Greek amphitheatre (specifically, that at Epidauros or Delphi).

The hall is almost stark in its simplicity. It is plain, almost devoid of ornamentation (certainly no nude figures) except for its Corinthian columns. The floor is uncarpeted and unvarnished, and the proscenium is undecorated. (Wagner wanted people to pay attention to the opera.) There are no galleries on the sides of the hall. The sight lines are excellent from all seats. The orchestra pit is in a deep well under the stage, obscured from the sight of the audience. This was, as Wagner said, to "separate the real from the ideal." It also allows

Finally, in 1876, with the financial aid of King Ludwig, Wagner was able to produce the *Ring* in its entirety, three times. Because of a huge financial deficit, six years passed before Wagner could stage another festival. In 1882 the festival was devoted entirely to *Parsifal*, a work he had written expressly for the Festspielhaus, with its vast, covered orchestra pit. (In fact, because of its excessive orchestral demands, Wagner intended that *Parsifal* should be performed nowhere else, *ever.*) Sixteen performances were given, and for the sixteenth, Wagner took the baton and conducted the final scene, the only time he conducted in his theatre. He died the next year.

Over the years the whole Wagner family partook in the realization of Richard's dream, and the festival remained under the exclusive control of the family until 1973. At that time the Richard Wagner Foundation Bayreuth was created to assume responsibility for the festival in perpetuity. Wolfgang Wagner (Siegfried's son, Richard's grandson, born in 1919) has been festival director since 1973. It was Wolfgang's British-born mother, Winifred, who was close to Adolph Hitler.

Wagner premieres in the Festspielhaus: August 13 through 17, 1876, the *entire Der Ring des Nibelungen* was premiered August 13, 1876, *Das Rheingold* (premiered alone in Munich in 1869); August 14, 1876, *Die Walküre* (premiered alone in Munich in 1870); August 16, 1876, *Siegfried* (premiere); August 17, 1876 *Götterdämmerung* (premiere); July 26, 1882, *Parsifal* (premiere).

Festspielhaus
guided tours: Tuesday through Sunday—April through September,
10:00–11:30 A.M. and 1:30–3:00 P.M.; November through March,
10:00–10:45 A.M. and 2:15–3:00 P.M.
tel: (49–921) 78–780
admission: DM 2
Closed in October.

For tickets for the summer Wagner Festival, you must write *at least* a year in
advance:

Kartenbüro, Festspielleitung Bayreuth, Postfach 10062
8580 Bayreuth, Germany

Wagner bought a plot of land adjoining the margrave's former residence, the
Neues Schloss, and built his family home, called Wahnfried (Peace from
Torment). Wahnfried housed the Wagner family up to the death of Wieland
Wagner (Richard's grandson, son of Siegfried) in 1966. Today the villa is the
Richard Wagner Museum. A music lover or history buff should plan on a stay of
at least three hours, and a dedicated Wagnerite should spend the whole day.

The museum bursts with information and details pertaining to Wagner's life:
manuscripts, handwritten librettos, letters, paintings, drawings, photos, books,
sculptures, mock-ups of stage sets, costumes, and much, *much* more. A
concert–lecture room downstairs in the library is filled with Wagner's books and
his piano. The family photos of the 1870s are not to be missed, and the

Festspielhaus

chronology of Wahnfried itself is fascinating. Along with a letter from Wagner to Pauline Horson, there is even a picture of this *Siegfried* Flower Maiden with whom he was flirting, and whose arrival in Venice precipitated the argument with Cosima that led to his fatal heart attack. And there are pictures of his funeral cortege in Bayreuth. Richard and Cosima (Liszt von Bülow Wagner) are buried together in the garden under a mound of ivy topped by a simple slab of marble. Connected to Wahnfried is the Siegfriedhaus, home of Wagner's first son.

Villa Wahnfried, Richard Wagner Museum, Richard-Wagner-Strasse 48
Open daily, 9:00 A.M.–5:00 P.M.
tel: (49–921) 757–2816
admission: DM 4 (for DM 6 one can visit both the Wagner and Liszt museums)
   Wagner's music is played at 10:00 A.M., noon, and 2:00 P.M.
   There are video presentations of performances in the Festspielhaus at 11:00 A.M. and 3:00 P.M.

The composer, conductor, and pianist Franz Liszt (October 22, 1811, Raiding, Hungary—July 31, 1886, Bayreuth), father of Cosima, was a great Wagner champion and conducted the Weimar premiere of *Lohengrin* in 1850. Liszt died in Bayreuth, where he had come to attend the premiere of his daughter Cosima's new production of *Tristan und Isolde* on July 31, 1886. A Franz-Liszt-Museum, containing his piano and many other artifacts, opened in 1993. The

Wahnfried

museum is filled with information about both opera and the very fruitful life of the astonishingly attractive Liszt (a life mask made in 1839 attests that paintings of him do not exaggerate his beauty!). Liszt was a lay priest of the Catholic Church and wore priest's clothing when he conducted. Of particular note is a portrait of the "mother of Liszt's children," Gräfin Marie d'Agoult. The collection also offers many beautiful paintings and uncirculated photos of composers other than Liszt, but especially striking are the photos of Liszt with his students. His death mask is in the sunny room in which he died.

Franz-Liszt-Museum, Wahnfriedstrasse 9
Open daily, 9:00 A.M.–noon; and 2:00–5:00 P.M.
tel: (49–921) 757–2818

Details of the Festspielhaus premieres

Der Ring des Nibelungen

Der Ring des Nibelungen spans four operas and is thus known as Wagner's tetralogy. In a nutshell, the saga describes the theft of the mystically powerful gold ring of the Rhine River and its consequences to mortals and gods alike. The fourth opera ends with the gods and their abode, Valhalla, going up in flames and the return of the ring to the Rhine. The journey fills about eighteen hours with some of the most exciting music ever written.

Das Rheingold, *Vorabend* (introductory evening) of *Der Ring des Nibelungen,* in four scenes, premiere as part of the *Ring,* August 13, 1876 (premiered as a single opera in Munich, September 22, 1869).
Libretto by the composer.

Das Rheingold is the first opera Wagner wrote in accordance with the theoretical principles set down in his book *Oper und Drama.* The rigor with which he adhered to them here makes *Das Rheingold* quite different from the other three operas of the *Ring.* Its first, and inadequately prepared, performance was given in Munich at the insistence of Wagner's patron King Ludwig II.

Die Walküre, first day of *Der Ring des Nibelungen,* in three acts, premiere as part of the *Ring,* August 14, 1876 (premiered as a single opera in Munich, June 26, 1870).
Libretto by the composer.

Die Walküre achieved an unprecedented organic relationship between music, text, and drama. This opera is easily the most approachable and engaging opera Wagner ever wrote. Its first performance, in Munich, given at King Ludwig's insistence, suffered—as did the premiere of *Das Rheingold*—from underrehearsal. Of course, *Die Walküre* contains Wagner's best known music, the "Ride of the Valkyries."

Siegfried, second day of *Der Ring des Nibelungen* in three acts, world premiere, August 16, 1876.
Libretto by the composer.

Wagner spent more than fifteen years on this opera, so that stylistically the first act is quite different from the last. Whoever plays Siegfried is on stage four full hours, singing the most taxing music in all the tenor repertory. Jokes abound about the role, culminating in a cartoon by the French artist-humorist Sempé in which a timid theatre director peeks between a proscenium's curtains, asking: "Excuse me, is there anyone in the house who can sing Siegfried?"

Götterdämmerung (Twilight of the Gods), third day of *Der Ring des Nibelungen,* in a prologue and three acts, world premiere, August 17, 1876.
Libretto by the composer.

Wagner began work on the libretto in 1848, completed the score in 1874, and saw the opera's premiere in 1876, twenty-eight years after its conception. The longest of all the operas in the *Ring, Götterdämmerung* lasts more than five hours. It requires great stamina from the singers , the orchestra, and the public. Nonetheless, the opera is very compelling and moving.

Parsifal, Bühnenweihfestival (Festival Play for the Consecration of the Stage), in three acts, July 26, 1882.
Libretto by the composer, after Wolfram von Eschenbach's poem, *Parzivâl.*

The world premiere of *Parsifal* was given for the Society of Patrons of the Bayreuth Festival. Wagner knew how to be charming and raise money. In *Mein Leben* (My Life), he wrote that the idea for *Parsifal* came to him on Good Friday and that he considered the opera a religious work. It concerns the quest for the Holy Grail, the striving for purity and regeneration, and is still most often performed in the week before Easter. Modern thinkers have uncovered a darker side to the opera—elements of racial purity and regeneration. However that may be, the music is Wagner's most sublime.

For more information contact:

Bayreuth Tourist Office (Fremdenverkehrsbetriebe), Luitpoldplatz 9, 95444 Bayreuth, Germany
tel: (0921) 88–588   fax: (0921) 88–555

Many of Bayreuth's shops have a Wagner angle: The Siegfried Pharmacy, the Tannhäuser Bakery, and so on.

FOOD

Zollinger "Opern Café," Opernstrasse 16, Bayreuth
tel: (49–921) 65–720

This lovely café stands in Bayreuth's center almost next door to the Markgräfliches Opernhaus. Its architecture reflects the theatre's. There's a wonderful selection of cookies and cakes, and during the summer months they also serve light meals.

LODGING

Hotel Goldener Hirsch Garni, Bannhofstrasse 13, D–95444 Bayreuth
tel: (49–921) 23–046   fax: (49–921) 22–483

This unpretentious hotel is almost directly across the street from the train station (Bayreuth is a small town). It is a five-minute walk to the center of town and a pleasant fifteen-minute walk up to the Festspielhaus.

Hotel Goldener Löwe, Kulmbacher Strasse 30, D–95445 Bayreuth
tel: (49–921) 41–046   fax: (49–921) 47–777

This hotel is closer to the center of town but slightly further from the Festspielhaus.

Hotel Zur Lohmühle, Badstrasse 37, D–95444 Bayreuth
tel: (49–921) 53–060   fax: (49–921) 58–286

This hotel is in the center of Bayreuth and quite near the Wagner and Liszt Museums.

DRESDEN

Dresden was a wealthy commercial city, and the list of famous premieres it presented approaches the offerings of Venice, Milan, or Vienna. From 1685, when a permanent Italian opera company was installed, opera played a leading role in the life of Dresden. In 1719 an Italian-style theater seating 2,000, one of the largest in Europe, was built for the court. In 1723, when a famous castrato refused to sing a role in an opera written by a local composer, the Elector of Saxony fired all his Italian singers; two years later, he hired a completely new Italian troupe, led by Faustina Bordoni, wife of the composer Johann Adolf Hasse. From 1734 to 1756, Hasse wrote, rehearsed, and conducted at least one opera for each Karneval season. In 1750 Giuseppe Galli-Bibiena, of Mantova and Bologna fame (see pages 28 and 68), supervised renovations to the court opera

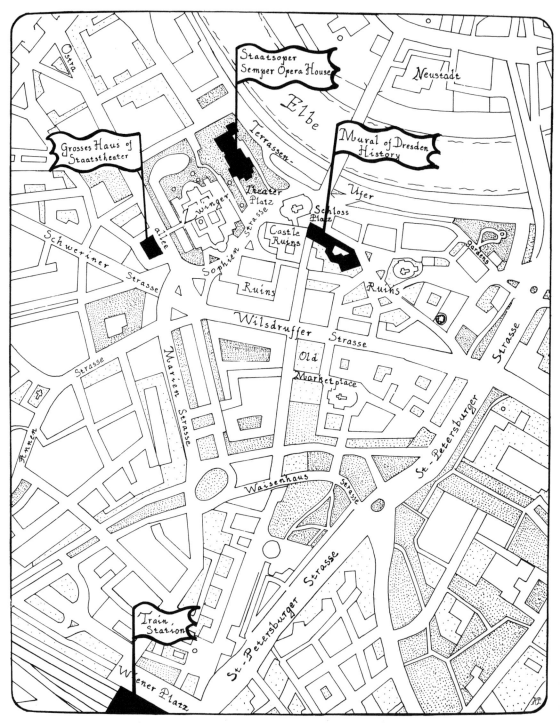

Operatic Dresden

house. Outside the court, starting in 1746, Italian operas were offered to paying audiences.

Dresden was devastated by the Seven Years' War between Prussia and Saxony. The Elector of Saxony was also the King of Poland, so he spent the war years in

Poland. The 1756 Prussian bombardment of the city destroyed everything Hasse wrote during his Dresden years. At the war's end in 1763, the elector returned to Dresden, and the opera house, which had served the Prussians as a storage depot, was reopened. In 1765 an Italian opera buffa troupe was installed in the court's Kleines Kurfürstlisches Theater, where it stayed, giving three performances a week, until 1777. Opera seria was seldom performed in the city. During the War of the Bavarian Succession (1777–79), the opera buffa troupe was replaced by a German company that presented *Singspiels*. Then, during the last twenty years of the eighteenth century, opera buffa again dominated the theatrical life of Dresden. Even Mozart's famous German *Singspiel, Die Zauberflöte*, was given in Italian!

By the beginning of the nineteenth century Dresden had almost surpassed Paris as the intellectual center of Europe. On January 1, 1817, the Dresden Hoftheater was formed when the court merged the city's Italian and German opera theatres. A glorious opera house was commissioned from and named after Dresden's leading architect, Gottfried Semper (his architecture was said to have made Dresden "the Florence of Germany"). The house was completed in 1841, burned down in 1869, then rebuilt by Semper's son Manfred and opened in 1878, again called the Semper Opera House.

Dresden was virtually untouched by World War II until the firebombing air raids of February 13 and 14, 1945. The Semper Opera, all of the city center, and all of Dresden's theatres, libraries, and many artistic treasures were destroyed. Over 35,000 civilians died. Reflecting the indomitable passion of the wounded city for its cultural life, on August 10, 1945, a performance of Mozart's *Le nozze di Figaro* was given in a temporary space. In 1948 the Grosses Haus of the Staatstheater reopened with a performance of Ludwig van Beethoven's *Fidelio*. (The Grosses Haus has 1,103 seats, and the Kleines Haus has 525.) Kurt Sanderling was principal conductor from 1964 to 1966, and Herbert Blomstedt was principal conductor from 1975 to 1985. The Staatstheater now houses the symphony.

On February 13, 1985, forty years to the day after the bombing raid that destroyed the city, the Staatsoper (Semper Oper) reopened with a production of Carl Maria von Weber's *Der Freischütz*.

The following premieres took place in Dresden's Semper Opera House (variously called the Königliches Sächsisches Hof, Hof Theater, or Sächsiches Staatstheater) *Arabella* (1933), Richard Strauss; *Die Ägyptische Helena* (1928), Richard Strauss; *Cardillac* (1926), Paul Hindemith; *Daphne* (1938), Richard Strauss; *Doktor Faustus* (1925), Ferruccio Busoni; *Elektra* (1909), Richard Strauss; *Feuersnot* (1901), Richard Strauss; *Der fliegende Holländer* (1843), Richard Wagner; *Intermezzo* (1924), Richard Strauss; *Orfeo* (1940), Carl Orff; *Der Protagonist* (1926), Kurt Weill; *Rienzi* (1842), Richard Wagner; *Der Rosenkavalier* (1911), Richard Strauss; *Salome* (1905), Richard Strauss; *Die schweigsame Frau* (1935), Richard Strauss; *Tannhäuser*, first version, (1845), Richard Wagner; *Tannhäuser*, second version, (1847), Richard Wagner.

Sächsischen Staatsoper Dresden (Semper Opera House), Office of Information, Postfach 12 09 08, 01008 Dresden
Box Office: Theaterplatz 2
Open Monday–Friday, 10:00 A.M.–noon and 1:00–5:00 P.M.
tel: (49–351) 491–1705
tel, recorded daily information: (49–351) 491–1731
tel, ticket reservations: (49–351) 491–1705
tel, information: (49–351) 491–1730   fax: (49–351) 491–1700

Monday through Sunday, from 2:00 P.M. to 4:00 P.M., the Staatsoper gives wonderful hour-long guided tours of its beautifully restored interior. The overall effect of the reconstruction is simply breathtaking, and the acoustics of the hall are perfect (the varnished hardwood floor is uncarpeted). Great attention was paid to each detail in the highly decorated hall and corridors. Take it all in, but do not expect too much from close inspection of the details, which are rendered in a workmanlike style reminiscent of the art of the American WPA. During the rebuilding of the Semper Opera House, operas were performed at the Schauspielhaus (originally called the Sächsischeshoftheater), rebuilt in 1948 on the other side of the Zwinger (Palace).

Semper Opera tour
Open Monday–Sunday, 2:00–4:00 P.M.
admission: DM 8

Semper Opera

On January 17, 1817, Carl Maria von Weber (November 18, 1786, Eutin—June 5, 1826, London) took on the post of conductor of Dresden's newly founded Deutsche Opera. From then until 1826 he was in the forefront of the popular movement for German opera, supported by Dresden's citizens, in what became a full-fledged rivalry with the court-supported Italian Opera. Under the same roof, the Italian composer Francesco Morlacchi oversaw the well-established tradition of Italian opera. The fragile, tubercular Weber championed the cause for a sophisticated German-style opera that would be a complete and unified art form, as opposed to the Italian style, which he regarded as an uneasy compromise between drama and music, resulting in the trivialization of both. He completed his opera *Der Freischütz* in 1820 in Dresden (see Berlin, Schauspielhaus page 264).

Carl-Maria-von-Weber-Museum, Dresdenerstrasse 44, 01326 Dresden
Open Wednesday–Sunday, 1:00–6:00 P.M.
tel: (49–351) 39–234
admission: DM 3

Weber set the stage for Richard Wagner (May 22, 1813, Leipzig—February 13, 1883, Venice), who came to Dresden some twenty years later. After the extraordinary success of his opera *Rienzi*, presented by the Dresden Hoftheater on October 20, 1842, Wagner was appointed *Kapellmeister* to the court of the King of Saxony. He remained in the position from 1843 to 1849 and was conductor of both the opera and the orchestra. Thus he became the spiritual successor to Weber. In 1844 Wagner acknowledged his debt to Weber by contriving to have Weber's body exhumed from its London resting place and returned to Dresden. For the reburial Wagner composed an ode for men's choir, "Am Weber's Grabe."

In 1848 Wagner joined an insurrectionist movement of German liberals and presented the king with a plan for organizing a German national theatre. Wagner was profoundly convinced that art, especially music, was the highest and potentially the most fruitful form of human endeavor. He delivered a speech to the *Vaterlandsverein* (Fatherland's Society) on the evils of capitalism as barriers to the emancipation of the human race. He predicted the downfall of the aristocracy. After the failure of the Dresden May Rising in 1849, when Prussian troops began to gain control of the city, Wagner had to flee for his life. He went into exile in Switzerland, where he lived with his wife Minna, her illegitimate daughter, and Minna's parents.

While in exile Wagner was supported by a retired silk merchant, Otto Wesendonck, who built him a small house adjacent to the villa he was building for himself and his wife in Enge, a suburb of Zurich. In 1857, Wagner and Minna moved in, and Wesendonck's wife Mathilde and Richard began an intense, but probably chaste, love affair which became the model on which the libretto of *Tristan und Isolde* was based. This tale celebrates and idealizes the extraordinary passion of unconsumated love. It was also during this period that *Der Ring des*

Nibelungen began to take shape. Wagner was not able to return to Germany until August 1860. (There are pictures of the ethereally beautiful Mathilde Wesendonck in Bayreuth's Wagner Museum.) After a crisis caused by Minna's discovery of the relationship, Richard began to set Mathilde's poems in what was his only song cycle, the "Wesendonck Lieder."

Between 1882 and 1914, under the musical directorship of Ernst von Schuch, Dresden gave fifty-one operatic premieres and 120 German or local first performances. In 1886, in the face of severe disapproval from the court on musical grounds, von Schuch produced three complete *Ring* cycles. With the 1901 premiere of Richard Strauss's *Feuersnot* began the relationship on which the twentieth-century fame of the Dresden opera rests. Nine Strauss operas premiered in the theatre, including the very popular *Elektra*, *Der Rosenkavalier*, and *Salome*.

Details of some premieres at the Semper Opera House (Königliches Sächsisches Hof, Hof Theater, or Sächsiches Staatstheater)

Die ägyptische Helena, opera, June 6, 1928.
Richard Strauss (June 11, 1864, Munich—September 8, 1949, Garmisch-Partenkirchen)
Libretto Hugo von Hofmannsthal.

Several factors contributed to *Die ägyptische Helena's* unsuccessful premier. The conductor, Fritz Busch, was ill and missed many rehearsals. In addition, the opera house refused to pay for Maria Jeritza, the soprano for whom both Strauss and Hofmannsthal had written the title role. The drama presented problems for both the composer and the librettist, and Strauss failed in a last-minute attempt to rewrite Act II. Only five days later, on his sixty-fourth birthday, Strauss conducted the Viennese premiere with Jeritza in the title role, and the opera was slightly better received, but it has never entered the standard repertory.

Arabella, Lyrische Komödie in three acts, July 1, 1933.
Richard Strauss (1864–1949)
Libretto by Hugo von Hofmannsthal.

Arabella is the last Strauss-Hofmannsthal collaboration. In 1929, only days after Hofmannsthal sent Strauss the final version of Act I, his only son committed suicide, and within thirty-six hours Hofmannsthal suffered a fatal stroke. Strauss decided to set Acts II and III from the librettist's draft. As a consequence, the opera suffers from lack of a finely honed plot, although it still has the appeal of late nineteenth-century Viennese operetta. In fact, much of *Arabella's* music is very simple, akin to tuneful folk songs but gloriously orchestrated. As are many of Strauss's feminine protagonists, Arabella is an all-forgiving wife portrayed in rapturous music.

Daphne, *Bukolische Tragödie* in one act, October 15, 1938.
Richard Strauss (1864–1949)
Libretto Joseph Gregor.

Gregor became Strauss's librettist after Nazi anti-Semitism made it impossible for him to contine to work with Stefan Zweig. Zweig and Strauss remained close, and Gregor never really gained Strauss's respect. The libretto to *Daphne* misses the mark, but Strauss's music is subtle and voluptuous.

Doktor Faust, *Opera* in a prologue, two preludes, a scenic intermezzo, and three scenes, May 21, 1925.
Ferruccio Busoni (April 1, 1866, Empoli, Italy—July 27, 1924, Berlin)
Libretto by the composer, based on sixteenth-century puppet plays.

Busoni died before completing *Doktor Faust,* and the missing music was added for the premiere by Philipp Jarnach. Busoni drew on much of his earlier work in assembling his "Faustian vocabulary." Like Wagner, he published theoretical writings to support what he did in the opera. The work is a modern mystery play, part folk festival, part passion play. In 1985 a new edition of the opera was presented by Bologna's Teatro Comunale, with a score assembled from sketches of the missing musical material by Antony Beaumont.

Elektra, *Tragödie* in one act, January 25, 1909.
Richard Strauss (1864–1949)
Libretto by Hugo von Hofmannsthal, after Sophocles's *Electra.*

From youth, Strauss was a Hellenist. At seventeen he set a chorus from Sophocles's *Electra* to music. When Strauss saw a Max Reinhardt production of the Sophocles play, rewritten by Hofmannsthal, he loved it and asked the writer if he could set the play as an opera. Thus began a fruitful relationship that lasted until Hofmannsthal's death in 1929. *Elektra's* premiere took place three years after the premiere of *Salome.* Both operas contain some of the most arresting music Strauss ever wrote. For that matter, they contain some of the most daring music of the first half of the twentieth century. His kind of atonality had nothing to do with the theories of the Second Viennese School but everything to do with the terrifying psychological state of his characters. It is precisely this that makes *Elektra* compelling, hair-raisingly so. The premiere and subsequent productions were well received by some, detested by others. After composing the daring music of *Elektra,* Strauss reverted to his own version of late ninteenth-century harmony, beautiful but dated.

Feuersnot (Fire-Famine), *Singgedicht* (sung poem), in one act, November 21, 1901.
Richard Strauss (1864–1949)
Libretto Ernst von Wolzogen.

After the fiasco of his first opera, *Guntram*, in Munich, Strauss wrote *Feuersnot*. The opera is a risqué anti-Munich comedy. Although the premiere and several subsequent productions were successful, it took Strauss four years to get Munich to agree to produce it. (Berlin banned the opera after seven performances because the Kaiser was not at all pleased with it.) In Bavaria the opera is still in the repertory.

Der fliegende Holländer (The Flying Dutchman), *Romantische Oper* in three acts, January 2, 1843.
Richard Wagner (1813–83)
Libretto by the composer, after Heinrich Heine's *Aus den Memorien des Herren von Schnabelewopski*.

Wagner identified with the persecuted, uprooted, sexually unfulfilled Dutchman who sees in a good woman's love a chance at a normal life. In his autobiography he writes that he got the idea for the opera during a stormy sea crossing in July and August 1839. *Der fliegende Holländer* is Wagner's first mature opera; it offers moments of Belliniesque vocality mixed with snatches of future Wagnerian majesty. The premiere was conducted by the composer.

Intermezzo, *Bürgerliche Komödie mit sinfonischen Zwischenspielen* (A Middle-Class Comedy with Symphonic Interludes), November 4, 1924.
Richard Strauss (1864–1949)
Libretto by the composer.

Strauss was no Wagner when it came to librettos, and he should have left his plots to real dramatists. He was somewhat self-indulgent and *Intermezzo* is based on a marital infidelity of his own that took place in 1903 (the characters in the opera are modeled after his wife and himself). The music is beautiful, but the opera is too long for its trivial material. He returned to this kind of domestic autobiography in his last opera, *Capriccio*.

Rienzi, der Letzte der Tribunen (Rienzi, the Last of the Tribunes), *grosse tragische Oper* in five acts, October 20, 1842.
Richard Wagner (1813–83)
Libretto by the composer, after Edward Bulwer-Lytton's novel of the same title.

Wagner conceived *Rienzi* as a grand opera. It is filled with marches, processions, and ballets. He thought Rienzi should "outdo all previous operas with its sumptuous extravagance." In his autobiography, *Mein Leben*, Wagner wrote that the premiere of *Rienzi* lasted over six hours! Notwithstanding, the premiere was a huge success and the opera remained one of his most popular throughout the nineteenth century. Dresden had given two hundred performances by 1908.

Der Rosenkavalier, *Komödie für Musik* in three acts, January 26, 1911.
Richard Strauss (1864–1949)
Libretto Hugo von Hofmannsthal.

Der Rosenkavalier was Strauss's third opera in a row to achieve enormous success. Hofmannsthal and Strauss collaborated very closely, albeit almost exclusively by correspondence. The opera, about an aging Marschallin and the loss of her adolescent lover to a girl his own age, contains some of the composer's most beautiful and poignant music. The years between 1905 and 1911, with *Salome, Electra,* and *Der Rosenkavalier,* bore compelling witness to the versatility and breadth of Strauss's compositional and dramatic talent. The premiere was a tumultuous triumph, and since then many singers have made characters from the opera their signature roles—Elisabeth Schwarzkopf and Kiri Te Kanawa as the Marschallin, and Christa Ludwig as Octavian, just to name three.

Salome, *Musikdrama* in one act, December 9, 1905.
Richard Strauss (1864–1949)
Libretto Hedwig Lachmann's translation of Oscar Wilde's play *Salome.*

Salome is Strauss's third opera, his first to score a riotous success (on the opening night the protagonist had thirty-five curtain calls!), and the first to become part of standard repertory. Strauss wrote that he imagined Salome as a "sixteen-year-old princess with the voice of an Isolde," which of course has always been a dilemma for opera houses presenting the work. The singer of Salome must sing over large orchestral forces, full of brass instruments, yet have the youth and allure to perform the Dance of the Seven Veils. For some fans of *Salome* (myself included), implicit eroticism is much more alluring than an obvious statement, but others prefer a more explicit interpretation— Maria Ewing as Salome, for example, has bared all at the end of the dance.

Die schweigsame Frau, *Komische Oper* in three acts, June 24, 1935.
Richard Strauss (1864–1949)
Libretto Stefan Zweig, after Ben Jonson's play *Epicoene.*

This opera contains more "light" music than any other Strauss opera. Ben Jonson's comedy *Epicoene* is also the basis for Donizetti's *Don Pasquale.* The *epicene* refers to a person who adopts a disguise of the opposite sex, in this case in order to pull off a prank. Karl Böhm conducted the premiere's stellar cast, but because the name of Zweig, a Jew, appeared on the posters announcing the performances, Hitler and Goebbels did not attend the opening. As a consequence, after its fourth performance in 1935, *Die schweigsame Frau* was banned.

Tannhäuser, *Grosse romantische Oper* in three acts, first version, October 19, 1845.
Richard Wagner (1813–83)
Libretto by the composer.

The story of *Tannhäuser* describes the spiritual journey of a young man who goes from enjoying erotic pleasures in the Venusberg, the home of Venus, to being saved after condemnation by the Pope. The premiere was performed by singers who found their voices taxed and their musicality challenged by the demanding score. It was also attended by an uncomprehending public. Wagner himself conducted the premiere, after which he spent three months analyzing the conditions under which all music was performed in Dresden's court.

Tannhäuser, second version, August 1, 1847.

Two years later, after making extensive revisions, Wagner again conducted the opera. The praise and acceptance he wanted for it were still not forthcoming, so he took the work out of circulation.

For more information write:

Dresden Fremdenverkehrsbetriebe, Prager Strasse 10–11, 01069 Dresden, Germany

FOOD

Italienisches Dörfchen, Theaterplatz 3, Dresden
tel: (49–351) 498–160 or 498–1629   fax: (49–351) 498–1688
Right on the Elbe river, this lovely restaurant café is just across the street from the Semper Opera House. Its name means Italian Village, a reference to Italian masons who lived on the site while they built the Hofkirche that stands in the Theaterplatz across from the opera. You can have anything from a complete meal to a cup of coffee here. The restaurant also caters to large groups, for which reservations should be made in advance by fax.

LODGING

Hotel Terrassenufer, Terrassenufer 12, 01069 Dresden
tel: (49–351) 440–9500   fax: (49–351) 440–9600

HALLE

The city of Halle, just east of Leipzig, was chosen to be the capital of the province (Land) of Saxony-Anhalt in 1947. Halle was almost unscathed by World War II and today is the one German city that has retained most of its prewar self.

Although the opera house of Halle premiered no operas in today's standard

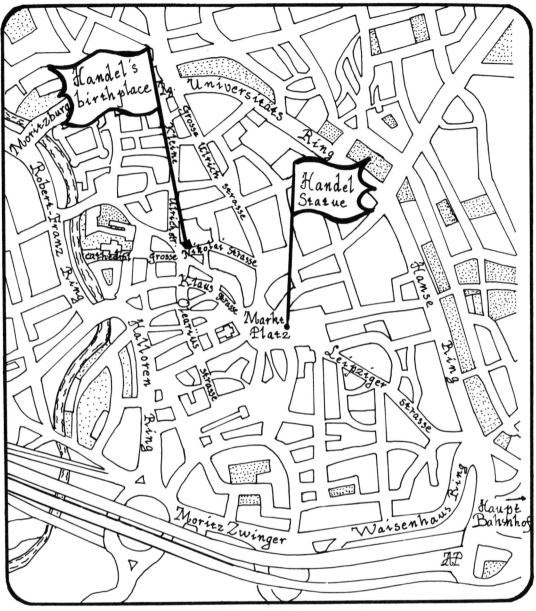

Operatic Halle

repertory, the city was the birthplace of George Frideric Handel (born Georg Friedrich Händel, February 23, 1685—April 14, 1759, London), undeniably one of the most influential opera composers during the first half of the eighteenth century.

The young Handel rejected the normal career opportunities open to a musician of his caliber. He did not become a *Kapellmeister* to a court or *Kantor* in a cathedral, the path chosen by his exact contemporary, Johann Sebastian Bach. Handel instead chose a unique route that led him to become the greatest composer of Italian-style opera of his day and to master all the compositional styles of the period.

In 1703, after a short stint as organist at the Calvinist Cathedral of Halle, Handel went to Hamburg, home of the only German opera company flourishing outside a court. There he took the position of second violist and then continuo harpsichordist in the opera orchestra. In 1705, Hamburg performed his first opera, *Almira,* and from then until 1741 opera was his principal compositional preoccupation. Handel's success as an opera composer was immediate, and in 1706 he was invited to Florence by the Prince of Tuscany. He also spent time in Rome, Venice, and, most important, Naples.

This trip to the heartland of Italian opera set him firmly on the path to becoming a great Italianist, and in 1707 his third opera, *Roderigo,* was performed in Florence at Teatro Cocomero (see Florence, page 54). In 1709, *Agrippina* was performed in Venice's Teatro San Giovanni Grisostomo (see Venice, Teatro Malibran, page 132).

Early in 1710 Handel slowly made his way back to Germany, where he took the position of *Kapellmeister* at the court of Hanover in the spring of that year. By autumn of the same year, he was in London. There he wrote the first Italian-style opera premiered in London (see London, page 208).

In Halle's beautiful and monumental Marktplatz stands a statue of a pensive Handel. Immediately to the north of Marktplatz is the Händelhaus, now a museum, the baroque-style house where the composer was born. The museum contains a great deal of documentation on the life and times of Handel that the visitor can peruse while listening to recordings of some of his most famous works.

Händelhaus, Grosse Nilolaistrasse 5–6
Open Tuesday, Wednesday, and Friday–Sunday, 9:30 A.M.–5:30 P.M.;
Thursday 9:30 A.M.–7:00 P.M.
admission: DM 1.50

LODGING

Hotel Europa, Delitzscher Strasse 17, 06112 Halle, Germany
tel: (49–345) 570–050   fax: (49–345) 510–1777

Hotel Kastanienhof, Beesenerstrasse 226, 06110 Halle, Germany
tel: (49–345) 42–790   fax: (49–345) 48–166
   Located in the center of town, this charming hotel also has a *Biergarten* (beer garden) restaurant.

Hotel Am Wasserturm, Lessingstrasse 8, 06114 Halle, Germany
tel: (49–345) 512–6542   fax: (49–345) 512–6543

Hotel Rotes Ross, Leipzigerstrasse 76, 06108 Halle, Germany
tel: (49–345) 37–271   fax: (49–345) 202–6331

HAMBURG

On January 2, 1678, the city of Hamburg hosted the opening of the first public opera house in Germany. The theatre was adjacent to the city center's Gänsemarkt, hence its name: Theater am Gänsemarkt. Premieres of about twenty operas by Georg Philipp Telemann and three by George Frideric Handel—*Almira* (1705), *Nero* (1705), and *Florindo* (1708)—took place in the Theater am Gänsemarkt in the eighteenth century. The theatre was demolished in 1763 and rebuilt in 1765. In turn, this theatre was torn down and replaced by a new one in 1827, called Theater am Dammtor, or the Neues Stadt-Theater in Dammtorstrasse.

Although the Staatsoper did not premiere any of the operas in today's standard repertory, its operatic connection to Handel and Telemann is very important. Today the theatre is perhaps the best repertory opera house in the world. Do not miss the opportunity to attend an opera performance here.

Throughout the city's history, its operatic life was dominated by Italian opera. Between 1827 and 1836, works by Rossini, Bellini, and Donizetti were central to the theatre's repertory. It also presented some operas by local composers that never entered the standard repertory. In 1844, Richard Wagner conducted the second performance of his opera *Rienzi* (about the Roman tribune Cola di Rienzi) following its Dresden premiere on October 20, 1842. *Rienzi* went on to be his most popular work in the nineteenth century! And, in 1845, Hamburg mounted its first Verdi opera, *Nabucco*. In 1891 Gustav Mahler became conductor of the Hamburg Stadtsoper, and from 1906 to 1913 Enrico Caruso appeared regularly at the theater and was enormously popular. Premieres of operas by Ferruccio Busoni, Erick Wolfgang Korngold, and Ottorino Respighi took place in the early twentieth century.

In 1934 the theatre was renamed the Hamburgische Staatsoper. In August 1943, it was destroyed in an air raid. The new Hamburg Staatsoper was reconstructed on the same land and reopened in October 1955 with a performance of *Die Zauberflöte*. Since its postwar reopening, the opera house has hosted quite a number of major premieres. Among them are *The Devils of Loudon* (1969), Krzysztof Penderecki; *The Flood* (1963), Igor Stravinsky; *Help, Help the Globolinks!* as "Hilfe, hilfe, die Globolinks!" (1968), Gian Carlo Menotti; *Der Prinz von Homburg* (1960), Hans Werner Henze; *The Visitation* (1966), Gunther Schuller; and works by many other contemporary composers.

The Hamburg Staatsoper still stands adjacent to the Gänsemarkt on Dammtorstrasse. The theatre seats 1,675 and the acoustics and sight lines from all seats are excellent.

Hamburg Staatsoper Tageskasse (ticket office)
tel: (49–40) 351–721   fax: (49–40) 356–8454
Open Monday–Friday, 10:00 A.M.–2:00 P.M. and 4:00–6:30 P.M.; Satur-

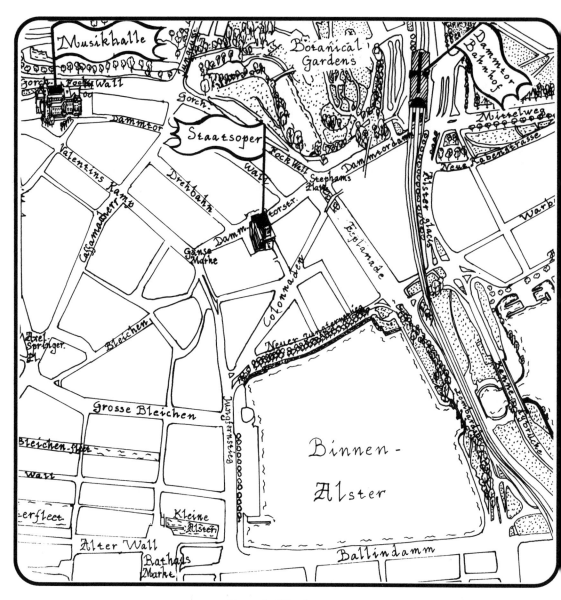

Operatic Hamburg

days, 10:00 A.M.–2:00 P.M.; and an hour before the beginning of each show.

The ticket office is located down the Grosse Theatrestrasse, on the left side of the opera house.

LODGING

Hotel Vorbach, Johnsallee 63–67, 20146 Hamburg
tel.: (49–40) 44182–0   fax: (49–40) 4418–2888

A tip: Stay just outside the circle of the city center, a fifteen-minute walk or five minutes by taxi to the Staatsoper or the Dammtor train station, at Hotel Vorbach. This beautifully renovated nineteenth-century building has all the modern comforts and is in the area of Hamburg's elegant villa-lined *Allees*.

Baseler Hof, Esplanade 11, 20354 Hamburg
tel: (49–40) 359–060   fax: (49–40) 3590–6918
This hotel is right in the heart of Hamburg, a three-minute walk to the Staatsoper; five minutes to the Musikhalle; three minutes by taxi from Dammtor train station.

Hotel Alster-Hof, Esplanade 12, 20354 Hamburg
tel: (49–40) 350–070   fax: (49–40) 3500–7514
Also a three-minute walk to the opera in the city's center.

Hamburg Marriott, ABC Strasse 52, 2000 Hamburg 36
tel: (49–40) 35050   fax: (49–40) 3505–1777
A five-minute walk to the Staatsoper across the Gänzeplatz in the city's center.

Hotel Alameda, Colonaden 45, 20354 Hamburg
tel: (49–40) 344–000 and 344–290   fax: (49–40) 343–439
Also a five-minute walk to the Staatsoper.

LEIPZIG

A preeminent publishing trade and an excellent university, founded in 1409, made Leipzig a leading intellectual center by the eighteenth century. The town has always been famous for its relationship with music. From 1723 until his death in 1750, Johann Sebastian Bach was *Kapellmeister* of the Saint Thomas Church, the church in which Martin Luther delivered the 1539 sermon that began the Reformation. A Bach museum is located at Thomaskirchhof, 16. The city has two monuments to Bach: the Old Bach Monument, on the Martin-Luther-Ring, was paid for by Felix Mendelssohn in 1843, and a New Bach Monument, built in 1908, stands nearby on the Burgstrasse 8.

Although Leipzig's opera house presented no premieres of operas in the standard repertory, the operatic importance of the city is undeniable. Richard Wagner was born in Leipzig on May 22, 1813 (he died in Venice on February 13, 1883; see Venice, Palazzo Vendramin, page 135). Wagner's background is filled with ambiguity. His putative father died only months after his birth; the baby Richard was adopted by Carl Geyer, an actor and painter who some believe was his real father. Recently it has been discovered that his mother was not the illegitimate daughter of a local prince, as Wagner claimed, but rather the prince's mistress! In 1828 Wagner entered Leipzig's Nikolaischule but was far more interested in pursuing his theatrical and musical passions than in undergoing a

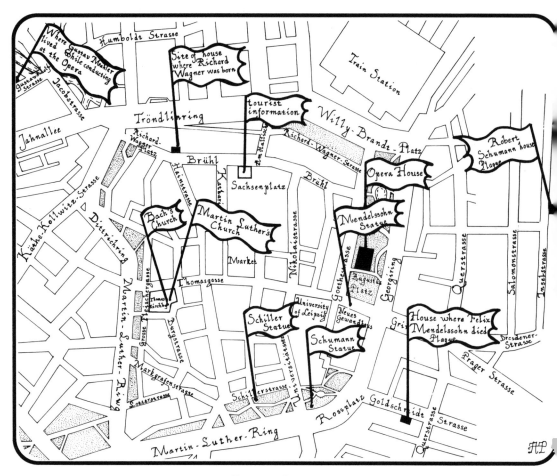

Operatic Leipzig

typical liberal education. His formal musical education was short though not nonexistent, as he would have us believe in his autobiography, *Mein Leben*.

Of all the composers in this book, Wagner most certainly possessed the greatest breadth of interests. Besides his autobiography, he wrote books on German opera, including *Die Deutsche Oper* (1834), a book on Italian bel canto entitled *Bellini* (1837), essays on art, *Kunstwerk der Zukunft* (1849), an immense discourse on the aesthetics of drama and music, *Opera und Drama* (1850–51), an anti-Semitic discourse on Jewish musicians, *Das Judentum in der Musik*, as well as all his own librettos and extensive prefaces to each opera, more than two hundred assorted books, articles, and lectures.

On top of all this, he invented a new operatic form—*Musik Drama*—which reconsidered the importance of opera as an art form; evoked Greek tragedy by imbuing his operas with a passionate, near religiosity; changed the role of the operatic orchestra; and revitalized the spirit of the early creators of opera (see Florence, page 46).

Whether one likes him or not, after Wagner opera and all music was changed. Even Giuseppe Verdi was influenced by Wagner's use of the orchestra, and the verismo composers, in particular Puccini, could never have written the way they did without his example. Leipzig performances of works by the city's native son began in 1853 with *Tannhäuser* and *Lohengrin*. The third performances (after Bayreuth and Munich) of the *Ring* were also staged in Leipzig.

The house where Richard Wagner was born in 1813 was called Haus zum Roten und Weissen Löwen (House of the Red and White Lion). A warehouse, bearing a plaque, occupies the site today on the southeast corner of the Brühl and Richard Wagner Platz. The area has been built up with the ugliest apartments imaginable.

Klinger Grove in the Clara-Zetkin Park offers a modern (1983) and unfinished monument to Wagner, with a bust of the composer and depictions of scenes from *Ring des Nibelungen* and *Parsifal*.

Leipzig did not have a resident court but was a prosperous commercial town. At first, traveling Italian opera companies performed at the town's annual commercial fairs. But in 1693, an opera theatre was built on the Brühl, very near where today's opera house stands. Touring Italian companies vied with local German companies for a paying public until 1817, when a Stadttheater, housing a permanent opera company, was established on what is now Richard-Wagner-Platz by the Brühl. In 1833, the actor, singer, composer Albert Lortzing was hired as director of the Stadttheater, and eight of his operas had their premieres there between 1837 and 1845. Although little known today outside Germany, Lortzing was well respected as a consummate musician. A plaque commemorating his thirteen years (1833–46) in Leipzig can be seen on the wall at Funkenburgstrasse 8.

Felix Mendelssohn (February 3, 1809, Hamburg—November 4, 1847, Leipzig) was the nineteenth-century composer who rediscovered the greatness of Bach's music. He spent the last twelve years of his short life in Leipzig as director of the Gewandhaus, one of the most famous musical institutions in Europe. Mendelssohn wrote seven operas, none a great success, so he turned his attention to other types of "dramatic" musical forms, such as symphonies and concert overtures written with a "program," cantatas, and incidental music. For these last twelve years of his life, Mendelssohn lived in:

Mendelssohn Haus, Goldschmidtstrasse 12

A plaque with a relief profile of the composer states:

In diesem Haus starb	In this house died
Felix Mendelssohn	Felix Mendelssohn
Bartholdy	Bartholdy
Am 4 November 1847.	On November 4, 1847.

The house is one block east of Solomonstrasse, which suggests the area might once have been part of the ghetto. Today the building is decrepit and has only the small plaque mentioned above.

A Mendelssohn Monument was erected in front of the Neue Gewandhaus in

1993 to commemorate the 150th anniversary of the Gewandhaus Orchestra. The Neue Gewandhaus is directly across the large Augustusplatz from the Opernhaus. (Kurt Masur conducted the Gewandhaus Orchestra before becoming conductor of the New York Philharmonic.)

In 1850, the Stadttheater presented the premiere of Robert Schumann's (June 8, 1810, Zwickau, Saxony—July 26, 1856, Endenich, near Bonn) only opera, *Genoveva*, a work in four acts, June 25, 1850, from his own libretto based on *Leben und Tod der heiligen Genoveva* by Ludwig Tieck and *Genoveva* by Friedrich Hebbel. Schumann himself conducted. He makes use of leitmotivs, and many of the arias are like the beautiful songs for which he is so famous. When Liszt conducted the second production of the opera in Weimar, he put his finger on the problem: It lacks "dramatic vitality," he said, but still he appreciated the work for its musical value. Today the work is rarely, if ever, performed. I chanced to see a production given by the Rome Opera in 1966 and it was indeed beautiful—but boring!

A Robert Schumann Monument stands near the Moritz Bastion, Youth and Student Center. While in Leipzig Schumann lived with his wife Clara and their eight children at Inselstrasse 18, just outside the city's center. Today the whole area seems to be under reconstruction. A plaque written in the stucco of the house states:

Hier wohnten   Robert and Clara
Robert und Clara   Schumann
Schumann   lived here from
1840–1844.   1840–1844.

The large Neues Theater complex was built on Augustusplatz in 1867. Gustav Mahler was conductor of the opera house in the Neues Theater from 1886 to 1888; a plaque at Gustav-Adolf-Strasse 12 marks his residence during this period. Just across the street is a memorial to Leipzig's Jews on the building that was the "collection center" for the city.

During the first two decades of the twentieth century, the Neues Theater was very forward-thinking, reviving and reforming the performance tradition of Mozart operas and presenting premieres of the following daring and provocative operas.

The Neues Theater premiered *Aufstieg und Fall der Stadt Mahagonny* (March 9, 1930), Kurt Weill; *Catuli carmina* (November 6, 1943), Carl Orff; *Jonny spielt auf* (February 10, 1927), Ernst Krenek; *Leben des Orest* (1930), Ernst Krenek; *Der Zar lässt sich photographieren* (1928), Kurt Weill.

Of these premieres, Kurt Weill's *Aufstieg und Fall der Stadt Mahagonny* is the only opera that remains on the edges of standard international repertory. The score is jazz-influenced and the libretto is satiric, merciless, and very funny. The "immorality" of Bertolt Brecht's provocative text caused an uproar at the premiere, where Nazi sympathizers mounted protests in and out of the opera house. When the opera went on to be performed in other German opera houses, *many* cuts had to be instituted for moral, political, and religious reasons. Brecht said that *Mahagonny* was "the pleasure city," which was in "every sense international." After 1933 the opera was banned in Germany until the end of the war. In the last fifty years *Mahagonny*, unlike any other opera, has been successfully staged in both opera houses and legitimate theatres. New York's Metropolitan Opera produced it in its 1995–96 season.

December 4, 1943, the center of Leipzig was heavily bombed, destroying all the buildings making up Stadttheater and Neues Theater. In 1960 the Opernhaus, in Augustusplatz, was the first opera house to be rebuilt in East Germany, outside of Berlin. It is the largest opera theatre in Germany, and it opened with Wagner's *Die Meistersinger*. The Leipzig Gewandhaus Orchestra plays in the Neue Gewandhaus, which opened in 1981 and is situated directly across Augustusplatz from the opera house.

Opernhaus, Augustusplatz 12, 04109 Leipzig
Open Monday through Friday, 10:00 A.M.–6:00 P.M.; Saturday, 10:00 A.M.–1:00 P.M.
tel: (49–341) 12–610

For more tourist information and maps write:

Leipzig Fremdenverkehrs-und Kongressamt, Sachsenplatz 1, 04109 Leipzig, Germany
tel: (49–341) 71–040   fax: (49–341) 281–854

LODGING

Maritim Hotel Astoria, Willy-Brandt-Platz 2, 04109 Leipzig
tel: (49–341) 128–4811   fax: (49–341) 128–4747
   This elegant, comfortable hotel is a stone's throw from the train station and just across the street from where the old city begins. There are two restaurants on the premises.

Hotel Inter-Continental, Gerberstrasse 15, 04105 Leipzig
tel: (49–341) 98–80   fax: (49–341) 988–1229
   This sleek, modern hotel is conveniently located in the old part of Leipzig and has a fine restaurant, a *Bierstube*, and several bars.

Hotel Corum/Holiday Inn, Rudolf-Breitscheid-Strasse 3, 04105 Leipzig
tel: (49–341) 125–100   fax: (49–341) 125–10–100
   Down the street from the train station, this hotel is within walking distance of all the old town's treasures.

MAGDEBURG

Magdeburg was the traditional capital of the province of Saxony-Anhalt before 1947 when its seat was changed to Halle. Opera came to the city quite late, when touring companies introduced it around the middle of the eighteenth century. The Magdeburg Nationaltheater opened in 1795. Although only a provincial opera house, it presented the premiere of *Das Liebesverbot,* a comedy by the young Richard Wagner, his first opera to be staged.

> **Das Liebesverbot,** *Grosse komische Oper* in two acts, March 29, 1836. Richard Wagner (1813–83)
> Libretto by the composer, based on William Shakespeare's comedy *Measure for Measure.*
>
> *Das Liebesverbot* relocates Shakespeare's *Measure for Measure* in a pleasure-filled, sun-soaked Sicilian setting. A celebration of free love and a humorous attack on sexual puritanism and bourgeois morality, the plot scandalized the good burghers of Magdeburg. On top of this, the premiere was a musical fiasco because the singers had not learned their parts thoroughly. As a consequence, Magdeburg suffered only one performance of the opera. The premiere was conducted by Wagner himself, a lad of twenty-three, and this early composition greatly resembles the music of Bellini or Auber. *Das Liebesverbot* was not performed again in Germany until 1923.

In 1876 the city built a Stadttheater, which was destroyed in 1944 and replaced in 1950 by a new Maxim-Gorki-Theater, now called the Theater der Landeshauptstadt. The main theatre's *Grosses Haus* seats 904 and the *Kleines Haus* 314.

Georg Philipp Telemann, (Magdeburg, 1681—Hamburg, 1767) in his day the most important composer of operas *in German,* was born in Magdeburg. Since 1962 the Theater der Landeshauptstadt has hosted a Telemann festival devoted principally to the revival of Telemann's twenty-nine extant operas. This artist was noted for the rare ability to write comedy into music, which makes him very much an opera composer with whom to become acquainted. Magdeburg's Music Conservatory is also named after Telemann.

Theater der Landeshauptstadt, Universitätsplatz (Erzbergerstrasse)
tel: (49–391) 551–835

All tickets can be purchased at:

Magdeburg Information, Alter Markt, 39104 Magdeburg
tel: (49–391) 541–4794   fax: (49–391) 541–4830

For information about the Magdeburg Telemann Festival write:

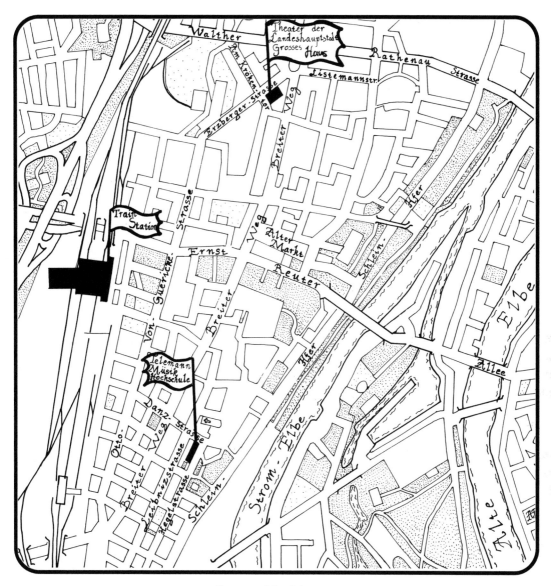

Operatic Magdeburg

Magdeburg Fremdenverkehrsbetriebe, Alter Markt 9, 39104 Magdeburg, Germany
tel: (49–391) 31–667   fax: (49–391) 30–105

LODGING

Residenz Joop, Jean-Burger-Strasse 16, 39104 Magdeburg
tel: (49–391) 62–620   fax: (49–391) 626–2100

MUNICH (München)

Munich is in Bavaria, the southeastern province of Germany, on the banks of the river Isar. Historically it appears that the rulers of Bavaria preferred to spend their money and time on artistic patronage rather than on territorial expansion, unlike most other leaders of the areas that make up what we call Germany today. As a result, the city has always been host to great music. Munich began its operatic patronage in 1653, and Italian opera presentations flourished until 1691 when the Elector Maximillian II Emanuel was appointed governor of the Spanish Netherlands. He and his entire court repaired immediately to Brussels, and operatic life in Munich languished until his return in 1715.

The Residenz, the large palace complex in the center of Munich, contains four theatres: two opera houses, the Cuvilliéstheater and the Nationaltheater; a large concert hall, the Herkulessaal; and a prose theater, the Residenz-Theater. The Cuvilliéstheater (also known today as the old Residenztheater) opened in 1753 and was named after the architect François Cuvilliés. (Cuvilliés was a dwarf who proved his architectural mettle by designing systems of defense for Maximillian's court in Brussels and was then sent to Paris to study architecture. The Residenztheater is one of the finest examples of his flamboyant rococo style.) The theatre was reserved for opera seria. The Munich public took this reservation seriously and did not appreciate the operatic "reforms" of Christoph Willibald Gluck. They insisted that an Italian touring company presenting Gluck's masterpiece *Orfeo ed Euridice* there in 1773 change the style of the recitatives in order to make the work more similar to the style of opera seria that Gluck was trying to reform!

The Cuvilliéstheater presented the premiere of Wolfgang Amadeus Mozart's *Idomeneo* on January 29, 1781. Mozart came to Munich in the fall of 1780 to write the opera and work with the singers. *Idomeneo* is the first opera, ever, to use clarinets in the orchestral score. Mozart was able to encompass many ideal elements of a "reform" opera—a noble, classical subject, much use of chorus, and mostly orchestrated recitative—but the work comes across as a highly stylized baroque opera seria. Mozart knew his public and gave them what they wanted. He wrote his father that the premiere of the opera was a great success.

The Cuvilliéstheater is a rococo gem, with a seating capacity of 463. The theatre is often used by the Bayerische Staatsoper and for occasional chamber concerts.

The Cuvilliéstheater (in the Residenz), Residenzstrasse 1
Open Monday–Saturday, 2:00–5:00 P.M.; Sundays, 10:00 A.M.–5:00 P.M.
tel: (49–89) 225–754
admission: DM 2

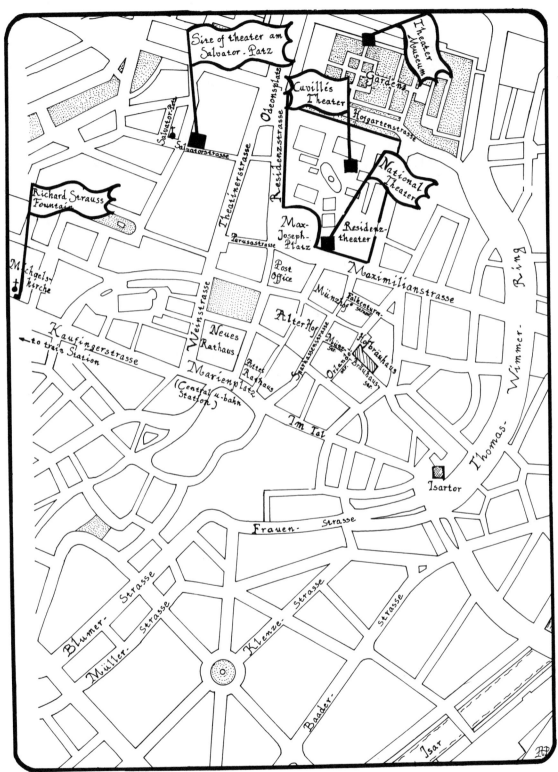

Operatic Munich

Interior of the Cuvilliéstheater

Earlier, on January 13, 1775, Mozart's *La finta giardiniera* was premiered at the Opernhaus am Salvatorplatz, Munich's opera buffa theatre, catering to the tastes of middle-class audiences. (Both Mozart works were commissioned as pre-Lenten operas, thus their January premieres.) The popular Opernhaus am Salvatorplatz presented operas from 1654, when it was built, until disrepair forced its closure in 1799. The theatre stood on the northeast corner of Salvatorplatz and Salvatorstrasse across from the Salvatorkirche.

In 1864 the eighteen-year-old Ludwig II ascended Bavaria's throne. One of his first acts as King was to pay off the enormous debts that Richard Wagner had incurred while in exile and to give him a yearly stipend equal to that earned by a ministerial councillor. Strangely enough, especially considering Wagner's political past, Ludwig welcomed his political advice. In at least one instance Wagner was very astute, urging the King to maintain Bavaria's neutrality during the war between Prussia and Austria. But the King sided with Austria and was defeated, which brought on the collapse of the German Confederation and Prussian hegemony. By the mid–1860s, Wagner was estranged from his wife Minna (Wilhelmine), with whom he had had a famously fiery relationship. Minna died in January 1866, in Dresden, where Wagner had set her up with a generous allowance in 1862.

Meanwhile, Wagner, by all accounts a magnetically attractive man, was in Munich surrounded by admiring women. He purchased a new home overlooking nearby Lake Starnberg in Kempfenhausen, where Cosima Liszt von Bülow came to visit him on June 29, 1864, eight days before the arrival of her husband. Cosima was the daughter of Franz Liszt and wife of the well-known Wagner champion, the conductor Hans von Bülow. Cosima arrived, seemingly well chaperoned by her two daughters and their nursery maid.

Sometime during the eight days before her husband joined them, however, Cosima became pregnant. Her daughter Isolde was born on April 10, 1865. So great was von Bülow's admiration for Wagner that he seems to have willingly yielded even his wife to the master, for Cosima and Richard's second child, Eva, was born in 1867, and their third, Siegfried, was born in 1869. Cosima finally obtained a divorce from von Bülow and married Richard on August 25, 1870.

Kempfenhausen lies fifteen miles southwest of Munich, outside the larger town of Starnberg. The villa in which Wagner lived is a boys' dormitory in a school situated directly on the Starnberger See, at 49–63 Münchnerstrasse. Take the S6 from Marienplatz (direction Tütsing) to Starnberg and then a taxi to Kempfenhausen. Enter the gates of the school and go to the left.

A plaque on the villa states:

Wagner-Haus	The Wagner House
Ehemalige Villa Pellet	(Formerly Villa Pellet)
Hier fand	Where lived
Richard Wagner	Richard Wagner
Vom 14. Mai bis 3 Oktober 1864	From 14 May until 3 October 1864
als Gast König Ludwig II	As guest of King Ludwig II
Es war da Beginn	This was the beginning
Der Grosszügigen Förderung	Of a generous patronage
Wagners durch den Bayernkönig.	By the Bavarian King.

King Ludwig II drowned in the Starnberg See, most likely at the hands of his ministers, because his infatuation with grandeur was bankrupting the Bavarian state's coffers.

Munich's native son Richard Strauss (June 11, 1864, Munich—September 8, 1949, Garmisch-Partenkirchen, in the Alps just south of Munich) was the leading figure in German opera during the first half of the twentieth century. He was no relation to the operatic Strausses of Vienna, either in blood or in style. Notwithstanding the inescapable influence of Wagner, Strauss managed to develop his own unique operatic voice. Only his first opera, *Guntram*, can be considered Wagnerian.

During his first thirty years, Richard Strauss wrote the majority of his instrumental music: tone poems (*Don Juan, Tod und Verklärung, Till Eulenspiegel, Also sprach Zarathustra, Don Quixote, Ein Heldenleben*, etc.), concerti, serenades, and other programmatic works such as ballet. Only after this did he begin his

Villa Wagner, Kempfenhausen

auspicious operatic career, writing fifteen operas, many of which are part of
today's standard repertory. At the end of his life he again wrote some purely
instrumental works. He composed *Lieder* (songs) throughout his life; his wife was
a singer, and he acted as her accompanist during her career.

As a composer, Strauss said he always needed a text to get him going. He
loved the classics, an enthusiasm that can be seen in his first two really successful
operas that remain today in repertory: *Salome* (1905) and *Electra* (1909).

Strauss had an active career as a conductor, first as assistant to Hans von
Bülow (of Wagner fame and notoriety) in Meiningen, then in Munich at the
Hofoper, and finally in Weimar at the Hoftheater, where he met his wife, the
singer Pauline de Ahna.

The Munich Conservatory of Music, located across the Isar River from the
city center in the Gasteig Arts Center, is called the Richard Strauss Conservatory and the Richard Strauss-Brunnen (fountain) stands next to the St.
Michael Jesuit church, in front of the Alte Akademie in the city center.

The Bayrische Staatsoper does not have a theatre of its own and uses both
the Nationaltheater and the Cuvilliéstheater for its productions. The

Königliches Hof und Nationaltheater, also called the Bayrische Hofoper, first opened in 1818 but burned down in 1823. It was rebuilt on a grander scale in only two years, and this enlarged theatre hosted many of the great premieres of Richard Wagner in the nineteenth century and of Richard Strauss in the twentieth century.

Königliches Hof und Nationaltheater (Bayrische Staatsoper, the Nationaltheater) premiered *Capriccio* (October 28, 1942), Richard Strauss; *Die Feen* (June 29, 1888, five years after his death in 1883), Richard Wagner; *Friedenstag* (July 24, 1938), Richard Strauss; *Die Meistersinger von Nürnberg* (June 21, 1868), Richard Wagner; *Das Rheingold* (September 22, 1869), Richard Wagner; *Tannhäuser*, fourth and final version (August 1, 1867), Richard Wagner; *Tristan und Isolde* (June 10, 1869), Richard Wagner; *Die Walküre* (June 26, 1870), Richard Wagner.

Mozart, Wagner, and Strauss are called "the three house gods" of Munich's Cuvilliéstheatre and Nationaltheater because of their importance and the number of their works premiered by the two theatres.

The Nationaltheater was destroyed in an air raid October 3, 1943. After the war, operas were performed in the Prinzregententheater, which had been built at the beginning of the twentieth century and still stands in Prinzregentenplatz 12. The Nationaltheater was rebuilt and reopened on November 21, 1963. The theatre hosts an annual opera festival in July and presents a fabulous opera season from September through June. The Nationaltheater holds 2,123, including standing room.

Nationaltheater, Max-Joseph-Platz 2
Open Monday–Friday, 10:00 A.M.–1:00 P.M. and 2:00–6:00 P.M.; Saturdays, 10:00 A.M.–1:00 P.M.
tel: (49–89) 2185–1920 or 2185–1919

Tickets are also available at the *Abendkasse* (box office), one hour before the beginning of the opera; a street entrance is located to the right and around the corner from the theatre's main doors.

The Prinzregententheater occasionally still presents opera. The theatre stands just across the Isar River from the city center and seats 1,070.

Prinzregententheater, Prinzregentenplatz 12, 81675 Munich
Open Monday–Friday, 10:00 A.M.–1:00 P.M. and 2:00–6:00 P.M.;
Saturdays, 10:00 A.M.–1:00 P.M.
tel, (49–89) 2916–1414
tel, program information: (49–89) 470–6270.

Munich hosts yet a fourth opera house, the Staatstheater am Gärtnerplatz.

Nationaltheater

Theater am Gärtnerplatz, Gärtnerplatz 3
Open Monday–Friday, 10:00 A.M.–6:00 P.M.
tel: (49–89) 201–6767
Tickets: Maximillianstrasse 11–13
Open Monday–Friday, 10:00 A.M.–1:00 P.M. and 3:30–5:30 P.M.; Saturday, 10:00 A.M.–1:00 P.M.

Tickets are also available at the *Abendkasse* in the theatre's lobby one hour before each performance.

Tickets for the Bayerische Staatsoper, at either the Nationaltheater or the Cuvilliéstheater, are also available through:

München Ticket GmbH
Open Monday–Friday, 9:00 A.M.–6:00 P.M.; Saturday, 10:00 A.M.–3:00 P.M.
tel: (49–89) 5481–8181   fax: (49–89) 5481–8154

Munich's Deutsche Theater Museum offers interesting information about Germany's operatic past. For example, it exhibits designs by Gottfried Semper, the architect of Dresden's Semper Opera House, and has a large Richard Wagner archive, including designs of original scenery and costumes and stage models of Munich's Wagner premieres.

Deutsche Theater Museum, Galeriestrasse 4a (Hofgartenarkaden), 80539 Munich
Open Tuesday–Friday, 10:00 A.M.–4:00 P.M.; Saturday and Sunday, 10:00 A.M.–6:00 P.M.
tel: (49–89) 222–449 or 222–554

For more information write:

München Tourist Office (Fremdenverkehrsbetriebe), Sendlinger
Strasse 1, 80331 Munich, Germany
tel: (49–89) 233–0300   fax: (49–89) 233–0233

Details of a premiere at the Residenztheater (Cuvilliéstheater)

Idomeneo, re di Creta, January 29, 1781.
Wolfgang Amadeus Mozart (January 27, 1756, Salsburg—December 5,
1791, Vienna)
Libretto by Giovanni Battista Varesco, based on Antoine Danchet's
Idomenée.

Idomeneo is a basic return-from-the-Trojan-War story with proper inter-
vention of the gods. Its premiere featured the Italian castrato Vincenzo dal
Prato in the role of Idamante. Mozart had been told of the beauty of dal
Prato's voice and was somewhat nonplussed to discover the young man was
quite inexperienced and had to be fed his music by rote "as if he were a
child." After three performances in 1781, *Idomeneo* was not performed again
until the early nineteenth century in Vienna and Berlin. It then languished
until the early twentieth century, when it found an audience in Paris, Italy,
Great Britain, and the United States. Richard Strauss arranged (reorchestrated) the opera for its 150th anniversary in 1931, as he did many Mozart
operas. Several arias are regularly excerpted, most notably Illia's "Zeffiretti
lusinghieri" and Elettra's fabulous fury aria "D'Oreste d'Ajace." *Idomeneo* is
often revived by better opera companies, but it is by no means in the
standard repertory.

Details of premieres at the Nationaltheater (Staatsoper, or Bayrische Staatsoper)

Die Meistersinger von Nürnberg, Music drama in three acts, June 21,
1868.
Richard Wagner (May 22, 1813, Leipzig—February 13, 1883, Venice)
Libretto by the composer.

Die Meistersinger, the only comedy Wagner wrote as a mature composer, is
about a singing contest held in medieval Nuremberg. (For details about how
Wagner got the idea for the opera, see Nürenberg, page 238.) The Munich
premiere, conducted by Hans von Bülow, was an enormous success, and the
opera was immediately performed throughout Germany. On the one hand,
the work is admired for its humanity, but on the other, many feel the libretto
is anti-Semitic and reflects Wagner's crusade to cleanse the German spirit of
"foreign elements." To commemorate the five-hundredth anniversary of the
birth of Hans Sachs (November 5, 1994), the opera's protagonist, Bavaria

issued a Hans Sachs postage stamp. Sachs, a shoemaker, wrote hundreds of poems and dramas and was the first German author to base a drama on the Nibelungen tale.

Tannhäuser, fourth and final version, August 1, 1867.
Richard Wagner (1813–83)
Libretto by the composer.

This final revision of *Tannhäuser* was completed six years after the Paris debacle and some twenty-two years after the Dresden premiere of the opera's first version. Hans von Bülow (January 8, 1830, Dresden—February 12, 1894, Cairo) conducted. By 1867 the public was able to appreciate the opera, and it was a great success.

Tristan und Isolde, *Handlung* (drama) in three acts, June 10, 1869.
Richard Wagner (1813–83)
Libretto by the composer.

Tristan und Isolde is considered the idealized operatic embodiment of the unconsummated erotic love between Wagner and Mathilde Wesendonck, which arose during the composer's exile in 1857. He wrote the libretto from August 20 to September 18, 1857, obviously in the heat of passion. The music for the whole opera was completed by August 1859. The emotional expression made possible by the opera's long stretches of unresolving harmonies forever changed the course of operatic history. It also makes the opera one of the most erotically charged pieces of music ever written. *Tristan und Isolde* was conducted by Hans von Bülow.

Das Rheingold, *Vorabend* (preliminary evening) of *Der Ring des Nibelungen,* in four scenes, September 22, 1869.
Richard Wagner (1813–83)
Libretto by the composer.

Wagner had completed the initial prose sketch for *Das Rheingold* by 1851. He then reworked it, wrote the final poem, and published it in 1853. The score was complete in 1854. The opera begins with a seven-minute introduction that sounds like the original example of "minimal music," made up of swooping arpeggios of E-flat major triads. The opera was Wagner's first written according to the theoretical principles he set forth in his book *Oper und Drama.* It is also his most rigorous treatment of those principles and has dramatic and musical characteristics not found in the other operas in the *Ring.*

Die Walküre, first day of *Der Ring des Nibelungen,* in three acts, June 26, 1870.
Richard Wagner (1813–83)
Libretto by the composer.

Die Walküre, the second opera in the *Ring* tetralogy, contains "The Ride of the Valkyries," a piece of music nearly everyone—at least in the Western world—has heard in some context. Wagner completed the opera in 1856. Although the premiere suffered from underrehearsal, *Die Walküre* is the most successful of Wagner's operas, perhaps because of its total synthesis of poetry and music. It is just this synthesis that makes the opera the most approachable piece in the *Ring*.

Die Feen (The Fairies), *Grosse romantischer Oper* in three acts, June 29, 1888.
Richard Wagner (1813–83)
Libretto by the composer, based on Carlo Gozzi's story *La donna serpente*.

Wagner completed the score to *Die Feen*, his first opera, in 1834 at the age of twenty-one. Stylistically the work has its roots in both Weber and Marschner. The opera has some very nice parts, however eclectic it may be. The premiere took place five years after Wagner's death in 1883.

Friedenstag, *Oper* in one act, July 24, 1938.
Richard Strauss (June 11, 1864, Munich—September 8, 1949, Garmisch-Partenkirchen)
Libretto Joseph Gregor.

The ideas behind the libretto of *Friedenstag* came mainly from Stefan Zweig, librettist of Strauss's *Die schweigsame Frau*. Because of the anti-Semitic Nazi regime he and Strauss could not collaborate, and Zweig urged the composer to work with his friend Joseph Gregor. Strauss originally conceived of the opera as a double bill with his *Daphne*—still to be written (see Dresden, page 281)—but each work proved far longer than planned. Today each is often paired with a short ballet or a tone poem by Strauss. Because *Friedenstag* was praised by the Nazis as giving operatic expression to their ideals, the piece is seldom performed today. (In fact, the work carries a pacifist message, a daringly brave gesture from Strauss and Gregor in 1938.)

Capriccio, *Konversationstück für Musik* in one act, October 28, 1942.
Richard Strauss (1864–1949)
Libretto Clemens Krauss (the conductor).

Capriccio is Strauss's fifteenth and last opera and, like the earlier *Friedenstag*, sprang from an idea by Stefan Zweig. While doing research in the British Museum, Zweig found the libretto to Salieri's opera *Prima la musica e poi le parole* (First the Music, Then the Words), which had shared a double bill with Mozart's *Der Schauspieldirektor* in a premiere at Vienna's Schönbrunn Palace. (See Vienna, Schönbrunn Palace, page 157.) The Strauss opera is a kind of "theoretical discussion," a wry debate about the nature of opera. Strauss, of course, believed that the words must come first. Ironically, although the opera has no real drama, it has settled on the margins of the international repertory because of its music: a wonderful finale sung alone by the soprano, a fabulous sextet, and a beautiful interlude.

FOOD

The old city center abounds with *Stuben,* wine bar–restaurants, including *the* Hofbräuhaus, which dates from 1886. These are jolly places to have something to eat if you can tolerate a smoky atmosphere.

LODGING

All of the following hotels are in Munich's historic center and within walking distance of the Residenz complex.

Hotel An der Oper, Falkenturmstrasse 10, 80331 Munich
tel: (49–89) 290–0270   fax: (49–89) 2900–2729

Platzl Hotel, Sparkassenstrasse 10, 80331 Munich
tel: (49–89) 237–030   fax: (49–89) 2370–3800   toll-free from the U.S.: (1–800) 488–8355
The Pfistermühle Restaurant, connected to the Platzl Hotel, is an excellent place for a light meal before the opera. The Galleria Restaurant is just a bit further down Sparkassenstrasse at the corner of Ledererstrasse 2.

Hotel Rafael, Neuturmstrasse 1, 80331 Munich
tel: (49–89) 290–980   fax: (49–89) 222–539

Hotel Torbräu, Tal 41, 80331 Munich
tel: (49–89) 225–016   fax: (49–89) 225–019

Hotel Schlicker, Tal 8, 80331 Munich
tel: (49–89) 227–941   fax: (49–89) 296–059

NUREMBERG (Nürnberg)

Half an hour south of Bayreuth by train is the city of Nuremberg, and to behold Nuremberg is to enter the world of Grimm's fairy tales. Its center, thoroughly bombed during World War II, was rebuilt as a perfect replica of the original medieval town. Although never more than a small city, Nuremberg has held a position of great importance since the Middle Ages. From the fourteenth century onward, a distinctive form of lyric poetry called *Meistergesäng,* practiced mainly by the artisan class, flourished. Today the most well-known Meistersinger is undoubtably Hans Sachs. Nuremberg was also home to Albrecht Dürer, the painter and engraver.

In the thirteenth and fourteenth century when Nuremberg was part of the Holy Roman Empire, the imperial jewels were housed there. In the seventeenth century the city was devastated in the Thirty Years' War. By the nineteenth century the town had become wealthy and hosted Germany's first railroad. In the twentieth century Hitler loved Nuremberg because it was traditional, conservative, beautiful, and represented Germany's illustrious past.

Like its founders who named the Weimar Republic (1918–33) to honor the greatness of Goethe, Schiller, and Bach, Hitler designated Nuremberg the symbol of the German nation under the Third Reich. On *Reichsparteitag* (Reich's Party Day) each year, ceremonies opened with a performance of *Die Meistersinger von Nürnberg*, at which attendance by all party members was mandatory.

It appears that in 1835, when he was conductor of the Magdeburg opera, Richard Wagner went to Nuremberg in search of singers to augment his company. On this particular trip he chanced upon a singing contest in a bar, which then led to a free-for-all, and finally to order again: a nutshell description of Act II of *Die Meistersinger!* In order to establish who was the best singer in Nuremberg, the *Meistersänger* had to adhere to rigorous rules, many of which are clearly set out in Wagner's opera. In 1866, with the opera nearly completed, Wagner offered the premiere to Nuremberg's opera house, but the director thought it too modern.

Hans Sachs, Wagner's protagonist, was a real shoemaker, but he is remembered for his more than a hundred full-length plays and the many poems he wrote. In a striking conjunction with Wagner, Sachs was the first German author to base a drama on the Nibelungen tale. In 1994, to commemorate the five-hundredth anniversary of Sachs's birth (November 5, 1494), Bavaria issued a postage stamp bearing his portrait. Sachs was a propagandist for the Reformation and coined Martin Luther's nickname, "the Nightingale of Wittenberg." The Gothic church of St. Martha was the hall where the *Meistersänger* performed and competed.

Most productions of Wagner's *Die Meistersinger von Nürnberg* attempt to portray the town as it looked in medieval times, which is how it actually looks today. Nuremberg is well worth a visit if you are in nearby Bayreuth or Munich.

FOOD

Nuremberg is well-known for its gingerbreadlike treat called *Lebkuchen*, which makes ordinary gingerbread dull by comparison. It is also famous for its bratwurst, and several establishments serve great bratwurst.

Historische Bratwurstküche von 1419, Zinkelschmiedsgasse 26, 90402 Nürnberg
tel: (49–911) 222–297   fax: (49–911) 227–695

Bratwurst-Häusle, Rathausplatz 1, 90403 Nürnberg
tel: (49–911) 227–695   fax: (49–911) 227–695

LODGING

Hotel Kröll, Hauptmarkt 6 (fourth floor), 90403 Nürnberg
tel: (49– 911) 227–113   fax: (49–911) 241–9608

Burghotel-Kleines Haus, Schildgasse 14, 90403 Nürnberg
tel: (49–911) 203–040   fax: (49–911) 226–503

STUTTGART

Stuttgart is the capital of the state of Baden-Würtemberg. Opera really began in Stuttgart in 1700 when a pupil of Jean-Baptiste Lully became *Kapellmeister* to the court. By 1730 the city's taste had distinctly changed from French to Italian opera. In 1764, in the wake of much political unrest, Duke Carl Eugen responded to public animosity by removing his whole court to Ludwigsburg, about ten kilometers north of Stuttgart. There, he used all his resources to build an enormous opera house. Eugen also established a theatrical school as part of the military academy and an Ecole des Demoiselles that supplied singers for the court opera. In 1777 the court began to charge admission to opera and theatrical events. During the first twenty years of the nineteenth century, opera in Stuttgart was impeded by financial difficulties of the court, and even though Carl Maria von Weber worked as secretary to the duke from 1807 to 1810, theatre and opera suffered a terrible decline.

The city began to mount distinguished premieres only after building the new Hoftheater, made up of two theatres—Grosses Haus and Kleines Haus—in 1912. Kleines Haus opened October 25, 1912, with the premiere of *Ariadne auf Naxos* by Richard Strauss. Grosses Haus, one of the only German theatres to survive World War II, was used as a club by the occupying French and American forces. Kleines Haus, destroyed in an air raid in 1944, was rebuilt and reopened in 1962.

Details of a Hoftheater Kleines Haus premiere

Ariadne auf Naxos, Oper in one act, October 25, 1912.
Richard Strauss (June 11, 1864, Munich—September 8, 1949, Garmisch-Partenkirchen)
Libretto Hugo von Hofmannsthal.

Produced by the famous Max Reinhardt, the most important theatre director of the early twentieth century, the opera's premiere was as a "third" act to a previous Reinhardt production of a two-act version of Molière's *Le Bourgeois Gentilhomme*. In the opera's original single act, characters from comedia dell'arte collide with operatic stereotypes from the eighteenth century to make a mockery of the Greek myth, even though the opera-within-the-opera's composer has vowed to disallow his impresario's additions.

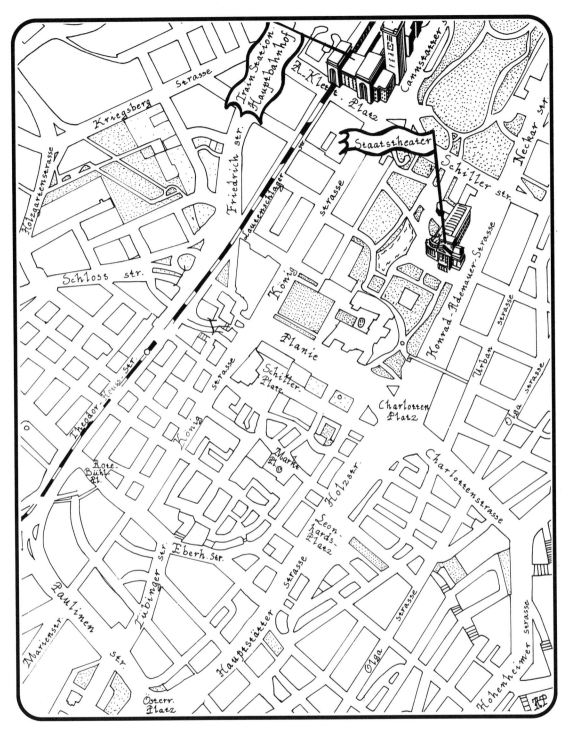

Operatic Stuttgart

Public and critical reception of the premiere was mixed. The public felt the Molière two-acter was too long, so Strauss and Hofmannsthal reworked the drama into the prologue and one act known to us today. This 1916 version was premiered in Vienna (see Vienna Staatsoper, page 159). The opera is scored for a chamber orchestra of only thirty-six players. *Ariadne auf Naxos* is not considered a Strauss masterpiece, but when an opera house has access to the singers the score calls for, including a fabulous comedienne-coloratura soprano, and a clever director, it is a delight.

Since World War II, Stuttgart has been in the vanguard of twentieth-century opera and has, among many others, produced:

Akhnaten (1984), Philip Glass
Einstein on the Beach (1988), Philip Glass
The English Cat (1983), Hans Werner Henze
Die Erschöpfung der Welt (1980), Maurizio Kagel
Satyagraha (1981), Philip Glass

Stuttgart Staatstheater, Ticket Office, Postfach 10 43 45, 70038 Stuttgart
Open Monday–Friday, 9:00 A.M.–1:00 P.M. and 2:00–5:00 P.M.
tel: (49–711) 221–795

Or purchase through **Easy-Ticket-Service:**

tel: (49–711) 255–5555   fax: (49–711) 255–5566

For specific information, contact:

Stuttgart Fremdenverkehrsbetriebe, Lautenschlagerstrasse 3, 70173 Stuttgart, Germany

LODGING

Hotel Unger, Kronenstrasse 17, 70173 Stuttgart
tel: (49–711) 20–990   fax: (49–711) 209–9100

Hotel Rieker, Friedrichstrasse 3, 70174 Stuttgart
tel: (49–711) 221–311   fax: (49–711) 293–894

WEIMAR

Because of its illustrious artistic past, Weimar is a city beloved by the majority of Germans. Weimar was the home of Johann Wolfgang von Goethe (1749–1832) from 1775, when he first came to the city from Frankfurt. He, of course, wrote the play upon which all Faust and Mephistopheles operas are based. He himself wrote the librettos to two operas, and some thirty other operas are based upon his novels and dramas. His Weimar home has been made into a large and fascinating museum.

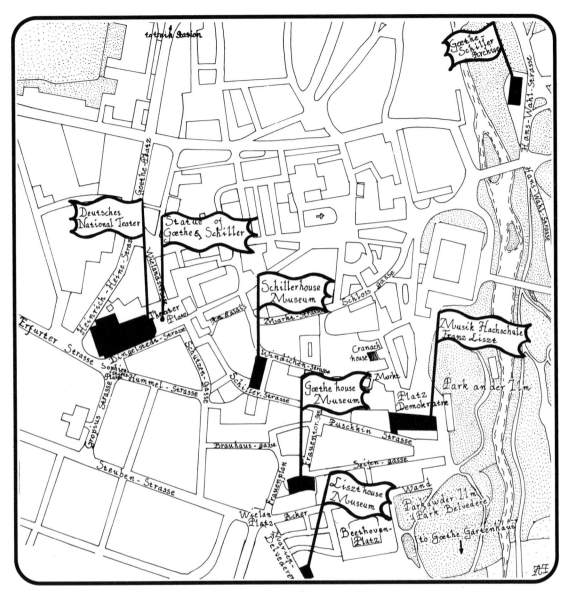

Operatic Weimar

The Goethewohnhaus and National Museum, Frauenplan 1
Open March through October, 9:00 A.M.–5:00 P.M., last admission 4:45;
November through February, 9:00 A.M.–4:00 P.M., last admission 3:45.
Closed Mondays.
admission: DM 3

The Goethes Gartenhaus, Park Belvedere, also called Park an der Ilm
Open March through October, 9:00 A.M.–noon and 1:00–5:00 P.M.;
November through February, till 4:00 P.M.
Closed Mondays.

Weimar was also the birthplace and home of Friedrich von Schiller, whose plays were the departure point for Rossini's *Guillaume Tell*; Verdi's *Giovanna d'Arco, I masnadieri, Luisa Miller, La forza del destino,* and *Don Carlo*; and his adaption of the Gozzi play used for Puccini's *Turandot;* and many more! Well over sixty-six opera librettos were culled from his stories. His home has been made into a splendid museum.

The Schillerhaus, Schillerstrasse 12
Open March through October, 9:00 A.M.–5:00 P.M.; November through February, till 4:00 P.M. Closed Tuesdays.
admission: DM 4

And, of course, Johann Sebastian Bach, born in nearby Eisenach, also lived in Weimar and was violinist in the court orchestra for a brief period in 1703, then leader of the court orchestra and organist from 1708 to 1717. His association with the city ended only with his month-long imprisonment for expressing fury at being passed over as musical director!

The first opera house was built in the Schloss Wilhelmsburg in 1696. Both Goethe and Schiller directed the Weimar Staatstheater from 1791 to 1817 (even sharing the position from 1799 to 1805). Under their direction the theater presented all the great operas of the period, including Mozart's works in their entirety (with the exception of *Idomeneo*), and premiered two by the woman composer Regentess Anna Amalia, based on dramas of Goethe. When the regentess's son Carl August came of age, he appointed Goethe his adviser and senior minister.

The composer-conductor champion of new music Franz Liszt expanded the operatic life of the city. He came to Weimar in 1848 as conductor of the Grossherzogliches Hofoper, where he remained until 1858. There he conducted the premiere of Wagner's *Lohengrin* in 1850, while Wagner was in exile in Switzerland. Liszt was champion of great music, recognized or not, and he also conducted the posthumous premiere of Schubert's opera *Alfonso und Estrella* as well as introduced Weimar to Russian opera.

Liszt's passionate devotion to new music and his demands on singers and orchestra alike for excellence in performance, combined with his fiery character, made his tenure at Weimar fraught with difficulties. He resigned from his position in 1858 after conducting the premiere of Peter Cornelius's *Der Barbier von Bagdad*, which the audience hated so thoroughly it staged an anti-Liszt demonstration. Cornelius had written the opera under Liszt's tutelege, and the piece is the first opera written in the manner of the Liszt "school." After Liszt resigned, he maintained his relationship with the theatre and returned from time to time between 1869 and 1886. He oversaw the premiere of Camille Saint-Saëns's *Samson et Dalila* on December 2, 1877.

The house Liszt lived in while in Weimar has been made into a museum. Most notable is the beautiful room containing his piano.

The Liszthaus, Marienstrasse
Open March through October, 9:00 A.M.–1:00 P.M. and 2:00–5:00 P.M.;
November through February, till 4:00 P.M. Closed Mondays.
admission: DM 2

The Franz Liszt Hochschule für Musik is the former Fürstenhaus (Prince's House) and stands in the Platz der Demokratie. It was built in 1770.

In 1889 the young Richard Strauss (June 11, 1864, Munich—September 8, 1949, Garmisch-Partenkirchen) was hired as *Kapellmeister* to the Grand Duke of Saxe-Weimar-Eisenach to direct Weimar's Grossherzogliches Hoftheater. During his tenure he conducted the premiere of Engelbert Humperdinck's (September 1, 1854, Siegburg—September 27, 1921, Neustrelitz) *Hänsel und Gretel*, December 23, 1893, in which his future wife, Pauline d'Ahna, was to have appeared as Hänsel but bowed out owing to ill health. He also conducted the premiere of his own first opera, *Guntram*, May 10, 1894, in which d'Ahna did appear.

Because of the great influence of the arts in the city, Weimar was called the German Athens. The Weimar Republic (1918–33), Germany's first democratic experiment and which adopted the most liberal constitution the world has ever known, was so named in the hope the republic would emulate the greatness of Goethe, Schiller, and Bach. A plaque on the Nationaltheater states:

In diesem Hause gab sich das	In this house
Deutsche Volk durch seine	On August 11, 1919
Nationalversammlung die	The German People
Weimar Verfassung	Adopted the Weimar Constitution
vom 11 August 1919.	Approved by their National Assembly.

The Deutsches Nationaltheater (Grossherzogliches Hoftheater), destroyed in an air raid in 1945, was rebuilt and reopened on August 28, 1948, with a performance of Verdi's *Otello*. Today the Nationaltheater has 857 seats and continues to present premieres of contemporary opera. A monument to Goethe and Schiller built in 1857 stands in front.

Nationaltheatre, Theaterplatz, 99423 Weimar
tel: (49–3643) 755–301

Details of the Nationaltheater (Grossherzogliches Hoftheater) premieres

Guntram, *Opera* in three acts, May 10, 1894.
Richard Strauss (June 11, 1864, Munich—September 8, 1949, Garmisch-Partenkirchen)
Libretto by the composer.

Guntram is Strauss's first opera, and he had hoped it would premiere in his native Munich, not in provincial Weimar. The opera reflects much of the Wagnerian influence from which his father had hoped to shield the student.

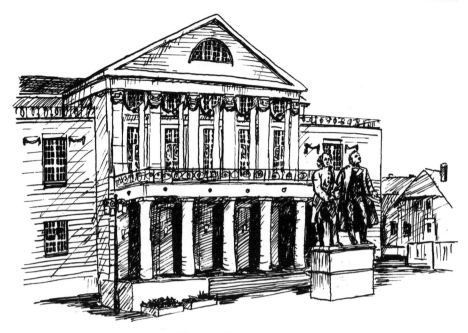

Nationaltheatre

Strauss conducted the successful Weimar premiere and finally arranged a performance in Munich, a much larger and more important city with a very discerning public. A single performance elicited an icy public reception, November 16, 1895. The problem was a clumsy libretto lacking in dramatic interest. Another six years passed before Strauss again tried his hand at opera, but he quoted heavily from *Guntram* in his tone poem *Ein Heldenleben,* in the section called "The Hero's Works of Peace."

Hänsel und Gretel, *Märchenspiel* (Fairy Story) in three acts, December 23, 1893.
Engelbert Humperdinck (September 1, 1854, Siegburg—September 27, 1921, Neustrelitz)
Libretto Adelheid Wette, after a fairy tale by the Brothers Grimm.

Although the overture at the opera's premiere had to be left out because the parts had not arrived, the young Richard Strauss scored a resounding success conducting the premiere of *Hänsel und Gretel.* The opera was immediately welcomed into the repertory of theatres throughout the world; seventy-two theatres staged it in its first year. The richness of the orchestral score reflects Humperdinck's debt to Wagner, but in his vocal lines the composer paid great attention to the simplicity of the fairy tale. *Hänsel und Gretel* is by no means a work just for children but a sophisticated operatic masterpiece that can be appreciated on many levels by people of all ages. The success of the opera, Humperdinck's first, proved a hard act to follow, and he was never able to repeat it in his next eight operas. Opera companies throughout the world regularly present it as part of pre-Christmas musical festivities. The best known part is The Evening Prayer, known to many as "Now I lay me down to sleep."

Lohengrin, *Romantische Oper* in three acts, August 28, 1850.
Richard Wagner (May 22, 1813, Leipzig—February 13, 1883, Venice)
Libretto by the composer.

Wagner had encountered the legend of Lohengrin's search for the Holy Grail at a meeting of the Königsberg Germanic Society. He became fascinated, and, of course, he used the Holy Grail theme again in *Parsifal*. Franz Liszt conducted *Lohengrin's* premiere while Wagner was in exile in Switzerland. The premiere was a success and the opera began to be performed throughout Europe. The potential of Wagner's future works is audible in the music of *Lohengrin*. The influence of Bellini is also apparent. *Lohengrin* is Wagner's last work that can be called an *opera;* all subsequent works are *Musik Dramas*. Because of his exile, the composer was not able to attend a performance of the opera until 1861, in Vienna.

Samson et Dalila, December 2, 1877.
Camille Saint-Saëns (October 9, 1835, Paris—December 16, 1921, Algiers)
Libretto Ferdinand Lemaire, loosely based on Judges 16.

Saint-Saëns admired Handel's dramatic oratorio *Samson* and in 1867 started to write *Samson et Dalila* as an oratorio but quickly developed an operatic conception. He was discouraged, however, when an audience invited to a presentation of Act II in his own home expressed alarm at putting a biblical subject on the stage, and he abandoned the work. Saint-Saëns finally completed the opera in 1876, but no opera house in France would produce it. The canny Liszt, however, knew it was a potential masterpiece and oversaw its successful premiere in Weimar. The score is intensely emotional and theatrical, and in it Saint-Saëns reflects his musical debt to both Berlioz and Wagner. The opera had to wait till 1892 for a Paris Opera performance. At the beginning of the twentieth century, Enrico Caruso made the role of Samson a vehicle for his great artistry. Considering the trials and tribulations of *Samson*, it is ironic that it is Saint-Saëns's only opera to remain in standard repertory.

For more Weimar information write:

Weimar Fremdenverkehrsbetriebe, Marktstrasse 4, 99423 Weimar, Germany

FOOD

Goethe-Café, Weilandstrasse 4, 99425 Weimar
tel: (49–3643) 34–32
   This charming café in the town's very center has excellent cakes and serves light lunches.

LODGING

The following hotels all have restaurants.

Flamburg–Hotel Elephant, Marktstrasse 19, 99423 Weimar
tel: (49–3643) 80–20   fax: (49–3643) 65–310
   This elegant hotel is in the old city center near the opera house and the museums. Its restaurant is excellent.

Intercity Hotel, Carl-August-Allee 17, D–99423 Weimar
tel: (49–3643) 23–40   fax: (49–3643) 234–444
   This convenient, modern hotel is right across from the entrance to the train station. Its restaurant is good.

Hotel Russischer Hof, Goetheplatz 2, 99423 Weimar
tel: (49–3643) 77–40   fax: (49–3643) 62–337
   This hotel, right in Weimar's historic center, is a three-minute walk to the Goethe and Schiller houses and ten minutes to the Liszt house. Its restaurant is pleasant.

MONACO

⮞ ⮜

MONTE-CARLO

In the sixth century B.C., the area now known as Monaco was colonized by the Monoikos Ligurians. The way the land and sea meet, in a high promontory jutting into the ocean, affords Monaco both a natural harbor and a fortress. The Romans used these attributes to their advantage. By the thirteenth century most of the western Mediterranean was ruled by the Genoese fleet. In this period, the land which now makes up Monaco became the property of the Genoese Grimaldi family. Monaco is something of an anomaly in the twentieth century: it is tiny and occupies some of the choicest real estate along the French Riviera; a good portion of the country's revenue comes from gambling and tourism—and most important, there are no taxes.

The capital city of Monaco, Monte-Carlo, was founded April 26, 1856. In 1864 the luxury Hôtel de Paris opened, and in 1876 Charles Garnier, architect of the Paris Opera, began to design the opera house that stands next to the Casino and shares the same entrance hall. The theatre was inaugurated in 1879 with a performance by the famous French actress Sarah Bernhardt (although built as an opera house, the theatre was also used for dramatic productions). Called Salle Garnier today, in the past it has been known as the Grand Théâtre de Monte-Carlo, the Théâtre du Casino, and the Opéra de Monte-Carlo. The theatre is gemlike and seats 524. Unlike his design for the Paris Opera, Garnier's plan called for stalls and very few boxes.

By the 1870s Monte-Carlo had become a very popular beach resort for Europe's elite. Nietzsche, while on holiday in Nice in December 1885, attended a concert in the Salle Garnier and heard for the first time the Prelude to Wagner's *Parsifal*.

Between 1893 (fourteen years after the Opéra de Monte-Carlo opened) and 1929, the company presented the premieres of twenty-three operas by twelve composers. Of these twelve, some are very well-known today whereas others are

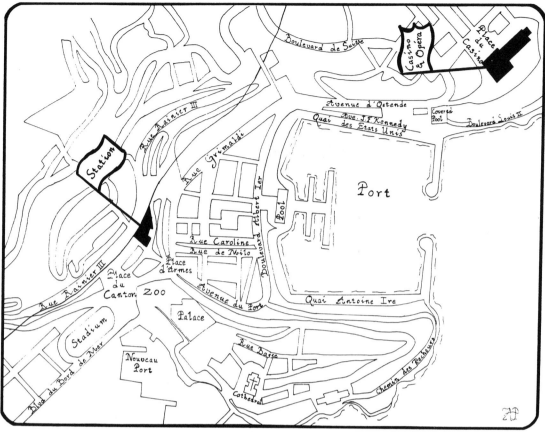

Operatic Monte-Carlo

virtually unknown, or at least unknown as opera composers. They are: Hector Berlioz, Georges Bizet, Lili Boulanger, Gabriel Fauré, César Franck, Raoul Gunsbourg, Reynaldo Hahn, Arthur Honegger, Jules Massenet, Giacomo Puccini, Maurice Ravel, Camille Saint-Saëns.

The operas are *L'Ancêtre* (1906), Camille Saint-Saëns; *Amadis* (1922), Jules Massenet; *Amica* (1905), Pietro Mascagni; *Cherubin* (1905), Jules Massenet; *Cléopatre* (1914), Jules Massenet; *Déjanire* (1911), Camille Saint-Saëns; *La Damnation de Faust,* complete and staged (1893), Hector Berlioz; *Don Procopio* (1906), Georges Bizet; *Don Quichote* (1910), Jules Massenet; *L'Enfant et les sortilèges* (1925), Maurice Ravel; *Faust et Hélène* (1924), Lili Boulanger; *La Foi* (1909), Camille Saint-Saëns; *Ghiselle* (1896), César Franck; *Hélène* (1903), Camille Saint-Saëns; *Hulda* (1894), César Franck; *Le Jongleur de Nôtre-Dame* (1902), Jules Massenet; *Judith* (1926), Arthur Honegger; *Nausicaa* (1917), Reynaldo Hahn; *Pénélope* (1913), Gabriel Fauré; *Roma* (1912), Jules Massenet; *La rondine* (1917), Giacomo Puccini; *Thérèse* (1907), Jules Massenet; *Vieil Aigle* (1909), Raoul Gunsbourg.

Raoul Gunsbourg, the Monte-Carlo Opera's astute director (and also a composer) from 1893 to 1951, is responsible for this illustrious list. During what is surely the longest directorial reign in the history of opera, he also hired the finest

Opéra and Casino de Monte-Carlo, 1900

singers from fin-de-siècle Europe. Among others, Enrico Caruso, Geraldine Farrar, Francesco Tamagno, Tito Schipa, Beniamino Gigli, Claudia Muzio, and Lili Pons appeared again and again. In the first two decades of the twentieth century, Monte-Carlo Opera casts were rivaled only by those of Italy's La Scala, New York's Metropolitan Opera, London's Covent Garden, and Argentina's Teatro Colón. Today the theatre has only a short season, from December or January through March, and presents a mere four productions of three performances each.

In April and May, the theatre hosts a festival, Le Printemps des Arts Monte-Carlo, during which at least one opera and several recitals by opera singers are presented.

Although the Casino is open daily, Salle Garnier is open only during performances. But it is possible and well worth the trouble to obtain special permission to see the hall by contacting the Fondation Prince Pierre de Monaco.

Fondation Prince Pierre de Monaco, L'Opéra de Monte-Carlo, 8, rue Louis Notari, Monte-Carlo 98000 Monaco
tel: (33) 9315–8303   fax: (33) 9350–6694

For opera information, contact:

L'Opéra de Monte-Carlo, Salle Garnier, Casino de Monte-Carlo, Monte-Carlo 98000 Monaco
tel: (33) 9216–2299
Closed Mondays.
    The box office is in the atrium of the Casino.

Details of some of the premieres given at L'Opéra de Monte-Carlo

La Damnation de Faust, *légende dramatique* in four parts, fully staged as an opera, February 18, 1893.
Hector Berlioz (December 11, 1803, La Côte-St. André, Isère—March 8, 1869, Paris)
Libretto by the composer and Almire Gandonnière, after Goethe's *Faust.*

The 1893 premiere of the staged version of *La Damnation de Faust* established the Monte-Carlo Opera as one of the leading opera companies in Europe. Within a year, this production of Berlioz's opera had been presented from Milan to New Orleans. The Monte-Carlo Opera revived *La Damnation de Faust* in 1902 to star the famous Nellie Melba.

Cherubin, *comédie chantée* in three acts, February 16, 1905.
Jules Massenet (May 12, 1842, Montaud, St. Etienne—August 31, 1912, Paris)
Libretto Henri Cain and Francis de Croisset.

Cherubin, one of the many sequels to Beaumarchais's *Figaro* plays, takes place on Cherubin's (Cherubino's) seventeenth birthday. He is now a young man well past puberty and amorously involved with several women (but the Cherubino role is nevertheless still played by a soprano). The premiere starred the soprano Mary Garden. One occasionally has the chance to hear *Cherubin* today.

La rondine (The Swallow), *commedia lirica* in three acts, March 27, 1917.
Giacomo Puccini (December 22, 1858, Lucca—November 29, 1924, Brussels)
Libretto Giuseppe Adami, based on a libretto by Willner and Heinz Reichert.

La rondine was commissioned by Vienna's Carltheater, but because of European political upheaval and the continuing war in 1917, Puccini's publisher suggested the opera should receive its premiere on neutral territory. Puccini had written many waltzes to please the Viennese but here lacks his usual compelling musical imagination. It is not a masterpiece, but the aria "Il bel sogno di Doretta" has achieved recent renown because of its prominence in the 1985 movie *A Room With a View.*

L'Enfant et les sortilèges (The Child and the Magic Spells), *fantaisie lyrique* in one act, March 21, 1925.
Maurice Ravel (March 7, 1875, Ciboure, Basses Pyrénées—December 28, 1937, Paris)
Libretto Colette.

L'Enfant et les sortilèges is a wonderfully entertaining fantasy opera in which all the desires of a lonely child are satisfied. Ravel worked on the opera's music until five days before the premiere. The young Balanchine choreographed the ballet sequences, and the premiere was a great success. When the opera was taken to Paris, Colette wrote that it played twice a week to packed houses while "modernists applaud, and shout down the others." "The others" were responding to, among other things, the "meowed" duet by two cats. Perhaps the conservatives had never heard the Cat Duet by Gioacchino Rossini!

LODGING

The principality of Monaco—and Monte-Carlo in particular—is wealthy and very tourist-oriented. Because the whole country consists of 482 acres, everything in Monaco is more or less in the center.

Hotel du Louvre, 16, boulevard des Moulins, 98000 Monte-Carlo, Monaco
tel: (33) 9350–6525   fax: (33) 9330–2368
This hotel is a nineteenth-century mansion filled with beautiful antique furniture. Each room is unique. The price is right for all you get.

Hotel Mirabeau, 1, avenue Princesse-Grace, 98000 Monte-Carlo, Monaco
tel: (33) 9216–6565   fax: (33) 9350–8485
This hotel stands next to the Casino. It is more expensive than Hôtel du Louvre and half the price of Hôtel de Paris.

Hotel de Paris, Place du Casino, 98000 Monaco
tel: (33) 9216–3000   fax: (33) 9325–5917
This fin-de-siècle hotel opened in January 1866. If you can afford it, you should spend a night here in splendor. It is very expensive, very posh, and part of the complex that includes the Casino and the opera house.

FOOD

La Coupole, In Hôtel Mirabeau, 1, avenue Princesse-Grace,
98000 Monaco
tel: (33) 9216–6565
La Coupole is known as one of the best restaurants on the Riviera.

The Grill de l'Hôtel de Paris, Place du Casino
tel: (33) 9216–3000
One of the swankiest places to eat in the world, this restaurant is quite expensive and appears to be *the* place to be seen.

Le Café de Paris, Place du Casino
tel: (33) 9116–2020   fax: (33) 9216–2020

Directly across the square from the opera house, the Casino, and the Hotel de Paris, this restaurant offers affordable and good food.

Glossary

accademia
    A type of private club, usually with some kind of intellectual basis, that flourished in Italy from the sixteenth through the eighteenth centuries. A few still exist today.

ballad opera
    English form in which spoken dialogue alternates with traditional popular songs that flourished during the first third of the eighteenth century in reaction to Italian-style opera.

bel canto
    Beautiful singing; the virtuoso singing style required for eighteenth-century opera, full of vocal display, improvisation, ornate cadenzas, and lyrical line.

biglietteria
    Ticket office.

Brighella
    The astute servant of commedia dell'arte, dressed in white with green trim, whose home is considered to be Bergamo. Often accompanied by *Pierrot*, the white-faced clown with the white ruff, large buttons, and wide pantaloons, and *Arlecchino* (Harlequin), who is masked and clad in spangled garments of many colors.

cabaletta
    A short operatic aria; in nineteenth-century Italian opera, the final fast part of a two-part aria or duet, e.g., "Sempre libera," from *La traviata*.

Camerata
    The group of intellectuals, poets, musicians, and theorists that met in the house of Count Giovanni Bardi in Florence in the late sixteenth century and invented opera.

castrato, castrati
    Male singers who retained their high boys' voices by undergoing quasi-elective surgery before puberty. In the seventeenth century, they performed opera and church music in areas under papal control; in early eighteenth-century opera they were the predominant voice; in the nineteenth century they went out of vogue. The last castrato was still singing in the choir of Rome's St. Peter's in 1910.

cavatina
A short aria without a da capo; often the slow part of a two-part aria or duet, e.g., "Ah! fors' è lui," from *La traviata*.

commedia
A play or a comedy.

commedia dell'arte
Italian semi-improvisational professional theatre (as opposed to folk or popular theatre) with stock characters, often containing rather grotesquely exaggerated comedy.

commedia lirica
Lyric (sung) comedy.

commission
A work commissioned by a theatre, impresario, or performers. From the mid-nineteenth century to the 1960s operatic commissions also came from publishers, in Italy most notably Ricordi and Sonzogno. Italian music publishers in the late nineteenth century not only commissioned new operas but also held competitions to search out exciting, new, and young talent. The object was to sign up these potential composer stars, guaranteeing the publishing company all the profits of their future operas. Because opera was still *the* popular art form in Italy, these contests were good investments.

da capo
The recapitulation of the first section of an ABA aria, which in the eighteenth century had to be lavishly ornamented by the singer; the predominant aria form in bel canto opera, from the end of the seventeenth to the middle of the eighteenth century.

diva
Italian for goddess; applied to great women opera singers; a great male opera singer may be called a divo.

dramma
Drama or play; or, in opera, a sad story often with a happy ending.

dramma giocoso
Playful drama (comic opera).

dramma in musica
The seventeenth-century term for a play set to music (opera).

dramma lirico
Sung drama (opera). Nineteenth-century term.

dramma musicale
A drama set to music (opera).

dramma serio
Serious drama (opera).

fermata
The sign on a piece of music shaped ⌒ that tells the performer to prolong whatever notes are beneath it; also, a bus stop in Italy.

Gesamtkunstwerk
A "total work of art," a term Wagner invented in his essay, *Kunstwerk der Zukunft* (The Future of Art, 1849) and which is used to describe his operas

from *Das Rheingold* onward; operas in which the drama, music, and text are inseparable. (See Musik Drama.)

grand opera

A French opera of five acts, sung throughout, with at least one ballet, and based on an ennobling historical or mythological subject. Composers such as Cherubini, Meyerbeer, and Spontini are considered the greatest in this genre.

intermezzo

A miniature comic opera in Italian, seldom involving more than two characters and usually performed between the acts of a longer work, usually an opera seria. The *intermezzo* was the immediate predecessor of opera buffa.

Italian-style opera (eighteenth century)

Commonly called: bel canto opera (see *bel canto* above); "singer's opera" because it depended completely on the vocal prowess and flamboyant imagination of singers; "number opera" because of the long string of arias (numbers) it comprised, during which the action of the drama in effect came to a stop.

leggenda drammatica

An operatic setting of a dramatic legend.

leitmotiv

Musical motifs, found in Wagner's later operas in association with particular characters, situations, and ideas. Unlike the many composers who copied him, Wagner combines and transforms the motifs throughout the opera (or in the case of the *Ring* cycle, operas).

librettist

The writer(s) who creates a concise drama and a singable text, often from a play, novel, or poem by another writer.

libretto

The text of an opera. Also the book containing the text.

lirica

Sung; also a synonym for *opera* in Italian (e.g., "Canta la lirica?" Do you sing opera?)

maestro di cappella

Master of the musicians who played in a nobleman's private chapel.

masque

An elaborately staged English court entertainment of the late sixteenth and entire seventeenth centuries, combining vocal and instrumental music, dancing, lavish costumes, and "special effects"; the subject matter was mythological and allegorical. Today the best-known masque is John Blow's *Venus and Adonis* (1681).

melodrama

Spoken text over orchestral accompaniment as in Act II of *La Traviota*.

melodramma

In Italian, a term virtually synonymous with *opera*.

melodramma eroico, giocoso, tragico

Heroic, playful, tragic opera.

monodrama

An opera for one person, such as Arnold Schoenberg's *Erwartung* (1924).

monody

The opposite of polyphony; in the context of the history of opera, the term for solo vocal music from ancient Greece that members of the Camerata used to describe how they thought opera should be written: to enhance the intelligibility and affect of the words.

Musikdrama

A term used to distinguish Wagner's later works, from *Das Rheingold* (1854) onward, from all other operas.

opera

Plural of *opus;* melodrama.

L'Opéra

The Parisian opera house that presented all *grand opera* in the nineteenth century.

opéra-ballet

French: a dramatic-musical art form combining singing and dancing, popular in the seventeenth and eighteenth centuries and in part responsible in the nineteenth century for the presence of at least one ballet in every opera performed at the Paris L'Opéra.

opéra bouffe

French comic opera.

opera buffa

Eighteenth-century term for Italian comic opera, in which recitativo secco predominates.

opéra comique

French: all operas with spoken dialogue and generally more "popular" in subject matter.

opera semiseria

Half-serious opera; the equivalent of French postrevolutionary opera, comic operas with serious qualities; often "rescue operas."

opera seria

Eighteenth-century term for "serious" opera, in which *recitativo accompagnato* predominates.

operetta, operette

In the eighteenth century, a short opera; in the nineteenth and twentieth centuries a theatrical work of light operatic style, comic, often sentimental or satirical, containing spoken dialogue; the style originated with Jacques Offenbach in Paris but by the end of the nineteenth century had become synonymous with Vienna.

opus

A work or composition.

politeama (polivalente)

Synonymous with *theatre* in Italian; used as a name for theatres throughout Italy.

proscenium arch

Proscenium: Greek for stage; *proscenium arch*: the arch that holds the stage
curtain; as we know it today, developed in England in the 1670s.

recitar cantando

The singing speech (dialogue) of early seventeenth-century opera where the
words are master of the music.

recitativo accompagnato

Recitative accompanied by the orchestra in which the music mirrors and
accentuates the passion of the text; mainly used in opera seria.

recitativo secco

Recitative accompanied only by a keyboard instrument; mostly used in opera
buffa, Italian-style comic opera; sounds like rapid speech (chatter); secco (dry)
refers to its unemphatic accompaniment.

Renaissance

Period of rebirth that followed the Middle Ages; in music, 1450–1600, the age
of polyphony.

Risorgimento

Resurgence of national pride that characterized the nineteenth-century
movement for a free and united Italy.

Singspiel

German: popular opera, usually on light subjects, in German with spoken
dialogue.

sopranist

A male voice singing in the soprano register. During the seventeenth and
eighteenth centuries some cities prohibited women from appearing on the stage
so women's parts were played by young castrati or *sopranisti.*

Sprechstimme

A type of voice production halfway between speech and singing.

Staatsoper

German: state opera house.

Stadtsoper

German: city opera house.

stile concitato

Term coined by Claudio Monteverdi to describe an agitated style of music.
Following the writings of Plato, Monteverdi believed that music should express
the three principal emotional states: agitation or anger (*stile concitato*),
moderation (*temperato*), and humility or softness (*molle*). *Stile concitato* should
imitate the utterances and accents of a man engaged in warfare.

teatro all'italiana

Horseshoe-shaped theatres with excellent acoustics and sight lines.

Théâtre des Italiennes

The popular forum for Italian-style opera in Paris from the early eighteenth
through the mid-nineteenth centuries.

tragedia lirica

Italian: lyric (sung) tragedy.

tragédie en musique
> French tragic opera, from the late seventeenth to the mid-eighteenth century; composers such as Lully and Rameau.

tragédie lyrique
> French: lyric (sung) tragedy.

Veglione (Sylvester Nacht)
> The grand vigil, or grand ball held in many of Europe's opera houses on New Year's Eve; often the theatre's seats are removed for dancing.

verismo
> A movement in Italian literature, and subsequently in opera, begun in the 1870s; in opera, characterized by regional and rustic characters using down-to-earth language and usually describing low-life and crimes of passion.

Weimar Republic
> Germany's first democratic experiment (1918–33), which adopted the most liberal constitution the world has ever known, was so named to link it to the greatness of Goethe and Schiller.

Index